NURTURING THE VISION: FIRST BAPTIST CHURCH, RALEIGH, 1812–2012

MERCER
UNIVERSITY PRESS

Endowed by
TOM WATSON BROWN
and
THE WATSON-BROWN FOUNDATION, INC.

Nurturing the Vision

First Baptist Church, Raleigh, 1812–2012

W. Glenn Jonas, Jr.

MERCER UNIVERSITY PRESS

MACON, GEORGIA

The James N. Griffith Series in Baptist Studies
This series on Baptist life and thought explores and investigates Baptist
history, offers analyses of Baptist theologies, provides studies in
hymnody, and examines the role of Baptists in societies and cultures
around the world. The series also includes classics of Baptist literature,
letters, diaries, and other writings.
Walter B. Shurden
Series Editor

© 2012 Mercer University Press
1400 Coleman Avenue
Macon, Georgia 31207

First Edition

Books published by Mercer University Press are printed on acid-free paper
that meets the requirements of American National Standard for Information
Sciences—Permanence of Paper for Printed Library Materials.

Mercer University Press is a member of Green Press Initiative
(greenpressinitiative.org), a nonprofit organization working to help
publishers and printers increase their use of recycled paper and decrease their
use of fiber derived from endangered forests. This book is printed on recycled
paper.

Library of Congress Cataloging-in-Publication Data

    Jonas, William Glenn, 1959-
    Nurturing the vision : First Baptist Church, Raleigh, 1812-2012 /
W. Glenn Jonas, Jr. -- 1st ed.
       p. cm.
    Includes bibliographical references and index.
    ISBN 978-0-88146-283-8 (hardback : alk. paper) -- ISBN 0-88146-283-7
(hardback : alk. paper)
    1. First Baptist Church (Raleigh, N.C.)--History. 2. Raleigh (N.C)—
Church history. I. Title.
    BX6480.R386J66 2012
    286'.175655--dc22

                             2011050963

MUP/H845

To: Hardy, Judy, Moses, Nancy, Zilpha, John, Lisbon, Nelly, Elhannon, Flora, Jack, Elizabeth, Jenny, Hannah, Samuel, Jethro, Joseph, Dolly, Hasty, Mary, Tabbytha, Siddy, and Elisha. They were the founders. The vision began with them.

Contents

Preface and Acknowledgments

Baptist historian Walter B. Shurden, when speaking of the value of writing local church history, has said, "In the future, Baptist historians probably should spend far more time on local than global history. The latter is almost impossible to do correctly, but the former is manageable, so helpful, and serves to correct our generalizations about our spiritual family."[1] Writing local church history can be rewarding for a congregation. It allows the congregation to see and understand better its historical context. It can shed light on the roots of certain controversies or the seeds planted that may be reaped many years later with positive results. A church's history also provides a witness for the local community to the grace of God during both good times and bad.

A celebrated text from the Old Testament prophet Habakkuk reads, "Write the vision; make it plain on tablets, so that a runner may read it. For there is still a vision for the appointed time; it speaks of the end, and does not lie. If it seems to tarry, wait for it; it will surely come, it will not delay."[2] In this book, I attempt to use the analogy of a "vision" anticipated by the twenty-three founders of the First Baptist Church of Raleigh, North Carolina, which began when they constituted their church on 8 March 1812. This book is an attempt to "write that vision" from the perspective of looking back over the intervening two centuries. Throughout the book, I have attempted to follow the "founders' vision" through two centuries as the church has grown and ministered in the heart of downtown Raleigh. I have also made an effort to contextualize the First Baptist story within the broader context of Raleigh history and the history of the United States.

There are numerous individuals who deserve thanks for making this book a reality. Thanks to the members of the 200th Anniversary Committee composed of: Carolyn Dickens (chair), Jim Clary, Charles Barham, Austin Connors, and Elizabeth Barnes. I appreciate the

---

[1] Walter B. Shurden, e-mail message to author, 1 April 2011.
[2] Hab. 2:2–3 (New Revised Standard Version).

confidence you had in me when you selected me as the historian to write your history, thereby entrusting me with this project.

I am grateful to my employer, Campbell University, for providing me with a research sabbatical during the fall 2010 semester. The staff of the Wiggins Memorial Library at Campbell University was also helpful and supportive. In particular, I would be remiss if I did not say a special word of thanks to Dr. Derek Hogan, Theological Reference Librarian and Assistant Professor of New Testament at the Campbell University Divinity School. He gave valuable assistance to me in securing the information and interlibrary loan materials that were necessary to complete this work.

I am grateful to the faculty and staff of the Campbell University Divinity School, especially my colleagues in the Department of Religion. My religion department colleagues "covered" for me during my sabbatical and never once complained about the extra work. Thank you!

Several individuals were valued readers of either the full manuscript or various chapters. Dr. Mel Hawkins from Carson-Newman College provided some early insights. Dr. Dan Day, my colleague in the Campbell University Divinity School and former pastor of First Baptist Church of Raleigh, provided valuable suggestions. He shares a love of the church's history and I am grateful for the many late afternoons that he allowed me to sit in his office and ask questions or share discoveries. Dr. Doug Weaver from the Baylor University Religion Department read the manuscript and wrote the foreword, for which I am appreciative. Dr. Chris Chapman (the church's current pastor) and Mr. Don Kline were also readers of the manuscript and made very helpful suggestions.

One other member of First Baptist Church deserves a special word of thanks. Mrs. Fannie Memory Mitchell, longtime member, provided a good "critical eye" as she read the manuscript. Her attention to detail helped make this book even better. She also contributed to this project in another important way. Her husband, Thornton, was the state archivist for North Carolina from 1973 to 1981. Years ago, he and Fannie Memory began to organize the church's records. Following his death in 2003, Fannie Memory and the history committee of the church carried the project to completion, resulting in what arguably could be the best local church archive collection in the state. Records of all church conference meetings exist, with only the exception of a few years in the 1830s and a few months scattered throughout the church's two centuries. There is a good collection of deacons' meeting minutes, WMU minutes, Sunday-school records, weekly bulletins, newsletters, photographs, and scrapbooks, along with miscellaneous records from important committee work throughout the years. All of these resources have been carefully organized and protected in a safe location in the church. The careful organization and preservation of the church's historical sources made this project much easier to manage.

Dr. Bill Summers and Ms. Taffy Hall, on staff at the Southern Baptist Historical Library and Archives in Nashville, Tennessee, provided me valuable information whenever I asked. Ms. Julia Bradford, archivist for the North Carolina Baptist Collection at the Z. Smith Reynolds Library at Wake Forest University, worked diligently to fulfill any request and, on at least one occasion, entrusted me with some original materials for use.

I extend gratitude to Mercer University Press and its editor Dr. Marc Jolley. This is now the fourth project we have worked on together and I appreciate the professionalism you always exhibit. Thank you for accepting this project.

Two graduate students at the Campbell University Divinity School also worked as my "personal assistants" and provided valuable help chasing down sources. Brittany Jackson helped me in the early stages of the project. Jonathan Lee provided important help in proofreading the final document. His ability to see grammatical and stylistic problems was necessary and helpful in the final stages of preparing the manuscript for publication. I doubt the manuscript would have been ready by the deadline without his help. Jonathan is a gifted editor and if the reader finds the book to be enjoyable, part of the credit must be given to him for making it a better read.

A word of gratitude and love is also extended to my family for the many, many nights I was away working in my office on this project. Thanks for understanding!

    —W. Glenn Jonas, Jr.,
       Easter 2011

Foreword

I sit here with my laptop computer to write this foreword after just having been a guest on a radio station's program that discussed why certain religious people attempt to predict a date for the end of the world. End-time predictors all seem to see the world as a terrible place to live, the past something to forget, the present something to escape, and the future something to fear and avoid. In the process, Christianity ceases to be about a journey of faith, grace, struggle, and love of God and others.

Reading a local church history is a breath of fresh air in an environment where concern for day-to-day ministry has been devalued. At the local church level, we read how Christians take their faith in Jesus Christ seriously day to day, week to week, month to month, year to year. We see how ministry has not simply been defined, but how it has been practiced. Active local church Christians might dream about the future but have feet planted in the joys and sorrows of their past experiences and present realities. Reading a local church history reminds us that our past has helped shape the understanding of who we are. The past is not something to forget, but to celebrate and to learn from so that growth can occur in the present and the future.

In recent years, the writing of local church history has increased dramatically in terms of the quality of research. Professional historians have been called upon to use their craft to tell a church's story in proper historical context. The histories are not simply "three cheers" for what a church believes it has accomplished, but the narratives have been honest assessments of the successes and failures of church life, the difficulties and the joys of doing ministry.

First Baptist Church, Raleigh, should be complimented for taking their history seriously. Its archives are a historian's goldmine. The church's commitment to publishing a 200th-anniversary history is evidence that the congregation understands the importance of assessing and celebrating the past in order to do effective ministry in the future. And the church should be complimented for choosing as the history's author Dr. Glenn Jonas, gifted scholar and historian, and well-known in

Baptist churches of North Carolina for his preaching, his love of the church, and his strong support for historic Baptist principles.

As you read the history of First Baptist Church, Raleigh, you will learn just how important the church has been to the history of Baptists in North Carolina. The histories of the church, Meredith College, Wake Forest University, and the news journal *Biblical Recorder* are inextricably intertwined. For example, Thomas Meredith, editor of the *Biblical Recorder* and one of the organizers of the North Carolina Baptist state convention, was an influential church member. Many of the church's pastors were connected to Wake Forest; almost all of the editors of the *Biblical Recorder* joined the congregation. One of the most influential women in Southern Baptist missions history, Fannie Heck, and other women involved in North Carolina missions were church members as well. Even prominent political figures—Governor W. W. Holder and Jesse Helms—are part of the church's story. But as important, or perhaps more important, the church's history is filled with the story of the commitment and service of "nameless" faithful believers, those Christians whose testimonies will not be found in textbooks or general history books, but whose experience of faith is the story of most Christians who follow Jesus.

Jonas tells the Baptist story well. He puts the church's history into the larger historical contexts of America, Raleigh, and Baptist life. He highlights the role of women, a corrective to the way older histories were written, and he understands Baptists and the importance of freedom to the Baptist witness. Jonas is not afraid to mention difficult struggles in the church's history, but he also is gracious and celebratory of the church's achievements.

First Baptist Church, Raleigh: it is time to celebrate. For you, the world has been God's place for service; the past has been something to remember, honor, learn from, and celebrate; the present something to journey in and minister to; and the future something to engage—with hope that God will continue to be faithful.

—Doug Weaver
May 2011

1

Defining a Tradition

To the non-Baptist world, Baptists may be better known for how they act than for what they believe. Baptists certainly have had their share of negative press in recent years, ranging from the Southern Baptist Convention's call in June 1997 for a boycott of Disney World, to outrageous activities perpetrated by individuals such as Reverend Creighton Lovelace, pastor of Danieltown Baptist Church in Forest City, North Carolina, who in 2005 posted a sign in front of his church that said, "The Koran Needs to Be Flushed."[1] In spite of some of the negative impressions left by the movement at times, Baptists do have positive attributes, such as their championing of individual freedom in spiritual matters, local church autonomy, religious liberty and believer's baptism, missions, and matters related to social justice.

The Beginning of the Baptist Tradition

Unlike Lutherans who have Martin Luther, and Methodists who have John Wesley, Baptists do not have a single founder to whom the entire tradition can be traced. John Smyth was the founder of the earliest branch of English Baptists. These early Baptists are called the General Baptists because of their Arminian belief in *general* atonement—the idea that the death of Christ is applicable to all who will believe. Educated at Cambridge (usually considered more radical than Oxford), John Smyth considered the Church of England to be the "Antichrist."[2] He was an agitator who became outspoken about the Church of England and Queen Elizabeth's *via media*, publicly denouncing all sorts of practices, but most

---

[1] For discussion about the call for a boycott of Disney World, see "Southern Baptists Vote for Disney Boycott," http://www.cnn.com/US/9706/18/baptists. disney/(accessed 13 August 2005). For information related to the Lovelace incident, see W. Glenn Jonas, Jr., ed., *The Baptist River: Essays on Many Tributaries of a Diverse Tradition* (Macon GA: Mercer University Press, 2006) xi.

[2] W. T. Whitley, *The Works of John Smyth*, vol. 1 (Cambridge: Cambridge University Press, 1915) lxvi.

frequently the clergy, whom he considered to be too similar to Catholic priests. He became so outspoken and bold that he was arrested and spent a short period of time in prison for refusing to conform to the practices of the Church of England.[3] One of Smyth's contemporaries described him as "a learned man, and of good ability, but of an unsettled head."[4]

In 1606 Smyth made a formal break with the Church of England. He moved to Gainsborough and identified with a Separatist (radical Puritans who broke away from the Church of England) congregation there, soon becoming its pastor. Encountering persecution, the congregation first divided into two different churches in order to be less conspicuous, but eventually both Separatist groups decided to leave England and become expatriates in Amsterdam, Holland, where they could worship freely. Smyth's group, which included a prominent layman named Thomas Helwys, arrived in 1607 and was befriended by a Mennonite named Jan Munter. Helwys and Smyth, along with the other English expatriates in their group, took jobs at Munter's place of business, called the East India Bakehouse, where they worked making hardtack, a type of biscuit that was used on the numerous ships coming in and out of Amsterdam.[5]

The circumstances suggest that Smyth was influenced by the Mennonites and their distinctive practice of believer's baptism. Sometime in 1609 he baptized himself in the congregation's presence, thereby publicly rejecting his infant baptism.[6] Then he proceeded to baptize the other members of the group, giving birth to history's first Baptist church. Not long after this experience, however, Smyth began to regard this self-baptism as invalid because he believed it had no apostolic authority. He suggested that the group seek membership with the Mennonites and be baptized into their fellowship because he believed they possessed the proper authority for their baptismal practice.

---

[3] H. Leon McBeth, *The Baptist Heritage: Four Centuries of Baptist Witness* (Nashville: Broadman Press, 1987) 32.

[4] Daniel Neal, *The History of the Puritans*, 4 vols. (London: Richard Hett, 1732–1738) 1:243, as cited in McBeth, *Baptist Heritage*, 33.

[5] McBeth, *Baptist Heritage*, 34.

[6] Smyth's *se-baptism* (self-baptism) was by the method of *affusion* or pouring. The practice of believer's baptism by immersion did not become standard until around 1641 when the Particular Baptists adopted immersion.

This unrest in Smyth's spirit eventually led to a significant amount of unrest in the congregation, so much so that they did *what Baptists have been famous for ever since: they split!* Smyth and part of the group remained in Amsterdam and sought membership with the Mennonites. He died of tuberculosis in 1612, unaffiliated with any church. Helwys, a much more stable leader, took the remnants of the group back to England and in 1612 established the first Baptist church on English soil in the Spittalfields district outside of London.[7]

The Particular Baptists also arose in England but developed from a much more moderate expression of English Separatism. Calvinist in their theology, Particular Baptists got their name from their belief in *particular* atonement—the concept that Jesus' death is only for those whom God has elected to salvation. The first Particular Baptists can be traced to a Separatist congregation in London established in 1616. Historians usually refer to this church by using the initials of its first three pastors—Henry Jacob, John Lathrop, and Henry Jesse—resulting in the "JLJ Church." Evidence suggests that this Separatist church began having discussions about baptism as early as the 1630s, and some of the members opted for believer's baptism about 1633. The church remained in harmony for the next five years until the group rejecting infant baptism separated in 1638, creating the first Particular Baptist church. Records from this church, though sketchy, indicate that by 1641 their mode of baptism changed from affusion (pouring) to immersion, making the Particulars the first Baptists to baptize by immersion.[8] While General Baptists gave future generations of Baptists their understanding of the "meaning" of baptism (believer's baptism instead of infant baptism), the Particular Baptists provided them with the "mode" (immersion).

General and Particular Baptists continued in England separate from one another for the next two centuries. During the eighteenth century,

---

[7] McBeth, *Baptist Heritage*, 35–39. The Helwys group actually wrote two letters and made a personal visit to the local Mennonite congregation with whom Smyth was trying to affiliate, warning them not to receive him as a member. See James R. Coggins, *John Smyth's Congregation: English Separatism, Mennonite Influence, and the Elect Nation* (Scottdale PA: Herald Press, 1991) 77.

[8] William H. Brackney, *Historical Dictionary of the Baptists* (Lanham MD: The Scarecrow Press, 1999) s.v. "Particular Baptists."

Particular Baptists experienced numerical decline as a result of controversies over their Calvinist beliefs. An exaggerated form of Calvinism caused some Particular Baptists to reject efforts to evangelize. Andrew Fuller and William Carey in the late eighteenth and early nineteenth centuries, both proponents of a much more moderate form of Calvinism, are usually credited with bringing a renewal to the Particular Baptist tradition. General Baptists, on the other hand, faced problems from the theological left. Rationalism leading to universalism and anti-trinitarianism caused a decline among General Baptists during much of the eighteenth century. Dan Taylor, who was greatly influenced by the Wesleyan revivals, began a movement called the New Connection among General Baptists, which served to revive its numbers. In 1891 General and Particular Baptists formally united with each other in England.[9]

In addition to the influence of English Separatism on early Baptists, several Baptist scholars have maintained that the Anabaptist tradition also contributed to the birth of the Baptists.[10] The support for this argument is based more on circumstances than documentation, but the circumstantial evidence is strong. While in Amsterdam, the Smyth-Helwys group clearly developed a close association with Jan Munter and his fellow Mennonites. Although there is no specific document to indicate that Smyth developed his ideas on believer's baptism from the Mennonites, it can be argued that he borrowed their mode of baptism (affusion); logically the close contact between the two groups led to influence. However, as previously noted, the dearth of documentation on the matter causes many historians to discount Anabaptist origin.[11]

While a variety of historians can be found who argue the presence of Anabaptist influence on the rise of the General Baptists, very few have

---

[9] See McBeth, *Baptist Heritage*, 153–99 for a general discussion of the General and Particular Baptists in eighteenth-century England.

[10] Ibid., 52–58. The Anabaptists were part of the radical wing of the Reformation in the sixteenth century. They rejected infant baptism and proclaimed that the New Testament only teaches baptism of adult believers who have professed faith in Christ.

[11] Excellent discussions of the historiography of this issue can be found in McBeth, *Baptist Heritage*, 49–63; Bill J. Leonard, *Baptist Ways: A History* (Valley Forge PA: Judson Press, 2003), 10–15; and Robert G. Torbet, *A History of the Baptists,* 3rd ed. (Valley Forge PA: Judson Press, 1980) 18–21.

ventured to argue that Anabaptists influenced the rise of the later Particular Baptists. One Baptist scholar, Glen Stassen, argued convincingly that the theological foundation of the Particular Baptist tradition lay in the work of Menno Simons, a leading sixteenth-century Anabaptist leader. Elements of *The Foundation of Christian Doctrine*, Simons's most widely distributed work, can be seen in the first confession of faith written by the Particular Baptists. Stassen argues the "Particular Baptists should not be ignored in our assessment of Anabaptist influence on Baptist origins."[12]

If Anabaptist influence played a part in the origin of the earliest two groups of Baptists (and enough evidence seems to suggest it is a strong possibility), then the early Baptists came about as a synthesis of two divergent traditions: Dutch Anabaptism and English Separatism. This synthesis has created a tension in the Baptist tradition similar to the tension between General and Particular Baptists, which occasionally serves as a root cause for disputes and diversity among different groups of Baptists.

The Baptist Tradition in the United States

The extant records do not reveal who the first Baptist in America was. What is known is that Baptists in early America were diverse, reflecting the diversity of the tradition in England at the time. There were Particular Baptists, General Baptists, and Seventh-Day Baptists in the colonies. There were also some uniquely American versions of Baptists that developed as well. For example, the Rogerenes in New England were similar to the Seventh-Day Baptists in their view of the Sabbath but also believed in and emphasized divine healing. The Keithians in the Middle Colonies were heavily influenced by Quakerism and evidenced a

---

[12] Glen Stassen, "Opening Menno Simons's Foundation-Book and Finding the Father of Baptist Origins Alongside the Mother—Calvinist Congregationalism," *Baptist History and Heritage* 33/2 (Spring 1998): 34. Another version of this article was published by Stassen in an articled titled, "Anabaptist Influence in the Origin of the Particular Baptists," *The Mennonite Quarterly Review* 36/4 (October 1962): 324–33.

similar type of spirituality, while at the same time holding Baptist views of baptism and ecclesiology.[13]

With all this in mind, the story of the early Baptists in America must include Roger Williams, originally a minister in the Church of England who migrated to Puritanism and eventually to Separatism. Williams's radical Separatist views caused him to run afoul of the Puritan establishment in Massachusetts Bay when he arrived from England in 1631, resulting in his banishment from the colony. Rather than be forced back to England, Williams fled into the wilderness in January 1636. He would not have survived the harsh New England winter had he not been taken in and sheltered by the Native Americans in the area, with whom he had previously developed a cordial relationship.

In June 1636 Williams and a few friends from nearby Salem established Providence Plantations (eventually to become the colony of Rhode Island). From the beginning the colony respected liberty of conscience and separation of church and state, concepts that had initially caused Williams conflicts with the Puritan establishment in nearby Massachusetts Bay. Sometime before 1639 Williams became a Baptist. Unfortunately, there are no records of his baptism, but records do indicate that sometime before 16 March 1639, Williams and his friends had organized a Baptist church, the very first Baptist church on American soil. The church still exists today as the First Baptist Church in Providence, Rhode Island.[14]

Williams, like John Smyth, had a restless soul. After only a few months, he came to reject his baptism, believing that the ordinances could only be legitimately performed by an actual apostle of Jesus. Since the apostles were dead, the ordinances of Christ could not be truly performed. Williams in his theological restlessness vowed to become a "seeker," seeking after the true New Testament Church, which could only be reconstituted if Christ sent a true apostle to do so, or if Christ

---

[13] McBeth, *Baptist Heritage*, 123.

[14] Ibid., 129–30. For two excellent biographies of Williams, see James P. Byrd, *Challenges of Roger Williams: Religious Liberty, Violent Persecution, and the Bible* (Macon GA: Mercer University Press, 2002) and Edwin S. Gaustad, *Liberty of Conscience: Roger Williams in America* (Grand Rapids MI: Wm B. Eerdmans, 1991).

himself returned. For the rest of his life Williams refused to affiliate with a local church.[15]

The Baptist tradition in New England, while initiated by Williams, owes much more credit to the efforts of John Clarke. Clarke, a friend of Williams whose spiritual pilgrimage was similar, became the founder of the second Baptist congregation in America in 1644, the First Baptist Church in Newport, Rhode Island. Unlike Williams, Clark remained a loyal and committed Baptist for the rest of his life and did more for Baptists in New England in the seventeenth century than anyone else. His *Ill Newes from New-England* (1652) remains an important early Baptist defense of religious liberty, as important as Roger Williams's *The Bloudy Tenent of Persecution* (1644). Clark wrote the book chronicling religious persecution by the Puritan establishment in Massachusetts Bay and then sent it to England so that Parliament could be aware of such abuses. Its impact was powerful, especially as it reported the vicious whipping of Obadiah Holmes in Massachusetts for illegal preaching.[16]

Baptists in the Middle Colonies enjoyed greater religious freedom than their neighbors to the north. None of the Middle Colonies had state churches, and consequently there was a greater religious diversity in that region, including the Quakers in Pennsylvania who were traditionally advocates for religious freedom. The most influential Baptist presence in this region was centered in Philadelphia. The Philadelphia Baptist Association, organized in 1707, became the first organized association in

---

[15] McBeth, *Baptist Heritage*, 129–30.

[16] See Edwin S. Gaustad, ed., *Baptist Piety: The Last Will and Testimony of Obadiah Holmes* (Valley Forge PA: Judson Press, 1994) 22f; see also McBeth, *Baptist Heritage*, 140–41. John Clarke, John Randall, and Obadiah Holmes made a pastoral visit to a Baptist named William Witter who lived in Lynn, Massachusetts, in July 1651. During the course of the visit the men, along with several neighbors, conducted a worship service in Witter's home. The authorities interrupted the meeting and arrested Clarke, Randall, and Holmes for conducting an illegal worship service. They were all sentenced to be fined or publicly whipped. Clarke's fine was paid by an anonymous donor. Randall paid his own fine. But Holmes, who was a bit more outspoken, was given a stiffer fine. Although the offer was made by a donor to pay it, Holmes refused, opting instead to take the whipping. On 5 September 1651, Holmes was publicly whipped thirty times. For several weeks the pain and wounds were so severe that he could only rest on his elbows and knees. The scars remained on his back for the rest of his life.

America. In 1742 the association produced a confession of faith that shaped Baptist theology in America for the next century.[17] In 1770 the Philadelphia Association founded a Baptist college in Rhode Island (eventually to become Brown University) in order to educate Baptist clergy and missionaries.

In the South Baptist development was much slower due to the Anglican establishment in many of the Southern colonies. It is impossible to know who the very first Baptist in the South was. There is evidence that in the 1680s dissenters began moving from England to Charleston, South Carolina, and presumably, a number of Baptists were among them. The real boost to Baptist activity in the South was the establishment of the First Baptist Church in Charleston in 1696. The church, though new to the South, was really the continuation of the Baptist church in Kittery, Maine. The aged Pastor William Screven (1629–1713) moved with the entire congregation from Kittery to Charleston and re-established the church there in 1696. Leon McBeth suggests several reasons for their move: (1) Native American raids on them in Kittery, which made their existence there precarious; (2) an available supply of timber needed for their shipbuilding business, which had been exhausted in Kittery; (3) the warm climate; and (4) the likelihood that Screven was familiar with many of the settlers already present in Charleston.[18]

Baptist historian Walter Shurden has argued that from the First Baptist Church of Charleston a distinct "Charleston Tradition" developed among Baptists in the South.[19] The Charleston Association was organized in 1751—the first Baptist association in the South. According to Shurden, the tradition that developed from the Baptists in Charleston can be characterized with the word "order." They desired *theological* order and adopted the Philadelphia Confession of Faith and its requisite Calvinism. They also wanted *ecclesiastical* order that sought to balance local church autonomy with associational cooperation. *Liturgical* order characterized the worship services, providing "a style in public worship that was

---

[17] McBeth, *Baptist Heritage*, 241.

[18] Ibid., 147.

[19] Walter B. Shurden, "The Southern Baptist Synthesis: Is It Cracking?" *Baptist History and Heritage* 16/2 (April 1981): 3–4.

ordered and stately, though pulsating with evangelical warmth."[20] Finally, *ministerial* order became a trait of this tradition as it fostered interest in an educated clergy. Richard Furman was the most influential pastor from First Baptist Church, Charleston. Although never formally educated himself, he argued that a sermon should "smell of the lamp," indicating his preference for well-organized and theologically reflective sermons.[21] The Charleston Tradition's emphasis upon an educated clergy led to the organization of numerous Baptist colleges and universities, and seminaries, in the South such as Furman (1826), Mercer (1833), and Wake Forest (1834), and eventually the Southern Baptist Theological Seminary in 1859.

The Baptist Tradition in North Carolina

Although no records confirm it, the assumption can be made that Baptists were among the earliest settlers to North Carolina. Morgan Edwards, an early chronicler of Baptists in Colonial America, wrote in the 1770s, "Next to Virginia, southward, is North-carolina; a poor and unhappy province.... In this wretched province have been some baptists since the settlement in 1695."[22] The earliest recorded reference to a Baptist presence, however, can be found in a letter written on 12 June 1714 by Reverend John Urmstone. Urmstone, a missionary of the Church of England's Society for the Propagation of the Gospel in Foreign Parts, complained in this letter that two of his vestrymen in the Chowan precinct were "professed Anabaptists."[23]

---

[20] Ibid., 4.

[21] Ibid.

[22] Morgan Edwards, *Materials Toward a History of the Baptists*, 2 vols. (Danielsville GA: Heritage Papers, 1984) as cited by McBeth, *Baptist Heritage*, 222.

[23] *Colonial Records*, II, 131, as cited in G. W. Paschal, *History of North Carolina Baptists*, vol. 1 (Raleigh NC: The General Board of the North Carolina Baptist State Convention, 1930) 131. See also Torbet, *A History of the Baptists*, 218. The use of the term "Anabaptist" beyond the sixteenth century to describe the Baptist movement of the seventeenth and eighteenth centuries can be confusing. The enemies of the Baptist tradition did not make a distinction, although a significant difference existed between the two groups.

The earliest Baptist churches in North Carolina were Arminian in theology from the General Baptist tradition. The first Baptist church to be organized in North Carolina resulted from the efforts of Paul Palmer, an itinerant General Baptist evangelist who came to the colony sometime before 1720. Originally a native of Maryland, Palmer was baptized by the Welsh Tract Baptist Church in Delaware, was ordained in Connecticut, spent some time in New Jersey, and eventually returned to Maryland where he gathered a group of Baptists who eventually became the first Baptist church in that colony. Sometime before 1720 Palmer came to North Carolina where he married the widow of Thomas Peterson, one of the wealthiest men in the colony. By 1726, when his itinerant preaching began to gain recognition, he had also become a wealthy man, amassing a large amount of land holdings along with that of his wife. The following year he organized the first Baptist church in North Carolina, located in Chowan County near the town of Cisco.[24]

Information about this first church is sketchy except for a short reference in the *Diary* of John Comer, the pastor of the Baptist church in Newport, Rhode Island, at the time. In an entry dated 27 September 1729, Comer states: "This day I received a letter from ye Baptist church in North Carolina, settled about two years ago (in ye year 1727) since by Mr. Paul Palmer, This church consists of 32 members, it meets in Chowan."[25] This places the date of the church's organization to be in the year 1727. While Palmer organized and gave birth to the church in Chowan, he was not its first pastor. That responsibility fell to Palmer's younger disciple Joseph Parker, also a member of the church. Parker's personality was less volatile than Palmer's, making him better suited for the life of a pastor.[26] However, only three years after its organization, Parker moved to

---

[24] Torbet, *History of the Baptists*, 218–19. See also McBeth, *Baptist Heritage*, 222. For a fuller account of Paul Palmer's activities in North Carolina, see Paschal, *History of North Carolina Baptists*, vol. 1, 131–60.

[25] C. Edwin Barrows, ed., *The Diary of John Comer* (Philadelphia: The American Baptist Publication Society, 1892) 84–85, as cited by McBeth, *Baptist Heritage*, 222.

[26] See Paschal, *History of North Carolina Baptists*, vol. 1, 134–38. Paschal indicates that Palmer and his wife on one occasion were accused of stealing a slave in a case that brought much public attention to the couple. The charges were eventually dropped.

Meherrin, and the absence of the Chowan church's name in records from the time leads historians to conclude that it lived a very short life.[27]

The distinction of being the oldest Baptist church in North Carolina that still survives to the present belongs to the Shiloh Baptist Church in Camden County, founded by Palmer in 1729. Palmer is listed as a charter member of the church, but the first pastor was William Burges. The Shiloh church was very active, evidenced from the fact that it produced nine ministers and eventually spawned six other Baptist churches from its membership.[28]

Yet as important as Paul Palmer was for the early organization of the Baptist movement in North Carolina, the early growth of the Baptist movement in the colony can be credited more to the tireless efforts of Joseph Parker, William Sojourner, and Josiah Hart. After his move from Chowan to Meherrin, Parker organized a thriving Baptist congregation there and was probably instrumental in the organization of churches at Bertie (Sandy Run), Lower Fishing Creek, and Swift Creek. William Sojourner moved from Burleigh, Virginia, in 1742 with a number of Baptists from the church there and organized the Kehukee church in Halifax County near the present city of Scotland Neck. This area became one of the most important Baptist presences in Eastern North Carolina during the eighteenth century. Josiah Hart is credited with organizing the Pungo church in Beaufort County and the Fishing Creek church in Warren County, but is best remembered for the large number of Baptist preachers whom he either ordained or baptized. The work of these early General Baptist preachers was so successful that, by 1755, there were sixteen General Baptist churches in North Carolina.[29]

During the decade between 1750 and 1760, Baptists in North Carolina went through a major theological shift. Almost all of these early

---

[27] Torbet, *History of the Baptists*, 219. See also Paschal, *History of North Carolina Baptists*, vol. 1, 131–42, 160.

[28] Torbet, *History of the Baptists*, 219; Paschal, *History of North Carolina Baptists*, vol. 1, 143–48; McBeth, *Baptist Heritage*, 223.

[29] Robert A. Baker, *The Southern Baptist Convention and Its People* (Nashville: Broadman Press, 1974) 45. For a much more detailed discussion of the General Baptist presence in the eighteenth century in North Carolina, see Paschal, *History of North Carolina Baptists*, vol. 1, 123–203.

General Baptist churches, originally Arminian in theology, radically shifted toward the Particular Baptist tradition and its resultant Calvinism. The story of how this shift occurred is much too long to chronicle here, but much of it can be credited to the work of Robert Williams, a Baptist pastor and native North Carolinian who went to the Welsh Neck area of South Carolina in 1745. Five years later he returned with Calvinist views and was highly successful in turning other North Carolina pastors from Arminianism to Calvinism. Robert Baker argues that the theological ignorance of most North Carolina Baptist pastors at that time, along with the lack of assurance of salvation on the part of the laity and lack of church discipline in the churches, contributed to the easy theological shift.[30]

To help in his efforts, Williams also contacted the Philadelphia Baptist Association and requested that other more learned preachers be sent to North Carolina. John Gano, one of the most prominent Baptists of the eighteenth century, made a trip southward to preach in North Carolina as a result. There were also others from Philadelphia who came south, such as Peter Van Horn and Benjamin Miller. These efforts to change the theological persuasion of the early North Carolina Baptist churches were so successful that, by 1755, all but three churches— Meherrin, Pungo, and Grassy Creek—had been reconstituted as Particular Baptist.[31] It should be noted, as G. W. Pascal indicates, that this transformation was not without controversy. In almost all the cases, the pastor's theology changed, but only a small portion of church members actually joined the newly constituted churches, so that "hardly more than five per cent of the General Baptist members were in the newly constituted Particular Baptist churches."[32] Nevertheless, the Calvinistic influence brought a lasting change to North Carolina Baptists, strengthening their understanding of regeneration and church discipline.[33]

---

[30] Baker, *Southern Baptist Convention*, 45–46.

[31] Ibid., 46.

[32] Paschal, *History of North Carolina Baptists*, vol. 1, 212. He describes some of the individual church disputes on pp. 211–23.

[33] Baker, *Southern Baptist Convention*, 46.

Along with the theological infusion of Particular Baptist theology in North Carolina from 1750–1760, during that same decade the rise of the Separate Baptists represents another dominant movement that occurred in the North Carolina Baptist family. Leon McBeth calls the Separate Baptist movement possibly "the most dynamic event among North Carolina Baptists in the eighteenth century."[34]

During the First Great Awakening, just as Presbyterians and Congregationalists had, the Baptists in Colonial America divided into two different groups. "Regular Baptists" tended to be located more in the urban areas and were critical of the excessive emotionalism of the revivals. "Separate Baptists," on the other hand, embraced the emotionalism of the revivals and appealed more to the rural folk.

In the early 1750s two brothers-in-law from New England, Shubal Stearns and Daniel Marshall, having embraced Separate Baptist beliefs, migrated southward with their families and other friends, first to Virginia and then in 1755 to North Carolina. They settled in Guilford County in a region known as Sandy Creek and there built a church. From this humble beginning eventually grew the "Sandy Creek Tradition," as Walter Shurden named it. As he characterized the Charleston Tradition with the word "order," he characterized the Sandy Creek Tradition with the word "ardor" and argued that they "released a devotion to freedom which is without parallel in Baptist history."[35]

These enthusiastic Baptists experienced rapid growth. Morgan Edwards, writing about the Separate Baptists in the 1770s, said that very soon after their arrival in North Carolina, "the neighbourhood was alarmed and the Spirit of God listed to blow as a mighty rushing wind in so much that in three years time they had increased to three churches, consisting upwards of 900 communicants, viz: Sandy Creek, Abot's Creek, Deep River."[36] Shurden describes the Separate Baptists' ardor with four terms. First, they were *revivalistic*. "Unlike the city slickers at Charleston, they did not praise God by praising God; they praised God

---

[34] McBeth, *Baptist Heritage*, 223.

[35] Shurden, "The Southern Baptist Synthesis: Is It Cracking?" 4.

[36] Morgan Edwards, *Morgan Edwards's Notebook on North Carolina Baptists*, published in Paschal, *History of North Carolina Baptists*, vol. 1, 227.

by reaching women and men. They had a mourner's bench and they expected public groaning, not polite amens."[37]

Second, they were *charismatic*. By this, Shurden means that they placed great emphasis on the internal presence of the Spirit. Conversion was more than just an intellectual decision. A calling to preach was truly a divine calling, not a "professional choice." Unlike the Charleston Tradition, the Separates *discouraged* ministerial education because they believed it had the effect of quenching the Spirit in both the preacher and, consequently, in the sermon. Their worship services each week were like revivals with tears and loud singing. Stearns was described by Morgan Edwards as

> but a little man, but of good natural parts, and sound judgment. Of learning he had but a small share, yet was pretty well acquainted with books. His voice was musical and strong, which he managed in such a manner, as one while to make soft impressions on the heart, and fetch tears from the eyes in a mechanical way; and anon to shake the nerves, and to throw the animal system into tumults and perturbations. All the Separate ministers copy after him in tones of voice and actions of body; and some few exceed him.[38]

Third, Shurden says that the Separate Baptists exhibited an ecclesiology that was fiercely *independent*. Even though they did form the Sandy Creek Baptist Association in 1758, which geographically stretched into several states, "the Sandy Creek Tradition did not spend as much time defining associational authority as they did declaring local church autonomy."[39] Finally, the Sandy Creek Tradition was *biblicist*, meaning that they approached the Bible with a literal interpretation and rejected all theological confessions of faith, which had become very important to Baptists in England and to the Regular Baptists, particularly in Philadelphia.[40]

***

---

[37] Shurden, "The Southern Baptist Synthesis: Is It Cracking?" 5.

[38] Morgan Edwards, *Materials Toward a History of the Baptists*, published in Paschal, *History of North Carolina Baptists*, vol. 1, 286–87.

[39] Shurden, "The Southern Baptist Synthesis: Is It Cracking?" 5.

[40] Ibid.

By the end of the American Revolution there were three groups of Baptists who were active in North Carolina: the General Baptists with their Arminianism, the Regular Baptists who populated the Kehuckee Creek area in Halifax County, and the Separate Baptists in Sandy Creek. These three groups shared a common experience as Baptists but expressed their faith and theology in very different ways.[41] At the end of the eighteenth century Regular Baptists and Separate Baptists in North Carolina began to find considerable common ground with one another and share fellowship together. As the nineteenth century dawned, the future looked bright for Baptists nationally and in the state of North Carolina. The nineteenth century brought an explosion of growth to Baptists, particularly in the South, forming the milieu within which the story of the organization of the First Baptist Church in Raleigh can now be told.

---

[41] McBeth, *Baptist Heritage*, 223.

2

Constituting a Church and
Struggling to Survive (1812–1840)[1]

If it were possible to set the dial on a time machine to the year 1800 and journey back, the world we would discover would be much different from our world in the early twenty-first century. The world population that year was 978 million, and it would be another two years before it topped one billion. The population of North America was a mere seven million.[2] In Europe, the French Revolution had run its course. Napoleon Bonaparte was on the rise in France and would be the major military/political player in Western Europe until his defeat at Waterloo in 1815.

The United States was still in its infancy in 1800. Twenty-one of the fifty-six signers of the Declaration of Independence were still alive. The nation was in the midst of grieving the leader of the Continental Army and first President George Washington, who had died just a few weeks before the dawning of the new century. The Constitution had only been ratified for twelve years. Washington, D.C. succeeded New York City as the capital of the United States and the nation's second president, John Adams, became the first to occupy the White House that year.

During the first three decades of the nineteenth century, several important events happened that brought tremendous change to the young nation. Thomas Jefferson defeated John Adams for the presidency in the Election of 1800, spelling the demise of the Federalist party and giving rise to the Democratic-Republican party, which would dominate

---

[1] For much of the organization and arrangement of the first century of the church's history, I am indebted to the work of L. J. Morris in his 1937 master's thesis from Wake Forest College. Morris used his thesis to chronicle the church's first century. See L. J. Morris, "The History of the First Baptist Church of Raleigh, 1812–1912" (master's thesis, Wake Forest College, 1937).

[2] United Nations Population Division, "Part 1—Introduction and Table 1-4," in *The World at Six Billion*, http://www.un.org/esa/population/publications/sixbillion/sixbilpart1.pdf (last accessed 14 September 2008).

American politics for the next several decades.[3] One of Jefferson's most important accomplishments was the Louisiana Purchase in 1803, which doubled the land size of the United States and represented a foreign policy victory over France. Several years later, the American victory over the British in the War of 1812 finalized America's complete break from Great Britain. Then in 1823 the United States further declared its sovereignty when James Monroe's address to Congress intoned the famous "Monroe Doctrine," a claim that has been the bedrock of American foreign policy since then. The young nation was clearly in the process of maturing in the first third of the nineteenth century.

The American religious landscape went through a momentous change during the first third of the nineteenth century as well. The Second Great Awakening brought a series of revivals to the Eastern seaboard as well as to the frontier. Historians differ over the exact dates for the Second Great Awakening, but the general consensus is that the movement began sometime after the American Revolution and continued until the 1840s.

Characterized by fervency and great emotionalism, and led by evangelists such as Charles Grandison Finney, the Second Great Awakening challenged religious Americans to implement moral reforms in numerous areas of society. In that regard, the Second Great Awakening awakened concern among American Christians for domestic ills such as slavery, alcohol abuse, and low literacy rates, which eventually mobilized them to work for a better society. Subsequently, the later decades of the nineteenth century witnessed the organization of new colleges, as well as the creation of a public school system, abolitionist organizations, and temperance societies. In addition to prompting general moral concern, it also motivated American Christians to think about carrying the Gospel beyond the borders of the United States to other nations in the world through foreign missions[4]

---

[3] See David McCullough, *John Adams* (New York: Simon and Schuster, 2001) 543–67 for more information on the Election of 1800.

[4] For an in-depth discussion of the Second Great Awakening, see Sydney E. Ahlstrom, *A Religious History of the American People* (New Haven: Yale University Press, 1972) 415–509; Mark A. Noll, *A History of Christianity in the United States and Canada* (Grand Rapids: William B. Eerdmans Publishing Company, 1992) 165–245;

The two Protestant denominations that benefited the most from the Second Great Awakening, especially on the frontier, were Baptists and Methodists, in large part due to the remarkable growth that the movement generated for each. In the midst of that tremendous growth, Baptists in the United States created their first national organization in 1814. Named the General Missionary Convention of the Baptist Denomination in the United States for Foreign Missions, the organization eventually came to be called the "Triennial Convention" because its meetings were held once every three years. The Triennial Convention had a solitary purpose in the beginning: to support foreign missions.[5] The Triennial Convention remained a united missions effort among Baptists in the United States until the Baptists in the South broke away in 1845 over slavery and formed the Southern Baptist Convention.[6]

As the new nation looked forward to a century of promise, the young city of Raleigh, North Carolina, also looked to the coming century with optimism.[7] The first mayor of Raleigh, John Haywood, was selected

---

Whitney R. Cross, *The Burned-Over District: The Social and Intellectual History of Enthusiastic Religion in Western New York, 1800–1850* (Ithaca NY: Cornell University Press, 1950); William G. McLoughlin, *Revivals, Awakenings and Reform: An Essay on Religion and Social Change in America, 1607–1977* (Chicago: University of Chicago Press, 1978) 98–140; and William G. McLoughlin, *Modern Revivalism: Charles Grandison Finney to Billy Graham* (New York: The Ronald Press Co., 1959) 3–165.

[5] The first missionaries supported were Adoniram and Ann Hasseltine Judson, who began their mission work in India but eventually moved to Burma. The story of their lives on the mission field and the support generated back in the United States by their close friend and colleague Luther Rice is a remarkable tale of missionary heroism.

[6] For a good discussion of the Triennial Convention, see H. Leon McBeth, *The Baptist Heritage: Four Centuries of Baptist Witness* (Nashville: Broadman Press, 1987) 343–91; Robert G. Torbet, *A History of the Baptists*, 3rd ed. (Valley Forge PA: Judson Press, 1980) 249–53; and Bill J. Leonard, *Baptist Ways: A History* (Valley Forge PA: Judson Press, 2003) 158–96.

[7] Elizabeth Reid Murray, *Wake: Capital County of North Carolina*, vol. 1 (Raleigh NC: Capital County Publishing Co.,1983). Although Murray's history of Wake County is the most comprehensive, there are several histories of the city of Raleigh that should be noted: Marshall Lancaster, *Raleigh: An Unorthodox History of North Carolina's Capital* (Asheboro NC: Down Home Press, 1992); David Perkins, ed., *The News and Observer's Raleigh: A Living History of North Carolina's Capital*

in 1795. Beginning in 1799 two newspapers were published weekly in the city—*The Minerva*, published by New Jersey native William Boylan until 1810, and the *Raleigh Register*, published by Joseph Gales. Gales, originally from England, came to Raleigh by way of Philadelphia. The *Raleigh Register* lasted as the major newspaper for the city from its inception in 1799 until 1863.[8]

Urban problems developed early in the life of the new city. Maintenance of roads was one example. In 1795 the General Assembly passed a law that any free male resident of the city of Raleigh would be required to work on the road in the city or supply three male slaves to do so in his place. That law was applicable to all free male residents of the city whether property owners or renters.[9] A suitable location for a cemetery created another urban concern for the young city. In 1798 the city commissioners set aside four acres of state-owned land near the city limit that became Raleigh's city cemetery.[10]

The religious climate in the city of Raleigh was slow to develop. During the years 1802–1804, a series of revivals swept through Wake County that captured first the Presbyterians and Methodists, and eventually the Baptists. Small Baptist churches began to spring up throughout Wake County as a result of the religious awakening. After 1810 an annual camp meeting was held by the Methodists on the property of the John and Samuel Whitaker Plantation, off of Fayetteville Road and south of the city. That event usually lasted for five or six days and brought a variety of people and commerce to the outskirts of the city.[11]

Despite the revivalist fervor within the county, more than a decade passed after the founding of the city of Raleigh before there were any

---

(Winston-Salem NC: John F. Blair, 1994); Steve Solpen, *Raleigh: A Pictorial History* (Norfolk: Donning Company Publishers, 1977); and James Vickers, *Raleigh, City of Oaks: An Illustrated History* (Woodland Hills CA: Windsor Publications, 1982).

[8] Murray, *Wake: Capital County of North Carolina*, vol. 1, 112–13. For a thorough history of the *Raleigh Register*, see Robert Neal Elliott, Jr., *The Raleigh Register, 1799–1863* (Chapel Hill: The University of North Carolina Press, 1955).

[9] Murray, *Wake: Capital County of North Carolina*, vol. 1, 111.

[10] Ibid., 112.

[11] Ibid., 168–73.

church buildings or regular worship services. The worship services that did take place usually were led by itinerant preachers in the courthouse. After its completion in 1794 the State House served as the location for most of the worship services and funerals in the city. In 1801 the General Assembly passed a resolution "that all regular Ministers of the Gospel, of any denomination whatever, should in the recess of the General Assembly, have the privilege and liberty of performing divine service, in either the Senate Chamber or Commons Hall, until the citizens of Raleigh have their church prepared."[12] The citizens of the city had earlier petitioned the General Assembly for a lot and sufficient funds to build a church building. The committee that dealt with the petition refused to allow the funds but did grant a parcel of land for such use, with the stipulation that when the church building was completed, it "shall be free and open to all ministers of every denomination."[13] Though the church building was never built, the property located at Moore Square was eventually used by the Baptists and later by the Christian Church.

The first minister to conduct regular worship services in the city was Reverend William Leftwich Turner, a Presbyterian minister who settled in Raleigh in 1806 to be principal of the Raleigh Academy. Turner held nondenominational services in the State House and ministered to the citizens of the city regardless of their religious affiliation. In 1810 he was succeeded by Reverend William McPheeters, who played an important role in establishing the first Presbyterian church in the city in 1816.[14] The first church building in the city continued the nondenominational tradition and was built in 1808 between Morgan and Hargett Streets. Instrumental in the building of the church named "Bethel" was Reverend William Glendinning, an eccentric man who donated the lot upon which the church was built.[15] The earliest

---

[12] *Raleigh Register* (North Carolina), 22 December 1801, as cited by Murray, *Wake: Capital County of North Carolina,* vol. 1, 173.

[13] *Raleigh Register* (North Carolina), 23 February 1802, as cited by Murray, *Wake: Capital County of North Carolina,* vol. 1, 174.

[14] Murray, *Wake: Capital County of North Carolina,* vol. 1, 174.

[15] Ibid., 175. See also Vickers, *Raleigh, City of Oaks,* for information about Glendinning. Apparently, Glendinning was prone to apocalyptic visions and considered quite bizarre until his death in 1816.

denominational group in the city to organize were the Methodists. Bishop Francis Asbury reportedly preached in the State House on 6 March 1800. By 1811 the first Methodist congregation had been organized.[16]

The Raleigh Baptist Church

Into that religious context, on 7 March 1812 twenty-three members from the Cool Spring Baptist Church, located several miles outside the city of Raleigh, came together to form the Raleigh Baptist Church.[17] The description of the organizational meeting as recorded in the church minutes reads:

> The following members were dismissed in full fellowship from the Baptist church of Christ at Cool Spring in Wake County. White male members: Hardy Sanders, Samuel Pearson, Elhannon Nutt, John Briggs. White female members: Mary Sanders, Nancy Card, Dolly Grayson, Elizabeth Briggs, Tabbytha Hutchins. Black male members: Jack, Moses, Elisha, Jethro, Joseph. Black female members: Siddy, Hannah, Hasty, Judy, Lisbon, Nelly, Flora, Jenny, Zilpha.[18]

---

[16] Murray, *Wake: Capital County of North Carolina,* vol. 1, 176.

[17] Church Conference Records, First Baptist Church of Raleigh, 7 March 1812. The church has done a remarkable job over the last two centuries of maintaining, organizing, and preserving its records. Church conference minutes exist from the beginning with only a few gaps in time. One unique source of information related to the church's first century was an account written by a former church clerk named Jordan Womble in 1873. Womble's history covers the first sixty-one years of the church's history and occupies forty-seven handwritten pages. Added to Womble's history is that of a later church clerk named J. C. Marcom, who continued the church's history from 1873 to 1893. His handwritten account also occupies forty-seven handwritten pages. Both accounts are joined together into one narrative and are appended in the church record book in the entry dated 29 September 1893. (Hereafter this will be cited as "Womble-Marcom History"). This early history is attached to the church minute book with a note that reads, "The history of the first Raleigh Baptist Church from 1812 as compiled by Jordan Womble, Jr. and ordered...on the minutes by the church in conference on Sept. 29th, 1893."

[18] Church Conference Records, 8 March 1812. The term "dismissed" used here does not carry a negative connotation. It was a common term used in the nineteenth century to describe the process of leaving one congregation for

The following day, the records state that these twenty-three people were examined in the State House by Elders Robert T. Daniel and Zadock Bell and, "being thought orthodox were regularly constituted into a Baptist church." Hardy Sanders and John Briggs were ordained as the first deacons and the church was named the "Raleigh Baptist Church." Elhannon Nutt was selected to serve as church clerk.[19]

For some reason unexplained within the minutes, the church existed for four months before calling Robert T. Daniel as its first pastor (9 July 1812). Presumably, the church met each Sunday in different locations with different ministers preaching. Following the entry describing the call of Daniel as the first pastor, there is a generalized statement that reads: "At sundry times a number were added to the church—some by baptism and some by letter." That statement is then followed by another listing of members, with other names added to the names of the charter members. Once again, the names are divided into the four categories of "White Male Members, White Female Members, Black Male Members and Black Female Members."

During the period from 1812 to 1835, eight pastors served the congregation with an average tenure of almost three years each. The story of the church must naturally include the story of these pastors.

Robert Thomas Daniel (1812–1815)[20]

The Raleigh Baptist Church was without clergy leadership for four months until Robert Thomas Daniel became pastor. He brought to the church a wealth of pastoral experience and excellence in preaching. A

---

another. The handwriting makes some of the names of the "Black Female" members difficult to read. "Siddy" may be "Liddy." "Lisbon" may be "Sisbon."

[19] Ibid. Although not stated in the church minutes, one tradition indicates that the organization of the church followed a sermon by Elder Robert T. Daniel, which was in itself a response to a sermon given earlier by a Universalist minister. See The North Carolina Historical Records Survey, Project Division of Community Service Programs, Work Projects Administration, Inventory of the Church Archives of North Carolina, Southern Baptist Convention, Central Association (Raleigh: February 1941) 7.

[20] Throughout the book the dates listed beside a pastor's name indicate the length of that pastor's tenure at the church.

native Virginian, born in Middlesex County on 10 June 1773, during his childhood his parents moved to North Carolina and settled in Chatham County.[21] He was converted and baptized in 1802 by the Holly Springs Baptist Church in Wake County. The following year he began preaching.

Sketchy accounts from Daniel's era indicate that he was a preacher of great fluency. The prominent Raleigh Judge Henry Seawell indicated that "he had never heard in the pulpit or in the court house or in the Senate Chamber a more eloquent speaker than Elder Daniel."[22] An account from the late nineteenth century says that Daniel "was an orator by nature but an uneducated man. His facille [*sic*] language flowed unhesitatingly and never in the pulpit did he betray his lack of education. He is probably the greatest preacher we have ever had in North Carolina."[23] R. B. C. Howell, pastor of First Baptist Church, Nashville from 1834 to 1850 and the second president of the Southern Baptist Convention, described Daniel as an "amiable, enlightened, and polished gentleman and Christian; the impassioned, eloquent, and successful minister of the cross."[24]

Much of Daniel's career was spent as a missionary for several early Baptist mission societies in the American South. In his own words just before his death, Daniel indicated that in his career he had traveled "60,000 miles; preached about 5,000 sermons; baptized about fifteen hundred persons, twelve of them ministers."[25] Daniel was in Raleigh in 1812 as a missionary of the Baptist Philanthropic Society (which was founded in 1805 as the first mission organization of North Carolina Baptists). His heart for missions and the legacy he left caused William

---

[21] Robert T. Daniel to R. B. C. Howell, letter reprinted in *Baptist Banner and Western Pioneer* (Kentucky), 30 July 1840, 1.

[22] Quoted in "Womble-Marcom History," 2b. The quotation is also cited by Morris, "The History of the First Baptist Church of Raleigh," 4.

[23] "Womble-Marcom History," 2b; Morris, "The History of the First Baptist Church of Raleigh," 4.

[24] R. B. C. Howell, "To Die Is Gain," *Baptist Banner and Western Pioneer* (Kentucky), 8 October 1840, 2.

[25] Robert T. Daniel to R. B. C. Howell.

Cathcart to say of him in 1881, "His was a missionary heart, a missionary tongue, and a missionary hand."[26]

Daniel served as the pastor of the Raleigh Baptist Church on two different occasions. Called as the founding pastor on 9 July 1812, he served until sometime in 1815. The date of his resignation is unknown, although a citation in the church minutes indicates that on 19 April 1815 he was dismissed by letter from the church roll. Seven years later, on 22 June 1822, the church once again selected Daniel as pastor. Daniel's tenure as pastor the second time lasted until 5 March 1826, when he and his wife, Penny, were dismissed again by letter, presumably due to Daniel's desire to further his itinerant mission work.

Few church records have survived from the years of Daniel's first tenure as pastor of the church. It was a few years before the congregation was able to construct a building for worship. Services were held at first in the State House and then in various members' homes.[27] Eventually, the congregation had the means to construct a small building on South Person Street across from Moore Square on a lot owned by Mrs. Mary Dudley. The date for the construction of the building is hard to determine, and several dates ranging from 1814 to 1819 are given by later interpreters of the church's history.[28]

Despite the limited number of records surviving from that period, it can be surmised that the church grew considerably during Daniel's first pastorate. Jordan Womble indicated that sometime around 1813/1814, the membership had more than doubled from the original twenty-three charter members to a total membership of fifty.[29] It is also clear that Daniel made a direct contribution to the congregation's worship services by producing the church's first hymnal, titled *A Selection of Hymns and*

---

[26] *Baptist Encyclopedia*, ed. William Cathcart, vol. 1 (Philadelphia: Louis H. Everts, 1881) s.v. "Robert Thomas Daniel"; also quoted in Morris, "The History of the First Baptist Church of Raleigh," 4.

[27] Inventory of the Church Archives of North Carolina, 7.

[28] See ibid., which gives a date of 1819 for the church's construction. See also Murray, *Wake: Capital County of North Carolina*, vol. 1, 177. Murray indicates that the church building was erected "about 1814." See Morris, "The History of the First Baptist Church of Raleigh," 6. Morris gives the date of 1818.

[29] "Womble-Marcom History," 2a.

Spiritual Songs. The hymnal included a number of hymns written by Daniel himself.[30]

At this time, it should be noted that as the congregation was adjusting to its new church and pastor, a significant event occurred for Baptist life in Raleigh and all over the state. During the first month of Daniel's pastorate, the North Carolina Baptist General Meeting of Correspondence convened at the State House in Raleigh on 24 July 1812, (making it the first statewide organization of Baptists in North Carolina and the forerunner of the Baptist State Convention). The "brain-child" of Martin Ross, the idea for the meeting was proposed before the Chowan association in 1809, which promptly approved it and invited the other nine associations in the state to participate. The Raleigh meeting in 1812 achieved the milestone of approving a new constitution for the fledgling organization.[31]

The North Carolina Baptist General Meeting of Correspondence met over the entire weekend and concluded on Sunday evening. Reports indicate that large crowds attended the sessions, and Sunday the numbers were so large that the meeting had to be moved to the yard outside the State House. Among the worship and business conducted by the organization, the Baptists also approved a resolution supporting President James Madison's call for a national day of prayer, as the country was at the time involved in the War of 1812. The entire resolution reads:

> *Resolved*, That the Proclamation of the President of the United States, in recommending the third Thursday in August next, to be observed as a day of Fasting, Humiliation, and Prayer, meets with our hearty approbation; and therefore, do respectfully recommend, that all the Associations and Churches in this State observe that day in the manner appointed by the President for the Religious Purposes disclosed in his Proclamation.[32]

---

[30] Murray, *Wake: Capital County of North Carolina*, vol. 1, 177.

[31] Henry Smith Stroupe, "North Carolina, Baptist State Convention of," in *Encylcopedia of Southern Baptists*, ed. Norman Wade Cox, vol. 2 (Nashville: Broadman Press, 1958) 994–95.

[32] *Raleigh Register* (North Carolina), 31 July 1812, 3.

Josiah Crudup (1815–1820?)

Following Robert T. Daniel's first tenure as pastor of the Raleigh Baptist Church, the congregation issued a call to Josiah Crudup on 28 August 1815. The following entry into the church minutes recounts the moment:

> We, the Baptized Church of Christ in Raleigh, in conference assembled this 28th day of August, 1815, being destitute of a pastor, and having prayed to God for direction in the choice of one, do agree to call our beloved Brother and Elder Josiah Crudup to minister unto us in holy things. And we will agreeably to our number and ability minister unto him of our earthly things.

The same entry into the church minutes also indicates that the new pastor requested that the date 26 October of that year should be set aside as a "day of humiliation, fasting, and prayer to Almighty God for direction in the choice of a pastor."[33] From the evidence it would seem to indicate that Crudup had a two-stage call in 1815, the first in August and the second a reaffirmation in October. Unfortunately, no church records exist from that point until 1821, so very little can be discerned about his work as pastor of the church, his style of leadership, or any events that may have happened during that time that could shed light on his personality.

There are facts about Crudup's life and career that are known from other sources. He was born in 1791 in Wake County, the youngest of nine children born to Baptist minister Josiah Crudup, Sr. and Elizabeth Battle. He was educated at the Raleigh Academy, which had been established in 1804 and had quickly developed a reputation as an outstanding educational institution. One early supporter of the academy wrote that "it not only offered an opportunity of education , at a moderate expence [*sic*], for all the male and female children of the city, but it was resorted to by youth of both sexes from the neighboring States, to the great benefit of our merchants, mechanics and boarding houses."[34] Crudup continued his

---

[33] Church Conference Records, 28 August 1815.
[34] Joseph Gales, as quoted in Murray, *Wake: Capital County of North Carolina*, vol. 1, 183.

education at Columbian College (now George Washington University), where he studied theology, an indication that he planned his education with a sense of calling to ministry in mind. Crudup was ordained in August 1813 with the Reverends John Purefoy, William Lancaster, and Robert T. Daniel serving on his ordination council. Daniel's presence on the ordination council suggests a close relationship, with Crudup perhaps considering Daniel a mentor. That same year, Crudup was married to Anne Maria Davis Brickell. They had four children.[35]

As previously mentioned, the lack of church records for Crudup's years of ministry at the Raleigh Baptist Church prohibits us from knowing about events that may have shaped his ministry. There is not even any indication as to when he left the pastorate of the church. He must have had some ministerial relationship to the church as late as 1820, because during that year he was elected to the state Senate to represent Wake County. Very soon after he occupied his senate seat, however, a dispute erupted when several senators contested his seat on the grounds that the state constitution originally adopted in 1776 prohibited ministers from holding office in the legislature while actively serving in a ministerial role. After a heated three-day debate in which Crudup declared himself not to be actively serving as the pastor of the Raleigh Baptist Church, a vote of thirty-six to fifteen was taken, and he was removed from office.[36]

---

[35] *Baptist Encyclopedia*, vol. 1, s.v. "Crudup, Rev. Josiah."

[36] "The Writer's Program of the Works Project Administration in the State of North Carolina," *Raleigh, Capital of North Carolina* (New Bern NC: Owen G. Dunn Co., 1942) 59, and Paul I. Chestnut, "Crudup, Josiah," in *Dictionary of North Carolina Biography*, ed. William S. Powell, vol. 1 (Chapel Hill, University of North Carolina Press, 1979) 467; Morris, "The History of the First Baptist Church of Raleigh," 5–6. See also Murray, *Wake: Capital County of North Carolina*, vol. 1, 388–89. The debate over Crudup must have been exciting and very heated at times. Following the debate and vote to remove Crudup, Thomas Person moved that Jesse Adams be removed on the same grounds as Crudup's removal. In retaliation, Adams argued that Person should be removed because he was an atheist. Adams was ultimately removed from his seat and requested to make a public apology for his attack on Person. The constitution for the state of North Carolina was amended in 1835, excluding that article as well as the article that prohibited anyone but Protestants from holding public office.

Crudup was not finished with politics after that frustrating experience, and his political career was at times colorful. In 1821 he was elected to Congress where he served for one term until 1823. There were rumors that during his campaign he bribed voters with liquor to influence their votes. Defeated for re-election in 1823, he tried again in 1825 and lost in a very close election to Willie P. Mangum. Crudup's loss might have been due to the fact that he had been scheduled to appear with Mangum at a meeting where both were to speak. A heavy rainstorm prohibited Crudup from attending, although Mangum was able to be present. Mangum was convinced that his presence at the meeting without Crudup was the factor that provided him the slender margin needed for the victory.[37] While Crudup's political career was short, his ministry was not. Rather, he served as a minister at various churches for more than fifty years and was described by one interpreter as a "cultivated Christian gentleman...[who] in his prime was a preacher of surpassing eloquence." He died in 1872.[38]

Thomas Crocker (1821–1822)

Unfortunately, the absence of church minutes also prohibits us from knowing much about the ministry of Thomas Crocker (the third pastor of the Raleigh Baptist Church) as well. In fact, the dates of his tenure cannot even be ascertained with a great amount of certainty. There is an entry in the church minutes dated 12 February 1821 that says the church was "under the pastoral care of Elder Thomas Crocker."[39] Beyond that there is very little to suggest either the tenure or the quality of his ministry as pastor of the church. His tenure must not have been long though, since

---

[37] Chestnut, "Crudup, Josiah," 467. As a further note on his political activity, Crudup was a lifelong member of the Whig party and owned a large number of slaves, but opposed Southern secession from the Union and opposed Lincoln's election in 1860 out of fear that his unpopularity in the South would give strength to the secessionist impulse. Yet, with the exception of representing Granville County at the constitutional convention in 1835, Crudup spent the rest of his life as a minister and farmer.

[38] *Baptist Encyclopedia*, vol. 1, s.v. "Crudup, Rev. Josiah."

[39] Church Conference Records, 12 February 1821.

Robert T. Daniel was called back for a second time to serve as pastor of the church on 20 June 1822.

Sources outside of the church records yield a few facts about Crocker's life and career as a pastor. One secondary source indicates that he was born in 1786 and died in 1848 and that "[f]or more than thirty years Thomas Crocker was a faithful and successful preacher of the gospel, and hundreds of persons in the counties of Wake, Warren, Granville, and Franklin, N.C. were brought to Christ by his labors."[40] His name also appears several times in the *Biblical Recorder* between the years 1835 and 1838, which indicates his activity in the newly organized Baptist State Convention.[41] In his history of North Carolina Baptists, G. W. Paschal reveals that Crocker was the son of Jacob Crocker, Sr., who resided about five miles north of Louisburg, North Carolina. He erected a church near his home and gave it the name "Crocker's Meeting House." He also played a role in the organization of the Wake Union Baptist Church located one mile west of Wake Forest, North Carolina. The elder Crocker had two sons, both of whom succeeded their father as Baptist preachers: Thomas, who spent his ministerial career in North Carolina, and his brother Jacob, Jr., who moved to South Carolina and ultimately migrated further west to Alabama.[42] Beyond this scant information very little else can be determined about Thomas Crocker.

Robert Thomas Daniel (1822–1826)

A reference in the church minutes dated 20 June 1822 marks the call of Robert T. Daniel to his second tenure as pastor, since "at that time [the

---

[40] *Baptist Encyclopedia*, vol. 1, s.v. "Crocker, Rev. Thomas."

[41] *Biblical Recorder*, "Proceedings of the Fourth Annual Meeting of the Baptist State Convention of North Carolina, Held at the Cashie Meeting House, Bertie County, November 1–5, 1834," 7 January 1835 (Newbern NC) 1, 3; "Proceedings of the Fifth Annual Meeting of the Baptist State Convention of North Carolina, Held at the Union Camp Ground, Rowan County, Commencing the 30th October, 1835," 25 November 1835 (Newbern NC) 1; "Report of Chs. McAllister, Trea. Dr." 10 February 1836 (Newbern NC), 3; 2 August 1837 (Newbern NC) 2; 27 October 1838 (Raleigh NC) 3.

[42] George Washington Paschal, *History of North Carolina Baptists*, vol. 2 (Raleigh: The General Board of the Baptist State Convention, 1955) 354.

church] was without anyone to go in and out before them." The entry indicates that Daniel "expected" the call, which may suggest that he had been filling the pulpit for several weeks before the actual call was made.[43]

During his second tenure as pastor, Daniel oversaw numerous projects and improvements to the church, which led to a period of significant growth. On 21 December 1823 the congregation adopted its first "Rules of Decorum" and a "Church Covenant," a signal that Daniel brought better organization to the church.[44] Jordan Womble indicated that the "recall of Elder Daniel was a matter of much joy for the church," because it had "for some time been in a very languishing condition" and he found the church "almost extinct."[45] He further indicated that most of the growth the church experienced since its founding had been additions of elderly people or people who joined during revival seasons. Very few "young" persons joined the church because the youth of the city considered it "unfashionable" to join a church only "suited to elderly persons."[46]

All of that began to change as Daniel "put new life into the church."[47] The baptism of Lucinda Briggs, the first young person ever to join the church, serves as an indication that the church was beginning to experience growth. No date is given for her baptism and her age is not indicated. Her baptism must have occurred very shortly after Daniel's second tenure began in 1822 because Lucinda Briggs's name is listed among the white female members for the first time in February 1823.[48] While the addition of Lucinda Briggs to the church membership is significant, the story of her baptism is almost legendary in the church's history. Jordan Womble recalled the tradition that she was baptized in the winter of the year in Rocky Branch, located near the city where "the ice had to be broken" in the water so that she could be baptized. In the modern era where most Baptist churches are equipped with baptisteries (which provide warm water for baptism), it is difficult to imagine how

---

[43] Church Conference Records, 22 June 1822.
[44] Ibid., 21 December 1823.
[45] "Womble-Marcom History," 4a.
[46] Ibid.
[47] Ibid.
[48] Ibid.; Church Conference Records, 1 February 1823.

baptismal ceremonies were once conducted in creeks and lakes with the congregation gathered on the banks to witness the momentous event.[49] After her baptism, Lucinda Briggs lived out her life as a faithful member of the Raleigh Baptist Church and became one of the church's most prominent members in the nineteenth century. A future pastor, Thomas Skinner, in 1897 indicated that "in her ninety-second year" she attended church services faithfully and that, "way back yonder in the twenties, was the voluntary sexton of the church when they worshipped in Moore Square."[50]

Having mentioned the particular case of Lucinda Briggs, it should be noted that during these early years of its history the Raleigh Baptist Church took great care to examine the faith experience of all of its new members. For example, in the church minutes entry from 25 January 1823, there is a reference that says that in the evening at candlelight the church "opened the way for reception of members." On that particular occasion Sister Mary Hendon "appeared and was received and appointed to be baptized tomorrow morning."[51] On another occasion (14 June 1823) the minutes indicate that the church "opened a way for experience [and] heard Sister Terry and approved her."[52] These two glimpses into how the church received members suggest that the typical method for receiving members today at the end of the regular worship service was not in

---

[49] "Womble-Marcom History," 4a. Womble also indicates that the baptisms usually occurred in Walnut Creek, but "heavy rains had raised Rocky Branch so that there was significant water for baptism."

[50] Thomas E. Skinner, *Sermons, Addresses and Reminiscences* (Raleigh NC: Edwards and Broughton, Power Printers, 1894) 367.

[51] Church Conference Records, 25 January 1823. The church was also concerned about members who moved away from Raleigh. On 30 September 1826, an entry into the church minutes indicates "that for the future no letter of dismission shall be granted to a member of this church who has been living from us a length of time until they give the church satisfaction that they are still in good standing amongst the brethren where they reside at the time of their making application." That action was prompted by two members, "Brother and Sister Lightfoot," who had made application for a letter of dismission from the church. The "letter of dismission" indicated that the couple had been members in "good standing" at the church, and was necessary before they could unite with another congregation.

[52] Church Conference Records, 14 June 1823.

practice then. Instead, during the church conferences, or during special occasions, the church would allow candidates to present themselves for membership, who were then examined carefully about their Christian experience, before becoming candidates for baptism and granted full privileges as members.

In addition to the baptism of Lucinda Briggs, Daniel's second tenure was marked by another key event in the life of the church. Shortly after his return, the church relocated. He petitioned the legislature for permission to move the church building across the street to Moore Square, property then owned by the state. Moore Square contained a number of oak trees and, with the presence of the church, the property was nicknamed "Baptist Grove." Jordan Womble recalled that the church building was placed on logs and rolled across the street to the new location. In addition to the move to the new property, the church also acquired a bell, which it purchased from Cook's Tavern. John Mason, who was not a member of the church, made and donated some new tin candlesticks to the church to replace the wooden ones that were being used. Furthermore, since the church had no paid custodian, the ladies of the church "washed, swept, and dusted the church and at such times they burnished the tin candlesticks until they shone like silver." He also reported that when the pulpit needed to be painted, Lucinda Briggs secured the donation of some black paint from a local paint shop, whereby "in this funeral color with her own hands she painted the pulpit."[53]

While the church included both black and white members from its inception, very little mention is made of the black members in the early minutes of the church. The minutes for 25 January 1823 do mention one important event when the church appointed a committee consisting of Elder Daniel and Brethren Hendon and Turner to "confer with the colored brethren of this church on the propriety of establishing certain rules and regulations for their future government and that they make report to the church at their next meeting."[54]

---

[53] "Womble-Marcom History," 4b.
[54] Church Conference Records, 25 January 1823.

The following month, on 1 February 1823, the committee made its report to the church. Included in the report was a suggestion for a standing committee composed of Brethren Hendon, Turner, and Lightfoot to examine the Christian experience of the black brethren who seek membership in the church, as well as to hear appeals for restoration in situations of church discipline. Finally, the report recommended that a deacon be appointed among the black brethren for the purpose of administering communion. "Brother Joseph," a slave who belonged to Sherwood Haywood, was appointed for the task. The report ended by stating that if "any black preacher of our persuasion and who shall be in possession of ample credentials, wishes to preach in this place that he have liberty of the meeting house, provided it be not occupied by the whites."[55]

In addition to the other aspects of church life already mentioned, church discipline occupied much of the church's attention during the second tenure of Daniel. It should be noted that church discipline was a typical practice for most Baptist churches in the nineteenth century. To some degree, the practice had been a part of the larger Baptist tradition since its inception in the seventeenth century. Some groups such as Primitive Baptists made church discipline more common than other Baptist groups. But the practice was quite common in many Southern Baptist churches in the late nineteenth and early twentieth centuries.[56]

Generally, the details of the accusations against the members are not revealed. Those complaints that are specified usually related to temperance matters, lack of church attendance, or disputes between members. One case that does stand out involved "Sister Dodd and drug abuse." On 17 September 1825 the minutes reveal that "an allegation against Sister Dodd for taking an over portion of Laudanum which

---

[55] Ibid., 1 February 1823. The minutes from that particular meeting state one other thing that is interesting: "Brother Lightfoot is requested to assist the clerk in arranging the records of the church." That may explain why the first record book of the church is not in chronological order and why certain records are missing.

[56] Morgan Patterson, "Discipline in Baptist Churches and Culture on the Early Frontier," *Review and Expositor* 61/1 (Winter 1964): 532–40; Stephen M. Haines, "Church Discipline As Practiced by Representative Southern Baptist Churches, 1880–1939" (Ph.D. diss., Southwestern Baptist Theological Seminary, 1984).

seemed for some hours to have taken away her senses and strength and seemed as though it might take her life but did not." The church members requested that she appear before them to answer to the charges, "it seeming to them to have been an act that a Christian should not have committed in their proper senses." Sister Dodd did not respond positively toward the church, but rather treated the church "with contempt" and remained "hard and obstinate."[57] After almost a year of longsuffering, the church eventually voted to excommunicate Sister Dodd on 2 September 1826.[58]

Another interesting case of discipline involved someone who had earlier been excommunicated from the church. On 21 April 1823 the church reported that a man named "William Harris," who had been excommunicated from the church's fellowship, "is preaching under the _____ [unable to read] of being a Baptist preacher and imposing on the public."[59] Signifying how seriously the church took proper credentials for both being a minister in the Baptist tradition as well as claiming membership in a Baptist church, it voted to publish advertisements in two newspapers in the state warning the public that Harris was an imposter.

Another important development in the congregation during Daniel's second tenure was the hiring of the church's first sexton, Robert T. Dodd. The church minutes for 6 March 1824 reported that Dodd was appointed to keep the meeting house in order and to prepare the church building for worship by lighting the candles and opening the doors, etc. Then on 5 June 1824 the church indicated that "Dodd should have something allowed to him for his services, as to sweeping the meeting house, lighting the candles, and wringing [*sic*] the bell." The following month the church agreed to gather a collection and paid Dodd $2.50 [$57.40][60] for his services.[61]

---

[57] Church Conference Records, 17 September 1825.

[58] Ibid., 2 September 1826.

[59] Ibid., 21 April 1823.

[60] The bracketed amounts in this book represent the amount of money needed in 2009 to have the same purchasing power, using the Consumer Price Index as a measure. One could calculate the *relative value* of construction costs using the GDP deflator (rather than Consumer Price Index) as a measure. However, for

In addition to discipline and administration, a key aspect of a church is its spiritual life. Some insight into the spiritual life and worship practices of the church can be gathered from Jordan Womble's account that the church held early-morning prayer meetings each Sunday morning, although they were sparsely attended. Womble reported that frequently the only attendants to the early prayer meetings were the elderly John Briggs and an aged sister. These meetings brought "much merriment" to the two worshippers, for "as neither could sing in tune and therefore in concert," they typically sang their favorite hymn, "Good Morning Brother Pilgrim," line by line with one leading and the other responding.[62]

One other action of the church from that time should be noted. On 4 September 1824 the records mention a relationship to the Raleigh Baptist Association for the first time. Brothers Hendon and Ragan were appointed to be messengers at the annual associational meeting that year. Brothers Turner and Ragan were commissioned to write the letter to the association that reported the church's vital statistics. The church also voted to send an offering of $1.00 [$22.90] to the annual meeting. Unfortunately, there are no surviving records from the Raleigh Baptist Association for that year. However, two years later (the date of the earliest record that exists), the associational minutes indicate that the Raleigh Baptist Church reported four baptisms, six members dismissed by letter, one member excommunicated, one member restored to fellowship, and one member dead, with a total membership of eighty-two.[63]

---

consistency, all bracketed amounts in this book will represent the amount of money needed in 2009 to have the same *purchasing power*, using the CPI as a measure. See Lawrence H. Officer and Samuel H. Williamson, "Purchasing Power of Money in the United States from 1774 to 2009," and Samuel H. Williamson, "Seven Ways to Compute the Relative Value of a U.S. Dollar Amount, 1774 to present," http://www.measuringworth.com (accessed 1 April 2011).

[61] Church Conference Records, 6 March, 5 June, and 3 July 1824.

[62] "Womble-Marcom History," 4c.

[63] Minutes of the Raleigh Baptist Association, 1826, microform copy located at the North Carolina Baptist Collection, Z. Smith Reynolds Library, Wake Forest University, Winston-Salem, North Carolina, 1.

There is no formal mention of Robert T. Daniel's resignation as pastor of the church, although the church minutes indicate that a "letter of dismissal" was granted to Daniel and his wife, Penny, on 5 March 1826. Daniel labored in ministry as a missionary for fourteen more years after he left the Raleigh Baptist Church. Records indicated that he served in North Carolina, Virginia, Mississippi, and Tennessee throughout his career. He died on 14 September 1840 at the home of his oldest son in Paris, Tennessee.[64]

Patrick W. Dowd (1827–1832)

Following Robert T. Daniel's second tenure as pastor, the church on 26 February 1827 issued a call to Patrick W. Dowd to assume pastoral duties. Dowd was born in 1799 and spent most of his ministry career in Wake County. Although the records for the church do not indicate the date when his pastoral tenure ended, it can be surmised that he served the church for approximately five years since the call of the next pastor came in 1832.[65]

Dowd had good contacts in the Baptist world of the early nineteenth century. He was baptized into the membership of the Friendship Baptist Church in the Raleigh Baptist Association by W. T. Brantly, Sr., one of the foremost Baptist ministers of that era. Dowd was educated at Columbian College and ordained by the Raleigh Baptist Church on 25 March 1827. The former pastor, Thomas Crocker, preached the ordination sermon.[66] It was during Dowd's tenure that the Raleigh Baptist Church experienced some of its most rapid growth. While associational records are missing for several of the years that Dowd served as pastor, the surviving records indicate that in 1826, the year before Dowd became pastor, the church

---

[64] Howell, "To Die Is Gain," 2.

[65] *Baptist Encyclopedia*, vol. 1, s.v. "Dowd, Rev. Patrick W."; Morris, "The History of the First Baptist Church of Raleigh," 14, 16.

[66] *Baptist Encyclopedia*, vol. 1, s.v. "Dowd, Rev. Patrick W."; Church Conference Records, 25 March 1827. Brantly also served as pastor of some of the most prominent Baptist churches in America, including the First Baptist Churches of Augusta, Philadelphia, and Charleston.

reported a total of eighty-two members. By 1832, Dowd's last year, the association records report a total membership of 189 members.[67]

Worship attendance seemed to be a great concern to the church during these years and the records indicate that the church had great expectations for their new, young pastor: namely, that he visit the absentee members and "admonish them to their duty." But within two months the church passed a resolution that represented a significant shift in its strict insistence on church attendance. At the church conference on 5 May 1827, the church "resolved that the article in our church discipline be entirely stricken out where it says that every member who fails to commune on days of communing shall be visited by the deacons and the reason inquired into by them."[68] That was the first indication that the church was easing up on its strict discipline. A legitimate question could be raised concerning the reasons for making that change. Could it be that the church had grown to the point where visiting the members who were absent had become too demanding? Or could it be that the church now realized there were legitimate reasons a member may miss worship services, and rather than call the member to account for the reason, it simply trusted that the members had legitimate reasons? Unfortunately, no further explanation is given in the church records.

One of the church's more interesting episodes of church discipline from that period involved a slave who belonged to prominent Raleigh citizen Sherwood Haywood. In the church minutes for 19 August 1827, the church charged that slave, named "Clabon," with "drinking too much spirits at a certain time and at the same time getting in a great passion and biting off the ear of one of his fellow servants." The accused appeared that day before the congregation in great remorse and admitted the error of his ways with "deep repentance." As punishment, the church excluded him from its membership for three months. There is no further mention of the incident in the church minutes.[69]

---

[67] Minutes of the Raleigh Baptist Association, 1826 and 1833, microform copy located at the North Carolina Baptist Collection, Z. Smith Reynolds Library, Wake Forest University, Winston-Salem, North Carolina.

[68] Church Conference Records, 31 March and 5 May 1827. The original bylaws of the church do not exist.

[69] Ibid., 19 August 1827.

Another interesting issue, the subject of footwashing, arose at the meeting of the church on 3 May 1828, with a very brief statement in the minutes that said "the subject of washing feet postponed till the next meeting."[70] The issue is not mentioned again until 27 February 1830, when the church voted unanimously that it was obliged to observe the practice. No evidence suggests that the decision caused any dissension in the congregation at the time, nor is there any information as to whether the church observed the practice regularly after that.[71]

Patrick Dowd's ministry at the church was not without controversy. Just after Christmas 1827, the church's records indicate that "Brother Dowd entered a complaint against J. L. Turner of being too intimate with Polly Matthews, a member of his family founded on a report which is generally believed." The minutes record that the church was so convinced of the "report" that it took action and excluded J. L. Turner from their membership. No further explanation is given. One question that might be raised is whether Polly Matthews was a member of Dowd's family or a member of Turner's family. The language of the entry is unclear. Whatever the case, it is clear that the church took the action seriously and responded swiftly.[72]

Another minor controversy began at the meeting of the church on 26 March 1830, when a "Brother Chandler" inquired as to the appropriateness of "communing with other societies." The church unanimously agreed that it was not appropriate.[73] Brother Chandler, evidently not pleased with the vote, then asked for his letter of dismission from the church, which was granted.[74] The matter of Brother Chandler resurfaced at the next meeting of the church, this time with some of the members dissatisfied at Dowd's treatment of Chandler. The church believed the pastor had not treated Chandler properly, forcing Dowd to defend himself and his actions before the congregation. In his defense, Dowd made reference to problems of Chandler's character, particularly mentioning that he had spread "lies and false reports"

---

[70] Ibid., 3 May 1828.
[71] Ibid., 3 May 1828 and 27 February 1830.
[72] Ibid., 29 December 1827.
[73] Ibid., 26 March 1830.
[74] Ibid.

against the pastor. He undoubtedly convinced the congregation of the propriety of his actions, as the minutes move on to another issue.[75]

The last mention of Chandler in the church records is found in the entry dated 26 July 1830. Unfortunately, this page is one of the most difficult pages to read in the entire first volume of the church minutes. From what can be read, Dowd inquired of the church about a favorable letter about Chandler that had been sent from the church to another church. Dowd proceeded by asking someone in the congregation (the name cannot be deciphered) if he wrote the letter, if he knew who wrote the letter, or if he had heard of the letter being written. The person responded "no" to all three questions. The matter then seemed to be dropped. Unfortunately, the details of that minor controversy cannot be fleshed out because there is simply not enough information contained in the records. The incident does seem to suggest that Dowd had developed something of a "heavy hand" in his leadership style with the church.

Problems within the fellowship began to appear beyond the Chandler case. On 17 August 1830, Sisters "Murden" and "Johnson" were censured for "whispering." That censure may refer to discussing matters of the church's business with people outside of the membership of the church.[76] The following month Sister Murden was excluded from the church with no explanation as to her offense, and Sister Johnson was excluded for falsely accusing one of the members of the church with an undisclosed indiscretion.[77]

Taking a slight pause for now from the increasing problems within the church's fellowship, the importance of missions in Dowd's ministry must be mentioned. Dowd's interest in missions beyond the Raleigh Baptist Church became apparent during his leadership of the church. The first mention by the church of contributing to missions (other than the local Raleigh Baptist Association) came at the church meeting on 5 July 1828, when Dowd proposed that the church provide money for "traveling preachers and other uses."[78] The suggestion was deferred until a later meeting, but the seeds were sown for mission commitment among

---

[75] Ibid., 14 May 1830.
[76] Ibid., 17 August 1830.
[77] Ibid., 4 September 1830.
[78] Ibid., 5 July 1828.

the members of the congregation. Several months later, on 22 January 1830, the minutes record the following: "The church feeling deeply impressed with the belief that it is the duty of all Christians to use exertions for the promulgation of the Gospel, therefore resolved that we become auxiliary to the North Carolina Baptist Benevolent Society and send up what money we can collect to aid them in their noble design."[79]

Dowd's interest in promoting the cause of missions is evident not only from his efforts as pastor of the church, but also from his involvement promoting missions statewide. He was selected as the president of the North Carolina Baptist Benevolent Society in February 1830. The following month, on 26 March 1830, Dowd and thirteen other men (six of whom were ministers) met in Greenville, North Carolina, and passed a resolution that the society should be transformed into a state convention, thereby giving birth to the Baptist State Convention of North Carolina. Dowd was selected as the first president of the convention as well.[80]

During the last several months of Dowd's tenure, the church minutes reflect a different tone than the earlier entries. The tenor of the meetings seemed to be harsh at times, reflecting the fact that the church

---

[79] Ibid., 22 January 1830. A few weeks later on 4 February, the minutes contain the following entry: "After lengthy exertion to do good, the church agreed to appoint agents to collect in the congregation a missionary fund." (See Church Conference Records, 4 February 1830.)

[80] Henry Smith Stroupe, "North Carolina, State Baptist Convention of," 997. The meeting occurred in the Baptist Meeting House in Greenville, North Carolina. Today that church is called "The Memorial Baptist Church" in recognition of that significant historical event it hosted. The seven ministers present were: Patrick W. Dowd of Raleigh, William P. Biddle of Craven County, Samuel Wait and John Armstrong of New Bern, Thomas Meredith of Edenton, James McDaniel of Cumberland County, and Thomas D. Mason of Greenville. The laymen present were: R. M. Guffee of Raleigh; Charles W. Skinner of Perquimans County (the father of Thomas Skinner, later pastor of the Raleigh Baptist Church); Henry Austin, Peter P. Lawrence, and R. S. Long of Tarboro; and George Stokes and Reading S. Blount of Greenville. Officers elected were: Dowd, president; Biddle, Meredith, and Charles McAllister, vice-presidents; Armstrong, corresponding secretary; Blount, recording secretary; and Austin, treasurer. A board of directors of eighteen men was elected and twelve men were named as agents of the convention.

was moving toward a period of conflict. Although the records give no date for Dowd's resignation, there is an entry indicating that on 12 March 1832 James G. Hall was called as pastor of the church.[81] During Dowd's ministry at the church, there was considerable numeric growth. However, according to Jordan Womble decades later, one of the aged members indicated "there was much unchristian feeling among the members and unsettled difficulties," the result of which was that "each member was a law unto himself."[82]

Patrick W. Dowd was one of the most influential North Carolina Baptist ministers of his era. In addition to serving as the first president of the Baptist State Convention of North Carolina, he remained throughout his career very active in the life and work of the Raleigh Baptist Association, serving as moderator on numerous occasions. Unfortunately, two decades after he left the pastorate of the Raleigh Baptist Church, controversies ensued that involved charges of immorality and plagiarism. As a result, he lived the twilight years of his life under a cloud of controversy and suspicion.

At the heart of these controversies, according to most interpreters of them, were the tensions in the middle of the nineteenth century between Baptists over missions. Sometime between 1850 and 1852, Dowd was accused of immorality involving charges that he made sexual advances toward the teenaged daughter of a man named George Poole. At the time, Dowd served as pastor of several rural churches in the Raleigh area and, when traveling, stayed in the homes of church members. Poole, a member of the Mt. Moriah Baptist Church, located then about seven miles outside of Raleigh, claimed that Dowd had been alone on the back porch with his daughter. Poole claimed that Dowd invited the girl to his room where he proceeded to grab and kiss her.[83]

---

[81] Church Conference Records, 12 March 1832.

[82] "Womble-Marcom History," 10a.

[83] Warren Lee Holleman and Carl Partin Holleman, "An Innocent and Injured Man: The Allegations of Impropriety Against the Reverend Patrick W. Dowd," *The North Carolina Historical Review* 69/3 (July 1992): 282–300. This is an outstanding, well-researched article based on the primary sources from the controversy.

The charges were aired at a meeting of the Mt. Moriah church, as well as in the Raleigh Baptist Association, where Dowd was exonerated both times. Failing to get satisfaction, Poole pressed charges in the Superior Court of Wake County, which charged Dowd with assault and battery against his daughter, "Rhoda Poole Lynch." The trial was set for 1 April 1852 but had to be postponed. When the case was called again, the jurors failed to arrive at a verdict. The case was tried once more with the same result. Then, interestingly, it was moved to Johnston County, where a jury heard the case and brought back a guilty verdict against Dowd in 1853. He was ordered to pay court costs and sentenced to twenty days in jail, but mysteriously Dowd was never arrested nor confined to the jail.[84]

During the same year that Dowd was battling charges of sexual impropriety, W. T. Brooks, a professor at Wake Forest College and a fellow Baptist minister, publicly accused Dowd of plagiarism in his sermons. Although the Raleigh Baptist Association again exonerated Dowd, that controversy, like the Poole controversy, played out in the pages of the *Biblical Recorder*, with both sides purchasing advertising space to press their claims.[85]

While exonerated by his ministerial colleagues, Dowd nevertheless lived with that taint upon his reputation for years. The plagiarism charge is difficult to dismiss, although Holleman and Holleman conclude that the motivation for the charge could have been professional jealousy. Brooks was a member of the faculty of Wake Forest College and Dowd was a trustee. Furthermore, Dowd was generally considered to be better educated and more erudite in his pulpit presence than Brooks.[86] Also,

---

[84] Ibid., 286–87.

[85] Ibid., 287. Also see the *Biblical Recorder* (Raleigh NC), W. T. Brooks, 19 November 1852, 3; Willima M. Crenshaw, 17 December 1852, 3; John F. Ellington and W. T. Brooks, 7 January 1853, 3; P. W. Dowd, 21 January 1853, 2–3; Isaac Winston, 11 February 1853, 2; "Trials of an Editor," and the reply to the editor from a committee appointed by Mount Moriah Church, 18 February 1853, 2–3; W. T. Brooks, 25 February 1853, 2–3; P. W. Dowd, 11 March 1853, 2; and George Poole, "To Whom it May Concern," 11 March 1853, 3.

[86] Holleman and Holleman, "An Innocent and Injured Man," 295–97. Murray, *Wake: Capital County of North Carolina*, vol. 1, 383–84.

In the realm of sermons, perhaps Dowd flaunted his divinity school knowledge more than he ought as a Baptist country preacher. Possibly by speaking in the erudite style…of prominent minister-theologians, Dowd appeared to be a plagiarist to persons unschooled in formal theology, unaccustomed to his mode of preaching, and uncomfortable with theology derived from literary sources other than Scripture.[87]

As for the charge of unwanted sexual advances, there is an interesting twist to the story that came to light years after Dowd's death in 1866. The account is located in the autobiography of Charles Houston Utley (1870–1944), state senator, educator, and Baptist preacher. According to Utley, the entire episode was a "setup" perpetrated by an anti-missions opponent of Dowd's. Many years after the fact, as he lay dying, a man (not identified by Utley) confessed to convincing the young woman to make the false charge against Dowd, her pastor, in an attempt to cripple the cause of missions among North Carolina Baptists.[88]

Dowd's longest tenure as a pastor was at the Mt. Pisgah Baptist Church in Durham for twenty-seven years. He died in 1866 and was buried in the Mt. Pisgah church cemetery.

---

[87] Holleman and Holleman, "An Innocent and Injured Man," 288–89.

[88] Charles Houston Utley, "The Education of Charles Houston Utley" (undated manuscript), Genealogy Vertical File, 33, as cited by Holleman and Holleman, "An Innocent and Injured Man," 295. The account reads: "The charge was made by a woman in the New Bethel section near Garner that the minister had made improper proposals to her when pastor of that Church. Years passed— a man in the community was dying. A young neighbor, Dave Buffaloe, sat with the dying man, calling the young man to his bedside he said: 'Dave, there is one thing on my conscience.' Then he related to the young astonished listener who himself at the time was not a Christian, how he a Hardshell had induced a woman to file the charge against the Missionary pastor [whom Utley specified as Dowd]. He assured the young man that the minister had been entirely innocent, that so far as he knew the minister has always deported himself as a Christian and a gentleman, however, his confession could not undo the harm done." See also Murray, *Wake: Capital County of North Carolina,* vol. 1, 383–84 for a condensed version of the account.

The "Silent" Years (1832–1840)

By 1832 the Raleigh Baptist Church was in the midst of significant internal dissension. Unfortunately, the church records for those years, if they ever existed, are lost. The records of the Raleigh Baptist Association are not very helpful either. During these eight years, the Raleigh Baptist Association records from six of those years (1831, 1833, 1834, 1835, 1837, and 1838) are missing. The associational records that exist do not contain any direct information about the Raleigh Baptist Church and its situation. It is interesting to note, however, that in 1832 the church is listed among the cooperating churches with a total membership of 189. In 1836 the church is listed with a total membership of 198. The church does not appear again in the association's list of churches until 1841, when it reported a total membership of ninety.[89]

Three Pastors. The Womble-Marcom history, based on eyewitness oral history accounts, is the best source for that difficult period in the church's history. The minutes do include just a few entries in 1832. On 12 March 1832 the church issued a call to James G. Hall to succeed Patrick W. Dowd as pastor. The following month on 7 April the minutes report that Hall responded positively to the call and agreed to serve "if he [could] be supported or get aid to support himself."[90] The Womble-Marcom history reports that Hall served the church for a year and that the membership grew in number during that time. Unfortunately, no further information is given about Hall's leadership or the events in the church during his tenure.[91]

Although Hall served the Raleigh Baptist Church for only one year, he did have a long and fruitful ministerial career. Born in 1801 in Currituck County, North Carolina, Hall attended school at Edenton Academy, graduating in 1817. He made a profession of his faith and was baptized at the Edenton Baptist Church in June 1817. Very soon thereafter, he moved to Chapel Hill where he furthered his education at the University of North Carolina. While in Chapel Hill, he roomed at a

---

[89] Minutes of the Raleigh Baptist Association, 1832, 1836, and 1841.
[90] Church Conference Records, 12 March 1832.
[91] "Womble-Marcom History," 10b.

boarding house operated by Reverend A. W. Clopton who, along with Robert T. Daniel, had profound influence on him. He graduated from the University of North Carolina in 1822 and felt a calling to ministry, which led to ordination by the Providence Baptist Church in Currituck County in 1830.

One biographer indicated that Hall stayed only a short time as pastor of the Raleigh Baptist Church, because the church was never able to raise sufficient funds to provide him a livable salary. That would seem to be true, given the dissension in the church following Dowd's ministry. Nevertheless, Hall moved from Raleigh to Tennessee and eventually on to Mississippi, where he spent the rest of his life and career. He served as pastor of several churches, most notably the First Baptist Church of Grenada, Mississippi, which he organized in 1838. He also helped establish the Yalobusha Baptist Female Institute in Grenada and served as its director from 1845 to 1855. He died in Grenada in 1878, a victim of a yellow fever epidemic that hit the town that year.[92]

Following the brief pastorate of James G. Hall, according to the Womble-Marcom history, the church called Quentin H. Trotman to be its next pastor. Unfortunately, the exact dates of his tenure are lost, and although his precise activities as pastor of the church cannot be ascertained, there are some basic facts about his life that should be mentioned.

Trotman was born in 1805 in Perquimans County, North Carolina. While he was still an infant, the family moved to Sandy Cross in Gates County. His father died very shortly thereafter, and for financial reasons, the young Trotman's opportunity for formal education was limited. For much of his early adult years he was a farmer, and according to several accounts, he soon developed a reputation for a wicked lifestyle. Through the witness of both his wife and mother, Trotman made a profession of his faith and was baptized into the membership of the Sandy Cross Baptist Church by Robert T. Daniel in 1828. Within two years the church both licensed and ordained him to the ministry. Most of Trotman's career

---

[92] Biographical information for James G. Hall obtained from a biographical file located in the North Carolina Baptist Collection, Z. Smith Reynolds Library, Wake Forest University, Winston-Salem, North Carolina.

was spent in the Chowan association where he labored as a minister for thirty years. Perhaps a sign that his health was beginning to fail, in 1859 he lost his vision, although he continued to preach. Three years later, in 1862, he died. Following his death, the Chowan Baptist Association included a tribute to Trotman in the minutes of their annual meeting in 1862. Included within a long, grandiose description of his preaching style, the account included this statement: "He borrowed nothing of others. Feeling the responsibility of his position, he leaned not upon learned theologians, but placing his trust in God from his word derived the waters of life."[93] The statement is interesting, given the charges of plagiarism leveled against Patrick W. Dowd and the public controversy surrounding that charge, which played out in the *Biblical Recorder* only a decade before.

Following Quentin Trotman's tenure as pastor, according to the Womble-Marcom history of the church, William Hill Jordan was chosen to lead the church. Again, due to the lack of church records from that period, very little is known about his ministry at the church. The *Biblical Recorder* dated 24 February 1836 indicates that Jordan had accepted the call of the church to serve as its pastor for a term of six months "with a view to a permanent settlement in that place."[94]

Jordan was born in 1803 in Bertie County, North Carolina. Little is known of his early life, although reports indicate that he was educated at the University of North Carolina. His profession of faith, baptism, and calling to preach all occurred within one month between December 1823 and January 1824. The Womble-Marcom account of the church's history indicates that Jordan was "a small _____ [unable to read] man of most wonderful attainments who preached most eloquent sermons frequently two hours in length."[95] Through his career Jordan served as pastor not

---

[93] "Quentin Hollowell Trotman," in the Minutes of the Chowan Baptist Association, 1862, 3. That account is reproduced from the original minutes and is contained in a biographical file on Trotman located in the North Carolina Baptist Archives, Z. Smith Reynolds Library, Wake Forest University, Winston-Salem, North Carolina. The original account is found on pp. 13–16 of the association's minutes.

[94] "Removal," *Biblical Recorder* (Newbern NC), 24 February 1836, 3.

[95] "Womble-Marcom History," 10c.

only of the Raleigh Baptist Church, but also in Wilmington, Lilesville, and Wadesboro in North Carolina; in Virginia at Clarksville and Petersburg; in Pennsylvania at Norristown; and in South Carolina at Sumter. He also served as corresponding secretary of the Baptist State Convention and was a trustee and agent for Wake Forest College.[96]

The Church Dissolved and Resurrected. According to the Womble-Marcom account, the division in the church began in 1832 and worsened to the extent that the very existence of the church became threatened. At that point, Jordan asked for the assistance of the Raleigh Baptist Association, which became involved, and after a great amount of discussion, a decision was made to dissolve the church.[97]

---

[96] *Baptist Encyclopedia,* vol. 2, s.v. "Jordan, William Hull." Jordan's middle name is "Hill." Cathcart's rendering of "Hull" is a typographical error.

[97] "Womble-Marcom History," 10c. "The dissension in the church, which instead of being healed had become worse, had now grown so fierce and the conduct of some of the members so unchristianlike [*sic*] that these serious matters which threatened the existence of the church could no longer be ignored. Elder Jordan asked the Association to examine the affairs of the church. After much discussion the church was declared dissolved." See also Minutes of the Raleigh Baptist Association, 1839, 5–6. (Unfortunately, the records for the Raleigh Baptist Association from the years 1831, 1833, 1834, 1835, 1837, and 1838 are missing.) The associational record for 1839 refers to a committee appointed in 1837 to investigate the situation in the church. The committee reported that it was "constrained to believe that this body is disorderly." The report continued: "For the very abusive and uncalled for letter, which that church sent up to the last Association, we believe they were justly considered as unworthy of further fellowship in this body. We consider that the printed communication sent up to this body makes nothing like a satisfactory acknowledgement for the offence. We deem it inexpedient to call upon their delegate for any further acknowledgement, as it would be unadvisable for him [to] make satisfaction for the whole church. We would advise that a committee be appointed to go and advise those brothers and sisters in this church, who are orderly, to leave that body and join some church in fellowship with this body. We propose that this Association advise the churches to whom any of these members may offer themselves (if they can fellowship the petitioner) to receive them without experience or letter."

Sometime after that, probably the latter months of 1839, John J. Briggs led the church to reorganize.[98] According to the account by Womble and Marcom, Briggs constituted "a church of one," and stood at the front of the pulpit extending a call for those who desired to join the reconstituted church to come forward and take his hand. More than half of the original members refused to take part in the new church fellowship, and the animosity toward the two groups was so great that they refused to allow the newly organized group use of the building located on Moore Square. L. J. Morris's history of the church's first century indicates that although the majority of the membership retained ownership of the building, most of them eventually united with the Christian Church.[99]

With no building where it could worship, the group began to worship in a room over a store located on the corner of Fayetteville and Hargett Streets, on property referred to then as "Ben Smith's Corner." The Baptist reputation in the city of Raleigh was sullied from that division in the church's fellowship, as indicated by Womble and Marcom that "all that the church had gained in position and influence was lost and it required much courage for a person to declare himself a Baptist. Baptist families coming to the city would not unite with the little flock and many of the prominent members had moved to Tennessee."[100]

Besides John J. Briggs, two other people should be remembered for their heroic devotion to the Raleigh Baptist Church during these difficult years. About the time of the church's reorganization, Mrs. Sarah A. Stone moved to Raleigh. Her first husband, son of North Carolina Governor David Stone (1808–1810), was deceased and she eventually married again to Alfred Williams. Womble and Marcom describe her as a "devoted Christian possessed of much worldly goods and a lady of high social position."[101] She was eventually elected as president of the Women's Working Society, an organization in the church devoted to raising money

---

[98] "Womble-Marcom History," 10. Briggs was one of the two charter deacons of the church and died in 1856 at the age of eighty-six. He was also the father of Lucinda Briggs, whose baptism is mentioned above.

[99] Morris, "The History of the First Baptist Church of Raleigh," 21.

[100] "Womble-Marcom History," 10d.

[101] Ibid., 10e.

for the pastor's salary and other expenses in the church by sewing and doing other types of work. The pastor's wife, Mrs. William Hill Jordan, was identified as another important member for the congregation during that difficult period. Womble and Marcom describe her as "a lady of much worldly goods and a model wife for a pastor."[102] The Womble-Marcom history also includes a general statement concerning the importance of female leadership in the church during that dark era:

> At this time, as is often the case in our churches, the female members outnumbered the male members; in this instance in the proportion of two to one. There were only two or three of the male members who were willing to lead in prayer. The church, though small being knit together in love, rapidly regained its lost position and soon attained more prominence than it had ever before enjoyed.[103]

The fact that the church experienced serious conflict in the early 1830s is evident. The exact nature of the conflict and the issues involved are much more difficult to ascertain since no records from the church survive, and because of the gaps in the associational minutes from the pertinent years. Toward the end of the century, one interpreter reported that "[a]bout 1835 a division occurred, partly from overgrowth, but partly also from differences of opinion."[104] Unfortunately there is no specificity regarding the exact nature of the division.

---

[102] Ibid.

[103] Ibid., 11.

[104] Kemp P. Battle, *Early History of Raleigh, The Capital City of North Carolina, A Centennial Address, October 18, 1892* (Raleigh NC: Edwards and Broughton, 1893) 65, as viewed at: http://books.google.com/books?id=DXEtAAAAYAAJ- &printsec=frontcover&dq=Early+History+of+Raleigh+the+Capital+City+of+Nort h+Carolina&source=bl&ots=rarHLI-56l&sig=OFee2Z1Fm7vxRB7cQIevXtlT- fDo&hl=en&ei=hZUHTd3UGoH88AbI-9TnAg&sa=X&oi=book_result&ct =result&resnum=1&ved=0CBoQ6AEwAA#v=onepage&q=Baptist&f=false (accessed 14 December 2010). On p. 66 Battle says that the part of the congregation that remained on Moore Square retained ownership of the building until the congregation dwindled down to one member, Mark Williams, who "sold the old building to a colored congregation who moved it to the trans-railroad southern suburb known as Hayti."

One possible cause of the problem was the strong anti-missions movement among North Carolina Baptists. As the Baptist presence in the United States became organized on the national level with the Triennial Convention in 1814, and as it became better organized on the state level with the birth of the Baptist State Convention in 1830, a powerful response arose in opposition to organized missions efforts, publications societies, and theological schools for ministerial training.[105] The anti-missions churches eventually coalesced into a segment of Baptist life known today as Primitive Baptists or "Hardshell" Baptists. The term "hardshell" refers to their refusal to cooperate with other Baptist groups in promoting missions.[106]

Shurden indicates that there were several things that caused the spirit of anti-missions to develop among Baptists in America. The first cause was jealousy. Anti-missions pastors tended to be uneducated while the missions-promoting pastors were usually well read and educated in the better theological schools of their day. A second factor causing an anti-missions spirit to develop was a general fear of missionary societies and organizations. Some Baptists feared that the missionary organizations, such as the Baptist State Convention of North Carolina, might eventually impose upon the local church's autonomy. A third factor motivating the anti-missions effort was money. Missionary organizations wanted the churches to contribute money to them so that they could pay salaries of their missionaries and representatives, all in an era when there were still Baptist churches that did not believe in paying the pastor a salary. Finally, theology played an important factor. Anti-missions advocates were frequently hyper-Calvinistic in their approach toward salvation, and to preach the Gospel and invite people to accept Christ were regarded by them as infringing upon God's work.[107]

---

[105] See Walter B. Shurden, *Not a Silent People: Controversies That Have Shaped Southern Baptists*, updated ed. (Nashville: Broadman Press, 1995) 19–28; McBeth, *Baptist Heritage*, 371–77; and Leonard, *Baptist Ways*, 180–82.

[106] See John G. Crowley, *Primitive Baptists of the Wiregrass South: 1815 to the Present* (Gainesville FL: University Press of Florida, 1998) for a good discussion of the Primitive Baptist movement in the South.

[107] Shurden, *Not a Silent People*, 22–28.

As already noted, the problems in the Raleigh Baptist Church began during the pastorate of Patrick W. Dowd. Dowd led the church to considerable growth during his five-year pastorate. He also is to be credited with motivating the church to support missions and the Baptist State Convention. He served as the first president of the Baptist State Convention and was instrumental in the founding of Wake Forest College, initially for the purpose of training ministers. It seems possible, then, that the problems within the fellowship, which ultimately led to the dissolution and rebirth of the church, could have stemmed from a spirit of anti-missions that may have become a part of the congregation. These problems might have been as much about opposition to Dowd's ministry and involvement in the Baptist State Convention as they were theological.[108]

Another possible cause for the dispute may be the controversy surrounding the Campbellite movement, which was beginning to make its way into North Carolina in the 1830s. "Campbellites," as they were called, taught that through centuries of corrupt entanglements with the state, the true New Testament Church had been lost and needed to be restored. In other words, the New Testament was the pattern for restoring authentic apostolic Christianity. Barton W. Stone, Thomas Campbell, and his son Alexander became the primary motivators and early spokesmen for the movement. They rejected all denominational names and preferred to call themselves "Christians." Alexander Campbell became the chief spokesperson for the movement in the middle decades of the nineteenth century with his journal *The Christian Baptist* (1823–1829), and later the famous *Millennial Harbinger* (1830–1863).[109] Doctrinally, he was very close to most Baptists, and even was a Baptist

---

[108] That may explain the issue between the Dowd-Chandler conflict described above. Interestingly, the controversy occurred in the church minutes on 27 February 1830, the very next month after the church voted to support the North Carolina Baptist Benevolent Society, which ultimately became the Baptist State Convention. Could it be that Chandler brought his supporters to the church conference and raised the question about footwashing (practiced by some Primitive Baptist groups) and then the following month the question about communing with other societies? If so, these entries in the church minutes could be early clues that an anti-missions presence was in the church.

[109] Leonard, *Baptist Ways*, 182–83.

for a period of time. He taught baptism by immersion, the authority of the New Testament for matters of faith and practice, local church autonomy, and the priesthood of the believer. However, Campbell rejected all creeds and confessions of faith, preferring instead "no creed but the Bible." He rejected mission boards and anything else that appeared to be "denominational" in practice. Campbell even rejected the use of the title "Reverend" to address ministers, although most ministers in the tradition continued to use the title. In addition, Campbell took an Arminian approach toward salvation, saying that mental assent plus baptism are all that is necessary for a salvation experience. Finally, Campbell and his followers observed the Lord's Supper every Sunday.[110]

Because of similarities with Baptists, Campbellism drew many adherents from Baptist churches, and competition between the two groups became intense in the middle of the nineteenth century.[111] That was also the case in North Carolina. After 1830 the movement began to spread in the state with numerous Baptist churches converting completely to Campbellite teachings.[112] Historian Mark Toulouse has concluded that "nearly all of the early Disciples of North Carolina were originally Baptist," and that "they did so without much thinking about it, without analyzing major differences between being Baptist and being

---

[110] Ibid.

[111] See Charles Crossfield Ware, *North Carolina Disciples of Christ: A History of Their Rise and Progress, and of Their Contribution to Their General Brotherhood* (St. Louis: Christian Board of Publication, 1927) 69–76. Thomas Meredith was particularly vigilant in his efforts to awaken the Baptists of North Carolina to the "dangers" of the Campbellite movement. Using their respective publications, *Biblical Recorder* and *Millennial Harbinger*, Meredith and Campbell became engaged in a debate that lasted for months and played out on the pages of their publications.

[112] See Ware, *North Carolina Disciples of Christ*; see also Mark Toulouse, "Once Baptists, Now Disciples: A Case Study of Rountrees Meeting House, North Carolina," *Discipliana* 60/1 (Spring 2000): 3–31. The restorationist Campbellite movement is generally referred to with the terms "Church of Christ," "Disciples of Christ," and "the Christian Church." Today, due to several splits in the movement, the Church of Christ tends to refer to the more conservative branch of the movement, whereas the Disciples or Christian Church denotes the more progressive wing.

Disciple."[113] Whether that was the issue that led to the dissolution of the Raleigh Baptist Church in the 1830s or not, it is perhaps a clue that when the church was dissolved, the majority of the membership did not become a part of the newly organized Baptist church in the city. Neither did it organize a rival Baptist church. Instead the majority retained the property on Moore Square, which by 1842 was occupied by the first Christian Church in the city.[114] Another clue is found in the words of Reverend Henry B. Hayes, a Campbellite and co-founder of the Christian Church in Raleigh. Hayes indicated that the preaching of Reverend Joseph B. Hinton, a former Baptist turned Campbellite, was very influential on the members of the Baptist church in the city:

> There is much due to Dr. Hinton for the change that has taken place. He preached to the old Baptist church before her change, and from a strict examination of our principles, he was strongly in favor of the new organization. He is a man of talent, and likely will unite with his brethren that have thus made a change in the name and order of their church.[115]

Murray indicates that seven former members of the Raleigh Baptist Church "formed the nucleus of the new church."[116] Could it be that these seven members had been the catalyst for the dissolution of the Baptist church?

The exact cause of the dispute, whether anti-missions or Campbellism, cannot be determined without the availability of the primary sources from either the church records or from the Raleigh Baptist Association. Perhaps the records will be discovered one day in an archive collection or in someone's attic. Until then, we can only speculate.

* * *

---

[113] Toulouse, "Once Baptists, Now Disciples," 4.

[114] P. J. Kernodle, *Lives of Christian Ministers* (Richmond: Central Publishing Company, 1909) 72–73, 126. Kernodle indicates that the Christian Church in Raleigh was organized by two ministers: Henry B. Hayes and Littlejohn Utley.

[115] Ibid., 225.

[116] Murray, *Wake: Capital County of North Carolina*, vol. 1, 378.

The Raleigh Baptist Church established a Baptist presence in the city of Raleigh and early on developed itself into a strong congregation. The church supported the formation of the Baptist State Convention of North Carolina, an indication that it intended to be a "missionary" Baptist church. Unfortunately, as is often the case with Baptist churches, conflict hit the nascent congregation in the 1830s. However, a remnant survived due to the leadership of John Briggs. The story of how these remaining members kept the vision alive is told in the next chapter.

3

Gaining a Foothold (1840–1855)

The election of Andrew Jackson to the presidency in 1828 signaled a political shift away from Jeffersonian Democracy to what came to be termed "Jacksonian Democracy." In addition to emphasizing a strong executive branch, Jackson's presidency marked the first time the "common man" gained political power. The electorate was extended during that time to include all white, adult males regardless of whether they owned land.

The Jacksonian era was also the age of Manifest Destiny—the belief that God had divinely ordained white Americans to expand across the North American continent. While the Westward movement was positive for many Americans and ultimately good for the nation as a whole, for the Native Americans it was disastrous. As whites moved westward, Native Americans were forcibly removed from their territorial lands. In 1830 Congress passed the Indian Removal Act. During the next eight years the peaceful, "civilized" tribes of the Southeast (Chickasaw, Creek, Choctaw, Seminole, and Cherokee) were forced westward to Oklahoma. The journey of the Cherokee, which commenced in 1838, was particularly tragic since the tribe had worked so hard to become "civilized" in the eyes of white settlers. During their journey westward more than one-quarter of the Cherokee nation died from disease and other hardships.[1]

Ultimately, the doctrine of Manifest Destiny and its application by the United States in the annexation of Texas led to war between the United States and Mexico from 1846 to 1848. A decade earlier Texas won its independence from Mexico and existed as an autonomous republic, although most Texans desired annexation with the United States. The Treaty of Guadalupe Hidalgo ended the conflict between Mexico and the United States and increased the territorial holdings of the United States.

---

[1] For a fuller discussion about the plight of the Native Americans in the middle decades of the nineteenth century, see Samuel Eliot Morison, *The Oxford History of the American People* (New York: Oxford University Press, 1965) 445–52.

Specifically, the treaty forced Mexico to cede control of Texas along with the present-day states of California, Nevada, and Utah, and parts of Colorado, Arizona, New Mexico, and Wyoming.[2]

The middle decades of the nineteenth century in America brought great advances in the areas of commerce. In 1830 a blacksmith from Illinois named John Deere invented the steel plow, which began to revolutionize farming. By 1858 Deere was manufacturing 13,000 plows per year. Cyrus McCormick and Obed Hussey invented reapers in 1831, which further increased agricultural growth as they began to be mass-produced. The garment industry became modernized after Isaac Singer began to mass-produce the sewing machine in 1851. That era also marked the beginning of collective bargaining with the formation of the National Trades Union in 1834.[3]

New frontiers in communications were emerging as well. For instance, in 1844 Samuel Morse developed the electronic telegraph and a system of codes so that messages could be communicated over great distances. Just fourteen years later the transatlantic cable was completed between the United States and Europe, allowing for instant communication between the two continents.[4] Transportation also saw great advances. For instance, the development of the clipper ship (the fastest sailing vessel on the seas in that day) significantly reduced travel time between the Atlantic and Pacific Oceans. That and other advances of its kind contributed to increased trade between the United States and other nations. In addition to advances in transportation for foreign trade, steam ships began to utilize waterways in the nation's interior, fostering trade between different regions of the country. Yet the most important advance in transportation during those decades was the development of the railroad, which eventually led to a system of tracks that spread across the country.

The middle of the century was also an era of great social change. Industrialism provided a promise of a new life and steady income that brought millions of immigrants to America from Northern and Western

---

[2] Ibid., 550–65.

[3] Rebecca Brooks Gruver, *An American History*, 4th ed. (New York: Alfred A. Knopf, 1985) 286–310.

[4] Ibid.

Europe before the Civil War. Between 1815 and 1820 more than 100,000 immigrants flooded into the United States. The numbers grew from there. In the 1830s more than half a million arrived at America's shores. During the 1840s one and a half million immigrants made the difficult six-week ocean voyage to America. Finally, during the decade of the 1850s, the number of immigrants who came to America was two and a half million. By 1860 more than 8 percent of all Americans were foreign born.[5]

The middle of the nineteenth century also marked the beginning of the struggle for women's rights. Opportunities for women to be educated began to be more plentiful by the 1830s. Oberlin College in Ohio became the first institution of higher education in America to allow women to matriculate as students. Shortly thereafter, in 1836, Wesleyan College was founded in Georgia as a college exclusively for women. In 1837 Mount Holyoke College was established in Massachusetts.[6]

As women became better educated, many also began to speak out about social ills in society. Two important early pioneers in the areas of abolition of slavery and women's rights were Sarah and Angelina Grimké. Those two sisters, daughters of a prominent slave-holding family in Charleston, South Carolina, eventually rejected their family's racial views and became important voices for social change.[7] Lucretia Mott and Elizabeth Cady Stanton were two other important advocates for the rights of women mid-century. Their activism eventually led to the first Women's Rights Convention, which met in 1848 in Seneca Falls, New York. While the work of those women was important in drawing attention to the rights of women, sadly it would not be until the twentieth century that women would win full suffrage and an equal place in American society.[8]

As noted, immigration and the Women's Rights Movement brought important social change to America in the nineteenth century. However, the institution of slavery proved to be the most significant, and

---

[5] Ibid., 294.

[6] Ibid., 329.

[7] See Pamela R. Durso, *The Power of Woman: The Life and Writings of Sarah Moore Grimké* (Macon GA: Mercer University Press, 2004).

[8] Ibid., 329–32.

ultimately divisive, issue of the century. There had been opponents of slavery since the Colonial era, most notably the Quakers. But by the 1830s slavery became the dominant issue of the day and remained so until the Civil War.

The abolition movement began to gather support in the 1830s, largely through the efforts of William Lloyd Garrison, a journalist from Massachusetts and publisher of *The Liberator*. Garrison was tireless in his efforts to denounce slavery, not only as a social evil but also as a sin, and his writings helped to generate a movement composed of Northern intellectuals and other notable reformers. The strength of the abolition movement in the middle of the nineteenth century eventually exacerbated sectional tensions between the North and South, which ultimately drove a wedge in the Union and led to the Civil War.[9]

Along with economic and social changes in the middle of the nineteenth century came significant religious developments. The large waves of immigrants, many of whom were Roman Catholic, spurred an intense anti-Catholic sentiment among many Protestants. Such competition between denominations led to the rise of certain indigenous religious traditions, including the Church of Jesus Christ of Latter Day Saints (begun by Joseph Smith in Western New York) and the Campbellite movement (started by a former Baptist minister, Alexander Campbell). Both of those traditions gained large numbers of members (many from Baptist churches) and grew into important traditions within American religion.[10] The Campbellite movement gained considerable strength and converts in North Carolina during that era. As we will discuss, one of the former pastors of the Raleigh Baptist Church converted to the Campbellites and spent the remainder of his career as an evangelist for them.

---

[9] Winthrop D. Jordan and Leon F. Litwack, *The United States* (Englewood Cliffs NJ: Prentice Hall, 1991) 261–63.

[10] For further discussion of the indigenous religious traditions that began in the famed "Burned Over District" of Western New York, see Whitney R. Cross, *The Burned-Over District: The Social and Intellectual History of Enthusiastic Religion in Western New York, 1800–1850* (Ithaca NY: Cornell University Press, 1950). This work is quite dated but is a classic interpretation of new religious traditions in America in the first half of the nineteenth century.

The most important religious development for Baptists in the South during the middle of the nineteenth century was the founding of the Southern Baptist Convention in 1845. Since the creation of the "Triennial Convention" in 1814, Baptists in the North and South had been unified in their work for missions.[11] However, the abolition movement and the growing wedge between North and South over slavery eventually "invaded" the major Protestant denominations. In fact, the Southern Baptist Convention was organized in Augusta, Georgia, on 8 May 1845 in reaction to the Triennial Convention's refusal to appoint a slaveholder as a missionary the previous year. William Bullein Johnson, pastor of the First Baptist Church in Columbia, South Carolina, was elected the first president of the new organization and served as an important leader during its early days.[12]

The Jacksonian era also brought change and growth to the city of Raleigh. The 1830s brought the development of the railroad to Raleigh and greater Wake County. By 1833 a rail line had been completed between Weldon, North Carolina, and Petersburg, Virginia, that brought connections with lines further north. Support for the railroad could be found in the editorials from the period. For instance, in 1835 the editor of the *Raleigh Register* encouraged citizens to support efforts to build more lines, arguing that the railroad would increase the value of real estate and ensure the general prosperity of the city. Furthermore, he argued, it would bring new citizens to the city and would prevent others from moving west in order to find better agricultural prospects. In other words, the railroad would "give you a certain market at your doors."[13] Eventually, a charter for a line from Raleigh to Gaston near Weldon was secured by 1836, and within four years passengers (and freight) were able to travel from Raleigh to Baltimore (338 miles) in thirty-two hours, including the stops.[14]

---

[11] See H. Leon McBeth, *The Baptist Heritage: Four Centuries of Baptist Witness* (Nashville: Broadman Press, 1987) 343–91.

[12] McBeth, *Baptist Heritage*, 388–89.

[13] *Raleigh Register* (North Carolina), 22 September and 29 December 1835, as cited by Elizabeth Reid Murray, *Wake: Capital County of North Carolina*, vol. 1 (Raleigh NC: Capital County Publishing Co.,1983) 245–46.

[14] Murray, *Wake: Capital County of North Carolina*, vol. 1, 246–49.

One of the most difficult challenges for Raleigh during those antebellum years was the containment of fires that broke out at various times in the city. In 1819 the city had purchased a small pumping engine. It was the responsibility of all citizens to respond and fight the fires whenever they broke out. However, the small engine and citizens' efforts with leather buckets were hardly able to contain fires of the magnitude that the city saw in 1831, 1832, and 1833, which destroyed much of the heart of the city's business district.[15]

During the early morning hours of 23 June 1831, Raleigh lost its most prized structure, the State House, to a fire. It was believed that the fire was accidently started by a worker who had been employed to install a new zinc roof on the building to replace the wood shingles (considered to be, ironically enough, a fire hazard). Fire had threatened the State House before, once in 1816 and again just five months before its final destruction in 1831. Joseph Gales, the editor of the *Raleigh Register*, caught the terrible irony of the building's destruction, saying, "It is a mortifying reflection that the very means adopted for the security of the building have been attended with a fatality that produced its destruction."[16] Rebuilding the structure took seven years and was completed in 1840 at a cost of $530,684.15 [$13.6 million]—more than ten times the original projected cost. The first legislative session met in the new building in November 1840.[17] Eleven years later the most destructive fire the city had ever experienced came on 15 December 1851. That night a fire erupted in H. A. Depkin's boot and shoe store located at the corner of Fayetteville and Hargett Streets. The fire ultimately spread to and destroyed more than seventeen buildings on Fayetteville, Hargett, and Wilmington Streets. Two months later the city employed Seymour W. Whiting as the first salaried fire chief.[18]

The middle decades of the nineteenth century also saw the establishment of a number of higher-education institutions, none more important for North Carolina Baptists than Wake Forest College,

---

[15] Ibid., 409–11.

[16] *Raleigh Register* (North Carolina), 23 June 1831, as cited by Murray, *Wake: Capital County of North Carolina*, vol. 1, 230.

[17] Murray, *Wake: Capital County of North Carolina*, vol. 1, 252–55.

[18] Ibid., 409–11.

established in 1834. Envisioned at first by North Carolina Baptist leaders as a school for training young men for the Baptist ministry, Wake Forest began with fifteen students. The campus was established about fifteen miles north of Raleigh on farmland purchased by the Baptist State Convention from Dr. Calvin Jones. Amazingly, by the end of the first year the fledgling school had seventy-two enrolled students. Samuel Wait and Thomas Meredith, two names associated with the organization of the Baptist State Convention four years earlier, were instrumental in the founding of Wake Forest. Wait was appointed to serve as the first president of the school. Meredith joined the faculty during the school's first year to teach mathematics and moral philosophy and became chair of the school's board of trustees in 1838.[19]

Meredith's vision for North Carolina Baptists did not end with the founding of the Baptist State Convention or with the establishment of Wake Forest College. While serving as pastor of the Edenton Baptist Church in 1833, Thomas Meredith began publishing the *North Carolina Baptist Interpreter*, a monthly publication that served as the first Baptist periodical in the state. Shortly thereafter, in 1835, it was followed by the *Biblical Recorder*, a weekly publication first produced in New Bern. Then in 1838 Meredith moved to Raleigh where he continued to serve as its editor until his death in 1850.[20]

Religious diversity also characterized the city of Raleigh during the antebellum years. A special census of the city taken in 1858 indicated that 962 residents of Raleigh were church members. The individual groups were categorized as follows:

---

[19] Ibid., 300–302. See also George Washington Paschal, *History of Wake Forest College*, 3 vols. (Raleigh NC: Edwards & Broughton, 1935–1943) for the definitive history of the school.

[20] G. W. Paschal, *History of North Carolina Baptists*, vol. 2 (Raleigh NC: The General Board of the North Carolina Baptist State Convention, 1930) 455. See also Murray, *Wake: Capital County of North Carolina*, vol. 1, 330–31. With just a few suspensions in publication (no issues published in 1842 or for about six months in 1865 as the Civil War ended), the *Biblical Recorder* has continued to be published since Meredith founded it. It currently serves as the official news periodical of the Baptist State Convention of North Carolina.

Christian Church—130
Baptists—240
Methodists—226
Presbyterians—180
Episcopalians—126
Roman Catholics—60[21]

The U.S. Census from 1860 reported a total of fifty-two churches in Wake County: twenty-nine Baptist, fourteen Methodist, four Presbyterian, two Episcopalian, one Lutheran, one Roman Catholic, and one "Free Church." The census failed, however, to include some of the county's churches, including those affiliated with the Christian denomination.[22]

The Raleigh Baptist Church 1840–1855
Amos J. Battle (1839–1841)

The absence of church records from 1832 to 1840 makes it impossible to determine exactly when the pastorate of Amos J. Battle began. However, secondary sources indicate that he became the church's pastor in 1839.[23] Battle was born in 1805 to a prosperous family in Edgecombe County. While his brother William Horn Battle served as an associate justice for the North Carolina Supreme Court, Amos Battle heard the call to ministry.

According to a story that is repeated in several sources, Amos was converted in a worship service at a small Baptist church in Georgia on a trip to his Florida plantation in 1828, and according to one tradition was

---

[21] The census was taken by John Spelman for the city commissioners the year following the city's extension of the city limits in 1857. See Murray, *Wake: Capital County of North Carolina,* vol. 1, 386.

[22] Murray, *Wake: Capital County of North Carolina,* vol. 1, 386.

[23] L. J. Morris, "The History of the First Baptist Church of Raleigh, 1812–1912" (master's thesis, Wake Forest College, 1937) 24. See also *Biblical Recorder* (Raleigh NC), 27 April 1839, 2, which reports: "Bro. A. J. Battle, having taken charge of the Baptist church in this place, has removed his residence to this city, where his correspondents will hereafter address him." See also A. J. Battle, "A Fair Proposition," *Biblical Recorder* (Raleigh NC), 22 April 1843, 2. In this biographical letter, Battle indicated that he came to Raleigh from Rocky Mount, North Carolina.

baptized by Jesse Mercer, the founder of Mercer University.[24] Ordained to the ministry in 1831 by the Rogers Crossroads Baptist Church in Wake County, Battle had already distinguished himself as a leader among North Carolina Baptists before he became the pastor of the Raleigh Baptist Church. He had been the pastor of the Nashville Baptist Church (North Carolina) and served in positions of recording secretary and treasurer for the Baptist State Convention. Battle had also served as a trustee and traveling agent for Wake Forest College from 1835 to 1838.[25]

Battle's ministry at the church marks the beginning of a difficult period for the congregation. The church would be led by seven pastors during the period from 1840 to 1855, and the records indicate significant financial struggle to pay the salaries of the pastors as well as the other expenses of the church. According to a later interpreter, the white membership of the church was not very sizable and a "large majority of the members were of the poorer class, and could ill afford to pay enough to support a pastor."[26]

Yet despite the meager means of most of the membership, the church began the period with great optimism. The remnants of the original Raleigh Baptist Church had survived the turmoil of the previous decade and emerged stronger with a determination to grow. Reflecting an earnest desire to put the difficulty of the past decade behind them, the first entry recorded in the church records after the "silent years" reads:

> On the fifth Sunday in May 1840 the new Baptist Church in the City of Raleigh was dedicated to the worship of Almighty God. Rev. Thomas Meredith preached the sermon and Rev. A. J. Battle offered up the didicatory [sic] prayer. May Almighty God bless that sermon

---

[24] Charles Crossfield Ware, *North Carolina Disciples of Christ: A History of Their Rise and Progress, and of Their Contribution to Their General Brotherhood* (St. Louis: Christian Board of Publication, 1927) 283; J. Kelly Turner and John L. Bridgers, Jr., *History of Edgecombe County North Carolina* (Raleigh NC: Edwards and Broughton Printing Co., 1920) 418–19. William Horn Battle was the father of Kemp P. Battle, president of the University of North Carolina at Chapel Hill from 1876–1891.

[25] Ware, *North Carolina Disciples of Christ*, 283. See also Paschal, *History of Wake Forest College*, vol. 1, 97–98.

[26] Richard H. Lewis, "Some Reminiscences of the Baptist Church in Raleigh Fifty Years Ago," *North Carolina Baptist Historical Papers*, 1/3 (April 1897): 256.

and answer that prayer, until the Church that worships in it shall be multiplied and the glory of the Lord be sent to rest upon it.[27]

New Building and Battle's Debt. Battle's commitment to the church as its new pastor is admirable. The fact that the congregation had no permanent building where it could worship made the construction of a new building to be of paramount importance. As a testament to his commitment, the story of Battle's personal financial investment in the church is recounted in several sources. They indicate that he purchased a lot at the southeast corner of Wilmington and Morgan Streets for $2,100 [$53,800] so that a new church building could be erected.[28] While the church records do not present the full picture of Battle's personal risk, the story is presented in the *Biblical Recorder*. In the week following the dedication service for the new building, Thomas Meredith, a member of the congregation, printed the following statement in the *Biblical Recorder* reflecting Battle's personal involvement:

> The Baptist church in Raleigh are [sic] mainly indebted, for their present neat and excellent place of worship, to the enterprize [sic] and disinterested benevolence of Rev. A. J. Battle, pastor of said church. When he took charge of this *little* flock, about twelve months ago, he found them not only without a preacher, but even without a house to worship in. By removing his family to this place, purchasing ground and materials, and employing workmen all on his own individual

---

[27] Church Conference Records, (no date given). Although the date included in the entry is 5 May 1840, the entry is on the first page of the record book, and no date of the entry is given.

[28] See D. DuPre, "To the Baptists of North Carolina," *Biblical Recorder* (Raleigh NC), 1 July 1843, 2. The deed for the lot was placed in the names of Madison B. Royster, Thompson Parham, James D. Nunn, James F. Jordan, and Joseph J. Biggs, who are listed as the church's trustees. See "Address by Willis G. Briggs on the 140th Anniversary of the First Baptist Church, Raleigh, North Carolina," 16 March 1942, located in file, "NC, Raleigh FBC," Southern Baptist Historical Library and Archives, Nashville, Tennessee. See also Morris, 24, and Inventory of the Church Archives of North Carolina, Central Association, 8. The exact figure for the original cost of the building was $5,572.64 [$143,000].

responsibility, he has succeeded in completing the above mentioned place of worship.[29]

By the following year Battle's personal and financial situation had changed drastically. He resigned as the church's pastor on 8 April 1841.[30] In July 1841 the *Biblical Recorder* published a letter written by Battle requesting that the Baptists of North Carolina aid in paying off the church's debt for the construction of the building. Appealing no doubt to Baptists' moral sentiments, Battle wrote,

> But if it [the debt] should be neglected, this House built for the worship of God, may go into such hands as will convert it into a common store or tavern, or it may be made of as a warehouse for storing away whiskey, and other intoxicating drinks. Should this happen to be the case, where is the Baptist in N.C. who has any regard for the character of his denomination, what would ever wish to show his face in Raleigh again?[31]

By September 1841 other North Carolina Baptists began to express concern that the church's debt should be paid, largely because of the

---

[29] *Biblical Recorder* (Raleigh NC), 6 June 1840, 2. The article continues with a statement about Battle's personal risk in the enterprise: "Subscriptions have been obtained as yet not to exceed, if even to equal, half the cost of building. The remainder, unless contributed by the friends of the cause, must of course come out of the pocket of the pastor. And when it is known that he has not even the prospect of receiving a fourth part of the annual expense of his family in the form of a compensation for his pastoral services, it may be seen how far it is right that he should be permitted to suffer loss on the building. It has been often said by brethren in different parts of the country, and with manifest justice too, that it was a shame that the Baptists could not have a good, substantial place of worship in the metropolis of the state. The object so long and so justly desired has at length been secured. It now remains to be seen how far those interested in its attainment, will bear a hand in meeting the expense thereby incurred."

[30] Church Conference Records, 8 April 1841. No specific reason for the resignation is given. However, it almost certainly was due to the church's debt and Battle's personal financial crisis. At the same meeting the church resolved that he be requested to work with "Brothers Wait and White" of Wake Forest on behalf of the church, presumably to help raise funds to pay the church's debt.

[31] A. J. Battle, "New Baptist Church in Raleigh," *Biblical Recorder* (Raleigh NC), 31 July 1841, 2. The same letter was published a second time the following week.

prominence of the church's location in the capital city—having been built diagonally across from the state capitol (which had just been completed in 1840). Many feared North Carolina Baptists would face embarrassment if such a prominently located church were to be sold to the highest bidder and then turned into a business, particularly if that business were a saloon. To prevent such an outcome, a future pastor of the church, J. J. Finch, put forth a plan to attract 300 subscribers from among North Carolina Baptists who would agree to give $10 [$254] each toward retiring the debt. He presented a list of five men (including himself) who had already done so.[32] Then in November 1841 D. D. Bumpass wrote a letter of support, published in *The Biblical Recorder*, describing how he originally thought the church building was overly lavish "but, on viewing the work, I am clearly of the opinion, that there is not ten dollars worth of unnecessary work done on it."[33] The following week T. B. Barnett published a letter that provided a list of subscriptions (pledges) from individuals committed to pay the debt. He called attention to the fact that five of the names were affiliated with the Presbyterians. "Now if our Presbyterian brethren will give $50 [$1,270] in one neighborhood, to pay for a Baptist church in Raleigh," Barnett said, "*surely* the Baptists of North Carolina will not suffer it to be sold."[34]

The obvious question is, how did the financial disaster for the church happen if Battle was from a wealthy family and originally pledged the funds for the church himself? The answer came in an article written by Lewis DuPre, which appeared in the *Biblical Recorder* in early 1843. DuPre indicated that Battle came to the church as pastor with a great concern that it should have a proper meetinghouse for worship. He was able to find contributors who pledged close to $1,000 [$25,400]. That allowed Battle to begin the construction of the building, believing that whatever he could not raise by pledge he would provide from his own resources. For those who may have wondered whether Battle had

---

[32] J. J. Finch, "A Plan to Save the New Baptist Church in Raleigh," *Biblical Recorder* (Raleigh NC), 18 September 1841, 2.

[33] D. D. Bumpass, letter to the editor, *Biblical Recorder* (Raleigh NC), 13 November 1841, 3.

[34] T. B. Barnett, letter to the editor, *Biblical Recorder* (Raleigh NC), 20 November 1841, 3.

sufficient financial resources to enter such an arrangement, DuPre said, "At this time our dear brother Battle had in his possession property enough to have paid for several such houses."[35]

DuPre continued describing how Battle's fortunes took a downward turn before the completion of the church building and how "he found himself to be much embarrassed, [as] his creditors forced his property into market when everything was very low, and of course his property was sold at great sacrifice, and did not bring enough to meet the demands against him."[36] When Battle's financial situation became precarious, the contractors who were building the church demanded some type of security for their work. Battle then "gave them a deed of trust upon the house for about $3,000 [$76,100], which has accumulated until it is nearly $4,000 [$101,000]."[37]

Battle's situation became so desperate in 1843 that he published a proposal in the *Biblical Recorder*, intended for all North Carolina Baptists, which offered his services to denomination for life with no pay if they would provide the funding to pay off the church's debt. He was motivated to make that frantic offer because of two concerns: (1) to save

---

[35] Lewis DuPre, "Once For All!" *Biblical Recorder* (Raleigh NC), 11 February 1843, 3. DuPre became the pastor of the church in 1842.

[36] Ibid.

[37] Ibid. See also A. J. Battle, "A Fair Proposition," 2. In a letter written to the Baptists of North Carolina several months later, Battle chronicled in detail his financial losses: "I was called from my engagements at Rocky Mount, to endeavor to build up an interest for the Redeemer in the Baptist Church here. To do this, a new house of worship became indispensably necessary. I undertook it upon the advice, and with the co-operation of many of our most judicious brethren. I had to sustain almost alone the whole burden and expense of its erection from beginning to end. About the time of its completion my misfortunes began. In the first place I had to pay twenty-five hundred dollars security money. I lost two thousand dollars by the Morus Multicaulis trees. [No doubt a business investment relating to raising silk worms]. I lost six thousand dollars by the Wilmington Rail Road. I lost near a thousand dollars at Mobile, Ala.—I had three thousand dollars due in Florida which could not be collected—I lost near four thousand dollars by the sale of property in Raleigh, over a thousand of which was lost on the adjoining lot to the Church, which was improved with a view that all the profits should be appropriated to the Church. In addition to all this, were the advance payments for the Church that could not be refunded."

the Raleigh Baptist Church and (2) his commitment to the Baptist State Convention of North Carolina and desire that it prosper.[38] Battle described in detail his financial losses and how he relocated to Wilmington, became pastor of the First Baptist Church in the city, and worked in secular employment as well. Things seemed to be improving as he said, "I had considerable business to transact, and flattered myself that it would not be long, before I would be able to meet all just demands against me."[39]

His optimism was shattered, however, when the proverbial "bottom fell out." He indicated that about a month prior to the writing of the article, "I was surprised with an arrest by the Sheriff of N. Hanover on a writ called a *Ca. Sa.* issued upon an old claim due to a citizen of Raleigh." Battle came back to Raleigh, appeared in court, and was "forthwith committed by the Judge to the custody of the Sheriff to be imprisoned."[40] Finally, laying his desperate situation into the open, he declared,

> I have thus been torn, by this cruel and barbarous feature of our laws, from pursuing a profitable business…which is now closed and suspended. I have been torn from the holy functions of a Pastor for God's people, who are now as sheep without a Shepherd. I have been torn by this unfeeling and oppressive act of human laws, from all the endearments of home, wife and children, who are by it bereft of their only earthly dependence for support, and thrown entirely upon the kindness of Christian charity for bread, and separated from them more than a hundred miles, to be kept in confinement for at least 20 days.[41]

Battle made an appeal once again to North Carolina Baptists for money to pay the church's debt. He promised that any extra money

---

[38] A. J. Battle, "A Fair Proposition," 2.

[39] Ibid.

[40] Ibid.

[41] Ibid. Although there are some later secondary sources that indicate that Battle never served time in jail for his indebtedness (see Morris, "The History of the First Baptist Church of Raleigh, 1812–1912," 27), this quote from Battle himself makes it clear that he did. The North Carolina Constitution of 1868 abolished the practice of imprisonment for debt. See also Paschal, *History of Wake Forest College,* vol. 1, 548.

beyond the church's debt would be given directly to the treasury of the convention because, as he said, "should this last appeal be disregarded, the Church will no doubt be lost, the whole denomination be reproached, and the Lord only knows what will become of me and my poor family."[42]

Battle's offer of lifetime employment to the convention with no pay in return for the church's debt being paid was shortlived. Within two weeks, another announcement from Battle appeared in the *Biblical Recorder* in which he withdrew his offer because,

> I have received such strong remonstrances [*sic*] from the members of the Baptist Church in Wilmington, against releasing me from my engagement to them as Pastor; and also such earnest remonstrances [*sic*] from my relations and others against that part of my communication which proposes to *sell myself for life*, that I feel it to be my duty to withdraw that part of my proposition.[43]

A few weeks later Reverend J. J. Finch, a future pastor of the church, provided a follow-up to Battle's "desperate" letter to North Carolina Baptists in order to give clarity to the issues involved. Knowing the church was on the verge of being sold at auction for payment of the debt, he began by asserting that some people might believe Battle's proposal was solely for the purpose of getting North Carolina Baptists to pay off his personal debt. Others, he said, will infer that it was so that the personal desires of his family might be attained. Still others might suppose it was for the purpose of saving the church. Finch explained the issue very succinctly with a question: "Will we purchase the church erected by Elder Battle, in the city of Raleigh, or will we suffer it to go into other hands?"[44]

Finch then projected a plan whereby the convention might purchase the church when it came up for sale, suggesting that "it would be best for some individual, or a few individuals...to *buy* the house, to be

---

[42] A. J. Battle, "A Fair Proposition," 2. It is ironic that Battle, while serving now as pastor of the First Baptist Church of Wilmington, was nevertheless being forced to appeal for funds to pay off the debt of the Raleigh Baptist Church.

[43] A. J. Battle, "To the Baptist Denomination," *Biblical Recorder* (Raleigh NC), 6 May 1843, 3.

[44] J. J. Finch, "For the Recorder," *Biblical Recorder* (Raleigh NC), 20 May 1843, 2.

transferred to the denomination as soon as they pay for it."[45] In summary, he reiterated, "The question then, is not will we buy brother Battle, by paying his debts, as some have understood it, or will we confer a favor on him…but will we favor *ourselves*—or the cause with which we are identified—with the use of a respectable and spacious church in the city of Raleigh?"[46] The anticipated auction of the church building was announced in the 24 June 1843 issue of the *Biblical Recorder*:

> To satisfy the provisions of a Deed of Trust made by Amos J. Battle, dated 17th July, 1841, will be sold publicly to the highest bidder for cash, on the premises, on Saturday the 22nd July next,
> THE NEW BAPTIST CHURCH,
> in the City of Raleigh, together with the land on which it stands,
> By order of two of the principal Creditors
> D. DuPre
> Acting Trustee

In the same issue of the *Biblical Recorder* that contained the advertisement, Daniel DuPre, one of the church's trustees, included an extensive letter of explanation about the church's situation. He began by reporting the exact amount of indebtedness that existed on the building. Originally, the exact cost of the building was $5,572.64 [$143,000]. To date, $1,562.50 [$39,600] had been raised, leaving a debt of $4,010.14 [$102,000]. DuPre said that the accumulated interest by the time of the auction would make the total debt $4,812.77 [$122,000]. DuPre encouraged the estimated 40,000 North Carolina Baptists to contribute 12 1/2 cents [$3.74] each, which would raise approximately $5,000 [$150,000] because "Our dignity as a religious community, is inseparably connected with the disinthralment of the Raleigh Church."[47]

DuPre's call for support motivated North Carolina Baptists to give more because, within a few weeks, a short notice appeared in the *Biblical Recorder* announcing that the creditors had decided to postpone the sale

---

[45] Ibid.

[46] Ibid., 3.

[47] Daniel DuPre, "To the Baptists of North Carolina," *Biblical Recorder* (Raleigh NC), 1 July 1843, 2.

of the church for several months to see if the necessary amount of money could be collected.[48] For the next five months, the *Biblical Recorder* published regular reports surrounding money pledged for the cause. However, in December a short notice appeared that must have been disappointing to all involved in the campaign: "The Baptist Church in Raleigh will be sold for cash on the 13th of January 1844; by virtue of Deed of Trust."[49]

Despite the debt and seeming disappointment, the story does have a happy ending for the Raleigh Baptist Church. On 20 January 1844 the *Biblical Recorder* reported the final result of the church's auction. According to the account, the church made a compromise with the creditors for the purchase of the building. The church was actually sold for the amount of $400 [$12,000]. The specifics of the compromise indicate that a total of $1,907 [$57,100] was paid to the creditors in return for a promise that only the church would bid for the property. The amount collected by subscriptions before the sale, $907.48 [$27,200], was paid to the creditors. The trustees of the church borrowed $1,000 [$29,900] from the bank, having been assured that donors would come forward to satisfy the debt once they were certain the building would end up in the hands of the Raleigh Baptist Church.[50] Within a year, a short article appeared in the *Biblical Recorder* indicating that most of the $1,000 debt had been paid by members of the church and that just a small amount was left.[51] By May 1846 the debt was finally retired on the building and the deed transferred to the membership.[52]

---

[48] A. J. Battle, "Baptist Church in Raleigh," *Biblical Recorder* (Raleigh NC), 29 July 1843, 2.

[49] *Biblical Recorder* (Raleigh NC), 9 December 1843, 3.

[50] "The Baptist Meeting House in Raleigh," *Biblical Recorder* (Raleigh NC), 20 January 1844, 2. The church appointed M. B. Royster, Thompson Parham, James D. Nunn, J. F. Jordan, and J. J. Biggs as trustees. See Church Conference Records, "Saturday Before the 1st Lord's Day, January 1844." For much of that period, rather than the actual date of the meeting, this designation was used.

[51] "The Raleigh Baptist Church Debt," *Biblical Recorder* (Raleigh NC), 18 January 1845, 3.

[52] "Fortitude Had Conquered All," *Biblical Recorder* (Raleigh NC), 2 May 1846, 2.

Resignation of Battle. In addition to the debt and looming foreclosure that the church faced in 1841, the congregation also was given the task that year of searching for a new pastor. Battle had resigned his pastorate of the church at a called church conference on 8 April 1841. His resignation came at the conclusion of a long meeting that took place at "Sister Parish's house." The meeting was originally called to consider a letter sent by the Bethel Baptist Church, a sister church in the Raleigh Baptist Association, dated 20 February 1841. The minutes of the meeting include the text of the letter:

> Dear Brethren, We have been informed by your Pastor bearing a letter to our last association that you were very much hurt with us. This hurt it appears has been occasioned by brother Battle and brother Bowers. We have requested brother Battle to come before us in our Church and we would attend to the charges made by him against brother Bowers. We now call on you as a church if you are hurt with us, to send two or three of your male members to our next church meeting which is on Saturday before the third Sunday in April. We as a Church wish to see into a matter of so great importance before we act, as we may be able to act according to the word of God.[53]

The reference to "brother Bowers" concerns a member of the Bethel church named Osbourne Bowers, with whom Battle evidently came into a financial conflict. The disagreement between those two men ultimately led to legal action by Bowers, who filed a civil suit against Battle. During the Raleigh Baptist Church conference, Battle conveyed his side of the conflict with Bowers and recommended that the church appoint a committee to meet with the Bethel church as the letter requested. The church affirmed his request by appointing J. J. Biggs[54] and M. B. Royster to the task.[55]

---

[53] Church Conference Records, 8 April 1841.

[54] The membership records from that period reveal that the church had two prominent leaders whose names were very similar: John J. Briggs, a charter member and one of the first two deacons, and J. J. Biggs. Both Briggs and Biggs were active during those years.

[55] Church Conference Records, 8 April 1841.

Battle had two points of contention against Bowers's action: (1) that Bowers's work on the steeple for the new church building was "unfit and unsafe for the purposes for which it was intended" and that he should have allowed the church a reduction in price to compensate for such poor workmanship; (2) and that he violated the letter of scripture by taking his claim to a secular court when an equitable solution might have been reached without such measures.[56] The Raleigh Baptist Church listened to Battle and then passed a strongly worded resolution of support for their pastor. The resolution took the Bethel church to task for not dealing with the Bowers matter internally (of particular concern, no doubt, was the supposed violation of scripture by virtue of the lawsuit) when it was called to their attention by Battle. Furthermore, they determined that the neglect of the matter by the Bethel church "was disrespectful toward [Battle] as a member of the Baptist Church and as a minister of the Gospel, and he being the Pastor of this Church justified this Church in sending the letter we did by brother Briggs to the Raleigh Association."[57]

Surprisingly, perhaps also to the congregation, Battle tendered his resignation as pastor of the church at the conclusion of the meeting. The only explanation conveyed in the minutes indicated that Battle, "after making a few brief, but affecting remarks in reference to his commission with this Church, and expressing the deep interest he felt in his success, tendered his resignation as Pastor of the Church, stating as his only reason, that he was unable to continue his residence in Raleigh."[58] As discussed, Battle moved to Wilmington where he found secular

---

[56] Ibid.

[57] Ibid. The reference to the letter delivered to the association is confusing. The reprinted correspondence from the Bethel Church mentioned above says that the letter was carried by Battle to the association. The church minutes then mention that it was carried by Briggs. See Minutes of the Raleigh Baptist Association, 1841, 2. The minutes of the Raleigh Baptist Association from 1840 mention nothing of that conflict nor of any letter delivered by Briggs. Battle is listed as a visitor at the associational meeting in 1840 because the reconstituted Raleigh Baptist Church did not rejoin the association until 1841.

[58] Church Conference Records, 8 April 1841. The personal financial woes encountered by Battle (discussed above) no doubt played a part in his decision to resign. No further information is given in the church records about the lawsuit or the controversy with Bethel Baptist Church.

employment and served for a time as pastor of the First Baptist church of that city. Following Battle's resignation, he suggested to the church that it contact the American Home Mission Society to see if it could send a missionary to serve the church in Raleigh who would be jointly supported by both the church and the society.[59]

As a final note about his life, Battle settled in Wilson, North Carolina, in 1853 where he resided for the rest of his life. He opened the first hotel in Wilson called the "Battle House." An interesting twist in his life occurred in 1852 when he became a minister in the Disciples of Christ denomination. One historian reported that he was especially known for his aggressive evangelization and eventually was appointed as their "State Evangelist," where "from the Dismal Swamp to the Swannanoa [he] sowed the good seed of the 'Restoration Movement.'"[60] His time among the Disciples, however, was not without controversy. As many ministers of that era had to do, Battle worked a secular job in addition to his ministry. In 1857 the Adams Express Company in Hertford, North Carolina, charged him with malfeasance while he was in the company's employment concerning some money he borrowed from the company and supposedly never returned. The Disciples proceeded to suspend Battle's ministerial credentials for the next decade, until 1866 when he was finally reinstated and, once again, became the denomination's traveling evangelist for the state. During the period of his suspension Battle preached at Christian Hope Church, a small Disciples congregation (which was itself suspended from the denomination for allowing Battle to preach). Following reinstatement of his ministerial credentials in 1866, Battle was able to serve the Disciples for only another four years. He died in Wilson on 24 September 1870.[61]

---

[59] Ibid.

[60] Ware, *North Carolina Disciples of Christ*, 283.

[61] Ibid., 178–79; Mark Toulouse, "Once Baptists, Now Disciples: A Case Study of Rountrees Meeting House, North Carolina," *Discipliana* 60/1 (Spring 2000): 26. See *Biblical Recorder* (Raleigh NC), 28 September 1870, 3. Amos J. Battle's life and career deserve more attention than can be given here. One question that needs exploring is his motivation for leaving the Baptists for the Disciples, especially in light of the intense competition between the two denominations in the antebellum years. The question is especially intriguing given the fact that Battle was such an important leader among Baptists in North Carolina in the antebellum years. It is

Lewis DuPre (1842–1844)

There were no church conferences in May, June, or July 1841. A short entry from August reports that Brother Briggs was asked and agreed to enlist the assistance of Samuel Wait of Wake Forest College to write to the American Baptist Home Mission Society for church aid.[62] Later that month the records report that the society responded positively to the church's request, and the church then appointed a committee to inquire about the possibility of Patrick Dowd returning as pastor.[63] There was no meeting in September, but by October the records indicated that Dowd had rejected the church's offer to return. Given the amount of turmoil that accompanied Dowd's first tenure as pastor, it is interesting that the church would consider extending him the possibility of a return. However, it should be kept in mind that Dowd was an important leader among North Carolina Baptists by 1841, and it would probably have paid dividends in public respect among Baptists had he accepted its offer. Given the debt and struggling condition financially, Dowd's stature could have helped the church.

Even though the church records report no significant business until February 1842, it is clear that the church was struggling to find a pastor. An offer was made to a former Wake Forest College professor, Daniel Ford Richardson, who declined.[64] Sometime later in the spring "Rev. Mr.

---

noteworthy that Battle was one of only three delegates representing North Carolina at the organization of the Southern Baptist Convention in Augusta, Georgia, on 8 May 1845. See "Proceedings of the Southern Baptist Convention," 8 May 1845, located in the Archives of the Southern Baptist Historical Library and Archives, Nashville, Tennessee. Battle and J. McDaniel were delegates from the First Baptist Church in Wilmington, while R. McNab represented the Kenansville Baptist Church.

[62] Church Conference Records, "Saturday Before the First Lord's Day, August, 1841."

[63] Ibid., 22 August 1841.

[64] Ibid., (no date given) February 1842. See Paschal, *History of Wake Forest College*, vol. 1, 125ff. Richardson was elected as professor of ancient languages at Wake Forest College by the board of trustees in 1837. He was ordained by the Wake Forest Baptist Church in 1838 and listed by the church as "Co-Pastor" in 1839. For some unknown reason, he was dismissed from the faculty of Wake Forest in 1840. Although no reason is known for his termination, he was given a

Pritchard" was offered the pastorate of the church—who also declined because of previous commitments.[65] By 1 September 1842, however, the church had offered the pastorate to Reverend Lewis DuPre, who accepted the call. The minutes indicate that "He came preaching Jesus and him crucified. May the blessing of God attend his ministry for his Son's sake."[66]

When DuPre assumed the pastorate of the church, the membership of the congregation was listed in the Raleigh Baptist Association records as 141. By the conclusion of his tenure, the church reported 281 members (eighty-two white and 199 "colored"), indicating a great amount of growth.[67] According to the church records, DuPre's ministry at the Raleigh Baptist Church was mostly consumed with the church's financial indebtedness. While the previous pastor, Amos J. Battle, was directly responsible for the debt on the building, the members were keenly aware that if the debt was not paid, they would lose the structure. Just after DuPre received his "annual call" to be the pastor for another year, he was asked to write a letter to the Home Mission Society to determine whether

---

letter of dismissal and recommendation from the Wake Forest Baptist Church and is listed among the ministers of the Baptist State Convention in 1842.

[65] Church Conference Records, (no date given) February 1842. No full name is given but this was most likely Joseph Price Pritchard, the father of Thomas H. Pritchard who would eventually become pastor of the church in 1867.

[66] Ibid. DuPre was no stranger to the church. His father, Daniel DuPre, was an active member and a trustee of the church. See Louis DuPre, "Once For All!" *Biblical Recorder* (Raleigh NC), 11 February 1843, 3.

[67] Minutes of the Raleigh Baptist Association, 1842 and 1844. The 1844 table delineated "white" and "colored" members. It is interesting that while white members are noted in the minutes when they were voted into the membership of the church, there is very little mention during that era of the slaves and their worship services, or even the names of the slaves as they joined and were baptized. While the earlier records of the church from 1812 to 1832 have various references to the black members and concerns for their meetings, the period from 1840 to 1855 rarely mentions them. In fact, the only reference to the black members' worship services occurred in 1854 in a cryptic message that read, "Brother Alex Moore appointed to take the superintendency of the colored meetings, the clerk [Jordan Womble, Jr.] having declined the appointment" (see Church Conference Records, 1 April 1854). Why Womble, a prominent leader in the church at the time, would decline the appointment is not known.

the church could depend on financial help for the coming year.[68] By November of that same year Thompson Parham and J. J. Biggs were appointed to raise by subscriptions (pledges) the funds necessary to pay the pastor's salary.[69]

Footwashing Discussed. One interesting issue that arose during Lewis DuPre's tenure was the question of footwashing. The question was not new to the church. It will be recalled from the last chapter that although details are sketchy in the minutes, the church dealt with the issue between the years 1828 and 1830. There was no further mention of the issue until DuPre's tenure as pastor. During the regular church conference in January 1844, John J. Briggs "requested that a time be appointed for the purpose of imitating our Lord and Savior in washing one another's feet." The request evidently brought considerable discussion, to the extent that the matter was "laid over" until the next meeting.[70] The next month the congregation decided to postpone the issue indefinitely. The next reference to the issue came two months later when M. B. Royster inquired as to whether the church's rules and covenant had been violated by the way in which Briggs's original motion had been dealt. After some discussion the church again decided to postpone the issue until the next meeting.[71]

A few days later at a special called meeting of the church, the following resolution was passed, which resolved Royster's concerns: "Resolved, that this church not censure the brethren who participated in washing feet as a religious observance in as much as they believed from the impression made upon their minds that they could do so without giving offense to the Church or any of the Brethren."[72] The compromise, however, did not seem to satisfy Briggs. Following its passage, Briggs asked the church if it would approve the washing of feet as a "Christian duty in a private capacity." This new perspective on the issue evidently fueled the controversy once again as the motion was postponed until the

---

[68] Church Conference Records, "Saturday Before the First Lord's Day, August, 1843."

[69] Ibid., "Saturday Before the First Lord's Day, November, 1843."

[70] Ibid., "Saturday Before the First Lord's Day, January, 1844."

[71] Ibid., vol. II, "Saturday Before the First Lord's Day, April, 1844."

[72] Ibid., 13 April 1844.

next meeting.[73] The minutes from the following month contain the final reference to the matter as the church decided it was "inexpedient to take any definite action upon Brother Brigg's inquiry relative to feet washing."[74]

Footwashing was a common practice among many Baptists in North Carolina in the nineteenth century, and still remains so today among some groups, such as some Primitive Baptists and all Freewill Baptists. Many Baptist groups regarded it as an ordinance to be observed, along with baptism and communion, based on Jesus' words in John 13:13ff. Since it was such a common practice in North Carolina, and since it seemed to be a matter of concern within the Raleigh Baptist Church, the issue of footwashing reflects a modicum of tension in the congregation at that time between the Separate and Regular Baptist traditions that were present in the state.

Resignation of DuPre. On 17 November 1844 Lewis DuPre resigned as the pastor of the Raleigh Baptist Church after just two years of service. The resignation must have caught the church members by surprise, since they immediately appointed a committee to investigate his motivation. The committee reported back that it did not think it was proper to inquire as to his motivation since the church had already accepted his resignation.[75] Interestingly, there was a resolution adopted by the church at that December meeting that may suggest some tension with DuPre:

> Resolved, that as a church, we hold ourselves responsible for eighty dollars which was collected in behalf of the church for the purpose of buying a bell and has been used by our late pastor Brother L. DuPre in payment of our church debt and also that Brother DuPre be requested to pay over to the treasurer of this church the balance of the bell fund in his hands and take the treasurer's receipt.[76]

---

[73] Ibid.
[74] Ibid., "Saturday Before the First Lord's Day, May, 1844."
[75] Ibid.,17 November 1844.
[76] Ibid., "Saturday Before the First Lord's Day, December, 1844."

No further word about the matter appears in the records. Without more information, it is difficult to determine whether or not the statement reflects the church's dissatisfaction toward its former pastor.

While the church records would not indicate a particularly eventful two years as pastor of the Raleigh Baptist Church, it should be remembered that the debt on the building was finally retired during DuPre's leadership. Given the financial difficulties and limitations of the congregation at the time, Lewis DuPre should therefore be remembered with appreciation for his leadership during that troubled period. Jordan Womble, who was a child during DuPre's ministry at the church, recalled that he had a "most pleasant recollection of Rev. Mr. DuPre as a warmhearted minister of the church and a very affectionate pastor."[77]

Josiah J. Finch (1845–1848)

Within one month of DuPre's resignation, the church extended a call to Reverend Josiah J. Finch to fill the pastoral vacancy.[78] At the regularly scheduled church conference the following month, Finch accepted the call for a salary of $700 [$20,700], an amount the committee believed had been pledged from several unnamed sources (which are not named). The minutes also suggested something that had not previously been mentioned in relation to the coming of a new pastor. In a gesture that may signal more open-mindedness in the congregation, they planned to invite the pastors of the Presbyterian and Methodist churches in the city to be present and witness the installation of Finch when he began his pastoral tenure.[79]

Finch was born on 3 February 1814 in Franklin County, North Carolina. Converted and baptized into the Maple Springs Baptist Church near Louisburg around the age of seventeen, he almost immediately began to have feelings of a call to ministry. When he was eighteen he was ordained to the ministry by the Maple Springs Church, and very soon thereafter enrolled as a student at what is now Louisburg College while preaching regularly at his home church. He was then called as pastor of

---

[77] "Womble-Marcom History," 15.
[78] Church Conference Records, 8 December 1844.
[79] Ibid., "Saturday Before the Fourth Sabbath in January, 1845."

the Edenton Baptist Church in 1835 where he served until he enrolled at Wake Forest College in 1837. Finch's giftedness for ministry must have impressed a number of influential people. After only two semesters at Wake Forest, he began receiving invitations to serve as pastor in churches located as far away as Mississippi. He chose, however, to move back to Edenton where he married Mary Louisa Wiles on 13 February 1838. The week following their marriage, he and his new bride moved to New Bern, North Carolina, where he became pastor of the First Baptist Church, a position in which he served until his call to the Raleigh Baptist Church seven years later.[80]

Disgruntled Members. Finch's tenure at the Raleigh Baptist Church was marked by several interesting and important events. The minutes from those years reflect the church grappling on a couple of occasions with the issue of disgruntled members. Thompson Parham, a prominent member of the church, first exhibited dissatisfaction in December 1845 when he abruptly asked the congregation for a letter of dismissal. No reason is given for the request but rather than approving it, the church referred the matter to a committee composed of three other prominent members—J. J. Biggs, M. B. Royster, and P. F. Pescud.[81]

The following month the committee reported that Parham's request for a letter of dismissal had been withdrawn and that he was now "satisfied" and no longer desired to leave. It is noted, however, that in the same meeting Parham made a motion that the church hold two prayer meetings each week instead of just one—a motion that was referred to a committee composed of Parham, M. B. Royster, and James F. Jordan. The issue seems to have been resolved, and Parham voiced no complaints. He was even selected by the church to serve on another temporary committee, indicating that the church believed he was content.[82] A month later, the minutes report that the church had decided not to change the number of prayer meetings per week and contain no

---

[80] G. M. L. Finch, "Biographical Sketch of Rev. Josiah J. Finch," *Sermons of the Rev. Josiah J. Finch* (Charleston SC: Southern Baptist Publication Society, 1853) v–vii.

[81] Church Conference Records, "Saturday Before the First Lord's Day in December, 1845."

[82] Ibid., "Saturday Before the First Lord's Day in January, 1846."

further comment about the matter.[83] Parham, however, was not happy. At the regular conference of the church in March 1846, the following resolution was passed by the congregation:

> Whereas Thompson Parham has declared himself no longer a member of this body, and has been guilty of other disorderly and schismatical [sic] conduct in *departing from the rules of the church in holding meetings contrary to the expressed instructions of official advisors, and absenting himself from the service of the church,* Therefore, resolved that he be expelled from the fellowship of this church.[84]

The matter was closed from that point forward. From what can be gathered from the church minutes, one could guess that Parham had become concerned about the spiritual fervor of the church and believed that adding an additional prayer meeting each week would solve the problem. Obviously, the majority of the members did not agree, and Parham's frustrations rose to the point that he had become a detriment to the fellowship of the congregation, resulting in his expulsion.

The second matter related to dissension within the fellowship of the church concerned J. G. Buffaloe, a member of the congregation. At the regular church conference in October 1846, Buffaloe called for the chairman of the executive committee to report on the status of a petition he had submitted to the committee relating to the pastor. The chair of the executive committee reported that the petition had been discussed and that the counsel of the committee had been to postpone the matter indefinitely. Buffaloe then appealed the decision of the executive committee to the congregation. After hearing the matter (the details of which were not recorded), the church voted to sustain the decision of the executive committee. Tempers must have flared at the meeting because the minutes record that J. J. Finch accused Buffaloe of "schismatical [sic] conduct" for circulating a petition about the pastor as he had done.

---

[83] Ibid., "Saturday Before the First Sabbath in February, 1846."

[84] Ibid., "Saturday Before the First Sabbath in March, 1846." (The emphasis is the author's.)

Finch's charge was then referred to the executive committee, which was to report on the matter at a later meeting.[85]

The following month, the executive committee reported back that it had rejected the charge of "schismatical [sic] conduct" concerning Buffaloe. It seems that other members wanted the matter against Buffaloe pressed further because a motion was made by one member for the matter to be reconsidered. Abruptly, the minutes indicated that the meeting was adjourned until the following Tuesday afternoon, when the issue was finally resolved by the church with this resolution:

> Resolved that in the opinion of this church, the circulating of petitions or any other instrument of writing designed to affect an officer or any other member of the church, is injurious, and schismatical [sic]. Resolved, as it is believed that Brother Buffaloe, acted without being fully aware of the nature and tendency of such acts, _____ [unable to read] would not under the circumstances, again do the same thing, that he be excused by the church from all further proceedings.[86]

In this case, the church reacted with grace, believing that Buffaloe was not aware his behavior would cause a problem in the congregation's fellowship (unlike the case of Parham).

Sunday-School Beginning. An important improvement in the life of the congregation during Finch's ministry was the addition of a Sunday school. The driving force behind that effort was Peter F. Pescud, a pharmacist by trade who remained active in the church as a deacon until his death in 1884.[87] Originally from Petersburg, Virginia, Pescud joined the Raleigh Baptist Church in 1844 at the age of twenty-two. Shortly thereafter he became Sunday-school superintendent and held the position until 1858. According to one source, Pescud was "commander-in-chief, and showed wonderful skill, tact and kindness of heart in so

---

[85] Church Conference Records, "Saturday Before the First Sabbath in October, 1846."

[86] Ibid., "Saturday Before the First Sabbath in November, 1846."

[87] "Church Receives Pescud Memorial," *News and Observer* (Raleigh NC), 22 February 1937, 10.

ordering the details that every little soul went home happy and glad of being a member of the Raleigh Baptist Sunday School."[88]

Pescud used several types of literature in the Sunday school, including Webster's *The American Spelling Book* and Judson's *Union Questions: A Compilation From Questions on the Selected Scripture Lessons*, a popular Sunday-school text among Baptist churches in the nineteenth century. He also introduced the tradition of Sunday-school picnics into the life of the church, observed annually in the middle of the summer. The church records briefly mention one such picnic that occurred on 4 July 1846, simply noting that the regularly scheduled church conference was cancelled on that day due to the "Sabbath School celebration."[89] In addition to its ministry to families, Pescud's Sunday school also provided an education for children whose families could not afford to do so otherwise. (There was no public school system in North Carolina at that point.) [90]

Resignation of Finch. Unfortunately, health problems associated with a chronic lung disease plagued Finch's ministry at the Raleigh Baptist Church. As a result, in 1848, after only three years as the church's pastor, he was forced to resign. Finch's letter of resignation was included in the church minutes:

> Having been unable in consequence of affliction to perform the duties of pastor among you for several months past, and seeing no reason to believe that I shall be for sometime to come, if ever, I feel it to be my duty to tender you my resignation as pastor which I hereby do. The Providential dispensation by which I am led to this step is so well known to you all that I need not detain you with explanations on so sad a subject. I therefore commend you to God and to the word of grace, with the earnest prayer that he may guide you with wisdom from above in all your plans and labors.[91]

---

[88] Lewis, "Some Reminiscences of the Baptist Church in Raleigh Fifty Years Ago," 258.

[89] Church Conference Records, "Saturday Before the First Sabbath in July, 1846." 4 July is inserted as the entry's date.

[90] "Church Receives Pescud Memorial," 10.

[91] Church Conference Records, 10 July 1848.

The resignation grieved the congregation, which responded by accepting his resignation and expressing "sympathy and regret on account of his afflictions." The church also voted to appropriate $100 [$2,800] to Finch to pay his expenses for a therapeutic visit to "White Sulphur Springs."[92]

Despite his failing health, Finch remained active in the life of the church and the Raleigh community after his resignation. Previously, in 1845, he and his wife had established the Sedgwick Female Seminary, an academy for young women located on Fayetteville Street. By all accounts the school was very successful.[93] Finch gave his remaining days to assisting his wife in the administration of the school. He tragically died at the age of thirty-six on 21 January 1850. Baptists all over the state mourned his loss. During its annual meeting in 1850, the Baptist State Convention of North Carolina included a special recognition of Finch's ministry.[94]

The Raleigh Baptist Church mourned the loss of their pastor the most. Following his death the church passed the following resolution:

> Whereas it has pleased Almighty God, in dispensation of His Providence, to remove from among us, our beloved Brother and late Pastor, the Rev. J. J. Finch; Therefore, Resolved that in the death of Brother Finch, the cause of Christ has lost one of its ablest advocates, and society one of its brightest ornaments;
> Resolved, that we have abundant reason to humble our hearts in prayer to our Heavenly Father, that with this affliction he would send His Spirit of Grace and consolation;
> Resolved, that we most sincerely sympathize with the bereaved family of the deceased, and pray that they may find in the _____ [unable to read] of Jesus that comfort and support which they so much need.
> Resolved, that as a token of our love and respect, for our late Pastor, we will erect a suitable monument of his memory and observe

---

[92] Ibid., 7 July 1848. Either this date or the date of the preceding entry in the church records that reproduced Finch's resignation letter is incorrect.

[93] Murray, *Wake: Capital County of North Carolina,* vol. 1, 313.

[94] "Report on Special Changes," *Annual of the Baptist State Convention of North Carolina* (1850): 23.

the usual emblem of mourning at our church for the space of thirty days.

Resolved that a copy of these resolutions be presented the family of the deceased, also a copy be forwarded to the "Biblical Recorder" for publication.[95]

The "monument" referred to in the resolution was a marker over Finch's grave in the City Cemetery.

The church remained without a pastor for the next two years. The minutes of the church business meetings during that time reflect an intense but fruitless effort to find a suitable pastor. One entry from the period reveals the state of low morale that must have existed in the church: "Brother Biggs briefly informed the church that the main object in calling it together was to inform them of its mournful conditions, and the necessity of speedy action and importunate prayers in order to avoid the _____ [unable to read] dark cloud which had so long hovered over us and to prevent closing the doors."[96]

The state of the church went from low morale to embarrassment in one incident related to the calling of a new pastor. In September 1848 the church was called into business session for the purpose of discussing candidates to serve as pastor. The names of Reverend James Holmes of New York and Reverend I. I. Brantley of Fayetteville were presented. The minutes reveal that the church's executive committee recommended Holmes be called as the pastor until 1 January 1849, and then that Brantley be called as the permanent pastor. The church voted to extend a call to Reverend James Holmes of New York, and it appointed a committee to inform him of the call.[97] Interestingly, there is no further mention of Brantley. Did the church choose Holmes as the permanent pastor at that meeting? Or did it follow the suggestion proposed? Unfortunately, the records are not clear. However, the following month the church records contain the following entry:

---

[95] Church Conference Records, (no date given) January 1850.

[96] Ibid., 8 April 1849. The missing word cannot be deciphered in the entry.

[97] Ibid., "Saturday Before the Second Sabbath in September, 1848."

It was explained that one of the objects of the meeting was to consider what action should be taken in regard to our late pastor, James Holmes, an impostor from the state of New York. The secretary and others made a statement of the facts and circumstances which led to the discovery that Holmes's credentials were forgeries. It was resolved that in as much as said Holmes left the city immediately upon being detected and as the executive committee had already appointed J. J. Biggs and W. W. Vass a committee to publish him as an imposter in the newspapers, no further action required now.[98]

The minutes from that period also report a curious and tragic episode of church discipline that should be recognized. Most of the issues relating to church discipline in the congregation, as in other churches of that day, concerned drinking, dancing, missing church meetings, or other minor violations. Frequently, the church appointed a committee to meet with the accused party, which would then report back to the church after the meeting and a vote would be taken as to the appropriate disciplinary action. But in 1849 a very serious charge was leveled against a prominent member of the church, J. G. Buffaloe. He was the same member who had been charged with schismatic behavior several years earlier. This time the charge was much more serious. The congregation leveled a charge of "conduct unbecoming a Christian in having formed a companionship for the purpose of speculating in negroes and recommended that said brother be required to cease from such a traffic and to make a suitable apology to the church."[99] A few weeks later the minutes report that Buffaloe refused to apologize for his actions or sever himself from that business enterprise, giving the church no choice but to expel him.[100]

Taking a pause from the other events in the church's life, the following involves the story of Raleigh native and slave Lunsford Lane. Lane's story is one of the most inspiring slave accounts from the nineteenth century, and interestingly, the Raleigh Baptist Church may have played a small role in the story. Lunsford Lane was born in 1803 into slavery on the Sherwood Haywood estate in Wake County. Lane

---

[98] Ibid., 2 October 1848.

[99] Ibid., 29 April 1849. It is interesting that the term "slave" is not used in the entry.

[100] Ibid., "Saturday Before the First Lord's Day in May, 1849."

became an astute businessman and possessed a remarkable entrepreneurial spirit. His benevolent owner allowed him to earn money through extra work, and with help from his father he developed a particular blend of smoking tobacco for which a local demand soon developed. Lane ultimately accumulated enough money to purchase his own freedom and move to the North. There he continued his business and amassed enough money to return to Raleigh where he sought to purchase freedom for his wife and children. When he returned to the city, a local mob of whites, angry about his success, abducted, tarred, and feathered Lane. With the aid of benevolent whites, Lane and his family boarded a train for Philadelphia and left the city. He spent the rest of his life in the North as an active leader in the antislavery movement. Although the exact date of his death is not known, most sources indicate that it was probably after 1865.[101]

Interestingly, along with other prominent Raleigh residents, Lane includes Amos J. Battle and Thomas Meredith as his supporters. Also, the evidence suggests that Lane was a member at one time of the Raleigh Baptist Church. In his autobiography, he relates that he "had been baptised [*sic*] and received into fellowship with the Baptist denomination."[102] Given that the Raleigh Baptist Church was the only Baptist church in the city at the time, it would be safe to conclude that he was a member of the church. That may also be confirmed by the church records. The name "Lunsford Haywood" appears in one of the "Black Members" lists in volume I of the church records as joining sometime around 1828 by baptism. The lack of the surname "Lane" is not unusual given that the slaves were listed by their first name and frequently identified by the surnames of their owners.[103]

---

[101] See "Narrative of Lunsford Lane, Formerly of Raleigh, N.C. Embracing an Account of His Early Life, the Redemption by Purchase of Himself and His Family From Slavery, and His Banishment From the Place of His Birth for the Crime of Wearing a Colored Skin," http://docsouth.unc.edu/neh/lanelunsford/lane.html (accessed 11 January 2011). See also Murray, *Wake: Capital County of North Carolina*, vol. 1, 274–75.

[102] "Narrative of Lunsford Lane," 20.

[103] See Orlando Patterson, *Slavery and Social Death: A Comparative Study* (Boston: Harvard University Press, 1985), 56, located at http://books.google.com/books?id=T2grY7NbnygC&pg=PA56&lpg=PA56&dq=slaves+surnames&source=

T. W. Tobey (1850–1853)

In July 1850 the church unanimously recommended the call of Reverend Thomas W. Tobey to be its next pastor at a salary of $500 [$14,200] or $600 [$17,000], if the Home Mission Board could assist with a supplement. Tobey and his wife, Isabella, had just recently returned to the United States from China where they served a brief stint as missionaries. The Tobeys, along with Matthew T. and Eliza M. Yates and J. L. and Henrietta Shuck, were among some of the first Southern Baptist missionaries to China.[104] Tobey and his wife originally went to China in 1847 to be career missionaries, but concerns about Isabella's physical and mental problems forced their return to the United States.

Thomas Tobey was born in Providence, Rhode Island, in 1819. In 1837 he was converted and baptized by his father, Reverend Zalmon Tobey, pastor of the Bristol Baptist Church in Rhode Island. Feeling a call to ministry himself, Tobey enrolled for a year at Brown University but eventually graduated from Columbian College in Washington, D.C. in 1844. The Lebanon Baptist Church in Lancaster County, Virginia, licensed him to preach, and he was appointed as a missionary to China in 1846. His ordination took place just before he left for China on 25 August 1846, at the E Street Baptist Church in Washington.[105]

Life in China had been difficult for the Tobeys. Although the exact nature of Isabella's problem is not specifically revealed in the sources,

---

bl&ots=_SjgzKM8jH&sig=uUboMDmVGZHpY2NkA0CM_s0ZO9w&hl=en&ei=L 4-jTbP0E8Hk0QG8m_zlDg&sa=X&oi=book_result&ct=result&resnum=10&ved =0CEcQ6AEwCTgK#v=onepage&q=slaves%20surnames&f=false (accessed 11 April 2011).

[104] See the Minutes of the Raleigh Baptist Association, beginning in 1846. Most likely, Matthew T. Yates, a North Carolinian and graduate of Wake Forest, was Tobey's contact in Raleigh. Beginning in 1846 with a recommendation to the Wake Forest Baptist Church for ordination, Yates enjoyed considerable support from the Raleigh Baptist Association. When he and his wife left for China, the association formed the "Yates Committee" from cooperating churches, which designated money for Yates's mission labors. Soon after he arrived in China, Yates began the practice of sending yearly reports back to the association to be included in the annual meeting records.

[105] H. A. Tupper, *Foreign Missions of the Southern Baptist Convention* (Philadelphia: American Baptist Publication Society, 1880) 168.

Matthew Yates provided a glimpse of the seriousness of her condition in his annual report to the Raleigh Baptist Association in 1849:

> Sister Tobey was in poor health when she sailed for China, but hopes were entertained that much benefit would be derived from the voyage. In this we were disappointed. She had suffered much by the way, and had not been here long, before it was evident that her whole nervous system was a wreck—Her mind was, at times, wholly deranged. These seasons of derangement grew more frequent and more violent, and Dr. Lockhart, of the London Mission Society, again and again urged brother Tobey to take his wife home; it being his (Dr. L's) opinion, that if they remained here, she would become a raving maniac.[106]

From Yates's observation it would appear that whatever physical ailments Isabella had suffered, the most critical problem related to some type of mental illness. Problems of mental illness were not uncommon among early missionaries. One of the most famous examples was the mental illness suffered by Dorothy Carey, the wife of William Carey, the great pioneer of Baptist missions in the early nineteenth century.[107]

Following his return to the states, Tobey settled into his pastoral work at the Raleigh Baptist Church at the end of summer 1850. His call as pastor marks the beginning of a new era for the church. While previous pastors were well known among the Baptists of North Carolina, Tobey, as one of Southern Baptists' first foreign missionaries, brought to the church a reputation that extended beyond just the state of North Carolina. Tobey's call as pastor, whether the church knew it at the time or not, can be seen as a significant milestone in the growth of the church's

---

[106] "Report of M. T. Yates," in Raleigh Baptist Association Minutes, 1849, 12.

[107] McBeth, *Baptist Heritage*, 186. Dorothy Carey had never been any more than a few miles from her home. Suddenly, she was forced to leave her home in England and sail to India where she would live the rest of her life. McBeth chronicles her problems and eventual insanity due to the harsh conditions she and William were forced to live with in India. For the last thirteen years of her life, Dorothy Carey was confined to a room with padded walls. McBeth says on p. 186, "Somewhere in missionary history a word of compassion should be written for Dorothy Carey, who paid a high price for Baptist missions and never knew why."

reputation. Without a doubt, as the year 1850 passed into the pages of history, the future looked brighter for the congregation than it had a decade earlier.

The year that Tobey began his ministry in Raleigh the church reported a total of 279 members, and the membership increased steadily while he was the pastor. By 1851 the membership had grown to a total of 310. The increase continued in 1852 as the church reported 384 members, and by the time of Tobey's resignation in 1853, the membership had doubled to a total of 558 members.[108] Not surprisingly, a motion was made by M. B. Royster on 3 April 1852 that a committee of five be established to consider the possibility of enlarging the church building. The committee was to suggest a plan and calculate the potential cost. W. W. Vass made an interesting amendment to the motion to include in the report the cost of adding a baptistery to the building. In a few years the church ultimately decided (under the leadership of Thomas Skinner) that it should construct a new building altogether rather than enlarge the old structure. The origin of the discussion that would eventually lead to that important decision can be traced to that meeting.[109]

Death of Thomas Meredith. Within a few months after Tobey became pastor, the church experienced the loss of one of its most prominent members, Thomas Meredith. During the first half of the nineteenth century there is no name that is more important among North Carolina Baptists than Meredith's. He was instrumental in the formation of the Baptist State Convention of North Carolina in 1830. He was also one of the first professors at Wake Forest College and served as chair of its board of trustees for several years. In 1838 Meredith was concerned enough about female education to propose to the Baptist State Convention that a "female seminary of high order" be established[110]—a dream that would not become reality until decades later (see chapter 5). Most importantly, Meredith was the founding editor of the *Biblical Recorder*, and he preached the dedicatory sermon in 1840 when the

---

[108] Minutes of the Raleigh Baptist Association, 1850–1853.

[109] Church Conference Records, 3 April 1852.

[110] Mary Lynch Johnson, *A History of Meredith College* (Raleigh NC: Meredith College, 1956): 4.

Raleigh Baptist Church dedicated its new building. The loss of Meredith in 1850 was a serious blow to the church.[111]

Meredith's funeral on 15 November 1850 was more than just an event observed by the Raleigh Baptist Church. Rather, his death was mourned by many Christians in the city of Raleigh, as evidenced by the participation of Dr. Drury Lacy, pastor of the First Presbyterian Church in the funeral. In addition, the choir of the First Presbyterian Church began the service with a hymn. Tobey read scripture and preached the funeral sermon based on Hebrews 4:9: "There remaineth, therefore, a rest to the people of God." Dr. Lacy then offered a prayer after the funeral sermon by Tobey.[112]

Meredith's death left the *Biblical Recorder,* one of the most important Baptist state newspapers in the South, without an editor. At a special called meeting of the congregation on 23 November 1850, Tobey revealed that the Meredith family had approached him with the possibility of assisting with the editorial duties, but believed he needed the church's consent before he agreed. The church subsequently voted unanimously to allow their pastor to serve as the *Biblical Recorder* editor "in order to sustain said paper."[113] The *Recorder* paid him a salary of $300 [$8,500] in addition to his salary of $500 paid by the church. Tobey continued as the editor of the *Recorder* until July 1852.[114]

While the church experienced unprecedented growth during Tobey's tenure as pastor, it continued to struggle financially. The records for those years frequently reveal a struggle to maintain a steady income, especially for the pastor's salary. The entry in the church records from a meeting in March 1852 expresses the church's problem most clearly. During that meeting the following resolution was offered and approved:

---

[111] Thomas Meredith's life needs attention from Baptist historians. To date, no complete biography of Meredith exists, although he is the most important figure in the first half of the nineteenth century for North Carolina Baptists. Furthermore, the history of the *Biblical Recorder* and its editors needs serious attention from Baptist historians as well.

[112] "Funeral Services on the Occasion of the Death of Rev. Thomas Meredith," *Biblical Recorder* (Raleigh NC), 23 November 1850, 2.

[113] Church Conference Records, 23 November 1850.

[114] Ibid., "First Lord's Day in August, 1851" and 11 July 1852.

"that for the future we adopt it as a fixed plan that each member subscribing to the pastor's salary be expected to pay at or previous to each church meeting one twelfth of his subscription and that a committee of six, three brethren and three sisters, be appointed whose duty it shall be to make these collections."[115]

Resignation of Tobey. Despite the church's financial struggles, Tobey enjoyed a good relationship with the congregation at the Raleigh Baptist Church. [116] However, concerns about his wife's physical health and mental illness persisted. On 10 May 1852 the church voted to pay the amount due on the pastor's salary through July 1 of that year "in order to enable him to make visit to the north with his afflicted wife." The church was greatly concerned about Isabella as well. The record for that meeting continues by saying that a committee was appointed to raise the money "at once," agreeing that if the amount could not be raised immediately, it would borrow the money so that Tobey could make the trip.[117] Unfortunately, Tobey's ministry at the Raleigh Baptist Church came to a close a year later when, in May 1853, he submitted his resignation. The records from the meeting indicate that of those voting, fifty-six were opposed to receiving it and seven favored accepting it.[118] In July, however, Tobey resubmitted his resignation and requested that the church grant it, which it did unanimously. The congregation then passed the following resolution showing their love and respect for Tobey and his wife:

> Whereas the resignation of the Rev. Thomas W. Tobey, pastor of this church has been tendered and accepted, "Resolved that we part with him with emotions of deep regret and that in him we have ever found a kind pastor and a pious Brother. Resolved further that as a church we regret that circumstances over which we had no control should have induced our beloved Pastor and Brother to take this step and that we cordially recommend him to the Christian love and friendship of our brethren in whose midst his lot may be cast. Resolved that the clerk be directed to have these resolutions published

---

[115] Ibid., 12 March 1852.
[116] Ibid., 10 May 1852.
[117] Ibid., 10 May 1852.
[118] Ibid., 29 May 1853.

in the "Biblical Recorder" on motions these Resolutions were unanimously adopted.[119]

After Tobey's resignation, he and his family left Raleigh and moved to Yanceyville, North Carolina, where he served as pastor of the Baptist church in that city. Tragedy followed the family with the move to Yanceyville. *The Biblical Recorder,* on 12 July 1855, continued a brief item indicating that Susan Caroline Tobey, daughter of Reverend T. M. Tobey, had died at the age of six months.[120] Two years later, on 11 October 1857, Isabella died, and just a few hours after Isabella's death, their one-month-old son died as well.[121]

The following year Tobey moved to Sumterville, Alabama, where he served as pastor of the Baptist church, and on 13 December 1858 he married a widow, Harriet A. Howard, who was from Tuskegee, Alabama.[122] Tobey eventually left the pastorate for the classroom and spent most of the rest of his life teaching at various Baptist colleges in Alabama (Judson Female Institute and Howard College) and Kentucky (Bethel College).[123] Tobey died on 7 February 1885 in Florida.[124]

A. M. McDowell and G. W. Johnson (1854–1855)

Tobey's resignation left the church once again in search of a pastor. As had become typical for that era of the church's history, the congregation met in a conference session, suggested possible candidates, and then voted. The candidate receiving the most votes was contacted by a committee to determine interest. For the next several months the same

---

[119] Ibid., 2 July 1853.

[120] *Biblical Recorder* (Raleigh NC), 12 July 1855, 3.

[121] "Death of Mrs. Tobey, Formerly Missionary to Shanghai," *Biblical Recorder* (Raleigh NC), 22 October 1857, 2. In the same issue of the *Biblical Recorder* there is a short entry that says, "In Yanceyville, N.C., on the night of the 11th of October, Robert H., infant son of Rev. Thomas W. Tobey, aged one month" died (3).

[122] *Biblical Recorder* (Raleigh NC), 23 December 1858, 3.

[123] *The Baptist Encyclopedia,* vol. 3, ed. William Cathcart (Philadelphia: Louis H. Everts, 1881) s.v. "Toby, Thomas W." Howard College is now known as Samford University, Judson Female Institute is now Judson College, and Bethel College is defunct.

[124] *Religious Herald* (Richmond VA), 26 February 1885, 1, 5.

process was followed and several candidates declined the offer. The church records indicate that during that time Professor W. T. Brooks from Wake Forest College filled the pulpit on an interim basis.[125] During that interlude a curious incident was reported in the church minutes involving a man named John Reynolds from Albany County, New York, who had contacted the church "expressing a desire on his part to take pastoral charge of this church if after becoming acquainted with the members such a relation should be mutually agreeable and also making a proposal to visit us if it should be the desire of the church for him to do so." That must have seemed a bit audacious for the church because the minutes indicate that the clerk was instructed to answer Reynolds's letter "in a cordial and respectful manner informing him of the refusal...to accede to his proposal."[126]

On 22 January 1854 the church voted to call Reverend Archibald M. McDowell to be their next pastor for the next twelve months at a salary of $400 [$10,500].[127] Although there is no specific mention of his acceptance in the record, the following month the church voted to pay McDowell's salary retroactively to the beginning of the year. Unfortunately, it is unclear from the church records how long McDowell served as pastor of the church.[128]

McDowell was born in Kershaw, South Carolina, on 10 April 1818. He was converted and baptized early in life, and in 1842 enrolled at Wake Forest College where he graduated five years later. In 1848 he became the principal of the Chowan Female Institute in Murfreesboro, North Carolina, when it first opened. The year after the school's opening,

---

[125] Church Conference Records, 17 July 1853.

[126] Ibid.

[127] Ibid., 22 January 1854. The reference to the call being for twelve months only reflects the church's practice during that era of the "annual call," whereby at the end of the year, if all was well between congregation and pastor, the call was extended for another year.

[128] During 1854 and 1855, the church record book has several blank pages, which upon careful examination reveal that at one time they had writing upon them. For some reason, perhaps the type of ink used, the writing has faded over time to the extent that the pages appear to be completely blank. These missing records would probably reveal information about when McDowell resigned and the circumstances surrounding it.

the town was hit with an outbreak of smallpox, which forced its closing temporarily. McDowell and his wife then moved to Milton, North Carolina, where he was ordained to the ministry and served as pastor of the Baptist church until his arrival in Raleigh in 1853. Most likely, McDowell had come from Milton to Raleigh in order to direct the Sedgwick Female Seminary. The school had been under the leadership of Mary Louisa Finch since Reverend J. J. Finch's death in 1850. She resigned in 1854 and McDowell, along with his wife, assumed the leadership of the school, which was renamed "Metropolitan Female Seminary."[129] Then in 1855 he returned to Murfreesboro where he became the chair of mathematics and natural science at the Chowan Female Institute. Following the retirement of William Hooper, the school's president, McDowell became the president, a position he maintained until his death in 1881.[130]

At the regular church conference on 1 September 1855, several items of interest appeared. First, the minutes indicate that "G. W. Johnston" was the pastor of the church. Second, letters of "dismission" were granted to McDowell and his wife. The church then appointed P. F. Pescud and Jordan Womble as a committee "to draw up resolutions commendatory of the course pursued by Brother McDowell in the discharge of his ministerial and Christian duties; also expressive of our regret that circumstances have rendered his withdrawal from our midst necessary and that said resolutions be published in the Biblical Recorder."[131] The laudatory resolution published in the *Biblical Recorder* is evidence of an amicable parting of the ways between McDowell and the Raleigh Baptist Church.

A short article from the *Biblical Recorder* may offer a reason for his resignation. In his article, the writer, after hearing McDowell preach at the Raleigh Baptist Church, seems to allude to McDowell's reputation as

---

[129] Murray, *Wake: Capital County of North Carolina*, vol. 1, 313.

[130] James Almerius Delke, *History of the North Carolina Chowan Baptist Association, 1806–1881* (Raleigh NC: Edwards, Broughton and Co., 1882) 54–60. The school is known today as Chowan University.

[131] Church Conference Records, 1 September 1855. The page immediately preceding the one containing this entry is one of the blank pages discussed above. Presumably, it contained the information about McDowell's resignation.

more of an educator than a preacher. He wrote, "We were gratified to observe the progress he had made in preaching, knowing that his attention has been chiefly called to literary and scientific subjects."[132] The writer also mentions the fact that he had "called at his Seminary and found him in readiness for the accommodation of our friends who may be disposed to patronize him," suggesting that McDowell was in the position as head of the school before he became the pastor of the Raleigh Baptist Church.[133] It is therefore not too much of a leap to assume that the chance to return to Murfreesboro would have been the reason for his departure from the pastorate of the church, since he seems to have been more suited for a life in the classroom rather than the pulpit.

As indicated, the exact date of McDowell's resignation is impossible to ascertain from the church records. For the meeting of the church on 1 September 1855, he is listed as the pastor of the church for the first time although one could surmise that he had served in that role for several months previously. As far back as September 1854 the church records contain this statement: "Brother McDowell, from the committee to address Brother Johnston, reported that duly having been performed, and that Brother Johnston was daily expected to visit this city, and would then give an answer to the call."[134] Unfortunately, this seems to be the report from something voted upon at the previous meeting, which would have been on 5 August 1854, and the writing for that page has completely faded except for the date.

The best guess that can be made, then, is that McDowell offered his resignation to the church sometime around August 1854, and the church made a decision to contact G. W. Johnston to see if he was interested in serving as pastor. The entry noted indicates that the church expected him to arrive in the city any day for a visit to the church, whereby he would then give them an answer. There is another blank page where the October 1854 minutes would have been written. McDowell is listed as the moderator of the business session on 4 November 1854. Nothing significant relating to the pastoral charge of the church is mentioned in

---

[132] "Sabbath," *Biblical Recorder* (Raleigh NC), 20 January 1854, 2. No author's name is given for the short article.

[133] Ibid.

[134] Church Conference Records, 2 September 1854.

December 1854. The January 1855 minutes are also missing. G. W. Johnston is listed as moderator in February 1855, suggesting that he began his pastoral duties at the beginning of that year. Johnston and his wife presented their letters of dismission from the Baptist church at Elizabeth City on 5 May 1855. McDowell and his wife were granted letters of dismission on 1 September 1855. It would seem that the pastoral transition therefore occurred at the beginning of 1855, but McDowell remained in the church as a member until the following fall.[135]

During Johnston's tenure the church records reveal that he was staunchly opposed to the plan passed by the church in March 1852, whereby the members would be required to pay one-twelfth of their "subscription" to the pastor's salary at each church conference (see above). There is a remarkable statement included in the church record book, opposite the entry on 6 May 1854, which was written and signed "G. W. J., 1855." It reads:

> A church of Christ is a voluntary association in which each member is morally bound to contribute to the support of the society according as the Lord has prospered him. Neglect of this duty is a sin; and a member so offending should be required to reform or be expelled. But the practice of taxing or assessing members (as mentioned on the opposite page) against their consent seems to be irregular and out of harmony with the spirit and practice of the Gospel. There is however, nothing wrong in the practice when all the members by formal vote agree to an assessment upon specified conditions. Coercion in matters of religion is always wrong. Freedom exercised within the requirements of the Gospel always right and hence most conducive to the interests of God and the church.[136]

Several important things should be noted about Johnston's statement. First, it is interesting that it is dated "1855," yet it is included in the record book the previous year. Did Johnston object to the policy for how to pay his salary when he became pastor and ask the clerk to include his objection in the church minutes? Why was it placed out of

---

[135] See ibid., 2 September 1854–1 September 1855.

[136] Ibid., 6 May 1854. The parenthetical phrase is contained within the original quote.

chronological order in the minutes? Is its location opposite the entry that mentions the "assessing" of church members intentional?

Second, this statement contains some elements of classic Baptist ecclesiology. The phrase "voluntary association" is important to the Baptist tradition. According to the tradition, a church is to be composed of individual members who profess faith in Christ and are baptized as believers. Furthermore, while the statement opposes coercion (in that case, paying the pastor's salary), it nevertheless recognizes the importance of members contributing to the financial upkeep of the church. It also recognizes that a Baptist church should be governed by a democratic process and that the members should have a voice in the church's policy. Finally, there is a general statement about the evils of coercion in matters of religion—a thoroughly Baptist-sounding sentence.

Unfortunately, Johnston's tenure at the church as pastor was extremely short. At a called meeting of the congregation on 25 November 1855, he submitted his resignation citing a "disease of his throat" that made him incapable of carrying out his responsibilities as pastor. The entry went on to describe that his physician had advised him not to preach and that he needed further medical treatment. The church then passed a resolution of appreciation:

> Whereas in the providence of God, our beloved and most esteemed pastor, Elder G. W. Johnston, is sorely afflicted with the throat disease, so that he is advised by his physicians to stop preaching in order to take such rest, and adopt such treatment as may be necessary therefore,
> Be resolved that we as a church and as individual members thereof, will have much cause of pleasure in the retrospect for the pastoral and social relations with him while in our midst, and we thank God for having crowned his ministry with such abundant success for having added through him instrumentally so many precious souls to this church and for having so largely increased the interests of the same:
> Resolved, that we fully endorse and approve his course of conduct in the management of the affairs of this church as its pastor, and the doctrines which he has taught, that we deeply deplore the necessity which thus forces him from our pulpit and from our midst, that we sincerely sympathize with him in his afflictions and its consequences

and that we promise to follow him with our prayers with the hope of an early recovery and restoration to the services of his heavenly maker.[137]

With Johnston's departure, the Raleigh Baptist Church closed out what might be called the "second era" in its history. Since its reconstitution in 1840, the church struggled financially but persevered. It reported ninety members to the Raleigh Baptist Association in 1841. By 1855 the membership had grown to 456. Without a doubt, the church overcame the adversity of the previous era. Yet the financial struggles were still, and would remain, a reality—especially during the coming years as the entire nation was plunged into the darkness of the Civil War.

In addition to what has been discussed, it must be said that it is striking the church records make so little mention of the church's black members during that era. While the church conference records from the period of 1812–1832 often mention the black members, report their worship needs, and even list the black members' names in the membership lists, hardly a thing is said about them between 1840 and 1855. Specifically, the membership lists in the church records between 1840 and 1855 no longer include the names of the black members. There are also only a few brief references to the existence of the black membership, while it is a fact that the black members made up a large part of the membership total.[138] Most likely, the growing movement toward abolition of slavery in the North and the Southern resistance to abolition in the middle decades of the nineteenth century could account for that silence. Slaves were treated differently and attitudes toward them began to change as the country moved closer to the Civil War. It could be that this change is reflected by the silence of the church records in this second era of the church's history.

* * *

---

[137] Ibid., 25 November 1855.

[138] As mentioned above, for some reason the Raleigh Baptist Association statistical table for 1844 breaks down the membership of the churches into "colored" and "white" members, although such a distinction is not made in other years. The Raleigh Baptist Church reported a total membership of 281 that year, with 199 "colored" members and eighty-two "white" members.

By 1855 the Raleigh Baptist Church was forty-three years old. It was poised for great things in the remainder of the nineteenth century, and strong pastoral leadership during the next three decades would carry the founders' vision to the next level in their history. Two pastors with strong leadership credentials would navigate the church through the Civil War, Reconstruction, and then through the decades leading to the twentieth century.

4

Developing a Legacy (1855–1886)

By 1850 slavery was the dominant political issue in the United States. While the nation could not have foreseen what was ahead for the next decade, looking back it is easy to see how the events of the 1850s laid the groundwork for the tragedy that was to be the Civil War.

The decade began with the Compromise of 1850, a series of five laws designed to ease the tension between the slaveholding South and the free states in the North. Unfortunately, the compromise did not work. Expansion brought settlement to new territories in the West, and the conflict of slave state vs. free state continued. Then in 1852 the publication of *Uncle Tom's Cabin* by Harriet Beecher Stowe brought the horrors of slavery into the consciousness of the average American in the North. Five years later, in 1857, the Supreme Court ruling in *Dred Scott v. Sanford* declared that blacks (slave and free) were not to be regarded as citizens of the United States. Two years later, in 1859, abolitionist John Brown led a raid on the federal arsenal at Harpers Ferry, Virginia, which further heightened the tensions between North and South.

Baptists in the South also experienced much activity in the 1850s. If the earlier decades of the century were marked by Baptist controversy over missions and the Campbellites, the 1850s saw the nascent Southern Baptist Convention consumed in controversy over Landmarkism. Historian Robert Baker called the controversy over Landmarkism the "greatest internal crisis" that Southern Baptists faced in the nineteenth century.[1] Led by the triumvirate of J. R. Graves, J. M. Pendleton, and A. C. Dayton, proponents of Landmarkism made the claim that Baptist

---

[1] Robert Baker, *The Southern Baptist Convention and Its People 1607–1972* (Nashville: Broadman Press, 1974) 208, as cited by H. Leon McBeth, *The Baptist Heritage: Four Centuries of Baptist Witness* (Nashville: Broadman Press, 1987) 447. McBeth provides a full discussion of the Landmark controversy on pp. 447–61. See also Walter B. Shurden, *Not a Silent People: Controversies That Have Shaped Southern Baptists* (Nashville: Broadman Press, 1972) 39–51.

churches are the only true churches and that the local Baptist congregation mirrors the New Testament church.

Other churches affiliated with different denominations have strayed from the New Testament model of the church and are false churches. In fact, Graves refused to use the term "church" to describe a non-Baptist congregation, preferring the word "society" instead. Since the only true church was a Baptist church, Baptists possessed the only valid preaching, ministers, and ordinances. Therefore, proponents rejected pulpit affiliation with ministers from other denominations and refused to participate in any "ecumenical" services. They further rejected the concept of the "universal church," placing all their attention on the local congregation only. In addition, Landmarkers believed there was an unbroken succession of Baptist churches throughout Christian history, from John the Baptist until the present. That "trail of blood," as J. M. Carroll called it, was a parallel track running alongside, and many times in opposition to, the Roman Catholic Church throughout church history.[2] While Landmarkers were never able to control the Southern Baptist Convention, their ideas became infused into the consciousness of Baptists in the South. Indeed, as Leon McBeth says, "it would be impossible to understand Southern Baptists apart from Landmarkism."[3]

Another important development for Southern Baptists in the 1850s was the founding of the Southern Baptist Theological Seminary in 1859, with four professors (James P. Boyce, John A. Broadus, Basil Manly, and William Williams) and twenty-six students.[4] Originally located in Greenville, South Carolina, after the Civil War (1877) it relocated to Louisville, Kentucky. Until 1907, Southern Seminary was the only seminary supported by Southern Baptists.[5]

As the political landscape in the United States was experiencing upheaval with disputes between North and South over slavery, and as Baptists in the South were experiencing turmoil with the controversy

---

[2] McBeth, *Baptist Heritage*, 450ff. See also J. M. Carroll, *The Trail of Blood* (Lexington KY: Ashland Avenue Baptist Church, 1931).

[3] McBeth, *Baptist Heritage*, 447.

[4] Ibid., 445.

[5] William A. Mueller, *A History of Southern Baptist Theological Seminary* (Nashville: Broadman Press, 1959).

over Landmarkism, the publication of Charles Darwin's *Origin of the Species* in 1859 changed the intellectual landscape. While its full impact would not be felt until decades later, *Origin of the Species* brought science and theology into direct conflict as it challenged the traditional literal interpretation of the creation stories in Genesis.

The tension between North and South over slavery finally erupted into full-scale war in 1861. The Civil War, which lasted until 1865, was the most destructive and costly war in American history, with more than one million Americans either killed or wounded. While the war itself lasted for four years, the tensions between North and South lasted for decades, and one could argue that they still exist in some quarters. In many ways, the war had devastating effects for the South in both rural and urban areas, from which it would take decades to recover.

One of the central questions of the Reconstruction period concerned how to assimilate the freed slaves into the mainstream of society. Unfortunately, when the federal troops were withdrawn from the South with the Compromise of 1877 (thereby ending Reconstruction), the federal government could no longer guarantee basic civil rights for freed slaves. Southern states then passed a number of "Jim Crow" laws, which segregated blacks from whites in Southern society. In 1896 the United States Supreme Court ruled in *Plessey v. Ferguson* that such segregation laws were constitutional, thereby giving legal footing to a completely segregated South and creating the "separate but equal" doctrine that dominated race relations for much of the twentieth century.

In 1869 the first transcontinental railroad was completed, joining both coasts. While that accomplishment brought rapid expansion to the West, it also brought conflict between white settlers and Native Americans over territory. Ultimately, the saga would end tragically for the Native Americans of the Western Plains who all but lost their way of life to white settlement and development.

Three inventions in the last quarter of the nineteenth century—Andrew Hallidie's cable car (1873), Alexander Graham Bell's telephone (1876), and Thomas Edison's light bulb (1879)—spurred revolution in the industrial sector of the nation and brought important innovations not only to the large cities but also to smaller towns. That urban growth, however, also created terrible living conditions in the cities, particularly in the tenement housing complexes that were home to the many new immigrants who had come to the cities to find employment.

By the 1850s the residents of Raleigh were aware that the nation's unity was at risk as tensions between North and South continued to grow, and they were naturally apprehensive about the current events of that day. The publication of Hinton Rowan Helper's *The Impending Crisis of the South: How to Meet It* (1857), which blamed the Southern support of slavery for the region's lack of financial progress, brought a swift reaction from Southerners. The fact that Helper was a native North Carolinian added to the local fury unleashed against the book.[6]

John Brown's raid at Harper's Ferry in 1859 also created tension among Raleigh residents, exacerbated by the fact that one of Brown's co-conspirators was a Raleigh native named John A. Copeland, Jr. Copeland, a freeborn African American who had moved with his parents to Oberlin, Ohio, was eventually executed along with the other conspirators for his part in the affair. Then when two fires broke out within a week—one at the store of prominent Raleigh Baptist Church member Jordan Womble and the other at the home of his son—many in Raleigh feared that Brown's raid was part of a larger conspiracy to encourage slave uprisings all over the South.[7] Evidence of such a fear in Raleigh could be found as early as 1855 when the Raleigh Baptist Association resolved, "That we recommend to our churches to request their ministers at their regularly monthly meetings, to preach a sermon *directly adapted* to our colored population on Saturday or Sunday afternoon, as may best suit their convenience, and the wishes of their owners."[8]

The Civil War and Reconstruction years were difficult for Raleigh residents. Although slow to accept the secessionist sentiment, when the war began at Fort Sumter, South Carolina, Raleigh citizens (like most

---

[6] Murray, *Wake: Capital County of North Carolina*, vol. 1, 452–53.

[7] Ibid., 453.

[8] Minutes of the Raleigh Baptist Association, 1855, 8. See also William Richard Eaton, *History of the Raleigh Baptist Association of North Carolina* (Raleigh NC: n.p., 1955) 38–39 for more background about that motion.

North Carolinians) became ardent supporters of the Confederacy.[9] The city joined the war effort in full force. John Lewis Peyton observed in the opening days of the war that the city seemed to possess "a good deal of the 'pomp and circumstance of glorious war.'"[10] Wake County historian Elizabeth Reid Murray reported that so much eagerness for the war effort existed in the county, such that even before North Carolina declared secession, four companies of volunteers were already prepared to deploy.[11]

The city's eagerness for the glories of war soon subsided as Raleigh residents began to realize the difficulties war brings. Of the nearly 125,000 soldiers North Carolina provided for the war effort, approximately 40,000 were killed, and when the war ended in 1865, thousands of soldiers returned home injured, maimed, sick, or mentally debilitated.[12] On the homefront, Raleigh citizens encountered shortages of almost all the necessities of everyday life. As the supply of goods dwindled, prices rose and along with them the tempers of many people. One citizen described the crisis in a letter to the *Observer* of Fayetteville: "People who cannot get enough to eat…grumble at everything [and] vent their spleen upon the war, which is the immediate cause of their suffering…. I do not wonder that the patriotism of some waxes cold and their wrath hot."[13]

Following the fall of Richmond and Lee's surrender at Appomattox in 1865, General Sherman ordered his army to move south into North Carolina. General Judson Kilpatrick's Third Calvary Division was ordered to move into and occupy the city of Raleigh. Fortunately for

---

[9] See Murray, *Wake: Capital County of North Carolina,* vol. 1, 457–542, for a complete summary of the impact the Civil War had on Wake County in general and the city of Raleigh in particular.

[10] John Lewis Peyton, *The American Crisis: or, Pages from the Note-book of a State Agent During the Civil War,* vol. 1 (London: Saunders, Otter and Co., 1867) 16, as cited by ibid., 470.

[11] Murray, *Wake: Capital County of North Carolina,* vol. 1, 470.

[12] "An Uncertain Future," http://ncmuseumofhistory.org/exhibits/civilwar/about_section8.html (accessed 23 June 2009).

[13] Mary Shannon Smith, "Union Sentiment in North Carolina During the Civil War," *Meredith College Quarterly Bulletin,* ser. 9 (November 1915): 14–15, as cited by Murray, *Wake: Capital County of North Carolina,* vol. 1, 485.

Raleigh residents, the city was spared the fate of complete destruction that befell the capital city of South Carolina. Sherman promised that the state capitol, as well as other buildings and benevolent societies, would be spared, along with the mayor and other local government leaders, as long as the Union troops met no resistance when they occupied the city.[14] The city was surrendered on 13 April 1865. The Federal occupation lasted until the end of 1865, but with the Congressional Reconstruction Acts, military rule was implemented again from March 1867 through July 1868. Troops remained stationed in North Carolina until 1870.[15]

The Raleigh Baptist Church 1855–1886

Thomas E. Skinner (1855–1867)

On 25 November 1855, when G. W. Johnston resigned as the pastor of the Raleigh Baptist Church, he "recommended and nominated Elder Thomas Skinner of New York…a native of North Carolina as his successor in the pastoral office." Johnston described Skinner as "one well-qualified to discharge the responsible duties of the same."[16] The church could not have known that evening in church conference the full impact that decision would have on the future of the congregation. The choice of Skinner as pastor proved to be the most important decision the church made in the nineteenth century. Like the church's founding pastor, Robert T. Daniel, Skinner served two terms as pastor (1855–1867 and 1879–1886). He became the longest tenured pastor in the church's history up to that point, and ultimately the second longest tenured in the overall history of the church.

Thomas Skinner was born in Perquimans County, North Carolina, on 29 April 1825. The Skinner name was well known throughout North Carolina in the early nineteenth century because his father, Charles, was one of the wealthiest farmers and businessmen in the state. The Skinner name became well known among North Carolina Baptists as well. Though Charles originally affiliated himself with the Presbyterians

---

[14] Murray, *Wake: Capital County of North Carolina,* vol. 1, 503–506.
[15] Ibid., vol. 1, 543.
[16] Church Conference Records, 25 November 1855.

following his conversion at age forty-three, through the influence of Thomas Meredith and Robert T. Daniel, he became a committed Baptist and soon a benefactor to Wake Forest College and other Baptist causes.[17]

In his "Reminiscences," Skinner describes himself as having been an impish child, so much so that at age eleven his father sent him to a private school near Hillsboro, North Carolina, run by William J. Bingham—"that celebrated bad-boy breaker."[18] Here he remained in study for a year until he was old enough to matriculate at Wake Forest Institute, which at that time was a manual labor school requiring each student to work for several hours per day on the farm owned by the school. Skinner related an episode in which he and two other young students were sent to the field to hoe corn. Instead of hoeing the dirt around the stalks, however, the three mischievous boys cut down the corn as a prank, which earned them each a whipping of twenty lashes.[19]

After four years at Wake Forest, Skinner returned to the school operated by Bingham and in 1844 he matriculated at the University of North Carolina. While in college, Skinner's mischievous antics continued. During the presidential election of 1844, he became involved in a rather large wager that Henry Clay would win the presidency. When James K. Polk was elected, Skinner suddenly owed a gambling debt of $600 [$17,800], which he could not pay. Having nowhere else to turn for financial help, he wrote "candidly" to his father explaining the trouble he was in. "O how tedious and tasteless were the days and hours which passed over my shadowed future—waiting for an answer to that imploring letter to the father from his impecunious son," Skinner wrote. When at last the letter from his father came, which included the $600, Skinner wrote, "I thought that I loved him more than I ever had done."[20] He received the Bachelor of Arts degree in 1847 and, perhaps with a bit of

---

[17] Thomas E. Skinner, "Reminiscences," in *Sermons, Addresses and Reminiscences* (Raleigh NC: Edwards and Broughton, Power Printers, 1894) 231–34. See also J. Daniel Day, *A Gentleman of the Old School: Thomas E. Skinner, Baptist Pastor, 1825–1905* (Holly Springs NC: Tarheelokie Products, 2010).

[18] Skinner, "Reminiscences," 335.

[19] Ibid.

[20] Ibid., 336–37.

self-deprecating humor, declared, "my diploma was granted—yes, granted—never earned."[21]

Skinner returned home to Perquimans County following his graduation and settled down to a life of farming and business. In 1848 he married Ann Eliza Halsey from Tyrrell County, North Carolina. By his own account, he declared himself "enthusiastically fond" of farming and seemed optimistic about the future. All of that was about to change, however. An encounter late in the year 1850 with a "Mr. Smith," a wheelwright in the county, brought Skinner to the point of accepting Christianity. Skinner met Smith one day and invited him to spend the night at his home, because a heavy rainstorm was about to occur. During the evening the two men engaged in conversation about Smith's faith and his host's lack thereof. Through the witness of Smith, two months later Skinner publically declared his faith and, on 19 January 1851, was baptized into the membership of the Bethel Baptist Church in Perquimans by the pastor Quentin H. Trotman.[22]

Change came rapidly for Skinner. Within four months of his baptism he embarked upon a career in ministry, enrolling as a student at Union Theological Seminary in New York City where his uncle Thomas Harvey Skinner was a professor. Tragedy then struck the young Skinner shortly after his move to New York when his wife Ann died. Remaining at the school with his daughter and young son, Thomas, Skinner graduated on 8 May 1854. The same evening as his graduation, he married Ann Stuart Ludlow, whom he had met in New York.[23]

A pastorate in Petersburg, Virginia, awaited the Skinners following graduation from seminary, but that pastoral tenure lasted only for eight months, due to the health of his new bride Ann who needed a warmer climate.[24] A call soon came from the First Baptist Church of Savannah,

---

[21] Ibid., 337.

[22] Ibid., 338–44. As discussed in ch. 2, Trotman served briefly as pastor of the Raleigh Baptist Church.

[23] Ibid., 347–49. Skinner does not mention his wife's death in his "Reminiscences," or any of the circumstances surrounding it. He only mentions that on the evening of his graduation, he remarried. See Day, *Gentleman of the Old School*, 19.

[24] Skinner, "Reminiscences," 349.

Georgia. The train from Virginia to Georgia stopped in Weldon, North Carolina, where Skinner met Reverend William Hooper, who invited him to travel to nearby Warrenton to attend the annual meeting of the Baptist State Convention. There he also met G. W. Johnston, at that time the current pastor of the Raleigh Baptist Church. Following the meeting of the convention, Johnston invited Skinner to preach in Raleigh. Skinner's account of the episode fills in some of the gaps from the church's records:

> Mr. Johnston had been pastor of the church in Raleigh for the past year, and being afflicted with a diseased throat had not been able to preach for some time, and was holding the pastorate only long enough to find his successor.... Upon invitation, I preached to the brethren of the Baptist church morning and evening of the next Lord's day. They seemed delighted with the new preacher, and called a conference meeting the next night and extended a unanimous call to their pastorate.[25]

After consulting with his wife, who agreed to settle in Raleigh, Skinner began his duties as the church's pastor on 1 December 1855, for a salary of $800 [$20,500].[26]

Skinner's ministry continued at the Raleigh Baptist Church until 1867 when he accepted a call to be the pastor of the First Baptist Church in Nashville, Tennessee. He remained in Nashville until 1870 and then left for Georgia where he served pastorates in Columbia, Athens, and Macon. In 1879 he returned to Raleigh and began a second tenure as the church's pastor that lasted until 1886. Tragedy struck the Skinner family in 1903 when his son, Ludlow, was shot and killed in front of the Raleigh post office. Thomas Skinner died two years later on 2 April 1905 after attending Sunday services at the Baptist church in Raleigh where he left a remarkable legacy.[27]

Within a few short months after calling Skinner as pastor, the congregation lost one of its most prominent members, John J. Briggs.

---

[25] Ibid., 351.

[26] Church Conference Records, 25 November 1855. See Skinner, "Reminiscences," 352. Skinner recalls that $400 [$10,200] of the salary was provided by the Home Mission Board of the Southern Baptist Convention.

[27] Day, *Gentleman of the Old School*, 111–17.

Briggs had been a charter member of the church and one of its first two deacons. He had been instrumental in the 1830s when the church was reconstituted after a major dispute within the congregation. In a sense, the death of John Briggs marked a transition to a new generation of leadership and growth, which coincided with Thomas Skinner's call as pastor. Accordingly, his life and impact on Raleigh Baptist Church deserve further mention here.

John Joiner Briggs was born in 1770, the son of Joel and Elizabeth Joiner Briggs. His parents' family had come from England to Massachusetts and then to Virginia. Eventually, John's parents settled in Scotland Neck, in Halifax County, North Carolina. In addition to John, they had another son and two daughters. Both parents died in 1770, the year of John's birth, which left the children under the care of a maternal uncle, Matthew Joiner, who taught John the carpentry trade. At the age of twenty, John reportedly left Scotland Neck and moved to Fayetteville, thinking that the city would become the capital of North Carolina. When Raleigh was chosen as the capital, Briggs relocated again for the final time. He was one of the first residents of the city at a time when, according to one account, "there were only five houses in the city, and Fayetteville Street was still in cedar growth."[28] According to Briggs's own account, he was one of the men who worked to build the early streets in Raleigh and clear them of trees. In 1795 he married Elizabeth Utley. Soon after his arrival in Raleigh, Briggs became one of the most celebrated builders in the city, known not only for the quality of his work but also for his honesty and fairness. He built some of the most prominent houses in the city and, perhaps most importantly, was one of the lead carpenters who worked on the reconstruction of the State House in the 1830s.[29] For forty-four years, John J. Briggs had been a steady presence and voice of leadership in the life of the Raleigh Baptist Church.

Constructing a New Building. In 1855 when Skinner began his pastoral duties, the church reported a total membership of 456 to the annual meeting of the Raleigh Baptist Association. Although strong in

---

[28] *Architects & Builders: A Biographical Dictionary*, 2009, s.v. "Briggs, John J.," http://ncarchitects.lib.ncsu.edu/people/P000038 (accessed 12 July 2009).

[29] Ibid.

number, the church had important needs, not the least of which was facilities. For several years the congregation had discussed the necessity of either renovating the present building or erecting a new structure altogether.[30] In fact, the most important church activity during the early years of Skinner's pastorate concerned the construction of a new building. In his "Reminiscences," Skinner indicated that he accepted the pastorate of the church "with the distinct understanding that they would, as soon as possible, erect a new meeting house in a more eligible situation."[31] On 31 May 1856, only five months after Skinner arrived in Raleigh, the church records report that he, along with church members A. M. Lewis and R. M. Jones, purchased a lot across from the state capitol, owned by Dr. James H. Cook, "on which it may be contemplated to build a new church edifice."[32] The three men used the services of attorney A. Williams, Esq. and purchased the property out of their own financial resources. Lewis spoke to the church and indicated that they had "purchased the lot for the sole use of the church" and offered to give a "sufficient portion of the lot" for the erection of a new church building and also pledged to give a generous contribution toward the expenses of the construction.[33]

Pleased with the report, the church members indicated their approval by unanimously passing the following resolution:

> Whereas in the Providence of God the Baptist church in Raleigh has been blessed for sometime past with a constantly increasing and larger congregation than our present house of worship can

---

[30] See, for example, Church Conference Records, 1 April 1854.

[31] Skinner, "Reminiscences," 351.

[32] Church Conference Records, 31 May 1856.

[33] Ibid. See Skinner, "Reminiscences," 352–53. Skinner gives details concerning the purchase of the lot and how he was able to convince Dr. Cook to sell it. It seems that Cook had promised to sell the lot on other occasions, but had never followed through with those plans. He had a "servant" (it is unclear whether he was a slave or a free black man) named Jim Atkins, a black member of the Raleigh Baptist Church. It was through the agency of Jim Atkins that Skinner was able to convince Cook to sell the property for the purpose of erecting a new church building. Skinner had warm feelings about Atkins, indicating that, "We could not have purchased it without the aid of that excellent Christian man."

conveniently or comfortably accommodate, therefore resolved that the church is fully sensible of the expediency and importance of speedily erecting a new house of worship in a more commodious style and in a more eligible situation and with the blessing of God in their efforts determined to do the same.[34]

Several members spoke positively about the new venture as did a former pastor, T. W. Tobey, an invited guest at the meeting that evening. There is no mention in the meeting minutes of any dissenting voices.

The church quickly appointed a committee composed of ten men and ten women to gather subscriptions (pledges) toward the new church building. The names of the male committee members were: M. B. Royster (chair), Lynn Adams, W. G. Upchurch, G. B. Bagwell, J. H. Kinkam, A. M. Lewis, W. W. Vass, P. F. Pescud, J. G. Williams, and A. Williams, Esq. The female committee members were: Helen Litchford, Sally Towler, Caroline Lougee, Mrs. A. M. Lewis, Mary B. Clark, Temperance Jones, Lydia Berry, Indiana G. Royster, Temperance G. Shaw, and Amey D. Womble.[35]

According to Skinner's recollection, the very first donation he received for the new building came from a non-Baptist, William Boylan, the father of one of his childhood friends. He described how he met Boylan "in the walk in the Capitol Square which leads from Fayetteville Street to Hillsboro Street, just where the oak stands nearly in the middle of the walk." There Boylan handed him a check for $100 [$2,610]. Skinner thanked him for the donation. About a year later, Boylan contacted Skinner to inquire as to why the check had never been cashed. Skinner replied, "Here it is, and it has been of great help to me in prizing up, as a fulcrum, many of our Baptist mudsills. I say to them, 'Why, look here at this check, given unsolicited to me by a gentleman who is not a Baptist, and can you withhold your aid to such a needful enterprise?'"[36]

The annual session of the Baptist State Convention met in Raleigh in November 1856 in the House chamber of the capitol building. Skinner's prowess as a fundraiser became obvious to the members of the Raleigh

---

[34] Church Conference Records, 31 May 1856.

[35] Ibid. The spelling of the names is difficult to decipher in this particular entry in the church records.

[36] Skinner, "Reminiscences," 365–66.

Baptist Church at the conclusion of the convention gathering. As the delegates to the annual convention gathered in the Raleigh Baptist Church building for a worship service the evening after the convention adjourned, Skinner sought to press several of the prominent members to increase their intended subscriptions. He told the congregation he wanted five people to pledge $2,000 [$52,200] each and that he already had two who had agreed to do so. By the time the evening's gathering had concluded, not only did he have pledges for $10,000 [$261,000] from the original five persons he targeted, but the other members of the congregation made pledges totaling $8,750 [$228,000]. The grand total pledged for the evening, according to Skinner, was $18,750 [$489,000].[37]

On 2 January 1857 the church authorized Skinner to appoint a building committee "consisting of five persons, members of the church, or if he should think proper, that he shall have the liberty of appointing A. Williams, Esq. as one of that committee in connection with four brethren."[38] A month later the church named a building committee consisting of Thomas Skinner, A. M. Lewis, Robert M. Jones, P. F. Pescud, and A. Williams, Esq. The next mention of the project came in June 1857 when Skinner reported to the congregation that the work had been delayed due to the sickness of the architect, but that the plan would be drawn very soon and turned over to the contractor. A few weeks later the building committee brought a report to the church in a special called meeting. At that meeting, they specified that the contractor for the project would be Thomas Coates of Petersburg Contractors, who had agreed to build the edifice for a cost of $18,750 [$489,000]. The architectural firm of Percival and Grant was secured to draw up the plans for $937.50 [$24,500] and the purchase of the lot was for the sum of $1,000 [$26,100].[39]

---

[37] Ibid., 362–65.

[38] Church Conference Records, 2 January 1857.

[39] See William B. Bushong, "William Percival, an English Architect in the Old North State, 1857–1860," *The North Carolina Historical Review* 58/3 (July 1980): 310–39. The details of William Percival's life have eluded historians for years. Records indicate that he worked in North Carolina for a short period of time designing several impressive buildings. He left Raleigh around 1860, and no further information can be gathered about him. No extant records exist concerning his birth, death, or any significant biographical details about his life.

The anticipated total cost of the building before construction began was $20,687.50 [$540,000]. The committee continued its report, stating that $15,433 [$403,000] had already been collected in subscriptions, leaving a deficit of $5,254.50 [$137,000] that the church needed to raise.[40] The committee expressed its confidence that the amount could be raised from "the liberality of those who feel an intent on establishing the Kingdom of Christ on earth."[41] Following the report of the building committee, Skinner resigned his position on the committee, likely feeling that it would be best to leave the planning matters to the laity. The church replaced him with J. G. Williams.[42]

Near the end of 1857 the church instructed the building committee to sell the old building as quickly as possible, with the exception of the bell and the seats, so that the money could be applied to the cost of the new building, which they expected to be completed by September 1858.[43] Earlier in the year it was reported that the estimated value of the building and land was $3,000 [$78,300].[44] Whether it was an oversight on the part of the building committee, or intentionally to be kept a separate expense, for some reason the church did not originally contract with the builder

---

[40] For information on how nineteenth-century Baptist churches raised money via the subscription method, see Gregory A. Wills, *Democratic Religion: Freedom, Authority, and Church Discipline in the Baptist South, 1785–1900* (New York: Oxford University Press, 1997) 132.

[41] Church Conference Records, 20 July 1857. The amount of $15,433 reported in the minutes that had been raised by subscriptions differs from the amount of $18,750 that Skinner reported in his "Reminiscences," which was raised in November 1856 at the conclusion of the Baptist State Convention meeting. The *Biblical Recorder* included a very brief mention of the meeting in its report of the Baptist State Convention annual meeting, which indicated that "The amount of subscriptions made by the church and visitors reached $13,000 [$339,000]" (see "The Baptist State Convention," *Biblical Recorder* (Raleigh NC), 13 November 1856, 2). The church records would probably be the more reliable figure since Skinner was writing years after the fact and the figure could have grown to more than $15,000 [$380,000] between November 1856 and July 1857. Furthermore, it appears that he may have confused the amount raised that evening with the amount contracted with Thomas Coates of Petersburg Contractors.

[42] Church Conference Records, 20 July 1857.

[43] Ibid., 4 December 1857.

[44] Ibid., 2 January 1857.

for a steeple. The first mention of the steeple came in February 1858 when a committee composed of W. M. Adams and J. D. Nunn were selected by the congregation to "get subscriptions and gather cash to build the steeple to the new church" and report the amount at the next meeting.[45]

The following month, at a called meeting, the records reflect that the contractor agreed to build the steeple for an amount of $1,470 [$39,500]. Subscriptions totaling $511 [$13,700] were already raised, leaving a balance of $959 [$25,800]. A committee of ten members was then appointed to collect pledges and report back at the next meeting.[46] Progress toward meeting that extra expense continued over the next several months. By July 1858 the deficit on the steeple expense had been reduced to $82 [$2,200].[47] There is no further mention of the steeple fundraising efforts in the records.

The steeple contained what is arguably the most impressive aspect of the new building: the sixteen-foot diameter rose window, which one observer said, "is composed of all the colors of the rainbow, and is most beautiful to look at."[48] There is a tradition in the congregation's lore that Skinner brought the rose window back from Europe after he journeyed there during the last year of the Civil War. There is no truth to the legend, however. There are multiple sources, one written by Skinner himself, that indicate the rose window was planned as the steeple was being constructed.[49]

After more than two years in the planning and building, the grand occasion of the new church's dedication came in November 1858. A special dedication ceremony was planned to coincide with the annual meeting of the Baptist State Convention, which met again in Raleigh that year as it had done two years before. Since subscriptions and funding for the building came from some North Carolina Baptists who were not members of the church, it was only fitting that a grand dedication

---

[45] Ibid., 5 February 1858.

[46] Ibid., 12 March 1858.

[47] Ibid., 9 July 1858.

[48] "The New Baptist Church," *Biblical Recorder* (Raleigh NC), 2 December 1858, 2.

[49] See ibid.; *Raleigh Register* (North Carolina), 13 January 1858, 3, and 14 September 1859, 3.

ceremony should be held in Raleigh. The indications are that the building was not fully completed by the time of the dedication ceremony, and it would be another ten months before the church was able to take possession of the building fully. Yet the ceremony in the new building, which was probably just a shell at that stage of its construction, was important to North Carolina Baptists—but especially to the Raleigh Baptist Church members.

The congregation was by then more than half a century old. Several generations had shared in that local family of faith and by then had passed on. There were still members like Lucinda Briggs who remembered the early days. They recalled the financial struggles of the past (a perennial problem for most of the rest of the nineteenth century). As they gathered with other North Carolina Baptists for that special ceremony, they must have reflected on their lives together and memories of their joy as well as difficulties. The new building was as much a testimony to the past as it was an avenue to the future.

The dedication ceremony occurred on the evening of 11 November 1858. All were invited to the ceremony to dedicate the new building. Reverend J. L. Burrows of Richmond, Virginia, preached the dedicatory sermon from Isaiah 60:7: "I will glorify the house of my glory." Though the weather that evening was stormy, the building, which reportedly could accommodate 1,000 people, was filled to capacity. A choir composed of some of the best voices in the city provided the music under the direction of Dr. W. D. Cooke. At the conclusion of the sermon, Burrows had the congregation stand as he spoke these words of dedication:

> It only remains that we solemnly, formally, and publicly declare this house dedicated, set apart for the glory of God and earnestly pray that He may ever dwell in it, reveal Himself from it, and gloriously work through it. To God, the omnipotent Father, we dedicate it that He may gloriously dwell in this temple made with hands here who reign over his people. To magnify His name, to fulfill His promises, to bless His truth, and to display His glory. To God the everlasting and incarnate Son that here He may subdue by His love his foes, exhibit the efficacy of his atoning sacrifice, reveal the wondrous mysteries of His cross, commune with his ransomed Saints, see of the travail of his

soul, and be satisfied. To God the omniscient Spirit that he may here convince the ungodly of sin, of righteousness, and of judgment, whisper pardon to the repentant, speak peace to the troubled, impart comfort to the distressed, light to the perplexed, strength to the weak, inspire the zeal, incite the prayer, confirm the faith, elevate the hopes, nourish the love of His Saints and purify to himself a peculiar people. To the great Jehovah, Father, Son and Holy Ghost, the one true and only God, do we now solemnly, joyfully dedicate this building. These lesser rooms we devote to the instruction of children, in the principles of his words, and to the assembling of his people for mutual edification and prayer. These pews, we devote to His worshippers; this choir, to those who sing His praise, this baptistry [*sic*] to those who observe His ordinance; this pulpit to such as shall declare all the counsel of God. This whole building we separate from ordinary and secular, to sacred and spiritual purposes. Holy Father, Gracious Redeemer, Blessed Spirit, accept the offering we humbly and gratefully make, and by the continued presence of power, glorify the House of Glory."[50]

Following the dedication, work continued in earnest to complete the building. In April 1859 the building committee asked for a special called meeting of the church to inquire as to whether the new building should be stuccoed or not. The cost would be $700 [$18,600] and would be due in the next five months, according to the committee. The church voted affirmatively on the matter.[51] Discussions also continued for the next several months about having pews built for the basement of the new building, a project that was not completed until long after the congregation had taken possession of the structure.[52]

Finally, the day arrived when the Raleigh Baptist Church worshipped in the old building for the last time. The date was 8 September 1859. At that time the church recorded a total membership of 438 (228 white members and 205 black members). The church clerk, J. H. Alford, could not help but include in the official record some of his personal thoughts:

---

[50] Church Conference Records, 11 November 1858.

[51] Ibid., 26 April 1859.

[52] See ibid., 5 October 1860. The last mention of the basement pews in the records was in October 1860.

There is always something solemn, and that which will excite melancholy emotions, when one knows that he is engaged for the last time in anything on earth. Such a thought leads the mind to meditate on the past, and recall pleasant memories that are associated with that which we are about to part. It was peculiarly so tonight with the church in her assembled capacity for prayer and praise for the last time in the house, in which the Lord has so often visited the hearts of his people with the refreshing of his grace, and where he had also often manifested his power in the conviction and conversion of sinners.[53]

Following the dismissal of that last worship service, the church went into a business session to discuss a few matters of importance, not the least of which was the fact that there was already a report of water damage from the pipes in the new building that needed to be fixed![54]

Three days later, on 11 September 1859, the Raleigh Baptist Church celebrated its first Sunday worship service in the new building (which is where the congregation continues to worship today). Although the plans initially were for the building to have been completed earlier, "owing to circumstances over which the church had no control; it was delayed until the present time."[55] Matthew T. Yates, Southern Baptist missionary to China and favorite son of the Baptists in Raleigh, was in town and delivered a lecture on "The Religious Elements in the Rebellion or Civil War in China" during the evening worship service. Alford captured the pride of all the members when he reported: "This was a proud day for the Baptists of Raleigh and an occasion which I believe did, and should have excited the deepest and most profound gratitude to Almighty God, for the prosperity with which he has blessed them, and for the peace and union which now reigns in their midst."[56]

Financial Woes. Despite the successful construction of the new building (or perhaps because of it), the church experienced serious financial strain during Skinner's first tenure. The records reveal a constant struggle month after month to pay not only the incidental costs

---

[53] Ibid., 8 September 1859.

[54] Ibid.

[55] Ibid., 11 September 1859.

[56] Ibid.

and church debts but also the pastor's salary. For most of its history the church used the "subscription" method for raising money. Typically, someone made a motion in a church conference concerning a project or other type of financial need. The church then appointed a committee to gather "subscriptions" or financial pledges toward that need. While not always an efficient process, nevertheless in the past it tended to be effective. Yet the problem with that system was that it did not allow for much money to be on hand to pay off small incidental expenses, which began to accumulate as the church grew.

The church became aware that the subscription method for fundraising needed to be modified as early as March 1856, just after Skinner's ministry began. A. M. Lewis made a motion before the church conference asking that "each member be assessed in proportion to his or her worth to be ascertained by the word of each…the worth to include all of each member's property, real or personal, exclusive of what is necessary for support."[57] Lewis's motion met with resistance, was tabled for two months, then subsequently withdrawn.

While assessment of the members' financial worth was unpopular, the method of pew rental proved to be successful for a while. In December 1858 the congregation called a special meeting of the church to discuss collecting rent on pews to pay for the incidental expenses of the church. "Sabbath contributions" were to be used to pay for other expenses of the church. Although that proposal generated a lot of discussion, it ultimately passed.[58] Two months later a plan was presented, which indicated that the pews ranged in price between $4 [$106] for the "least desirable" seats to $18 [$479] for the best seats. When a seat was desired by several people, it would be retained by the highest bidder.[59] On 27 March 1859 the church gathered in the new building for the purpose of renting pews and enlisted an auctioneer's services for the event. The available pews were rented while sixteen pews were "reserved for those who could and would not rent and for strangers."[60]

---

[57] Ibid., 8 March 1856.
[58] Ibid., 14 December 1858.
[59] Ibid., 10 February 1859.
[60] Ibid., 27 March 1859.

The event netted the congregation between $600 [$16,000] and $700 [$18,600] for the year.

Unfortunately, pew rental could not provide the church all the funding it needed, and the possibility of a congregational assessment returned. The issue surfaced once again in October 1862 as the church struggled to pay the pastor's salary, which had been in arrears for three years. The assessment plan was implemented and seemed to provide some relief, but by April 1863 some assessments had not been paid, prompting the collection committee to read the delinquent names publicly to the members assembled in the church conference. Some assessments were excused for various reasons. Others had their assessments lowered, while still others were given more time to pay. Families of soldiers serving in the Confederate Army were exempted from the assessment requirement.[61] Then in October 1866 the church began to move toward a unified budget method of raising finances. The church authorized the deacons to have "blanks printed," with "captions of the various objects for which we...are accustomed to contribute," which would then be distributed to each member of the church so that they "might subscribe as [they] wished."[62]

Perennially, the most pressing expense the church struggled to pay was the pastor's salary during the Skinner years. Skinner began his tenure with a salary of $800 [$20,500] per year.[63] The church set his salary at $1,000 [$26,100] for his second year.[64] Given that Skinner had been a successful businessman before his decision to enter ministry and that his father was wealthy, his salary at the church was probably not an issue during his first few years. By spring 1857 the church began to accumulate debt to the pastor for his salary.[65] In fact, the church was still indebted to G. W. Johnson for $30 [$783] at the start of Skinner's ministry.[66] As 1858 ended, it appears that Skinner's financial needs had increased. The

---

[61] Ibid., 3 April 1863.

[62] Ibid., 5 October 1866.

[63] Ibid., 25 November 1855.

[64] Ibid., 5 November 1856.

[65] See the references to the pastor's salary in ibid., 27 February 1857 and 7 March 1857.

[66] Ibid., 14 February 1856.

records on 3 December 1858 state that the "pastor signified his willingness to preach the coming year for the same salary; but gave the church to understand in kind but very plain terms that as soon as they were relieved of the present church debt,…he should require the sum of $1,500 [$40,300] per year should they require his services."[67]

A year later Skinner's position remained unchanged. An entry from 18 November 1859 reveals that the committee appointed to meet with the pastor to determine his salary needs for the next year reported that the pastor had "expressed himself affectionally [*sic*] to the brethren," but continued to insist, as he had on 3 December of the previous year, that his salary needs would be $1,500.[68] A few weeks later Skinner compromised with the church and agreed to a salary of $1,200 [$31,900] for the coming year until the pew rental time in September, whereby the church would reconsider the matter.[69] There was no mention of the pastor's salary in September 1860 although the pew rental that year netted the church $1,608 [$42,800].[70] The month before, on 3 August 1860, Skinner told the church that the agent secured to raise money among North Carolina Baptists for the planned establishment of the Baptist Female Seminary had resigned. The founding of the school in Raleigh depended upon the ability to raise $25,000 [$665,000]. Skinner requested from the church a leave of absence to work for the effort and pledged to them that he would take no salary from the Baptists of North Carolina for his labor, nor would he expect his salary from the Raleigh Baptist Church during that period. The church acceded to his wishes, granting him a leave of absence, although it is unclear how long this arrangement lasted.[71]

---

[67] Ibid., 3 December 1858.

[68] Ibid., 18 November 1859.

[69] Ibid., 2 December 1859.

[70] Ibid., 7 September 1860.

[71] Ibid., 3 August 1860. The venture was delayed by the onset of the Civil War. As discussed in ch. 3, the dream of a school for young women sponsored by the Baptist State Convention of North Carolina had been around since Thomas Meredith first mentioned the idea in a resolution before the convention in 1838. See Mary Lynch Johnson, *A History of Meredith College* (Raleigh: Meredith College, 1956) 1–21.

Skinner's financial situation became desperate during the years of the Civil War. The record suggests he did not anticipate that was going to be the case. In June 1861 the church records report that "Brother Skinner made a statement of the relations existing between him and the church. He said that in consequence of the troubles of the country growing out of the war,…that he would serve the church as pastor, without the usual salary."[72] But the summer took its toll on Skinner. In September 1861 he called for a special meeting of the church to read his resignation because "his eastern possessions [were] exposed to the marauding enemy and that it is his duty to give them more attention than would be consistent with his duties as our pastor."[73] The church refused to accept his resignation and offered him a leave of absence instead, but his intention to resign suggests that the Skinner family's fortune was at risk during the war.

For most of the war years, the church remained delinquent in paying the pastor's salary and tried numerous ways to raise the funds, but with little success. On 3 January 1866, Skinner again offered his resignation, saying he was "embarrassed financially" and "thought that it was his duty to leave the ministry and try by all the means in his power to relieve himself from his embarrassment."[74] After some discussion the church refused the resignation once again. But the next year, even though the church determined his salary to be $2,000 [$29,900], he informed them that he had accepted a call as pastor from the First Baptist Church in Nashville, Tennessee.[75] When Skinner resigned as the pastor of the

---

[72] Church Conference Records, 7 June 1861.

[73] Ibid., 10 September 1861. The church refused to accept the resignation at that meeting and appointed a committee to convey to Skinner that they were going to grant him a leave of absence. The following month (see Church Conference Records, 1 October 1861) the committee reported back to the church that Skinner wanted to address the church again. He then conveyed that there were other reasons for his resignation that related to the church's "cold and lukewarm state." He reminded them of their Christian duty to support the church and indicated that he "could and would not remain as pastor under current circumstances and would only withdraw his resignation in case the brethren would be more faithful and punctual hereafter."

[74] Ibid., 3 January 1866.

[75] Ibid., 26 September 1867.

Raleigh Baptist Church in September 1867, the church was indebted to him for the amount of $1,520.78 [$22,800].[76]

Church Discipline. In addition to financial hardship, church discipline dominated the pages of the church records during Skinner's first tenure as pastor. The typical disciplinary matters concerned the use of profanity, consumption of alcohol, and most especially, lack of attendance at church meetings. The church had clear expectations that its members were to attend worship services and church conferences regularly. Article Seven of the church's "Rules of Decorum" from that period stated that, "All the members of this church shall attend its conference meetings unless providentially hindered."[77] During the Skinner years the church clerk had instructions to make a notation of the members absent from church conference meetings. Members who were habitually absent were asked to appear before the church and justify their absences.

These disciplinary records provide rich insight into the cultural milieu of nineteenth-century Baptist life, an era very different from the twenty-first century in which personal privacy is paramount.[78] The discussion on 30 April 1858 provides a case-in-point. On that day the church passed a motion requesting that the "deacons inquire into the truth of the rumors against Mrs. Lougee of infidelity to her husband and report at the next meeting."[79] In early June the record shows that "Brother D. King and the clerk reported that they had a conference with Mr. W. J. Lougee with regard to the conduct of his wife in leaving him and he stated that he considered her a guilty person and that he never expected to live with her again." The church then proceeded to excommunicate "Mrs. Caroline E. Lougee" from its membership for

---

[76] Ibid.

[77] The "Rules of Decorum" are printed at the front of the Church Conference Records that cover the years 1840–1855.

[78] See C. Douglas Weaver, *Second to None: A History of Second Ponce de Leon Baptist Church* (Brentwood TN: Baptist History and Heritage Society, 2004) 33ff, for a good discussion of church discipline in nineteenth-century Baptist churches. See also Wills, *Democratic Religion*, 8–9, 17.

[79] Church Conference Records, 30 April 1858.

adultery.[80] Such personal family matters are rarely, if ever, brought into the domain of official congregational business in our era, and a modern church might even find itself in legal trouble if it pursued such a personal matter.

The church conference on 5 April 1856 involved an amusing case (perhaps to the modern reader) of discipline concerning Isaiah Perry. He appeared before the church that day to answer to a charge of drunkenness that had been brought against him several weeks earlier. Perry apologized for his intoxication and stated that "the unusual cold days of the weather" induced him to drink and that "he was deceived with regard to the effect that was produced by his use of it at the particular time referred to."[81]

A similar charge concerned Alsey Crocker. He steadfastly denied that he was or had ever been intoxicated and even referred to his wife as a witness. Yet several members testified that they had witnessed him intoxicated, and one member said he observed Crocker "in a reeling position." Crocker then stated that "he sometimes mimicked drunken people" and "drank spirits as a medicine" on the recommendation of a member of the church. He reported receiving "relief from a dropsical [sic] swelling" from its use and that a small amount sometimes affected him. The pastor then asked Crocker to refrain from using and selling intoxicating beverages, but for business reasons Crocker refused to comply.[82] After much discussion the case was deferred until the following month when Crocker's letter of repentance was read to the church. He continued to deny being intoxicated but indicated that he had quit using "spirituous liquors," and that he would agree to stop selling alcohol in his place of business. He must have been unable to abide by his promise, because after another month, Crocker was excommunicated from the membership of the church.[83]

The church also disciplined members for fornication, another matter that today is considered to be deeply personal. The case of P. O. Williams and Elizabeth Parham serves as an example. On 30 September 1859 the

---

[80] Ibid., 4 June 1858.
[81] Ibid., 5 April 1856.
[82] Ibid., 4 February 1859.
[83] Ibid., 4 March 1859 and 1 April 1859.

church reported that the couple had been married for only five months, but during that time Elizabeth gave birth to a child. Upon motion from the congregation, they were both expelled for fornication.[84]

African-American Members. The records from the decade preceding the Civil War also reveal a growing distance between the white and black members. On 5 September 1856 the church determined that the black members would have to be moved out of the "galleries" so that the "children and young persons of both sexes connected with the Sabbath School" would have a place to participate in the Sunday-morning services. A further note indicated the church's support for "the colored congregation to have a special service every Sabbath afternoon and permission to use the galleries at night."[85]

Almost three years later, as the church was about to occupy the new building, Skinner reported the presence of division among the black members in their reactions to the upcoming move. Some, he reported, wanted to worship in the new building and others wanted to stay in the old one. Still others were in favor of buying a separate lot and building their own building. The church appointed a committee composed of P. F. Pescud, William Adams, and _____ [unable to read] Crabtree to explore the options and bring forth a recommendation.[86] Several weeks later the committee reported that the black congregation had plans of purchasing the old building. No further reference exists to that planned venture except that the building was sold to the Roman Catholic Church, indicating that the black members may not have been able to raise the necessary funds for the purchase.[87]

An interesting addition to the church minutes in early 1861 indicates that a voluntary committee of twelve white members was appointed "to attend to the colored brethren" for the next three months.[88] There is no explanation given as to the reason for that committee, but it could serve as a clue that the two groups were growing apart, and it may be evidence

---

[84] Ibid., 30 September 1859.

[85] Ibid., 5 September 1856.

[86] Ibid., 4 February 1859.

[87] Ibid., 1 April 1859. The report that the building had been sold to the Roman Catholic Church came on 3 September 1859.

[88] Ibid., 4 January 1861.

of tension that began to exist in the minds of Southern whites regarding the slaves on the eve of the Civil War.

An important step in the eventual split between the black and white members came in 1865, following the conclusion of the Civil War. A report was presented stating that the black members of the church wanted to begin their own Sunday-school program. Believing they had come to the church "in the right spirit," J. C. Marcom offered a motion to approve their request and "give them all the aid we [can]." After "considerable discussion" and an attempt to postpone the matter, the church approved their request.[89] A few months later Skinner reported to the church that the black members sought permission to have their own pastor, "a colored man sent out by the society of colored brethren in the north." The church, not wishing to act too hastily in the matter, or perhaps rebuffed by the idea of a black minister "from the north" coming to their church, deferred the matter until later when it was indefinitely postponed.[90]

Women Deacons and the Civil War. There are two other items of interest that occurred in the life of the Raleigh Baptist Church during the first tenure of Thomas Skinner. First, upon the motion of Jordan Womble, Sallie Towles and Roxana Dodd were appointed to be deaconesses to visit the sick "where the company of ladies was more suitable and to collect the apportionments of the ladies with privilege of calling upon the sisters for assistance."[91] While those two women did not have the same authority and status as the male deacons, and while there is no indication of any kind of ordination service for them, they represented a major step forward in the congregation's attitudes toward women. Women had been appointed to serve on committees from time to time in the church up to that point. But the appointments of Towles and Dodd marked the first time the church gave a woman the title "deaconess" with certain ministerial responsibilities.

Second, the records provide a glimpse of the war's impact on church life. One of the most immediate effects of the Civil War was financial. The

---

[89] Ibid., 29 September 1865.
[90] Ibid., 1 December 1865 and 8 December 1865.
[91] Ibid., 18 January 1867.

church struggled to pay its bills and especially its pastor's salary during that period, a problem made more difficult with so many of the male members away on the battlefield. There are references, for example, to families being excused from having to pay their pew rental fee to the church because a member of the family was at war. One interesting reference to the Civil War in the church minutes is found in the entry on 4 April 1862: "The War Department having called for the church bells of the Confederacy in order that they might be molded into cannon for the public defense, it was moved by resolution introduced by Bro. Sykes, that the bell of this church be donated for the purpose named."[92] Although not mentioned in the church records, there is evidence that the basement of the church was used as a makeshift factory where the women produced "1,500 mattresses, 400 shirts, 300 jackets, 200 pairs of pants, and 200 haversacks at the beginning of the war."[93] Following the Battle of

---

[92] Ibid., 4 April 1862. The bell most likely became Confederate cannon. It is clear that the church sent the bell to the Confederate government with that intention. The bell that currently hangs in the church belfry was manufactured in 1886. Nevertheless, there are a couple items of interest in the *Biblical Recorder* related to the bell and the church's offer that at least raise the question about the fate of the bell. Following the church's offer of the bell, the *Biblical Recorder* printed a column titled "Church Bells Not Wanted," which included a letter, dated 15 April 1862, from W. S. Ashe indicating that he had received the bell with gratitude, but "as it is not desired to deprive the Churches of those dear instruments whose sweet tones have, for the ages, called to divine worship those faithful followers of the Gospel," he respectfully declined the offer (*Biblical Recorder* (Raleigh NC), 23 April 1862, 2). The following week the *Biblical Recorder* printed another column titled "Church Bells Accepted," which included another letter, dated 11 April 1862, from Smith Stansburuy of the "Confederate States of America, War Department Ordnance Office" indicating that the "offer is accepted with thanks," and asking the church to "please hold the bell subject to order." The letter continued to say that the Confederacy had enough metal on hand to keep the foundries busy for "two or three months to come" (*Biblical Recorder,* 30 April 1862, 2). It is interesting that the *Biblical Recorder* printed one letter saying that the bell was not needed, followed by another letter the following week saying that the bell was needed. But the *Recorder* reversed the order of the letters. Following the proper order, therefore, one might be led to believe that the church offered the bell and the Confederate government accepted, but then later declined, leaving the final fate of the bell a mystery.

[93] James Vickers, *Raleigh, City of Oaks: An Illustrated History* (Woodland Hills CA: Windsor Publications, 1982) 48, as cited by Day, *Gentleman of the Old School,*

Bentonville near the conclusion of the war, the church served as a makeshift hospital for more than 100 wounded soldiers.[94]

The spiritual condition of the soldiers in the Confederate Army was also of great concern to the Southern churches, and the same was true of the Raleigh Baptist Church.[95] Following the lead of the Central Baptist Association, in September 1862 the church appointed a committee to collect funds from among the members, which were then to be sent to the association for Army colportage.[96] Eventually, the church collected $520.25 [$9,170], an impressive amount given the church's financial

---

49. See also *The Daily Dispatch*, 26 April 1861, http://www.perseus.tufts.edu/hopper/text;jsessionid=54482A954076193B28889126B7734B9C?doc=Perseus%3Atext%3A2006.05.0103 (accessed 18 April 2011).

[94] *Weekly Conservative*, 29 March 1865, 1. This article lists names of the wounded soldiers, their units, and the nature of their wounds. See also Murray, *Wake: Capital County of North Carolina*, vol. 1, 464, who reports the reminiscences of Mrs. Jonathan McGee Heck, the mother of Fannie E. S. Heck who recalled that wounded soldiers came into the city regularly by train during the war and the "basement of the First Baptist Church" was used as a makeshift hospital. It should be noted that the church was not named "First Baptist Church" until 1883.

[95] There are scores of articles and books written about the Southern churches and their concerns for the spiritual well-being of the soldiers in the Confederate Army. For a sampling, see W. Harrison Daniel, "An Aspect of Church and State Relations in the Confederacy: Southern Protestantism and the Office of Army Chaplain," *North Carolina Historical Review* 36/1 (January 1959): 47–71; W. Harrison Daniel, "Bible Publication and Procurement in the Confederacy," *Journal of Southern History* 24/2 (May 1958): 191–202; Herman Norton, *Rebel Religion: The Story of the Confederate Chaplains* (St. Louis: Bethany Press, 1961); Herman Norton, "Revivalism in the Confederate Armies," *Civil War History* 6 (December 1960): 410–24; Charles F. Pitts, *Chaplains in Gray: The Confederate Chaplains' Story* (Nashville: Broadman Press, 1957); and Sidney J. Romero, "The Confederate Chaplain," *Civil War History* 1 (June 1955): 127–40.

[96] Church Conference Records, 5 September 1862. The Central Baptist Association was organized in 1860 with seven churches, including two that came from the Raleigh association: Mt. Vernon and New Hope. The Raleigh Baptist Church joined that new association in 1861 (see Church Conference Records, 19 August 1861). Providing the Confederate troops with religious periodicals and Bibles was of paramount concern to the churches of the Central Baptist Association during the war years. As early as 1861, the association unanimously passed a resolution that colportage "among our soldiers should be prosecuted with energy" (see Minutes of the Central Baptist Association, 1861, 13).

difficulties at that time.[97]

The most direct reference to the Civil War in the church records is an amazing entry recorded on 13 April 1865, the day the city of Raleigh was surrendered to Sherman's troops. This entry, unlike any other entry into the church's records up to this point, contains no reference to any church business. It provides modern readers with a window into the emotions and fears of the members of the church on that fateful day: "This morning, just before the rising of the sun, General W. T. Sherman at the head of a hundred and thirty thousand Federal soldiers entered the city of Raleigh; the city having been surrendered to him by the authorities."[98] The city was surrendered by Mayor William H. Harrison and City Commissioners Alexander H. Creech, C. M. Farriss, Hackney Poole, and W. R. Richardson. Prominent citizens Kenneth Rayner, Dr. Richard B. Haywood, Dr. William H. McKee, and Peter F. Pescud were also present at the surrender.[99] The account indicates that "little violence was offered by the citizens though all houses were seized and every kind of firearm was confiscated." Because of the recent Battle of Bentonville, "all of the hospitals and many private houses were full of wounded soldiers." The description further reports that the Federal army encircled the city for "some weeks" and that there were no regular church meetings held for several months. Since Thomas Skinner was away on a leave of absence, the pastoral duties were being performed by Thomas H. Pritchard at that time. The narrative recalls that Pritchard preached each Sabbath "at first to only a few of the citizens and no ladies but many soldiers." After a few weeks the people returned to their regular habit of church attendance.[100]

Thomas H. Pritchard (1868–1879)

On 26 September 1867 Thomas Skinner informed the congregation at a called meeting of the church that he planned to resign as pastor to

---

[97] Church Conference Records, 27 October 1863.

[98] Ibid., 13 April 1865.

[99] Murray, *Wake: Capital County of North Carolina,* vol. 1, 543. Pescud and Raynor were members of the Raleigh Baptist Church.

[100] Church Conference Records, 13 April 1865.

accept a call to the First Baptist Church of Nashville, Tennessee.[101] Skinner's reason for leaving is not recorded, but (as seen above) finances most certainly played a part because of the church's inability to pay his salary consistently. As mentioned above, by the time he resigned, the church owed Skinner $1,520.78 [$22,800] in salary, a debt the church promised to pay before it called a new pastor.[102]

He had been the church's longest tenured pastor up to that point, having served the congregation for twelve years. His years of faithful service included not only the baptizing, marrying, and burying of many from the congregation, but also critical leadership during the construction of a new building and the suffering of the Civil War. It is no surprise, then, that the church's resolution of appreciation called attention to the fact that his ministry embraced "perhaps one of the most marked and important periods in the history of the church since its formation." Furthermore, the members of the Raleigh Baptist Church celebrated Skinner as "the honored instrument in effecting much for the Kingdom of Christ in this State" and pledged that they "shall ever cherish the liveliest recollections of that enlarged liberality and earnest devotion to the service of our blessed Redeemer." They lamented not only their loss of a pastor but also the fact that the Baptists of North Carolina would be losing "a most zealous and ardent supporter." Finally, they concluded,

> although nature cannot repress emotions of sorrow, as we reflect that in the relation of pastor, his loved voice will call us no more to duty, we still have cause for consideration in the memory of his sterling virtues, of his kindness of heart, and of his deep love for the Brethren, and we bow in thankfulness to the great Head of the church for the bright example that he has enabled our Brother to leave us in works of benevolence, and in the zeal which he has constantly manifested for the promotion of the cause of Christ.[103]

---

[101] Ibid., 26 September 1867.
[102] Ibid.
[103] Ibid., 4 October 1867.

The church extended a call to Thomas H. Pritchard on 3 January 1868, although he was not their first choice. Following the standard procedure of that day for calling a pastor—very different from the modern Baptist church's process of appointing a search committee to narrow the possibilities down to one candidate—the church voted on 16 October 1867 to go into a formal election of a pastor. Several names were discussed, including Pritchard's. Four candidates were mentioned as potential pastors and the members voted on each one. Pritchard received the second highest total of votes. The highest total of votes went to a "Rev. Dr. Williams," who later informed the congregation that he would not be able to accept the call from the church, because the salary of $1,800 [$26,900] per year would not meet his financial needs.[104] At that point, the church turned its attention to the second choice, Pritchard, who agreed to the salary offered and began his service in January 1868.

Pritchard was no stranger to the Raleigh Baptist Church. From October 1863 until just after the conclusion of the Civil War in spring 1865, Skinner was on a leave of absence from the church "for the purpose of visiting Europe on a private and denominational character."[105] The exact nature of Skinner's visit to Europe is not stated in the church minutes; however, other sources indicate that he was in England purchasing Bibles for the soldiers and people in the Confederacy.[106] The

---

[104] Ibid., 16 October 1867 and 19 December 1867. Unfortunately, there is no first name recorded for Williams. Since it is such a common name, it is difficult to determine who the prospective pastor was.

[105] Ibid., 15 October 1863 and 13 April 1865.

[106] *Proceedings of the Baptist State Convention 1863*, 26: "Elder T. E. Skinner, who has recently run the blockade in the Advance, was entrusted with two one thousand dollar Confederate cotton bonds to be used in the purchase of a set of stereotype plates of the New Testament, which he is to have forwarded to us by one of the government vessels engaged in running the blockade at Wilmington. He is also commissioned as agent to purchase Bibles and Testaments in England on the credit of the Board of Missions to be paid for when the war shall have ceased. Let us pray that the Lord will through these channels give us an abundant supply of His precious word to distribute among our soldiers who are now flocking to his standard by thousands." See also G. W. Paschal, *History of Wake Forest College*, vol. 1 (Wake Forest: Wake Forest College, 1935) 630; and Day, *Gentleman of the Old School*, 56–64 for a fuller discussion of that episode in Skinner's life.

journey to Europe in the middle of the Civil War would have been adventurous, to say the least, and most certainly dangerous due to the Federal blockade of the port at Wilmington, Skinner's point of departure.

During the period of Skinner's absence, the church employed Pritchard as an interim to fill the pulpit and see to other pastoral duties.[107] The fact that Pritchard was known to the members of the congregation and had actually served them in the role of pastor may explain why he came in second in the balloting for a new pastor. Just as there probably would have been those who remembered him favorably and wanted him back, it is likely that there also would have been others who remembered him with the opposite impression.

Upon his arrival at the Raleigh Baptist Church, Thomas Pritchard brought with him a remarkable career among North Carolina Baptists. He was born on 8 February 1832 in Charlotte, North Carolina. His father was a Baptist minister and native of Charleston, South Carolina. Shortly after his birth the family moved to Mocksville, North Carolina, where as a youth he was instructed by the Reverend Baxter Clegg at the Mocksville Academy. Due to the financial generosity of a wealthy uncle, Pritchard was able to enroll at Wake Forest College at the age of seventeen.[108] By his sophomore year his financial support had dwindled to the extent that he had to leave at the conclusion of the year. Pritchard taught school during the hiatus with the intention of eventually returning to finish his bachelor's degree. Borrowing money, he was able to return to Wake Forest where he graduated with the B.A. degree in 1854. While enrolled at Wake Forest, he was president of the Philomathesian Literary Society, where his academic skills soon became apparent. One contemporary indicated that he brought "the joyfulness and energy of

---

[107] Church Conference Records, 15 October 1863.

[108] There are several short biographical sketches of Thomas Pritchard. See John R. Woodard, "Pritchard, Thomas Henderson," in *Dictionary of North Carolina Biography*, ed. William S. Powell, vol. 5 (Chapel Hill: University of North Carolina Press, 1994) 149–50; *The Baptist Encyclopedia*, vol. 3, ed. William Cathcart (Philadelphia: Louis H. Everts, 1881) s.v. "Pritchard, T. H., D.D."; and Paschal, *History of Wake Forest College*, vol. 2, 166–67 and vol. 1, 620. It should be recalled from the previous chapter that Pritchard's father received a call from the Raleigh Baptist Church to be its pastor in 1842 but declined.

abounding health, and gracious manners, the uplifting influence of noble ambitions, literary tastes, with a readiness and fluency of speech which came to him by inheritance, and an optimism which clung to him."[109]

During his time as a student at Wake Forest, two important spiritual events happened in Pritchard's life. First, he was baptized during his freshman year by W. T. Brooks at the Wake Forest Baptist Church. A short time later, he experienced a calling to ministry and was licensed to preach by the same church. Upon his graduation, the young Pritchard had so impressed his peers and administrators that the board of trustees appointed him as an agent for the college and gave him the assignment of traveling throughout the state to raise money on behalf of the college. That assignment lasted for a year, and upon its completion, he settled in Hertford, was ordained to the ministry, and became pastor of the Baptist church in the town.[110]

Pritchard served the church in Hertford for three years. Then in 1858 he left for Charlottesville, Virginia, where he studied theology with Dr. John A. Broadus. Broadus left the following year to join the faculty of the new Southern Baptist Theological Seminary in Greenville, South Carolina. Pritchard, on the other hand, served as an interim pastor at the Fredericksburg Baptist Church in Fredericksburg, Virginia, during 1859, and in 1860 he accepted a call to become the pastor of the Franklin Square Baptist Church in Baltimore, Maryland.[111]

Pritchard served for three years in Baltimore, and when the Civil War began, he made no attempt to hide his support for the South. He refused to swear allegiance to the federal government, was imprisoned as a rebel for a short period, and eventually was banished to the South.[112] At that point, he came to serve the Raleigh Baptist Church in Skinner's absence. Upon Skinner's return in spring 1865, Pritchard became pastor of the First Baptist Church of Petersburg, Virginia, where he remained until accepting the call again to Raleigh in 1867. Pritchard remained with the Raleigh Baptist Church until 1879, a tenure that matched Skinner's in longevity.

---

[109] Woodard, "Pritchard, Thomas Henderson," 149.
[110] Paschal, *History of Wake Forest College*, vol. 2, 166–67.
[111] Ibid., 167.
[112] Ibid.

Pritchard left the Raleigh Baptist Church to become the president of Wake Forest College, where he remained until 1884 when he returned to the pastorate, serving at First Baptist Church of Wilmington, North Carolina. He remained there until 1893 and then moved to Charlotte where he assumed his last pastorate at the Tryon Baptist Church (eventually renamed First Baptist Church). Pritchard died in May 1896 in the home of his son in New York City where he was visiting.[113]

During his career Pritchard was active among the Baptists in North Carolina. He served for seven years as the chairman of the state mission board and was corresponding secretary for much of that time. He served as associate editor of the *Biblical Recorder* for several years. He was also a trustee at seven different institutions, including Wake Forest College, the University of North Carolina, and the Southern Baptist Theological Seminary. He received the honorary Doctor of Divinity degree from the University of North Carolina in 1868.[114]

Although Pritchard's tenure as pastor of the Raleigh Baptist Church is bookended by Thomas Skinner, the student of the church's history should not forget the important contributions he made to the congregation. He served as the interim pastor of the church for more than a year during the Civil War and was with the church during the dark days of the city's surrender to General William T. Sherman. He also ministered to and led the church during the difficult period of Reconstruction.

First Colored Baptist Church. Despite the difficulties Raleigh residents encountered during those years, the Pritchard tenure at the Raleigh Baptist Church was a period of transition and growth. One of the first important events to occur soon after Pritchard became the pastor of the congregation was the establishment of the First Colored Baptist church, made up of former black members from the Raleigh Baptist Church. As noted above, as early as 1856 the relationship between the white and black members was changing, largely due to the tension developing between North and South over slavery. After the war, in 1865 the black

---

[113] Woodard, "Pritchard, Thomas Henderson," 149–50.
[114] Paschal, *History of Wake Forest College,* vol. 2, 167.

members had made a request that the Raleigh Baptist Church allow them to start their own Sunday school, which the church had granted.[115]

Three years later, on 5 June 1868, a delegation "from the colored church were at the door," according to the church's records. Upon the motion of P. F. Pescud, they were received, and the leader of their delegation, Henry Jett, "expressed the thanks of the church (Colored) for some favors received from us, and having made some remarks as to their condition and hopes, stated that the colored church wished our church to dismiss them in a body." The record further explains they had already "organized in a separate body under the name of the First Colored Baptist Church."[116] The church approved their request and formalized the break.

Additional sources indicate that the First Colored Baptist Church was comprised of some 200 members. Trustees included names such as Friday Jones, Richard and James Shepard, Isaac Vass, and Calvin Strickland. The first pastor of the church was Reverend William Warrick from Philadelphia. The first location for their church building was on North Salisbury Street between North and Johnson Streets. In 1896 they purchased the property originally inhabited by their mother church on the corner of Wilmington and Morgan Streets (which had been the location for the Roman Catholic Church of St. John the Baptist). In 1904 the First Colored Baptist Church began to erect a new building completed in 1909 on the property. The church continues to inhabit the building today as the First Baptist Church (Wilmington Street).[117]

Construction Projects. Another step forward for the Raleigh Baptist Church during Pritchard's pastorate was the addition of a parsonage for the pastor. On 4 March 1870 the congregation formed a committee to begin the discussion of building a parsonage. In the coming months the committee was enlarged and later in the year reported that it was considering several lots, which would provide a suitable location. By the

---

[115] Church Conference Records, 29 September 1865.
[116] Ibid., 5 June 1868.
[117] Murray, *Wake: Capital County of North Carolina,* vol. 1, 617.

end of the year a lot had been located near the church that the committee believed could be purchased for $200 [$3,390].[118]

Several months passed before the church returned to the topic of the parsonage. On 24 August 1871 the parsonage committee reported that everything was ready for construction to begin, except that the funds needed to be pledged and the church needed to give its final approval. The estimated cost of the house was $3,000 [$54,400]. That report generated considerable discussion, according to the church minutes, and the meeting seems to have closed without the church's approval.[119] Then, seemingly by surprise, the following month at a called meeting of the church, Thomas Pritchard resigned his position as pastor of the church, saying that he had received a unanimous call to the Baptist church in Savannah, Georgia. The fact that the Raleigh Baptist Church experienced perennial difficulty keeping his salary paid and seemed ambivalent about building a parsonage likely played a part in his decision. After hearing Pritchard's resignation, the church prayed and appointed a committee of five men to visit with the pastor and offer him an increase in salary from $2,000 [36,200] to $2,500 [$45,300], to take effect the following month. The committee also promised that a parsonage would be built. The committee then left to visit Pritchard and convey the offer while the church remained in session praying and singing hymns. Pritchard sent word back by the committee that he would give them a final decision the following Sunday. The congregation came to church that following Sunday in great anticipation of what his decision would be. He ended their suspense by agreeing to stay in Raleigh.[120] By the end of the year, money began to be collected for the construction of a parsonage.[121]

There is no information in the church records to indicate the exact date of the parsonage's completion, nor is there any suggestion of dedication ceremony. It is clear that by 1874 the structure had been completed and the debt it caused was problematic. On 16 August 1874 the treasurer reported a debt of $600 [$11,700] on the parsonage. One

---

[118] Church Conference Records, 4 March 1870, 3 June 1870, 30 September 1870, and 30 December 1870.

[119] Ibid., 24 August 1871.

[120] Ibid., 14 September 1871.

[121] Ibid., 7 December 1871.

person who seemed annoyed at the church's lack of financial interest in the project was J. M. Heck, an original member of the parsonage committee. The account reads: "Bro. Heck says that it has been suggested that the majority of the church did not undertake to build the pastor's home and he thinks it best to see whether the church really wants the home or not and to test this point he moves that it be sold." Only two people voted to sell the house. Everyone else voted to keep it. Heck had made his point![122] The debt on the parsonage continued to burden the church for most of the decade. As late as 1877 the minutes reveal that the church still owed money on the home, although no amount is mentioned.[123]

The church added another important structure in 1874. Called the "Infant Classroom," that facility was erected on the southwest corner of the church building, "extending ten feet on the lot of Sister Swepson (she having kindly granted the privilege for an indefinite period)."[124] That building, effectively the church's first education facility, was large enough to accommodate 300 infants and cost the congregation $1,000 [$19,400].[125] The Infant Classroom also became intertwined with the history of Meredith College. On 11 February 1890 the room hosted the school's first board of trustees when they selected Raleigh to be Meredith's host city from among offers by New Bern, Goldsboro, Durham, Oxford, Henderson, Greensboro, Winston-Salem, and Charlotte.[126]

Mission Congregation. Another project initiated by the church during Pritchard's pastorate, which had a far-reaching impact on the city of Raleigh, was the establishment of a mission congregation. Discussions about the mission endeavor began within the congregation as early as

---

[122] Ibid., 16 August 1874.

[123] Ibid., 5 January 1877.

[124] Ibid., 1 May 1874.

[125] See "Raleigh Baptist Church to the Central Baptist Association," contained in Church Conference Records, 4 September 1874. The quote reads: "Our infant department has become so large that we have been obliged to provide better accommodation for it and an addition has been made to our church of a beautiful semicircular room (which will seat three hundred children) at a cost of a thousand dollars—most of which has been provided for."

[126] Johnson, *History of Meredith College*, 28.

1872. By spring 1873 the church was actively raising money for the cause.[127] In May 1873 a committee was appointed to "make plans and estimates for a church building to be erected on Swain Street," with instructions to report at the next month's meeting of the church.[128] Two months later the committee was dismissed, and a board of trustees comprised of Governor W. W. Holden, J. H. Mills, A. J. Redd, Len H. Adams, and N. S. Mosely was appointed to raise money and "build the house according to their best judgment."[129] The following month the trustees recommended the building of the structure on Swain Street at a cost of approximately $2,500 [$46,200].

The building was dedicated on Sunday, 31 May 1874. The mission, originally begun as a Sunday school, was officially organized on the following Sunday. J. S. Allen was elected as superintendent with N. B. Broughton as his assistant. W. T. Womble was appointed librarian of the Sunday school. Clifford Harris became secretary and Henry Mitchell, treasurer.[130] The church's letter to the Central Baptist Association in 1874 described the work in more detail:

> Wishing to reach a class of persons with the benefits of the gospel who rarely attend any place of worship we have erected in the Eastern Ward of the city a neat chapel at a cost of about one thousand dollars and already have a flourishing Sabbath School in operation there. The gospel is also preached there on the Sabbath and a prayer meeting held on each Friday night. It is contemplated to organize a church at this place at an early day.[131]

---

[127] Church Conference Records, 2 August 1872, 28 February 1873, and 5 April 1873. The church also reported to the Central Baptist Association in 1873, "We have been holding five prayer meetings each week for some time: one in the church and four in different neighborhoods of the city" (see Minutes of the Central Baptist Association, 1873, 13).

[128] Church Conference Records, 5 May 1873.

[129] Ibid., 11 July 1873. Mosely was replaced by S. D. Harrison as a trustee the following month (see Church Conference Records, 1 August 1873).

[130] Ibid., 7 June 1874.

[131] Ibid., 4 September 1874.

The ceremony to constitute a church at the Swain Street property occurred on 15 November 1874. Ten members from the Raleigh Baptist Church requested letters of dismission, which were granted, so that they could be constituted as the charter members of the new church. That afternoon, in a special worship service, Reverend J. D. Hufham, editor of the *Biblical Recorder* and a member of the Raleigh Baptist Church, was selected as the first pastor of the new church.[132]

The new congregation grew rapidly. Originally constituted as the "Swain Street Baptist Church," from 1881 to 1887 it was called "Second Baptist Church." The name was changed a second time to "Tabernacle Baptist Church" in 1910. By 1900 it became the largest Baptist church in Raleigh, eclipsing its mother church in membership. By 1910 the church boasted an enrollment of 1,000—more than one-fifth the total membership of the entire Raleigh Baptist Association—with a Sunday-school enrollment of 1,600.[133]

One interesting footnote to the organization of the new church concerns Caroline Lougee. As noted above, Caroline Lougee was dismissed from the membership of the Raleigh Baptist Church for adultery in June 1858. Almost seventeen years later the church records report, "Request from 2nd church that Mrs. Caroline Lougee be restored to fellowship. On motion she is restored."[134] Evidently, Mrs. Lougee and her husband, W. J. Lougee, worked out the problems that were noted

---

[132] Ibid., 15 November 1874. The original ten members were: J. S. Allen and his wife, W. T. Womble, Henry Mitchell, J. M. Broughton, N. B. Broughton, Mary Broughton, Carrie Wilson, Mattie Harton, and Cornelia Burch. The property was deeded from the Raleigh Baptist Church to the new congregation the following month.

[133] K. Todd Johnson and Elizabeth Reid Murray, *Wake: Capital County of North Carolina*, vol. 2 (Raleigh: Wake County, 2008) 83. The success of the Swain Street Baptist Church propelled the congregation to begin discussion of establishing another mission (see Church Conference Records, 2 April 1875, 4 August 1876, and 1 September 1876). That mission enterprise, however, did not fully materialize until after Pritchard's ministry at the Raleigh Baptist Church had concluded. See also Day, *Gentleman of the Old School*, 87–88, for a discussion of the competition brought about by the other churches.

[134] Church Conference Records, 30 April 1875.

earlier. The couple is buried beside one another in Raleigh's Oakwood Cemetery.

Congregational Life. The annual letter sent by the church to the Central Baptist Association in 1876 provides an important glimpse into congregational life at that time. The church reported that the women were active in benevolent work, reflecting the growing spirit among Baptist women in the South that would eventually come to fruition in the organization of the Woman's Missionary Union:

> We deem it worthy of special mention that the sisters of our church are accomplishing much for the cause of the Master by their special organizations. They have a Missionary Society, a Sewing Society, and a Mite Society, and some of them propose with the help of our pastor, to attempt the better organization of the Baptist women of NC in working for Jesus.[135]

The church reported a total membership of 513 that year (199 men and 314 women) and a total of 645 involved with the Sunday school. Perhaps the most telling statement in that snapshot of the church in 1876, however, is the reference to "the remarkable peace and harmony which have prevailed among us for many years we are still permitted to enjoy."[136]

Women in the church began to move into greater positions of leadership during Pritchard's pastorate. However, that does not change the fact that American society at large in the nineteenth century was still male-dominated. Not only were women prohibited from voting in state and national elections, but they were also prohibited from other civic responsibilities such as jury service. In fact, it would be decades before the United States would amend the Constitution and pass the 19th amendment, giving women the right to vote. And even at the Raleigh Baptist Church, women were not allowed to participate in the regular monthly church conferences, except on occasions when a "mass meeting"

---

[135] Ibid., 27 July 1876.
[136] Ibid.

was called.[137] Still it should be reiterated that the church did begin to turn to some of its prominent women for important tasks. As mentioned previously, in 1867, for example, the church had appointed its first two deaconesses. On 21 August 1874 Pritchard announced he was going to "insist" that the church elect *deaconesses* at their next regular church conference.[138] The following month a motion came before the body that called for the election of four deaconesses. The motion passed by a vote of twenty-seven to four. Sallie Towles (one of the two deaconesses elected in 1867), Mrs. A. M. Lewis, Virginia B. Swepson, and Anna Justice were elected.[139]

The most prominent of those four women was Swepson. Virginia B. Swepson was the daughter of prominent North Carolina politician Bartlett Yancey. She was the wife of notorious scalawag George W. Swepson, who came to Raleigh following the Civil War speculating in a variety of business interests. George Swepson was baptized into the membership of the Raleigh Baptist Church in 1881 and seemingly became a committed member of the church until his death two years later.[140] Historian William S. Powell described him as "one of the chief Scalawags of the Reconstruction period," who was involved in banking, railroad speculation, distribution of liquor, manufacturing, as well as some other business interests. Because of Swepson's shady business dealings, Powell went so far as to categorize him as "one of the greatest rascals of North Carolina history."[141] Yet despite her husband's reputation as a scalawag,

---

[137] See ibid., 31 December 1869. Women were appointed to serve on committees from the early years of the church's history. However, a reading of the church records from the Pritchard era gives a clear indication that women were not participatory in the meetings. For example, included in the entry for 31 December 1869 is a notation that J. M. Heck moved that the female members be invited to attend a called meeting to discuss the issue of pew rental. The fact that the women had to be "invited" indicates that they were regularly excluded.

[138] Ibid., 21 August 1874.

[139] Ibid., 4 September 1874.

[140] See Day, *Gentleman of the Old School*, 87–88, for a good summary of Swepson's relationship with the church and Thomas E. Skinner, the pastor who baptized him in 1881. Skinner's "Reminiscences" provides a detailed description of Swepson's conversion to Christianity on pp. 373–78.

[141] William S. Powell, *When the Past Refused to Die: A History of Caswell County North Carolina 1777–1977* (Durham NC: Moore Publishing Company, 1977) 232–

Virginia was a devoted member of the Raleigh Baptist Church, whose generosity to the church included land as well as $1,000 [$26,000] to the Woman's Missionary Union upon her death in 1901.[142]

Another infamous person to join the Raleigh Baptist Church during Pritchard's tenure was W. W. Holden. Holden, who first made his name in Raleigh as a newspaper publisher, became one of the most controversial figures in North Carolina during the Reconstruction era. Holden held numerous controversial stances both during the Civil War and afterwards. He was also known to change his mind from one perspective to another. One example was his position regarding Southern secession. Holden originally favored North Carolina's secession from the Union, but as the war progressed he became a vocal opponent of the Confederacy, particularly the presidency of Jefferson Davis. During Reconstruction President Andrew Johnson appointed Holden to be the provisional governor of the state, and he won the office outright in the election of 1868. But again, his controversial stances on various issues of the day—no less his opposition to the Ku Klux Klan—brought the ire of his political enemies and eventually led to his impeachment and removal from office in 1871.[143] In Washington at the time of his impeachment and guilty verdict, Holden attempted to return to journalism in the nation's capital. He soon returned to North Carolina in 1872 and assumed the position of postmaster in Raleigh until 1883. He died from complications of a stroke in 1892.[144]

33, as cited by http://ncccha.blogspot.com/2006/11/george-william-swepson-1819-1883.html (accessed 16 August 2009). In another article, it is said estimates were that Swepson, who died in 1883, amassed a fortune of somewhere between $1 million [$22.1 million] and $2 million [$44.2 million] and he kept most of it in his wife's name in order to keep the authorities away from it (see Robert J. Wylie, "Swepson, George William," in *Dictionary of North Carolina Biography*, vol. 5, 490).

[142] Minutes of the Woman's Missionary Society, First Baptist Church of Raleigh, 2 December 1901.

[143] Horace W. Raper, "Holden, William Woods," in *Dictionary of North Carolina Biography*, vol. 3 (Chapel Hill: University of North Carolina Press, 1988) 170. See also Day, *Gentleman of the Old School*, 85–87.

[144] Ibid., 171. In 2011 the North Carolina General Assembly pardoned Holden for the judgment against him that resulted in his removal from office in 1871. See http://www.ncga.state.nc.us/Sessions/2011/Bills/Senate/PDF/S256v1.pdf (accessed 24 April 2011).

Though originally a Methodist-turned-Episcopalian, Holden sought membership in the Raleigh Baptist Church in 1871 as his political enemies were pressing toward his impeachment. His enemies were skeptical of his public profession of faith in Christ and his decision to become a Baptist, and claimed that it was a political stunt. However, Holden settled in as an active and dedicated member of the church where he served faithfully for the next fifteen years. He served in just about every major leadership role within the congregation, and his name appears frequently in the church records at the forefront of whatever issue was being decided.

In addition to local missions and outreach, the music ministry of the church received a boost during Pritchard's pastorate. In 1877 he notified the church that informal conversations had taken place concerning the possibility of purchasing an organ for the sanctuary. Out of those conversations, William Simpson and F. P. Hobgood were selected to "correspond with some of the principal organ builders in the country and ascertain upon what terms the church could secure a suitable instrument."[145] Simpson reported to the church the list of prices, which were all around $2,000 [$42,300]. The church then appointed a committee of women to raise money for the organ.[146]

The women quickly became busy in their fundraising efforts. The following month the church granted permission for the women to use the church basement for a "festival," the proceeds of which were designated toward the organ fund.[147] Two months later a formal report on the organ project was given to the church. A total of $2,200 [$46,500] would be needed for the organ. Additionally, it was reported that some changes would need to be made to the interior of the sanctuary to accommodate the instrument.[148] By November 1877 the church was anticipating the arrival of the organ at any time. The organ committee asked the church for permission to use the sanctuary for a concert of sacred organ music after its installation. The purpose of the concert was "to realize funds to be devoted to liquidizing the debt incurred in its purchasing and in

---

[145] Church Conference Records, 4 May 1877.

[146] Ibid.

[147] Ibid., 1 June 1877.

[148] Ibid., 31 August 1877.

making the necessary changes in the church building."[149] According to the letter sent to the Central Baptist Association the following year, the grand total of the organ purchase plus the renovations to the sanctuary ended up being $3,000 [$63,400].[150]

Another important action taken by the church during Pritchard's pastorate was the adoption of a new confession of faith. When the church reorganized in 1840, they saw the need to appoint a committee to revise the constitution, rules of decorum, and articles of faith that had previously existed.[151] In 1873 the church chose to revise the church covenant and bylaws and, perhaps more importantly, further define itself theologically by adopting the New Hampshire Confession of Faith.[152] Whereas the church's theological statement from 1840 was written by a committee within the church, the New Hampshire Confession came from outside the congregation. It was the most important Baptist confession in nineteenth-century America. Originally drafted in 1833 by the Baptists of New Hampshire, by 1850 it had a wide circulation among Baptists in America. Perhaps the confession's best-known attribute is its modification of the rigid Calvinism that had been so prevalent in the late eighteenth century in New England.[153]

The confession of faith produced by the church in 1840 contained fifteen articles that roughly correspond to the following topics: creation, Christ, mankind, sin, scripture, salvation (three articles), baptism, the holy spirit, proclamation, election, justification, perseverance of the saints, and resurrection of the dead.[154] The New Hampshire Confession of Faith is more comprehensive, adding articles on such topics as "A Gospel Church," "Baptism and the Lord's Supper," "The Christian Sabbath," "Civil Government," and the "Righteous and Wicked."

---

[149] Ibid., 30 November 1877.

[150] Ibid., 4 October 1878.

[151] These documents appear at the very beginning of the Church Conference Records for the years 1840–1856.

[152] Ibid., 28 February 1873.

[153] S. J. Grenz, "New Hampshire Confession of Faith," in *Dictionary of Baptists in America*, ed. Bill J. Leonard (Downers Grove IL: Intervarsity Press, 1994) 202.

[154] See pp. 3–5 of the Church Conference Records, 1840–1856.

The New Hampshire Confession, once adopted by the church, became part of a "church manual" published by the church in 1874. As early as 1871 the church had discussed the need of a "little book or pamphlet, containing a brief history of the church together with the church government, articles of faith, and names of all its members."[155] The booklet was finally completed and 800 copies were printed by 5 June 1874.[156] This booklet provides further insight into the life of the church in the postbellum years. It opens with a list of the officers of the church followed by a list of the weekly worship schedule, as well as regularly scheduled offerings. There follows a short history of the church and the Sunday school. The articles of faith (adapted from the New Hampshire Confession of Faith), the church covenant, the constitution, the financial plan of the church, the standing resolutions, and the rules of order then fall into sequence. There is a list of the church's membership, both male and female members, concluding with an appendix containing information about Baptists in general and, more specifically, information on baptism and communion.[157]

The reason the church deemed it necessary to produce the church manual can only lead to speculation since no official reason is stated in the church records. The church had experienced significant numerical growth during both the Skinner and Pritchard years. Perhaps the congregation wanted to use the church manual to introduce new members to the beliefs and practices of the church. Or the church manual could have been used as a way to introduce non-members to the church's traditions and beliefs. The growth in new members may also have created a need to become more organized around core principles, such as a more complete doctrinal statement and clearly established guidelines and expectations of members. Whatever the reason, the 1874 church manual provides an excellent window into church life among the members of the Raleigh Baptist Church during the late Reconstruction era.

---

[155] Church Conference Records, February 1871.

[156] Ibid., 5 June 1874.

[157] A copy is available among the church records housed in the church's vault.

All things considered, the church records from 1867 to 1879 reveal a congregation gaining strength after the devastation of the Civil War. There were financial struggles during the period to be sure, but the church persevered and seemed able to generate the financial resources for repairs on the building, the establishment of a mission congregation, the building of a parsonage, the growth of Sunday school, and the addition of an organ to the sanctuary.

With so many good things that had happened during his pastorate, the church was likely surprised on 20 July 1879 when Thomas Pritchard offered his resignation as pastor, effective 1 September. Pritchard left Raleigh for what may have seemed to him to be a "dream" position, the presidency of Wake Forest College. He had been a loyal alumnus of Wake Forest during his pastoral years and had sought to promote the school in every way possible. There is also ample evidence that he remained close to the president, W. M. Wingate, who filled the pulpit on numerous occasions when Pritchard needed to be absent. So the selection of Pritchard to succeed Wingate may have seemed like a natural choice. But for the church, bidding farewell to Pritchard must have been difficult. Pritchard had been the pastor for twelve years—as Skinner had been before. And the longevity of both those pastorates brought a sense of stability to the church that it needed, especially during the Civil War and Reconstruction era.

Thomas E. Skinner (1879–1886)

Finding a new pastor proved less difficult than many in the congregation might have assumed. The transition from Skinner to Pritchard in 1867 had been simple because Pritchard had already served the congregation as an interim pastor during the war. A similar situation existed following Pritchard's resignation in 1879. Thomas Skinner made visits back to Raleigh during the Pritchard years—most notably for a revival preached during April and May 1875. The timeline for Skinner's return to Raleigh reveals both a pastor and a congregation eager for a reunion. Pritchard resigned on 20 July 1879. Within fifteen days the Raleigh Baptist Church extended a call to Thomas Skinner. He accepted the call, notified the church within a week, and was in Raleigh ready to assume the pastorate of the congregation by the first week of September.[158]

In some ways, the church to which Skinner returned was different from the church he had left twelve years earlier. The membership had dramatically increased during Pritchard's pastorate, from 290 when Skinner left, to 502 when he returned.[159] The Sunday school also continued to grow from thirty teachers and 250 students in 1867, to thirty-nine workers and 488 students in 1879.[160] Furthermore, the church had birthed a mission congregation that grew rapidly and quickly began to compete with the mother church for members and prominence. Beginning his second tenure, Skinner faced a church with many people he had known before, but also one with many new faces and new challenges.

Within just a few months of his assumption of the pastoral duties over the church, Skinner invited Dr. T. C. Teasdale of Knoxville, Tennessee, to the church for an extended revival meeting. The revival lasted for twenty-two days and proved to be highly successful, bringing numerous additions to the membership and producing twenty-nine candidates for baptism. The following year, 1881, the church held another successful revival meeting that lasted from 4–28 February. The success of those two revival meetings in the first two years of Skinner's second tenure as pastor and the additions to the congregation are noteworthy.

New Converts. Among the names of new converts and baptismal candidates that are listed in the church records during the years 1880–1881, two young women stand out, although no one would have had any way of knowing the far-reaching impact their Christian conversions would bring. In the church conference records on 11 November 1880, the church clerk recorded the following sentence: "After the prayer meeting tonight, Miss Fannie Heck was received for baptism upon a statement of

---

[158] Church Conference Records, 20 July 1879, 4 August 1879, 10 August 1879, and 5 September 1879. See also Day, *Gentleman of the Old School*, 81.

[159] Minutes of the Central Baptist Association, 1867, 19; Church Conference Records, 24 August 1879.

[160] Minutes of the Central Baptist Association, 1867, 15; Minutes of the Central Baptist Association, 1879, 21.

her Christian experience."[161] Thomas Skinner baptized the eighteen-year-old the following month.[162]

Fannie Exile Scudder Heck was born on 16 June 1862 in Buffalo Lithia Springs in Mecklenburg County, Virginia. Her father, J. M. Heck, was a lawyer, a successful businessman, and a lieutenant colonel in the Confederate Army. Fannie's unusual second name came from her mother Mattie, whose hometown was Morgantown, West Virginia. She named her child "Exile" to symbolize her status of being away from her hometown during the war years. Because their sympathies lay with the Confederacy, the Heck family relocated south to Virginia when the war began. Fannie added the name "Scudder" herself, taken from her maternal great-grandmother, a descendent of the famous Scudder family, known for the number of ministers and missionaries who came from its ranks.[163]

Near the end of the Civil War, Fannie moved with her family to Raleigh where her parents united with the Raleigh Baptist Church. The church records reveal that Colonel J. M. Heck was baptized into the membership of the church in 1864.[164] J. M. Heck remained a prominent member and leader of the church, as well as generous contributor for the rest of his life. He and his wife, Mattie, must have been pleased that night in 1880 when their daughter Fannie made public her profession of faith, requesting baptism and full membership in the church.

Fannie's name eventually became legendary among North Carolina Baptist women for her ardent efforts to promote missions and social change. She served as the state president of North Carolina Woman's Missionary Union from its beginning in 1886 until her death in 1915. She also served as president of the Southern Baptist Woman's Missionary Union from 1892 to 1894, 1895 to 1899, and 1906 to 1915. And she was

---

[161] Church Conference Records, 11 November 1880.

[162] Her baptism was recorded in the record book on 5 December 1880.

[163] Catherine B. Allen, *Laborers Together with God: 22 Great Women in Baptist Life* (Birmingham: Woman's Missionary Union, 1987) 37; Minnie Kennedy James, "Heck, Fannie Exile Scudder," in *Encyclopedia of Southern Baptists*, vol. 1, 604–05; T. L. Scales, "Heck, Fannie Exile Scudder (1862–1915)," in *Dictionary of Baptists in America*, 142–43. See also Day, *Gentleman of the Old School*, 85.

[164] Church Conference Records, 6 March 1864.

instrumental in the founding of the WMU Training School at the Southern Baptist Theological Seminary in Louisville, Kentucky, which eventually became the Carver School of Missions and Social Work.

Another important young woman converted and baptized during the second tenure of Thomas Skinner was thirteen-year-old Sallie Bailey. Sallie was the daughter of C. T. Bailey, editor of the *Biblical Recorder* from 1875 to 1895. Sallie became a close co-worker with Fannie Heck in organizing the women of North Carolina to promote missions. When she was seventeen, Sallie participated in the initial organization of the North Carolina Woman's Missionary Union. Heck was elected the first president and Sallie was elected secretary. She also served as treasurer of the organization from 1900 to 1916 and then president from 1916 to 1938.[165]

Building Repair Needs. A careful analysis of the church records from 1879 to 1886 reveals a different congregational mood from that which existed during Skinner's first tenure as pastor. Perhaps that mood is symbolized in no better way than the urgent need to make major repairs to the building that began to surface the first year after Skinner returned. The "house that Skinner had built" was by that time in desperate need of repair. The first mention of the need for repairs came in December 1879— a mere four months after Skinner's ministry began, when a committee was formed to examine the floor of the basement. For the next several months the committee investigated the matter, discussed cost, and ultimately decided in November 1880 to "make a thorough examination of the church building and to report to the church an estimate of the cost to make necessary repairs."[166]

The notation in the church minutes in April 1881 that "a communication was read from the sisters of the church asking the church to take some steps to have the church building repaired as soon as possible" had the desired effect.[167] After only one more month of study

---

[165] S. L. Morgan, "Jones, Sallie Bailey," in *Encyclopedia of Southern Baptists*, vol. 1, 711.

[166] Church Conference Records, 5 November 1880. See also Church Conference Records, 5 December 1879, which is when the issue of repairs first arose during Skinner's second tenure.

[167] Ibid., 29 April 1881.

the committee reported that the major needs involved the basement floor, which had decayed along with the support posts, which had rotted as well. The south vestibule of the basement needed repair. The floor leading to the coal room in the basement needed repair as well. The basement also needed new plastering and paint, and the vestibule leading into the sanctuary needed floor repair because exposure to the weather had adversely affected the hardwood flooring. The seat cushions needed new padding and reupholstering. The windows of the church needed work. The roof needed some work as well, although the report indicated that much of the roof was still in good condition. The heating units needed to be replaced. The total cost for the repairs was estimated to reach $3,100 [$67,100]. A new committee was then appointed to raise the necessary funds for those needed repairs.[168] More than eighteen months later the committee reported that it had pledges in hand for $2,963.50 [$65,500]—less than $200 short of the goal needed to complete the repairs on the building.[169] It is unclear from the minutes when all the repairs to the church building were completed, but the records do show that as late as November 1883, the committee on church repairs reported "progress."

The church building was not the only structure needing repair. By 1885 the infant room of the Sunday-school building, built during Pritchard's tenure and located adjacent to the church structure, was reported to be in an unsafe condition and in need of either major repairs or a new structure altogether.[170] In February of the following year the church had a long discussion about how to finance a new structure, but no action was taken for several years.[171]

Fellowship Problems. The saga of the church bell, which played out during the last two years of Skinner's ministry as pastor, also symbolized the downbeat mood of the congregation. In September 1884 the church instructed the building committee to purchase a new bell to replace the original bell donated to the Confederate war effort.[172] By March 1886 the

---

[168] Ibid., 3 June 1881.
[169] Ibid., 2 February 1883.
[170] Ibid., 5 June 1885.
[171] Ibid., 5 February 1886.
[172] Ibid., 5 September 1884.

church's dissatisfaction with the new bell was evident from an entry in the church records. The entry indicates that the bell was broken and instructs the building committee to raise the necessary money to pay freight and other expenses to acquire a new bell immediately. The following month (undoubtedly as cooler heads prevailed) the building committee reported that an expert had examined the bell and determined there were no cracks in it. A motion was then made "that the committee be continued and that the Secretary, Bro. J. A. Briggs be requested to correspond with the bell co. and see if they can suggest any remedy for the grating sound of the bell."[173]

It would be interesting to know Skinner's thoughts on the dilapidated condition of the building, having been the chief promoter of its original construction. Unfortunately, his published reminiscences include no reflections about the state of the building during his second tenure. The building's condition would not have been his only concern anyway. From what can be gathered from the church records, there were other problems that needed his attention, as evidenced by this letter from the deacons in 1881:

> Dear Brethren,
> Our much beloved and esteemed pastor and the undersigned, your most unworthy deacons, feel increasing concern by reason of evidence that more than one half our membership exhibit yearly decreasing concern for the spiritual welfare of the cause of Christ, seeming indifference to the sustenance thereof, and neglect to arrest apparent decay in church edifice and in making it both comfortable and attractive. For a long time business of vast concern is deferred from one conference to another because the few in attendance feel reluctant in the absence of 2/3 of the members to adopt measures requiring either their money or their time. It is our impression that the situation above described is mainly owing to the non-enforcement of

---

[173] Ibid., 2 April 1886. The new bell was manufactured in 1886 by the Meneely Bell Foundry in West Troy (now Watervliet), New York. The company was established in 1826 and manufactured bells until it closed in 1952. At its peak, the Meneely Bell Foundry was one of the top producers of bells in the United States. See http://danart.home.mindspring.com/bellsite/html/ (accessed 27 January 2011) for a website devoted to the preservation of the company history.

that discipline which would result from a more perfect organization and an increased number of younger and more active deacons in place of ourselves to be nominated by the pastor, who like the President of the United States, should have the selection of his Cabinet. We would suggest further more sociability, frequent intercourse and sympathy between the brethren both around the fireside and in more frequent meetings of the church for music, reading and conversation. This would remove the stiffness and formality which increased prosperity has begotten and an interest in each other's comfort, and welfare, both spiritual and temporal, and that increase of love which would make discipline unnecessary, and cause an enlarged liberality in the support of the pastor and in making needed improvements to the church edifice.[174]

In spite of the appeal, the church voted against increasing the size of the diaconate in August 1881, prompting the resignation of two prominent and influential deacons, J. M. Heck and W. W. Vass.[175] They were replaced by equally prominent members T. H. Briggs and W. W. Holden.[176] The following year the deacons once again brought a request to increase the size of the diaconate "as some of the members of the present board of deacons by reason of infirmity cannot be as active as the nature of the office demands."[177]

Further problems within the fellowship are suggested by a report in 1883 from the delegates sent by the church to the annual meeting of the Central Baptist Association. They spoke very well of the meeting itself, but informed the church that "there seemed to be a lack of interest manifested by this church in the association work," and hoped that the church would become more motivated in its desire for cooperation with sister churches.[178] Also, about a year before Skinner ended his pastoral duties at the church, T. H. Briggs brought a resolution before the body

---

[174] Church Conference Records, 1 April 1881.

[175] Ibid., 5 August 1881. Heck was elected again in 1883.

[176] Ibid., 23 October 1881.

[177] Ibid., 3 November 1882. The request passed, and in February 1883 Henry Horton and T. B. Yancey were elected, although the following month Horton declined to serve. He was replaced by E. G. Harrell. (See Church Conference Records, 2 February 1883, 2 March 1883, and 30 March 1883.)

[178] Ibid., 31 August 1883.

that requested "to all who may have had any differences in the church to forgive all the wrongs of the past and that we all live in harmony and peace," suggesting that hard feelings existed among the fellowship of the church.[179]

Along with structural problems and dissension among the members, the church was forced to deal with inane discussions in church conference meetings, which must have tried Skinner's patience. Such conversations included a discussion about whether to continue the Sunday-evening collection for the orphans' asylum, followed by a discussion about the definition of "orphan"; whether to pay for offering envelopes to be printed; whether to relax church discipline so as to allow members to miss more than three consecutive church conferences without having to give an excuse; and whether to change the appointed time to observe communion to a separate Sunday-afternoon service. There was also a request to ask the governor "not to rebuild the state privies on that part of Union Square fronting this church."[180] The presence of the state privies across the street from the church may symbolically capture the church's mood at the time better than anything else.

In the midst of the church's difficulties during that period came the death of Peter F. Pescud in 1884—one of Skinner's closest friends and, for decades, a "bedrock" of congregational leadership. Born in 1824, Pescud came to Raleigh nineteen years later and established a drugstore. He quickly united with the Baptist church and served in almost every leadership capacity possible. As noted in an earlier chapter, he was instrumental in the establishment of the church's Sunday-school program, over which he served for fifteen years as superintendent. Pescud's death was a blow to the congregation but must have been especially difficult for Skinner.[181] Paying tribute to his life and contributions, the church declared: "A full and truthful sketch of Bro.

---

[179] Ibid., 1 May 1885.

[180] See ibid., 2 February 1883, 3 April 1885, 30 December 1881, 3 March 1882, and 5 November 1880 respectively.

[181] Ibid., 12 March 1884.

Pescud would embrace the history of the Baptist Church in this city for the last forty years."[182]

Name Change. The name of the church also became a matter for discussion during Skinner's second tenure. Since its inception the Raleigh Baptist Church had little competition from other Baptist congregations in the city. However, by the time Skinner returned in 1879, the First Colored Baptist Church had been established with the church's blessing, and the Swain Street Baptist Church had become so successful that it presented competition to the mother church. With an increased number of Baptist churches in the city, some members believed the church needed to distinguish the congregation with another name. For a short period of time the church used the name "Salisbury Street Baptist Church." One member finally moved that the church officially change its name to the "Salisbury Street Baptist Church," prompting a discussion that finally ended up with the deacons.[183] The following month the deacons recommended that the name of the church be changed to "The First Raleigh Baptist Church," which the congregation approved. However, the next month, for some unknown reason, they proposed that the name be recognized as "The First Baptist Church of Raleigh, N.C."[184]

Skinner's Tenure Ends. The trend of "birthing" churches continued during Skinner's second tenure. The idea of starting another mission had been presented back during Pritchard's pastorate.[185] In May 1884 the church affirmed the efforts of John T. Pullen to collect funds and purchase a lot to "erect thereon a building for a mission station." Along with Pullen, W. W. Jones and Eugene Harold were appointed to act as a committee to raise the money and purchase the land.[186] Pullen worked in earnest toward the project, announcing later in the year that a "third Baptist church would be organized soon."[187] The project came to fruition by the end of the year when the Fayetteville Street Baptist Church was formally constituted. Thomas Skinner, C. T. Bailey, and Alvin Betts were

---

[182] Ibid.

[183] Ibid., 5 January 1883.

[184] Ibid., 2 February 1883 and 2 March 1883.

[185] See ibid., 2 April 1875, 4 August 1876, and 1 September 1876.

[186] Ibid., 2 May 1884.

[187] Ibid., 31 October 1884.

constituted as a presbytery, ordaining Thomas W. Blake and John T. Pullen as deacons.[188]

Despite the fact that 1884 ended on a high note with the birth of a new Baptist congregation in the city, the new year would bring difficulty to the members of the First Baptist Church of Raleigh and to Thomas Skinner. First, John T. Pullen reported that the Fayetteville Street Church had just recently had a revival meeting that resulted in about twenty additions to the church.[189] Things did not fare so well with the mother church's annual spring revival the following month. Skinner had invited the Irish evangelist George Needham to the church for ten days of revival services. The services were disappointing to say the least. Previous annual revivals were reported in the church minutes with glowing accounts and long lists of new members' names following. It was different with the 1885 revival. The local newspaper called the revival "fairly successful" with "many distracting influences being at work, such as sickness, the pressures of the legislature, etc."[190] The clerk's report attempted to sound positive, but it was hard to disguise the disappointment:

> Began a series of meetings by Bro. Needham which lasted about 10 days. There were no special manifestations either among the membership of the church or among the unconverted although very ____ [unable to read] attention was given by both and it is to be hoped that much good may result from the labors of Bro. Needham who gave every evidence of a true and earnest and loving Christian.[191]

Other clouds began to appear on the horizon in 1885 as well. In July the church conference discussed a $35 [$806] bill received by the treasurer for offering envelopes someone had ordered to be printed. A committee

---

[188] Ibid., 28 December 1884. See Roger H. Crook, *Our Heritage and Our Hope: A History of Pullen Memorial Baptist Church* (Raleigh NC: Pullen Memorial Baptist Church, 1985). The church eventually became Pullen Memorial Baptist Church.

[189] Church Conference Records, 30 January 1885.

[190] *The News and Observer*, 15 March 1885, http://infotrac.galegroup.com/itw/infomark/724/946/74843129w16/purl=rc1_NCNP_0_GT3005566938&dyn=147!xr n_46_0_GT3005566938&hst_1?sw_aep=acd_ncnp (accessed 7 September 2009).

[191] Church Conference Records, 1 March 1885.

was appointed to investigate the matter and determine who the member was that placed the order. After several other unrelated matters were discussed, the last line of the record states that "a leave of absence was granted the pastor indefinitely."[192] The statement suggests dissatisfaction brewing among some of the membership toward Skinner. Was he the culprit of the $35 bill? Unfortunately, there is no further information given about the matter.

Skinner was still absent on 2 October when the church discussed how much debt had accumulated on the pastor's salary. On 30 October Jordan Womble read a letter from Skinner to the church. Though the contents of the letter were not recorded, the minutes give the impression that it was critical of the church. On 4 December resignations came from W. W. Holden as deacon and J. C. Marcom as purchasing committee member. The most surprising resignation, however, came by way of the deacons who reported Skinner's intent to resign. Perhaps most telling, however, is that the church refused to accept the resignation of Holden and Marcom but voted thirty-nine to thirty-four to accept Skinner's resignation.[193]

A bizarre called meeting occurred the following week. The tension among the members is evident from reading the minutes of that meeting, there being a considerable amount of disagreement reflected about Skinner and his successor. The most acrimonious debate during the meeting had to do with the call of another pastor. A. M. Lewis moved that the church elect a pastor to succeed Skinner and that a vote be taken without a customary list of nominations. After a considerable amount of debate and discussion, along with failed substitute motions, the church took a vote on the matter and, by a 103 to 48 majority, decided to proceed with calling another pastor. Further debate ensued, after which Thomas Skinner was called again to be the pastor. A committee was selected to inform him of the decision. Clearly, Skinner still enjoyed considerable support within the church.[194]

---

[192] Ibid., 3 July 1885. Also see Day, *Gentleman of the Old School*, 92ff, for a good summary of Skinner's last year as the church's pastor.

[193] Day, *Gentleman of the Old School*, 96ff; Church Conference Records, 2 October, 30 October, and 4 December 1885.

[194] Church Conference Records, 11 December 1885.

It is impossible to know all the causes for the discord that existed among various factions of the congregation, some of which were directed toward Skinner. A clue may be gathered from another letter sent by Skinner to the church and read at that discordant church conference. The letter described a $1,000 [$23,500] pledge Skinner made on behalf of the church to the endowment fund of Wake Forest College. He admitted that he made the pledge "without the consultation of or even the knowledge of the church."[195] Nevertheless, he called the members' attention to the fact that shortly after he had made the pledge, he had told the congregation about it, and he further reminded them that after being informed of the pledge, they had unanimously approved of it.[196] Skinner complained that the church had not paid the pledge and that he had borrowed money at 8 percent interest to pay it. Because of his own financial difficulty—no doubt the result of the church's debt on his salary—he was by then unable to pay.[197]

That pledge to Wake Forest seems to be at the root of Skinner's problems in the church during 1885. Perhaps the fact that he made the pledge without first consulting the church angered some of the members. J. Daniel Day suggests that it may be an indication that he went too far with his autocratic leadership style. Day also suggests other factors that may have created an atmosphere of discontent toward Skinner, including an "inter-church rivalry" that may have grown with the success of the Swain Street Church.[198] Whatever the cause of the turmoil, Skinner accepted the call and resumed his pastoral duties in January 1886. But things were never the same again.

The next month Skinner invited Irish evangelist George Needham back to the church for another series of revival meetings, which were

---

[195] Ibid., 11 December 1886. See also Day, *Gentleman of the Old School*, 93.

[196] Church Conference Records, 4 January 1884. The record of the meeting reads: "the meeting in regard to the pastor's pledge of one thousand dollars for the church in behalf of the endowment of Wake Forest was ratified by the church."

[197] Ibid.; Day, *Gentleman of the Old School*, 93.

[198] Day, *Gentleman of the Old School*, 96ff.

much more successful than the previous year.[199] But the success of the spring revival could not resolve the problems that would lead very shortly to Skinner's final resignation. At the April church conference the church's indebtedness became evident, particularly the amount owed to Skinner. The church had a total debt of $3,946 [$92,800] and owed Skinner $955 [$22,500] in back salary stretching back to 1883. He was not present at the meeting but requested that he be given "early recreation" (a reference to vacation). That request was "laid on the table"—effectively a denial by the church. It is understandable, then, that six days later Skinner called a special meeting of the congregation and gave them his final resignation.[200]

So ended the pastorate of the longest tenure thus far in the history of the First Baptist Church of Raleigh. Skinner served the church for a grand total of nineteen years. His leadership and determination were key elements in the building of the impressive structure that even today occupies the lot on Salisbury Street across from the state capitol. Skinner never served as pastor of another church. He maintained his membership in Raleigh's First Baptist Church until his death on 2 April 1905. For the rest of his life, despite the difficulties he faced in the early 1880s, Skinner would regard the church with fondness as "my old first love."[201]

* * *

Skinner's resignation in 1886 marks the end of an era. The following year the church celebrated a seventy-fifth anniversary. A new generation of leadership would be needed to lead the church into the twentieth century. As the founders' vision continued, great challenges, as well as the promise of great potential, lay ahead of the church.

---

[199] Church Conference Records, 2 April 1886. Jordan Womble, Jr. wrote an eight-page account of the revival's success, which is included in the church records.

[200] Day, *Gentleman of the Old School*, 101. See also Church Conference Records, 2 April and 8 April 1886.

[201] Skinner, "Reminiscences," 370.

March 7th 1812

The following members were dismissed in full fellowship from the Baptist Church of Christ at Cool Spring in Wake County.

White Male Members	White F. Members
1 Hardy Sanders	1 Mary Sanders
2 Samuel Pearson	2 Nancy Card
3 Elhanon Nutt	3 Dolly Grayson
4 John Briggs	4 Elizabeth Briggs
	5 Tabitha Hutchens

Black Male Members	Black Female Members
1 Jack	1 Liddy
2 Moses	2 Hannah
3 Elisha	3 Hasty
4 Jethro	4 Judy
	5 Lisbon
5 Joseph	6 Nelly
	7 Flora
	8 Jenny
	9 Zilpha

Raleigh, March 8th 1812

The above members were examined in the State House by Elders Robert T. Daniel and Zadock Bell; and being thought orthodox were regularly constituted into a Gospel Church.

Minutes from the organizational meeting of the Raleigh Baptist Church, 7 March 1812. Notice the list of charter members. (Church Archives)

First church building built between 1814 and 1819. It was located on South Person Street across from Moore Square on a lot owned by Mrs. Mary Dudley. Sketched by Barbara Jacobs from the original located in the Raleigh City Museum. (Used by permission)

Briggs Hardware Store originally located on Fayetteville Street. The church met at this location during the "Silent Years" discussed in chapter 2.

(Used by permission from the Raleigh City Museum)

Interior of the church sanctuary ca. 1860s as it would have originally appeared before later renovations. (Church Archives)

Interior of the church sanctuary ca. 1880s. Notice the addition of the organ and early choir loft located above the pulpit. (Church Archives)

Above, the interior of the church sanctuary ca. 1890s. Notice the change to the pulpit area with steps on each side rather than at the front. Notice also the more decorative railing around the organ loft. (Church Archives)

Below, the interior of the church sanctuary ca. 1930s. Notice that the pulpit area has changed once again. The side steps are gone, replaced with steps on the front again. (Church Archives)

Exterior view of the church taken from across Edenton Street in 1948. Notice the old education building attached to the back. (From *Raleigh Times* news article located in Church Archives. Photo used by permission of the *Raleigh News and Observer*)

Exterior view of the church taken from the Capitol grounds ca. 1930s.
(Church Archives)

Thomas E. Skinner who served as pastor from 1855–1867 and 1879–1886. The present structure, completed in 1859, was built during Skinner's first tenure. His length of service to the church was longer than any other nineteenth-century pastor. (Church Archives)

Thomas H. Pritchard, pastor from 1868–1879. (Church Archives)

Jacob L. White, pastor
from 1886–1888. (Church Archives)

John W. Carter, pastor
from 1889–1899. (Church Archives)

Alexis A. Marshall, pastor
from 1900–1902. (Church Archives)

William C. Tyree, pastor
from 1902–1910. (Church Archives)

Thomas W. O'Kelley, pastor
from 1911–1927. (Church Archives)

J. Powell Tucker, pastor
from 1927–1937. (Church Archives)

Sydnor L. Stealey, pastor
from 1938–1942. (Church Archives)

Broadus E. Jones, pastor
from 1943–1959. (Church Archives)

John M. Lewis, pastor from 1960–1987. Lewis's tenure was the longest pastoral tenure in the history of First Baptist Church. (Church Archives)

W. Randall Lolley, pastor from 1988–1990. (Church Archives)

R. Wayne Stacy, pastor
from 1990–1995. (Church Archives)

J. Daniel Day, pastor
from 1996–2007. (Church Archives)

Christopher C. F. Chapman, since 2009, the current pastor of the church. (Church Archives)

Fannie E. S. Heck (1862–1915). She was a member of First Baptist Church and president of WMU national for fifteen years. In North Carolina, she was the first president of the state WMU, a position she occupied for thirty years. (Church Archives)

Above, the Honduras Mission Group, February 2011. Throughout First Baptist Church's history, it has been committed to missions on the local, state, national, and international levels. (Church Archives)

Below, members of the Japanese mission church enjoying a weekend retreat at Fort Caswell in 2010. (Church Archives)

Above, youth mission trip to Mt. Airy, North Carolina, August 2004.
The youth are constructing a Habitat for Humanity home. The youth have
participated in various mission trips focusing attention not only on Habitat
for Humanity, but also on many other types of mission projects.
(Church Archives)

Below, Clothing Ministry. This is one of First Baptist Church's most vital
ministries in downtown Raleigh, 2008. (Church Archives)

Sallie Bailey Jones (1869–1943). She was one of the first female deacons elected by the congregation. She was involved with WMU in some capacity for fifty-seven years. Following Fannie Heck's death, she served as president of North Carolina WMU for twenty years. (Church Archives)

Lucinda Briggs (1802–1896) was the first young person to be converted and baptized into the membership of the Raleigh Baptist Church. She was a member for seventy-four years. (Church Archives)

Foy J. Farmer (1887–1971) was a member of First Baptist Church and the first foreign missionary that the church helped to sponsor. Upon her return from Japan, she later served as president of the North Carolina WMU from 1942–1945 and 1946–1951. From May 1945 until March 1946, she served as the interim and corresponding executive secretary.

Charles E. Johnson House located at 120 Hillsborough Street. The house was built around 1840 and purchased by the church in 1959. It was used for Sunday School space until it was demolished in the early 1970s to make space for the Lewis Education Building.

(Photo used by permission of the *Raleigh News and Observer*)

Above, a Sunday school attendance card from 1875. (Church Archives)

Below, the Berean Sunday school class (1919) taken in front of the state capitol. Several members of the class had just returned from service in World War I when the photo was taken. (Church Archives)

A youth Sunday school attendance card from ca. 1930. (Church Archives)

Above, the Livingston Johnston Sunday school class. This photograph was taken at the annual class picnic in 1957 at the home of Dr. and Mrs. J. Clyde Turner. (Church Archives)

Below, the main entrance to the Sunday school building which was demolished in the early 1970s and replaced by the Lewis Education Building. (Church Archives)]

Above, Mrs. E. H. Hostetler helps Jane Dunn prepare for the
Sesquicentennial Celebration in 1962. (Church Archives).

Below, the church choir group photo (1960). Notice John M. Lewis (pastor)
front row, left; Harry E. Cooper (organist) center; and Donald M.
Niswonger (associate minister) front row, right. (Church Archives)

Above, Girls Auxiliary Coronation (14 May 1958). This ceremony was once common for the girls' mission organization as a way to recognize their mission learning accomplishments. (Church Archives)

Below, John Lewis and Charles Ward. Ward served as pastor of the First Baptist Church, Wilmington Street. He and Lewis developed a close friendship and their mutual admiration served as a positive witness for racial harmony during the turbulent 1960s. (Church Archives)

Intermediate Youth group at the North Carolina Baptist Assembly at Fort Caswell (1960). The youth took a trip there for many years in the spring.

(Church Archives)

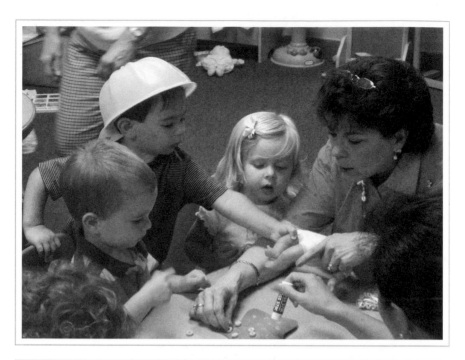

Above, vacation Bible school with the two-year-olds (2008). (Church Archives)

Below, children in the Infant Toddler Center. Founded in 1975, it remains one of the church's most important ministries. (Church Archives)

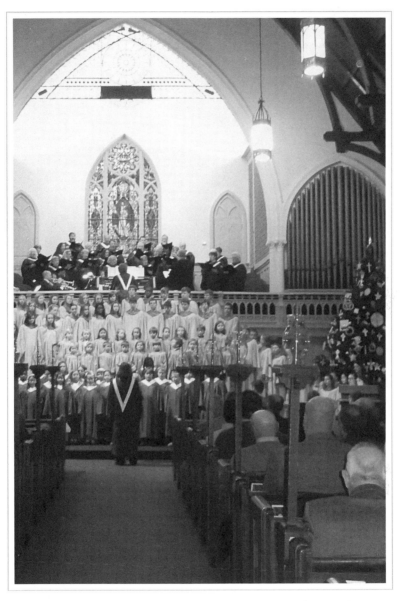

The Hanging of the Green (2010). This is an important Advent tradition at First Baptist Church. (Church Archives)

Exterior view of the church building taken from the Capitol Grounds
(2011). (Church Archives)

5

Emerging Stronger from the Turmoil (1886–1910)

At the conclusion of the Civil War many Americans began to look west for new land. Unwilling to leave their ancient lands, the Native American tribes of the Great Plains refused to vacate their homeland peacefully. For two decades, battles pitted Native American tribes—desperate to remain on their homeland—against white settlers. Yet by the 1880s the United States Calvary had successfully suppressed those tribes who refused to leave willingly, placed them on reservations, and made them submit to federal control. For those tribes the reservation system was doomed to fail since the land set aside was unfit for habitation and unable to sustain large numbers of people. Furthermore, reservation life was vastly different from the culture of the Great Plains, where many of the tribes roamed as hunter-gatherers. The destruction of the Native American culture of the Great Plains by white settlers remains one of the darkest moral failures in American history, rivaled only by the "peculiar institution" of slavery.[1]

Following suppression of the Native Americans of the Great Plains, the white settlers began to make the most of the land by mining operations. The Homestead Act of 1862 made land easy to acquire out west, and large ranches were established to provide beef to the growing cities back east. Towns were built around the economies of mining and cattle, many of which became legendary for their wild justice. Barbed wire was patented in 1874, and eventually the Great Plains were tamed as farmers began to fence in their land and crops—thereby creating the "breadbasket of America" and one of the world's leading centers of grain production.[2]

A satire written in 1873 by Mark Twain and Charles Dudley Warner gave the period from the end of the Civil War to the beginning of the

---

[1] Winthrop D. Jordan and Leon F. Litwack, *The United States*, 7th ed. (Englewood Cliffs: Prentice Hall, 1991) 419–36.

[2] Ibid., 436.

twentieth century its chief appellation, "The Gilded Age." In the novel Twain and Warner lampoon the corruption and excessive materialism that came to characterize the era.[3] *Laissez-faire* economics reigned supreme during the Gilded Age, producing names such as Cornelius Vanderbilt, John J. Astor, Andrew Carnegie, John D. Rockefeller, J. P. Morgan and Durham, and North Carolina's own James B. Duke—all captains of industry who dominated the business world. By the end of the first decade of the twentieth century, the "Robber Barons" controlled the vast majority of American industry, effectively squelching competition so that 2 percent of the population had gained control of 60 percent of America's total wealth.

During that period Charles Darwin's *Origin of the Species*, published in 1859, had far-reaching influence beyond the field of the natural sciences. Herbert Spencer, an English philosopher, proposed the idea of "social Darwinism," which transformed American culture and fueled a "gospel of progress."[4] *Laissez-faire* economics coupled with "social Darwinism" spurred the nation to become the greatest industrial society on earth by the beginning of the twentieth century. The industrial growth contributed to developments in transportation and communication. In 1869 the transcontinental railroad was completed, joining the East and West Coasts. In 1876 Alexander Graham Bell received a patent for the telephone. Soon other inventions such as the light bulb, the typewriter, and the adding machine became necessities in business. European capital began to flow into American corporations, adding to the massive wealth Americans were accumulating.

However, industrialism also brought misery to the working classes, especially in the large urban centers. The promise of the "American Dream" brought waves of new immigrants from Europe to shores of America. Without any government regulation of business or the workplace, workers were often subjected to long hours and difficult conditions in the factories, not to mention occupational safety hazards. To make matters worse, the tenement housing complexes created

---

[3]Mark Twain and Charles Dudley Warner, *The Gilded Age: A Tale of Today* (Hartford CT: American Publishing Company, 1874). See also Rebecca Brooks Gruver, *An American History*, 4th ed. (New York: Alfred A. Knopf, 1985) 564.

[4] Jordan and Litwack, *United States*, 540.

horrible living conditions where disease could spread rapidly. Confronted by those circumstances, not all social theorists accepted the status quo. Thorstein Veblen became a noted social critic, and his *Theory of the Leisure Class* (1899) was one of the most important studies of the late nineteenth century, challenging the assumptions made by the Social Darwinists. Churches also began to address the social ills of the large cities. The Social Gospel Movement, led by the German Baptist pastor Walter Rauschenbusch, sought to "Christianize" the social structures of society. Rauschenbusch believed that individual conversion through revivalism alone would not cure the nation's ills. He called for a "Christian socialism" whereby the wealth in society could be redistributed more evenly. Rauschenbusch laid out his vision in three books that soon made him a household name: *Christianity and the Social Crisis* (1907), *Christianizing the Social Order* (1912), and *A Theology for the Social Gospel* (1917). In addition, labor unions began to organize for workers' rights. For instance, the year 1869 saw the organization of the Knights of Labor. The American Federation of Labor was founded in 1886. Famous labor strikes from the period included a nationwide railroad workers' strike in 1877, the Homestead steelworkers' strike in 1892, and the Pullman railroad workers' strike in 1894. By 1900 labor and management had become willing partners at times and, at others, bitter enemies.

Corruption and conflict characterized the politics of the Gilded Age. Political campaigns (much like today) were riddled with personal attacks. Political bosses, such as the legendary "Boss Tweed" in New York City, were effective in manipulating the vote on the local level. On the national level, the Republicans dominated the presidency from 1876 to 1884 with Rutherford B. Hayes, James Garfield, and Chester A. Arthur. During those years conflict between those who advocated an expanded money supply and those who did not led to fights over the gold standard. The specific needs of farmers led to the formation of the Populist Party in the 1890s, which promoted affordable transportation, lower taxes, price controls, and cheap credit. The economic crash of 1893 served to strengthen the Populists who were successful in electing several congressmen and senators. In 1896 Populism reached its crescendo as it brought its support alongside of the Democrats in nominating William Jennings Bryan to be the Democratic candidate for president. His "Cross of Gold" speech—one of the greatest political speeches in American history—electrified the convention. Yet despite his oratorical skills, Bryan lost the election, marking the gradual decline of the Populists. Nevertheless, they were successful in achieving some reforms such as direct election of senators, the income tax, and an improved money and credit system.[5]

In addition to industry and finance, modernization left its mark on higher education and scholarship, introducing new methods and sparking heated debates. For example, as Darwin's work became more widely known, biblical scholars began to challenge traditional assumptions about the Bible, eventually leading to the intense theological battles between Liberals and Fundamentalists in the early twentieth century. Other academic disciplines such as law, philosophy, education, and history all experienced renewed interest and progress, and universities began offering graduate degrees to accommodate them.

Also during the 1890s, as Americans expanded westward and dominated the continent, they began to compete with European nations for territories in other parts of the world. The territory of Alaska was purchased from Russia in 1867, and Hawaii became an American territory in 1898. America also showed interest in the Caribbean, Central and South America, the South Pacific, the Philippines, and China. Following the Spanish-American War in 1898, America emerged as a world power (a new status that would eventually be tested in the second decade of the twentieth century as World War I broke out).

Like the rest of the nation, Raleigh experienced a transformation in the last quarter of the nineteenth century as the "sleepy state capital surrounded by remote farming communities in the 1870s was by 1900 transformed into a center of industry, higher learning, consumerism, and social activism."[6] The nationwide financial Panic of 1873 created a depression for a period of time, which kept the Civil War generation in a struggle to survive. Nevertheless, a new generation began to see the

---

[5] Ibid., 493–94.

[6] K. Todd Johnson and Elizabeth Reid Murray, *Wake: Capital County of North Carolina*, vol. 2 (Raleigh: Wake County, 2008) ix.

world differently in Raleigh. They began to see that, through industry, the city of Raleigh as well as the entire South could be changed. The key to the city's industrial growth was the railroad. The railroad provided new markets for farmers and new products to help reinvigorate their lands. The commercial success of the railroads also brought advantages to merchants and bankers as they found their places in the new economy. Finally, railroads brought new people to the city, which added diversity to the population. It became clear by the end of the century that Raleigh residents "were gradually abandoning an isolated agrarian way of life in favor of one that was increasingly industrial and urban."[7]

Such change was not without difficulty. The Gilded Age and the Progressive Era in Raleigh, along with economic successes, also brought sociological division. With the end of Reconstruction, racial tensions began to grow in the capital city. In September 1898, a race riot erupted in the city between some white soldiers stationed in Raleigh and some of the African-American population in the eastern portion of the city. Two skirmishes took place over a Saturday night and Sunday afternoon, resulting in a tense atmosphere but no significant injuries. By the beginning of the twentieth century the joy of the freed slaves had turned into the misery of a segregated city.[8]

Significant changes occurred in the Baptist world—particularly the Southern Baptist world—following the Civil War. Interest in foreign missions continued to increase. The era saw the birth of the Woman's Missionary Union, an auxiliary of the Southern Baptist Convention, whose promotion of foreign missions within the churches brought astonishing success. During the period from 1893 to 1914, giving to foreign missions among Southern Baptists increased from $110,000 [$2.71

---

[7] Ibid.

[8] Ibid., 18–20. See *Farmer and Mechanic*, 3 January 1878, as cited by ibid., 32. Governor Zebulon B. Vance, speaking to an Emancipation Day celebration on New Year's Day 1878, expressed the white sentiment: "You cannot, of course, expect me to join with you in celebrating this day, the anniversary of that emancipation which I struggled so long to prevent, and which I, in common with almost all the people of my race in the South, regarded as an act of unconstitutional violence to the one party and as an injury to the other." See pp. 32–46 for a discussion of race relations in Raleigh and Wake County during that era.

million] to $600,000 [$13.3 million], and the number of missionaries in foreign countries grew from ninety-two to 298.[9] Landmarkism was so pervasive in the Southern Baptist Convention that William Heth Whitsitt had to resign his position as president of the Southern Baptist Theological Seminary after he claimed that, based on historical research, Baptists did not baptize by immersion until the year 1641.[10] Whitsitt's claim was particularly unpopular west of the Mississippi River in Texas and was countered by Landmarkist Benajah Harvey Carroll, pastor of the First Baptist Church of Waco, who eventually founded Southwestern Baptist Theological Seminary as a "safe" place for ministerial students in the South to study.[11]

The First Baptist Church of Raleigh 1886–1910

Jacob Lee White (1886–1888)

Following Thomas Skinner's resignation as pastor in April 1886, the church wasted no time securing the services of a new pastor. At the church conference the following month Thomas H. Briggs moved that a committee of eighteen be appointed for the task of selecting a new pastor (seemingly an interim pastor) for the summer months and that the same committee should have the responsibility of finding a permanent pastor. An amendment to the motion suggested that the church extend a call to the Reverend J. L. White of Wake Forest College to serve for three months beginning 13 June. The amendment passed and a committee comprised of Jordan Womble, Thomas H. Briggs, and W. H. Pace was

---

[9] Robert A. Baker, *The Southern Baptist Convention and Its People* (Nashville: Broadman Press, 1974) 288.

[10] James H. Slatton, *W. H. Whitsitt: The Man and the Controversy* (Macon GA: Mercer University Press, 2009). This is an outstanding new book that chronicles Whitsitt's life and provides a detailed account of the controversy. Slatton utilized Whitsitt's personal journals and letters to tell the story.

[11] Alan J. Lefever, *Fighting the Good Fight: The Life and Work of Benajah Harvey Carroll* (Austin TX: Eakin Press, 1994); Robert A. Baker, *Tell the Generations Following: A History of Southwestern Baptist Theological Seminary, 1908–1983* (Nashville: Broadman Press, 1983).

selected to confer with White. The following month the church records report that White agreed to serve the church for the summer.[12]

White's preaching and pastoral skills impressed the congregation, because in August the "pastoral committee" recommended extending a call for a period of one year. White received seventy-six of seventy-seven votes when the recommendation came before the church for a vote. His one-year call was to begin in October following three weeks of vacation, provided that he could secure release from several previously scheduled preaching engagements in Northampton County. A letter from First Baptist to the Jackson and Sandy Run Baptist Churches requesting that they release White from his preaching obligations to them produced the desired results.[13] The *Biblical Recorder* contained the following brief entry on 22 September 1886: "Rev. J. L. White, who has been holding in abeyance the call to the pastorate of the First Baptist church, has at last signified his acceptance. He will enter upon his duties as pastor on his return from his vacation."[14]

At only twenty-four years of age, White was young and lacking in pastoral experience when he assumed the pastorate of Raleigh's First Baptist Church—a clear contrast with the long years of experience possessed by the church's previous two pastors. Although he was the valedictorian of his graduating class at Wake Forest College the previous spring, he had been ordained to the ministry only two years prior by the First Baptist Church of Shelby, North Carolina. Adding to the excitement of the young minister's exhilarating summer, White married Dovie Poston of Shelby on 22 September 1886. In fact, the "vacation" alluded to in the church minutes on 18 August 1886 must have been for White to travel to Shelby for his wedding. The *Biblical Recorder* commented on their arrival in Raleigh two weeks after their wedding: "Rev. J. L. White and wife arrived in Raleigh from their Western trip on Friday last. They received a joyous welcome to their new home, which, with the pastor's study had been splendidly fitted up by the good sisters of the First

---

[12] Church Conference Records, 19 May and 4 June 1886. White's salary for the three months was to be $75 [$1,760] per month.

[13] Ibid., 18 August, 26 August, and 1 October 1886.

[14] *Biblical Recorder* (Raleigh NC), 22 September 1886, 2.

church. Bro. White preached to a large and interested audiences [*sic*] on Sunday."[15]

Though his tenure in Raleigh was brief, J. L. White had a noteworthy career among Southern Baptists. From Raleigh he went on to serve as pastor of the First Baptist Churches of Elizabeth City, Durham, and Asheville. His longest tenures however, were outside of North Carolina at the First Baptist Churches of Macon, Georgia (1895–1907), and Miami, Florida (1916–1936). He also served as pastor of other churches in North Carolina, Texas, Tennessee, Georgia, and Florida.[16] White would also receive honorary doctoral degrees from Wake Forest College, Mercer University, and Stetson University. Through his long career he served in a variety of denominational positions, including president of the Florida Baptist Convention and vice-president of the Southern Baptist Convention. For much of his career he also served as a trustee for both the Home and Foreign Mission Boards. Known as a powerful pulpiteer, perhaps the most memorable moment in his career came on 21 May 1933 in Washington, D. C., when he preached the annual sermon for the Southern Baptist Convention. That day, he occupied the platform with four of his sons, themselves all ministers, who also participated with him in leading worship for the gathered messengers.[17] He died in Madison, Florida, on 25 November 1948. His obituary appearing in the *Florida Baptist Witness* declared that "Dr. White was a great gospel preacher. He believed and preached the Bible. Soul-winning was the passion of his life."[18] The membership of First Baptist Church of Raleigh can take pride that their congregation served as the launching pad for the ministerial career of that fine Southern Baptist minister.

---

[15] Ibid., 6 October 1886, 2.

[16] For biographical material about Jacob Lee White, see Charles W. Deweese, *The Power of Freedom: First Baptist Church, Asheville, North Carolina, 1829–1997* (Franklin TN: Providence House Publishers, 1997) 92–94; H. Lewis Batts and Rollin S. Armour, *History of the First Baptist Church of Christ at Macon* (Macon: First Baptist Church, 1991) 105–106; and Martha White Kunkel, "White, (J. L.) Jacob Lee," in *Encyclopedia of Southern Baptists,* vol. 3, ed. Davis Collier Woolley, vol. 3 suppl. (Nashville: Broadman Press, 1971) 2048–49.

[17] Deweese, *Power of Freedom*, 93.

[18] Quoted in ibid., 94.

Several important developments occurred within the congregation during White's pastorate. The saga of the bell finally reached a resolution. It will be recalled from the previous chapter that the church purchased a new bell in 1884, and just before Skinner's resignation the church had determined to correspond with the bell company about the "grating sound" the bell was making.[19] Two months later the company agreed to provide the church a new bell if the church paid the freight charges for delivery. A short entry in the church minutes in October indicated that the church expected the new bell to arrive any day. That was the last reference to the matter until 1893 when the Ladies Memorial Society requested that the church ring the bell on 10 May for the Confederate memorial observance and again on 30 May while Jefferson Davis's remains lay in the state capitol.[20]

Financial problems encountered during Skinner's second term as pastor continued to be a major concern during White's tenure. In July 1886 the church reported that it still owed more than $200 [$4,700] to Skinner for his salary the previous year, and a further debt of $250 [$5,880] to the bank for financing part of his salary. In addition, the church appointed a committee to collect pledges to raise $1,800 [$42,300] to pay incidental expenses that were not being covered by Sunday offerings.[21] The matter surfaced again the following year and resulted in a joint meeting between the deacons and the finance committee. The committee made several changes to the church's finance plan and recommended that the church discipline for covetousness any member

---

[19] Church Conference Records, 2 April 1886.

[20] Ibid., 4 June, 30 July, and 1 October 1886. See ibid., 5 May 1893. See also "Death and Burial," http://cohesion.rice.edu/humanities/pjdavis/Chron.cfm?doc_id=1468 (accessed 6 January 2010). Jefferson Davis died on 6 December 1889 in New Orleans, and he was temporarily buried there. However, in 1893 the decision was made to move his remains to Richmond for final burial. The train carrying his remains left New Orleans on 28 May 1893. The train stopped in Birmingham, Atlanta, and Raleigh, where the body lay in state before reaching its final destination and burial on 31 May 1893.

[21] Church Conference Records, 2 July 1886.

who failed to contribute to the church's financial needs.[22] The following month the church passed a strong resolution about its debt:

> Whereas we are taught by experience that a church in debt is greatly crippled in spiritual power, and to remain in debt, we believe, is contrary to the tenor of the scriptures, Resolved, that we will at once make an effort to relieve our church from this burden and to that end each member of this church is requested to give something for this special object and will also increase our regular contributions for current expenses.
>
> Resolved further, that we believe the Bible requires us to be just before we are generous therefore no collection shall be made in this church, until otherwise ordered, for any purpose whatever except it be for our current expenses, to redeem convention pledges already made or to liquidate this floating debt.
>
> Resolved further that our brethren and sisters are requested to make no further contributions to outside matters until our church is again enjoying the honorable and spiritual condition of freedom from debt.
>
> Resolved further that the treas. be requested to assume no obligations for gas, fuel or any other purpose except so far as he has funds on hand to meet said obligations at once. Resolved further that while our bills for lights remain unpaid the regular Sunday evening exercises shall be held at 5 oclock until further notice.[23]

The church postponed the resolution for several months, and eventually its author withdrew it, but it provides an example of how serious the church believed its financial problems were. In fact, the cash flow problem was so acute the church could not afford to purchase new hymnals![24] In November 1887 J. H. Holding made a motion, which was approved, to create a special "purchasing committee" comprised of one deacon, one trustee, one member of the finance committee, and one church member at large. The church gave the purchasing committee the responsibility of approving all expenditures. The church instructed the

---

[22] Ibid., 4 March 1887. Skinner's salary was finally reported to be paid in full at the church conference on 4 November 1887.

[23] Ibid., 29 April 1887.

[24] Ibid., 3 June 1887.

treasurer not to pay any bills that were not first approved by the committee, and the minutes include a specific statement that no individual member could incur debt on behalf of the church without first obtaining approval of the committee as well. The organization of that committee proved to be a wise move and for the coming years helped the congregation get better control of its financial affairs.[25]

Also during White's tenure, two of its most prominent members at the time—former Governor and Mrs. W. W. Holden—withdrew their fellowship. As mentioned in chapter 4, Governor Holden had been a member of the church since 1871 and had served in just about every leadership capacity possible. But in summer 1886 he gave notice at a church conference that he and his wife intended to join another church "that allowed open communion."[26] Having been raised in the Methodist tradition and even attending the Episcopal church for a period before he became Baptist, Holden must have been more open-minded than many of his fellow Baptists. He and Mrs. Holden followed through with their plans, as the church minutes record that fellowship was withdrawn from the couple for joining a "church of [a] different order."[27]

Another development during White's pastorate involved a variety of improvements to the church property, some of which represent the beginnings of modernization. In 1887 the church began to explore the cost of replacing the water cistern with city water and running pipes into the church building to carry the water. The members even voted to have pipes placed in the baptistery for the purpose of warming the water for baptisms.[28] The church also modernized its lighting with electricity, deemed to be less expensive than the gas lighting.[29] Larger pew racks

---

[25] Ibid., 4 November 1887.

[26] Ibid., 30 July 1886.

[27] Ibid., 3 September 1886. See J. Daniel Day, *A Gentleman of the Old School: Thomas E. Skinner, Baptist Pastor, 1825–1905* (Holly Springs NC: Tarheelokie Products, 2010) 86. Day suggests that Holden was a "Skinner man," indicating that he initiated many "pastor-friendly" actions toward Skinner on behalf of the church. Consequently, Holden's parting might be partially attributed to dissatisfaction with Skinner's departure as pastor.

[28] Church Conference Records, 30 September and 30 December 1887.

[29] Ibid., 2 September 1887.

were installed in the pews in order to hold the new hymnals that were purchased, and the parsonage received some sorely needed repairs.[30]

The most important event to characterize White's ministry at the church was a "union" revival that occurred in fall 1887. Involving the Protestant denominations of the city, Reverend R. B. Pearson, a Cumberland Presbyterian evangelist, was invited to preach. Pearson had just recently completed a successful revival in Charlotte, and the Raleigh churches were anxious to experience the same. The initial plan was for Pearson to preach for one week in each of the participating churches. First Baptist Church was assigned the first week and, for some unknown reason, the evangelist decided against moving to other churches. Consequently, the revival lasted for four weeks with all the services at the First Baptist Church. All reports indicate that the revival was a great success as "immense crowds thronged to hear the man of God from the 1st night." The "meetings began with great interest and continued to increase in interest and power until they closed." A total of 500 professions of faith were recorded at the end of the revival, causing the Baptists to proclaim, "Never in the history of Raleigh has there been such a religious awakening so say the oldest citizens."[31]

The success of the revival and recent modernization of the building notwithstanding, White offered his resignation in March 1888—less than two years after becoming the pastor. The announcement was a surprise, especially since the church had just increased his salary to $1,800 [$41,900] per year the previous month! His resignation was to be effective the second Sunday in March (the week following that meeting of the church conference). White's letter of resignation was copied into the church minutes by the clerk. While the church bylaws called for a resigning pastor to provide at least three months' notice before the resignation was effective, White suggested that the rule did not apply to his situation since he "was not called according to the first clause of the same article." Article III, paragraph 2 of the church bylaws, in effect during his tenure, stated that the "election of a Pastor shall be

---

[30] Ibid., 30 December 1887. The cost of the repairs to the parsonage was $148.72 [$3,460].

[31] Ibid. Of those making professions of faith, a total of eighty-eight were affiliated with the First Baptist Church for baptism and church membership.

understood to be for life."[32] In his resignation, White pointed out that he did not owe the church three months' notice because the church had violated its own bylaws by making his original call a one-year appointment only.

Why the church disregarded its bylaws at the time of White's call is not clear. It could be related to White's youthful age at the time he was called or to his relative lack of experience. Perhaps the church wanted to make sure he had the necessary skills to serve the congregation as pastor, given the church's status and size at the time. Regardless of the reason, it is clear that White never liked the arrangement. A postscript to his resignation letter was read to the membership, which contains a hint of bitterness:

> I thought when I sent my resignation to the deacons that it was best to give no reasons, but the great majority of the members desire to know them, so I give them and give them now. I have never been satisfied with the annual call. This is the first reason. The second, I am not content to labor for a reduced salary. These are the two considerations that made me resign. I don't think the church has done or is doing its duty to make such calls. So, I pray that you may remain united and change these conditions in calling my successor.[33]

His reference to the "reduced salary" as his second reason likely related to his predecessors (Pritchard and Skinner), both of whom had received at least $2,000 per year for their services while White's salary for the year 1888 was only $1,400.[34] In the church's defense it should be remembered that both Pritchard and Skinner had considerably more experience and seasoning as pastors than did White. Also, when White was called to be pastor, the congregation still owed several hundred

---

[32] "Principles of Government," in *Manual of the First Baptist Church of Raleigh, N.C.* (Raleigh NC: John Nichols and Co., 1874) 15.

[33] Church Conference Records, 2 March 1888.

[34] White's salary is listed in the church's annual letter to the Central Baptist Association for 1888, contained in the Church Conference Records, 3 August 1888. There is a contradiction in the minutes as to the salary amount. The associational letter says the salary was $1,400 [$32,600]. The month before White's resignation the church records indicate that his salary was being raised from $1,500 [$34,900] to $1,800 [$41,900].

dollars on Skinner's salary from the previous year. In fact, for years previous to White, the records continually show the church struggling to pay the salaries of Skinner and Pritchard. So it is no wonder that when the church decided to call the youthful and inexperienced White, the call would be on a trial basis and the salary lower than what had been paid to more experienced pastors.

J. W. Carter (1889–1899)

Following the reading of White's letter, the church regrettably accepted his resignation and proceeded immediately to appoint a search committee of twenty-five members to find a new pastor. It is interesting to note that the church asked Thomas Skinner to serve on the search committee.[35] The church's annual letter to the Central Baptist Association always listed him among the ordained members in the congregation, and his name appears in the church minutes on occasion, evidencing his continued involvement.

The first name put before the congregation for consideration as pastor was Dr. Charlton Hines Strickland, who was at that time serving as pastor of the First Baptist Church in Nashville, Tennessee. Thomas Skinner (who, as previously mentioned, had served as pastor of First Baptist Church in Nashville before returning to Raleigh) vouched for his character, and the church voted to contact him to inquire of his interest and to offer him a salary of $3,000 [$69,800] per year plus the parsonage. The following month the committee reported that Strickland had declined the invitation.[36] The second name suggested by the committee was J. M. Frost of Selma, Alabama. The church again approved of the candidate and instructed the committee to contact him. Unfortunately, Frost also rejected the invitation.[37] Shortly thereafter, Frost became pastor of the Leigh Street Baptist Church of Richmond, Virginia, and ultimately

---

[35] Church Conference Records, 2 March 1888.

[36] Ibid., 8 May and 1 June 1888. It is interesting that the salary offer was for $3,000, a higher salary than any pastor of the church had previously been paid. And the offer was higher than the salary J. W. Carter, the ultimate choice for pastor, would ever make.

[37] Ibid., 5 October 1888. It is worth noting that the church offered Frost a salary of $2,000 [$46,500] per year rather than the $3,000 offered to Strickland.

led the movement to establish the Sunday School Board of the Southern Baptist Convention in 1891.[38]

Following Frost's rejection of the church's offer, the committee finally turned toward Dr. J. W. Carter of Parkersburg, West Virginia. The church approved his candidacy and made an offer of $2,000 [$46,500] per year salary with the parsonage. Carter accepted the offer and assumed his duties as pastor the first Sunday in January 1889.[39]

John William Carter was born in Nelson County, Virginia, on 31 December 1836, the oldest of eleven children.[40] When he was very young his parents moved to Sago, West Virginia. In 1858 Carter made a profession of his faith and was baptized into the local Baptist congregation. Within two months the Sago Baptist Church licensed him to the ministry. His opportunity for schooling was infrequent in his early years; he was tutored by various itinerant teachers who traveled to and from his town. Carter experienced only two opportunities for formal education. The first came during a period of time when he lived and studied in Preston County, West Virginia, in the home of Reverend J. M. Purinton. (Education by such means was not unusual in the antebellum

---

[38] See H. Leon McBeth, *The Baptist Heritage: Four Centuries of Baptist Witness* (Nashville: Broadman Press, 1987) 432–40. Frost first proposed the idea at the meeting of the Southern Baptist Convention in 1890, but it raised so much opposition that the convention chose to appoint a Sunday-school committee to study the idea for a year. The following year the convention selected Frost, who favored a Sunday-school board, and J. B. Gambrell, who opposed the idea to be a committee of two and instructed them to work out a solution to the controversy created by the proposal. While the convention was in session, the two men met in a hotel room for several hours and worked out a compromise. Gambrell promised to support a Sunday-school board if Frost would let him write the last paragraph of the resolution. Frost agreed, provided that Gambrell allow him to write the last sentence of the last paragraph! With that compromise, forged by two great Baptist statesmen, the Sunday School Board of the Southern Baptist Convention was born.

[39] Church Conference Records, 30 November 1888.

[40] For a brief biographical sketch of Carter, see Truett Rogers, *West Virginia Baptist History: The Early Years: 1770–1865* (Terra Alta WV: Headline Books, 1990) 158–60; and *The Baptist Encyclopedia*, vol. 1, ed. William Cathcart (Philadelphia: Louis H. Everts, 1881) s.v. "Carter, Rev. John W." The two sources disagree as to Carter's county of birth. Rogers indicates Carter was born in Nelson County, while the entry for *The Baptist Encyclopedia* says it was in Albemarle County.

years for young men preparing for ministry.) The second came during a brief period of study at the shortlived Alleghany College.

The Sago Baptist Church ordained Carter on 13 April 1860. Recalling the solemn event, the Sago church minutes record: "The brethren and many of the sisters came forward and with warm hearts and melting tears extended the hand and invoked the blessing of God to rest on him. It was truly a time of great rejoicing to see one so young and so promising entering the field of the Gospel ministry. May he live long to preach the Word."[41] Carter served the Sago church and several other small congregations for the next four years until 1864, when he received a call to the Parkersburg Baptist Church. His ministry in Parkersburg lasted for twenty-five years until he accepted the call to First Baptist Church of Raleigh. Upon his resignation from the Raleigh church in 1899, Carter returned to West Virginia where he lived the remainder of his life. He died in October 1907.

Woman's Missionary Society. One of the most important developments in the life of the Raleigh congregation during Carter's ministry was the growth of the church's mission organizations. The church's women throughout the nineteenth century had been integral to the life of the congregation. It was noted in the previous chapter that in 1867 the church appointed two women deaconesses and gave them a particular ministry to perform. Then in 1874 four women were appointed to be deaconesses.[42] As previously noted, as early as 1876 there is evidence that the women of the church were involved in several ventures, such as a "Missionary Society," a "Sewing Society," and a "Mite Society," all of which were benevolent efforts on their part.[43] In 1883 the women of the church brought those three societies under the aegis of a new organization with a constitution and called it the "Working Women's Society." The purpose of the new organization was "to raise funds for state missions, foreign missions, the poor of the church or any special

---

[41] Quoted in Rogers, *West Virginia Baptist History*, 159.
[42] Church Conference Records, 4 September 1874.
[43] Ibid., 27 July 1876.

work the Society may decide upon."[44] Ann Skinner, Thomas Skinner's wife, served as the first president of the group.

Although it would be decades before the 19th Amendment to the Constitution was ratified (giving women full rights in American society), the last half of the nineteenth century saw women beginning to assert themselves within the male-dominated world. One of the most natural places for that to happen was in the life of the local church. The records reveal an active organization of devoted women aggressively dedicated to mission education and caring for the poor of the city. Their confidence and sense of importance are reflected in the society's minutes in early January 1884. Mrs. James Briggs, chair of the group's Committee on the Poor, gave a report that on the evening of the Sunday school's Christmas festivities, the women collected $28 [$619], which had been turned over to the deacons to be distributed to the poor. The record then reports: "The deacons, either wanting to get free from this work or else acknowledging the superior judgment and ability of the ladies to expend this money properly, turned the amount over to the ladies of our society to have the whole matter entirely in our hands." The entry continues that Mrs. Dodd and Mrs. James Briggs were selected to carry out the task and "it is sufficient to say that the work was well done and thanks come up from every direction for the relief and comforts given to those in need during Christmas week."[45]

In 1886 the Working Women's Society was restructured into a new organization called the "Woman's Missionary Society." According to the constitution, the purpose of the society was to "raise funds for the poor of the church and for missions." The money raised was to be divided into thirds, with one-third devoted to the poor, one-third devoted to foreign missions, and one-third divided equally between home and state missions. Membership in the society required a 10-cent-per-month contribution. The first officers elected were: Mrs. R. G. Lewis (president), Mrs. J. M. Heck (vice-president), Mrs. T. H. Briggs (2nd vice-president), Mrs. M. J. Norris (secretary), and Mrs. M. C. Williams (treasurer).[46]

---

[44] "Constitution of the Working Women's Society," located in the Minutes of the Woman's Missionary Society, 1883–1886. No date is given on the constitution.

[45] Minutes of the Woman's Missionary Society, 7 January 1884.

[46] Ibid., 1 November 1886.

Such were the beginnings of the organization that later became identified as the Woman's Missionary Union and was an integral aspect of the overall ministry of the First Baptist Church of Raleigh. The minutes of the Woman's Missionary Society provide a monthly chronicle of individuals in the church who were in need and the specific aid given to them. In addition to having a different tone than the minutes of the church conferences, the minutes of the Woman's Missionary Society reveal that the women who served were compassionate and highly dedicated to caring for the poor of the church and the city and promoting the cause of Baptist missions both at home and abroad. For example, for 2 May 1887 the minutes provide a detailed report of several poor families and individuals who received help from the Woman's Missionary Society. One member suggested that the society ask the physicians who were members of the church if they would be willing to divide those families among themselves and visit them "gratuitously" whenever there was sickness in the family. The following month it was reported that the physicians had "cheerfully agreed" to visit the poor when they were sick.[47]

In January 1888 the society reported that at Christmas the previous month, "Through the kindness of Mr. Royster we were able to carry apples and candy to all these homes and it was wonderful to see the pleasure and delight given by this most unexpected treat."[48] The Royster family had long been associated with First Baptist Church. The proprietor mentioned was probably V. C. Royster, younger brother of A. D. Royster and a member of the congregation. Following the Civil War A. D. Royster opened a general store on Fayetteville Street. Reports are that soon after opening his store, A. D. Royster began to make fruit-buying trips to Norfolk, whereupon he would load his goods on a flat railroad car and rode back to Raleigh on the flatcar, wearing a poncho and holding a gun to keep thieves away from his produce. A. D. Royster eventually decided to send his younger brother to New York where he learned the candymaking business. He convinced Jim Leonard, a master candymaker, to come to Raleigh and teach the craft to several locals.

---

[47] Ibid., 2 May 1887 and 6 June 1887.
[48] Ibid., 2 January 1888.

Beginning around 1873 Royster's store became famous for its candy. Although illness forced A. D. to leave the business in 1878, his younger brother V. C. kept it going. By 1883 the Royster store was employing thirty to forty men to make the candy in a small factory in the back of the business while several female employees sold to the public in the front of the store. A third brother, O.M., became a salesman for the company, peddling the goods throughout North and South Carolina.[49]

As expected, two of the most prominent names among the records of the Woman's Missionary Society are Miss Fannie Heck and Mrs. W. N. Jones (Sallie Bailey Jones). Both women's names appear in almost every entry during the last decade of the nineteenth century and the first decade of the twentieth. Their work on behalf of the poor of the city is evident but also revealed is their involvement in mission education. In June 1892 the society honored Fannie Heck with a reception celebrating her election as president of the Woman's Missionary Union of the Southern Baptist Convention. Also honored that day was Mrs. James Briggs, who had been elected as vice-president of the North Carolina Woman's Missionary Union.[50] Other important women in the early years of the society's leadership include Mrs. W. W. Vass, Mrs. J. W. Carter (the wife of the pastor), and Virginia Swepson, who upon her death in 1901 (as previously mentioned in chapter 4) had willed $1,000 [$26,000] to the society.

The society's influence extended to the children of the church as well. In 1889 the Young Ladies Auxiliary to the Woman's Missionary

---

[49] Johnson and Murray, *Wake: Capital County of North Carolina*, vol. 2, 187. The business lasted well into the twentieth century. The Royster family must have been an interesting bunch. The Royster boys were three of eight children born to James D. Royster and his wife, Mary Ashley. A fourth son, named Iowa Michigan, was wounded at the Battle of Gettysburg in 1863 and died ten days later. According to family lore, James grew tired of traditional names so he decided to name his children after states. The children's names were: "Indiana Georgia," "Vermont Connecticut," "Virginia Carolina," "Iowa Michigan," Oregon Minnesota," "Arkansas Delaware," "Wisconsin Illinois," and "Louisiana Maryland." For further biographical information, see "Royster Family Papers, 1840–1979," http://www.lib.unc.edu/mss/inv/r/Royster_Family.html#d1e884 (accessed 6 February 2010).

[50] Minutes of the Woman's Missionary Society, 6 June 1892.

Society was constituted and, through the efforts of Fannie Heck and some of the other leaders of the Woman's Missionary Society, the new organization became quite successful. Foy Johnson Willingham, one of the Young Ladies Missionary Society members, eventually became a foreign missionary to Japan.[51] The children were also incorporated into the overall mission education program of the church in 1886 when Mrs. James A. Briggs organized the Mission Workers. Originally, the group met in the home of Briggs, but when Carter became pastor of the church the name changed to the "Sunbeam Band" and the meetings moved to the church. Maggie Parrie and Sallie Bailey aided Briggs with the group. The organization changed its name again to the "Yates Mission Band" in 1895, but several years latter reverted to the "Sunbeam Band."[52]

Mission Churches. While the women cared for the city's poor and promoted state, home, and foreign missions, the entire church continued the spirit of "birthing" new congregations in the city. The previous chapter described the birth of both the Tabernacle and Fayetteville Street Baptist Churches. The desire to establish mission congregations continued to flourish after Skinner had stepped down as pastor. In May 1889 the church approved a committee to begin gathering subscriptions for the purchase of a lot "near the agricultural college and to erect a building suitable for mission work in that vicinity."[53] Several months later the committee reported that it had found a lot on the south side of Hillsboro Street for the price of $200 [$4,810]. During the next two years the congregation worked to raise the funds necessary for the purchase of the land and the construction of the building. Final approval to begin construction came in August 1890. By early spring 1892 the work on the "West End Mission" was complete.[54] Within two months the West End Mission had a thriving Sunday school with an average attendance of 100 and a mid-week worship service on Thursday evenings.[55] In fall 1894 the

---

[51] L. J. Morris, "The History of the First Baptist Church of Raleigh, 1812–1912" (master's thesis, Wake Forest College, 1937) 97.

[52] Ibid., 98.

[53] Church Conference Records, 3 May 1889.

[54] Ibid., 5 February 1892.

[55] Ibid., 1 April 1892.

West End Mission was constituted into a church and named the West Raleigh Baptist Church, signifying the success of the mission endeavor.[56]

The success of the West End Mission can be attributed partially to a cooperative effort between the First Baptist Church, the Tabernacle Baptist Church, and the Fayetteville Street Baptist Church. Just after discussion began within the membership of First Baptist, Reverend Columbus Durham, a member of the congregation and corresponding secretary of the Baptist State Convention at the time, made a suggestion that each of the three churches appoint several members to serve on a committee to oversee the mission work in the western part of the city. The proposal suggested that First Baptist Church provide nine members to the committee and the Tabernacle and Fayetteville Street churches supply seven and three members, respectively.[57] That arrangement proved to be a helpful way to oversee the work and served as the genesis of an arrangement between the three churches, which ultimately resulted in the hiring of a city missionary for the purpose of organizing and ministering to mission congregations within the city.

Following the success of the West End Mission, by 1895 the church began to discuss a new mission venture in the Pilot Mills section of the city.[58] A. D. Hunter, the city missionary employed by the cooperative efforts of First Baptist Church, Tabernacle Baptist Church, and Fayetteville Street Baptist Church, organized the effort. That work also proved to be highly successful. Three years after a small building was erected, the mission was constituted into a church with twenty-seven members.[59]

The city missionary provided regular reports to the members of First Baptist Church throughout the 1890s. Those reports are detailed and provide a good window into the decade of the 1890s and the organized efforts of the three Raleigh Baptist churches to reach out to areas of the fast-growing city that had no significant Baptist witness. For example, the city missionary's report for the first quarter of 1898 indicates that he preached forty sermons, conducted forty-eight prayer meetings, made

---

[56] Ibid., 31 August 1894.
[57] Ibid., 30 August 1889.
[58] Ibid., 1 February 1895.
[59] Ibid., 29 April 1898.

397 visits, and organized one new church (the Pilot Mills church). His report also provided a list of the mission churches he was serving at that time.[60]

There is evidence that the church, through the city missionary, became involved in one other mission congregation during the Carter pastorate. The work began sometime in 1898 and was located in the Caraleigh Mills area of the city. The Caraleigh Cotton Mill opened in 1892 and was one of the earliest textile mills in the city. Its presence, like that of the Pilot Mill that opened in 1893, created a burgeoning community that became fertile ground for local Baptist missions.[61]

L. J. Morris argued that during the years following the Civil War, "the missionary spirit had born fruit as never before known in the Raleigh Church." A total of five mission congregations had been established from the "Mother Church" by the century's end.[62] Perhaps more important than the number of congregations produced by First Baptist Church is the fact that the postbellum years produced within the congregation a passion for missions that grew during the twentieth century and continues to be sustained in the present.

Loss of Prominent Members. During the 1890s the church lost several of its most prominent members to death. On 15 February 1896 Sarah Williams (wife of Alfred) died. Upon her death, the church passed a resolution honoring her decades-long devotion to the congregation and recalling that, upon the church's reorganization in the 1830s, she identified with the congregation, incurring the wrath of her family. The resolution also noted that Sarah prayed faithfully "during long years for the conversion of her companion and after patient waiting received the desired answer."[63] She was also an important early contributor and active participant in the Woman's Missionary Society.

Within about six weeks the church lost another long-time "pillar" of the church, Miss Lucinda Briggs, who died on 29 March 1896. She was ninety-four at the time of her death. As discussed in chapter 2, Lucinda was the first young person to be converted and baptized into the Raleigh

---

[60] Ibid., 31 March 1898.

[61] Johnson and Murray, *Wake: Capital County of North Carolina*, vol. 2, 201.

[62] Morris, "The History of the First Baptist Church of Raleigh," 100.

[63] Church Conference Records, 15 February 1896.

Baptist Church and had been a member for seventy-four years.[64] She was also the daughter of arguably the most important member of the church during its first half-century, John Briggs. She was one of the church's first Sunday-school teachers and, like her father and other family members, actively involved in every aspect of the church's life.

Two prominent members, William Worrell Vass, Sr. and his wife Lillie, died on 1 September 1895 and 6 December 1896, respectively. The couple was involved in the church's life in almost every way possible. Their names appear frequently in both the church conference records and the records of the Woman's Missionary Society. William Vass was one of the most important railroad magnates of the late nineteenth century and had served as a member of the First Baptist Church for forty-nine years. In addition to being a longtime deacon in the church, he had been an officer in the Confederate Army; served as director for the Raleigh Institute for the Deaf, Dumb, and Blind; and had been a trustee for Wake Forest College. His service to the congregation, particularly during the difficult financial times of the postbellum years, was inestimable.[65] Lillie was memorialized by the church as the leader of the choir for twenty-six years "and was, it seemed to a good many of us, as near indispensable as someone could be."[66]

Another loss to the congregation was Dr. Columbus Durham, one of the church's ordained ministers. Durham died at an early age of fifty-one. After serving in the Confederate Army, he graduated from Wake Forest College and served as pastor of First Baptist Church in Goldsboro as well as the First Baptist Church of Durham. In 1887 he became the corresponding secretary of the Baptist State Convention of North Carolina and was serving in that role when he died.[67] Durham's name appears frequently among the church records after he joined the congregation in the late 1880s. An ardent opponent of dancing, Durham

---

[64] Ibid., 30 March 1896.

[65] Ronnie W. Faulkner, "Vass, William Worrell, Sr.," in *Dictionary of North Carolina Biography*, ed. William S. Powell, vol. 6 (Chapel Hill: University of North Carolina Press, 1996) 95.

[66] Church Conference Records, 1 September 1895.

[67] E. Norfleet Gardner, "Durham, Columbus," in *Encyclopedia of Southern Baptists*, vol. 1, 381.

at one time had been concerned that members of First Baptist Church were ignoring church policy and participating in the sinful amusement. In 1889 he proposed the following resolution to the church conference:

> Resolved, that three of the deacons be appointed a committee to make all needed investigation to know the facts and request any and all members of this church who, since our last church conference, have provided for or engaged in or attended dancing, to attend our next church conference and explain why they have failed to comply with the request of the church as expressed in its resolution on that subject.[68]

The following month the committee presented a report that shed further light on the issue at hand, which evidently involved many of the youth of the church. Desiring to support the church's official position on the matter, but at the same time attempting to be redemptive and even lenient, the members of the congregation decided that a "healthy sentiment and correct information on the matter of dancing should be disseminated." They encouraged all the members to assist in enforcing the church prohibition against dancing, "so that our young brethren and sisters who have been dancing should be counseled and dissuaded from the practice." Since "reveling" and "rioting" are deemed "works of the flesh" in the Bible, and "are grouped along with the worst sins of human nature," the church advised that no member engage in dancing, which "able expositors" agree would fall into that category. Finally, the church counseled that "a kind and decided stand should be maintained by the church urging the cessation of the practice of dancing by any of its members with the distinct understanding that if the practice is persisted in after admonition that the fellowship of the church will be withdrawn."[69]

Another prominent member who died during that period was Leonidas L. Polk. Polk was born in Anson County, North Carolina, in 1837. Orphaned at age fifteen, but with the inheritance of a portion of his father's plantation, Polk originally intended a vocation as a "gentleman

---

[68] Church Conference Records, 3 May 1889.

[69] Ibid., 31 May 1889.

farmer." However, the political turmoil of his era and ultimately the Civil War itself turned him toward a life of public service. Following service as a colonel with the Confederate Army (he served with the 81st North Carolina Militia at Gettysburg), Polk returned to North Carolina with a desire to help educate and organize the farmers in the state, recognizing the importance of their work for rebuilding North Carolina. He established the North Carolina Department of Agriculture and became the state's first commissioner of agriculture in 1877. Earlier experience in journalism gave him the knowledge he needed to begin publication of the *Progressive Farmer* in 1886. He was also instrumental in the establishment of the North Carolina State College of Agriculture and Mechanics in 1887 (which became North Carolina State University).[70] Polk gained national prominence with his election as president of the National Farmer's Alliance and Industrial Union in 1889, an honor that ultimately gave him a place of leadership in the growing Populist Movement taking root in American politics at the time. Had he not died suddenly in 1892, it is likely that he would have been a presidential candidate under the banner of the People's Party.[71]

As an active Baptist layman, Polk served as a messenger from First Baptist Church on several occasions to the Baptist State Convention of North Carolina, and in 1885 the convention elected him to the vice-presidency. His promotion of Thomas Meredith's long-dormant dream of a Baptist institution to educate women, however, was his most important contribution as a Baptist. On 16 November 1888, at the annual gathering of the BSC in Greensboro, Polk offered a resolution calling for the establishment of a Baptist female college. The motion passed unanimously. Two years later the Baptist Female University was chartered by the state of North Carolina. Doors opened to the school in 1899, and it was appropriately renamed "Meredith College" in 1909.[72] Polk and other prominent members of First Baptist Church were elected

---

[70] Stuart Noblin, "Polk, Leonidas LaFayette," in *Dictionary of North Carolina Biography*, vol. 5, 110–11; Mary Lynch Johnson, *A History of Meredith College* (Raleigh: Meredith College, 1956) 22–24.

[71] Josh Shaffer, "Voice of the Poor Farmer Rises Again," *News and Observer* (Raleigh NC), 18 November 2010, sec. b 1, 7.

[72] Johnson, *History of Meredith College*, 23.

to the original board of trustees for the school. Those names include J. D. Hufham, R. T. Vann, N. B. Broughton, Columbus Durham, W. G. Upchurch, the pastor J. W. Carter, and former pastors Thomas H. Pritchard and Jacob Lee White.[73]

Through the intervening years to the present twenty-first century, it is impossible to separate the history of Meredith College from the history of First Baptist Church. For decades the church has celebrated its annual summer picnic on the campus of the college. Students and faculty members from the school have enhanced the life of the church in numerous ways, such as the music program and the educational ministry. The church turned to the college throughout the twentieth century for guest preachers, teachers, and lecturers. In return, the church supported (and continues to support) the college financially through private donations, fundraisers, and cooperative program giving.

During the last month of the century, J. W. Carter submitted his resignation to the church after ten years as its pastor. His resignation letter was simple and a bit abrupt, but contained no bitterness: "The time approaches when my work as pastor of this church must close. Thanking you for kindness in the past and trusting God for the future I now present you my resignation to take effect on the 31st of December 1899 or sooner if you think best, but in no event later. Earlier if you desire, but certainly not later."[74]

As the nineteenth century came to a close, the First Baptist Church of Raleigh was about to enter its ninth decade. The world was moving rapidly and the church found itself once again without pastoral leadership.

Alexis Abraham Marshall (1900–1902)

By the first week of January a pastor search committee was organized, and the name of Dr. Alexis Abraham Marshall from Forsyth, Georgia, was presented to the church conference two months later. Of the total eighty-five votes cast, Marshall received seventy-two (85 percent). His salary was to be $2,000 [$52,700] per year (the same amount Carter

[73] Ibid., 25.
[74] Church Conference Records, 3 November 1899.

had been paid for most of his pastoral tenure), and the church provided him with the parsonage for his family's use. Marshall formally accepted the call a few weeks later.[75] His letter of acceptance, recorded in the church records, reveals something of his philosophy of ministry: "In coming to labor among you I come as the herald of no new creed, but rather as an under shepherd of my Master, to lead you along the old paths. In undertaking the work before me I shall count upon your prayerful sympathy and your hearty cooperation, relying at the same time upon the guiding providence of God to direct me in all things."[76]

Marshall was a native of Georgia, born on 17 July 1856 in Marietta. An interesting aspect of his family genealogy was that he was the great-great-grandson of Daniel Marshall of the North Carolina Separate Baptist fame.[77] Daniel Marshall was originally from Connecticut and a Congregationalist. After hearing George Whitefield preach during the First Great Awakening, he became an advocate of revivalism. Following the death of his first wife, in 1747 he married Martha Stearns, the sister of Shubal Stearns, and a preacher in her own right. During the early 1750s the couple, along with Shubal Stearns, embraced the tradition of the Separate Baptists, which allowed for much more religious enthusiasm than the more staid Regular Baptists, and they began a move toward the South. They settled for a while in Virginia where Marshall was baptized and licensed to preach. Eventually, they all ended up in Sandy Creek, North Carolina, which became the heart of the so-called "Sandy Creek Tradition" among Baptists in the South.[78] Following a period in North Carolina the Marshalls moved further south to Kiokee, Georgia, where in 1772 Daniel founded a Baptist church and became a leader of the early Baptist movement in that state. In 1784 he moderated the first meeting of

---

[75] Ibid., 5 January, 2 March, and 7 March 1900.

[76] Ibid., 26 March 1900.

[77] "Alexis A. Marshall," biographical file, located at the Southern Baptist Historical Library and Archives, Nashville, Tennessee.

[78] See McBeth, *Baptist Heritage*, 223–24, 227ff; and L. W. Hähnlen, "Marshall, Daniel (1706–1784)," in *Dictionary of Baptists in America*, 181–82. For a discussion of the Sandy Creek Tradition and the Separate Baptists, see ch. 1.

the Georgia Baptist Association, the earliest organized effort of Baptists in Georgia.[79]

Alexis A. Marshall received his B.A. and M.A. from Mercer University in 1874 and 1877, respectively. Two years before First Baptist Church, Raleigh called him (1898), he was awarded an honorary Doctor of Divinity degree from Mercer University. A seasoned minister having served in several pastorates in Georgia and South Carolina, Marshall was president of Monroe College in Forsyth, Georgia, at the time that he received the call to Raleigh. The school was originally organized in 1849 as the Forsyth Female Collegiate Institute. It changed its name to Monroe College in 1857 and again to Bessie Tift College in 1907. The women's school affiliated with the Georgia Baptist Convention in 1898. The school finally closed its doors and merged with Mercer University in 1986.[80] Given his experience as president of Monroe College, speculation might lead one to consider whether Marshall was drawn to Raleigh because of an interest in the new women's school in the city. Unfortunately, since those thoughts would have most likely been held in private, and since Marshall died in 1902 after serving only two years at the church, the real reason for his departure may never be ascertained.

Because Marshall's tenure was so short, no major events occurred in the life of the congregation while he was pastor. The mission endeavors begun under Carter continued to grow and be funded with great interest. Related to that, the church hired a Sunday-school missionary, Miss Harriett Blackstone, whose salary was to be $50 [$1,320] per month, split evenly between the church budget and the Sunday-school budget.[81] The church also received a request from the membership of Samaria Baptist Church to become a mission congregation of First Baptist Church. The Samaria church had struggled to maintain viability, and their membership had dropped to thirty. Marshall was very supportive of the concept, arguing that "for Samaria church to be an arm of this church

---

[79] Hähnlen, "Marshall, Daniel," 181–82.

Dictionary of Baptists in America, s.v. "Marshall, Daniel," by L. W. Hähnlen.

[80] "Tift College," http://www.hmdb.org/Marker.asp?Marker=25657 (accessed 11 February 2010).

[81] Church Conference Records, 29 June 1900, 3 August 1900, and 2 November 1900.

would give our members an opportunity to go there and engage in mission work." He continued to say that "this church needed to come in closer touch with the humble class of people."[82] The congregation granted the request and transferred the entire membership of Samaria to the church roll of First Baptist Church on 4 April 1902.[83]

The church also continued its support of the Baptist Female University during Marshall's tenure. The school, though chartered in 1891, was not able to open its doors until 1899 when nineteen faculty and more than 200 students began the new academic year. The first president, James C. Blasingame, resigned after only one year at the helm, and Richard Tillman Vann was selected as his successor. Vann's ability to raise money and his skill in administrative leadership proved to be the winning combination for the school as the twentieth century dawned.[84] In November 1900 Vann appeared on behalf of the Baptist Female University with a request that the church make a substantial pledge. Vann "spoke of the great need for a special effort to raise money to pay off the indebtedness of the university and for the other Baptist schools of the state." Vann requested $4,000 [$105,000] from First Baptist Church, which the church readily agreed to give. The records indicate that $1,000 [$26,400] toward the school had already been raised.[85]

The first sign of Marshall's illness came in early 1902. The church records simply report in January and February that the pastor was absent from the church conference. Then in April the deacons reported that W. B. Morton had been asked to supply the pulpit until the pastor was able to resume his duties. Morton was paid $15 [$386] per week for preaching, with the understanding that "he is to give his entire time to the church in

---

[82] Ibid., 29 November 1901.

[83] Ibid., 4 April 1902.

[84] "Meredith Timeline," http://www.meredith.edu/library/archives/ meredith_timeline.htm (accessed 12 February 2010). When Vann was twelve years old, he lost both arms in an accident at a cane mill. Coupled with that tragedy, Vann lost his mother when he was five years old, and his father died soon after the mill accident. That Vann could overcome such adversity, become well-educated, and serve as a successful college president is testimony to his character. (See also Johnson, *History of Meredith College*, 88–89.)

[85] Church Conference Records, 30 November 1900.

performance of regular pastoral duties."[86] During that year the church approved wiring the parsonage for electricity, but by July the work had to be postponed indefinitely "due to Dr. Marshall's illness." There was also discussion at that meeting about the advisability of employing another minister full time while Marshall was ill, although the church ultimately chose not to do so.[87] Unfortunately, Marshall was never able to return to his pastoral duties. Six weeks later, on 17 August 1902, he died. The church mourned his loss with a resolution recognizing that their "faithful minister has been removed and we feelingly recognize the great loss we have sustained as a church."[88]

William Cornelius Tyree (1902–1910)

Less than one week after Marshall's memorial service, the church unanimously called William Cornelius Tyree to be its next pastor. At the time Tyree was serving as pastor of the First Baptist Church in the neighboring city of Durham. The salary offered was the same $2,000 per year that Marshall had received. Tyree began his work as pastor in December 1902.[89]

Tyree was born in Danville, Virginia, on 13 October 1860. It may have been "in the stars" that Tyree would become a pastor. He was named for both his father (William) and his uncle (Cornelius), who were both highly respected Baptist preachers in Virginia. When he was twelve years old, Tyree made a profession of faith and was baptized into the membership of the Hunting Creek Baptist Church (the church his father was serving at the time) in Halifax County, Virginia. Tyree was educated at Richmond College, the University of Virginia, and finally at the

---

[86] Ibid., 4 April 1902. See ibid., 3 October 1902. The annual letter sent to the Central Baptist Association for the year 1902 contains this note about Marshall's illness: "He was sick continuously from the last Sunday in Dec. 1901 to the date of his death (17 August 1902) and was unable to serve the church at all. We were dependent upon such brethren as could be secured for our regular services and were so fortunate as to maintain the services during all this time. For this we feel very grateful."

[87] Ibid., 4 July 1902.

[88] Ibid., 20 August 1902.

[89] Ibid., 25 August, 5 September, 31 October, and 5 December 1902.

Southern Baptist Theological Seminary. While serving as pastor of the Baptist church in Amherst, Virginia, Tyree's father became ill and died in 1884. That prompted the congregation to ordain William on 29 March 1885.[90]

Tyree enjoyed a long and respectable ministerial career. He served five churches in Virginia and Kentucky (four in Virginia, one in Kentucky) and then moved in 1892 to North Carolina to become pastor of First Baptist Church in Durham. Following his tenure in Raleigh, Tyree moved to High Point where he served the First Baptist Church in that city. Then following a pastorate in Greenwood, Mississippi, from 1914 to 1922, he returned to North Carolina to finish his ministerial career as pastor of the First Baptist Church of Lenoir.[91]

Tyree's wife, the former Lonie Currin, was a native of Oxford, North Carolina. They were married on 18 April 1895. His death came tragically on a trip with his wife to visit her family in Oxford. About four miles outside of town on 20 December 1928, their car was involved in an automobile accident. Tyree died instantly. His wife, though injured, survived.[92]

Church Improvements. During Tyree's pastorate the church underwent several improvements. The parsonage, by that time old enough to need perennial attention, underwent repairs totaling $297.40 [$7,650].[93] High attendance at worship services necessitated the purchase of folding chairs to be used to accommodate the overflow.[94] The Ladies Improvement Society, very active during that time, gave a new communion set to the church, which prompted a change from the common cup to individual cups during the observance of the Lord's Supper.[95] A growing interest in the church's music program was evidenced by the purchase of new hymnals and the attention given to the employment of a new organist upon the resignation of former organist

---

[90] George Braxton Taylor, *Virginia Baptist Ministers*, 6th Series, 1914–1934 (Lynchburg VA: J. P. Bell Co., 1935) 275–77.

[91] Ibid.

[92] Ibid.

[93] Church Conference Records, 5 December 1902.

[94] Ibid., 1 May 1903.

[95] Ibid., 31 August 1903.

Sam Parrish.[96] Wade Brown, a professor at Wake Forest College, was employed with a salary of $40 per month [$984].[97]

The most important improvement of the period was a major enlargement of the church building. In October 1903 the church appointed a committee to investigate the possibility of "enlarging the Sunday School room" and determine the cost. It also empowered the committee, composed of J. E. Ray, C. J. Hunter, J. A. Briggs, W. N. Jones, and J. P. Wyatt, to secure the services of an architect.[98] Over the next several months the plans to enlarge the "Sunday School room" changed into a plan to enlarge the church structure itself. By the following summer the committee, by that time named in the minutes as the "Committee on Church and S.S. Enlargement," brought a bleak report back to the church. It seems there were problems with the church's neighbor to the south, R. B. Raney. According to the report, Raney refused to allow the church to purchase a strip of land necessary for the enlargement of the building.[99]

It was not the first time the church and Raney were at odds. The previous year there was a disagreement between the church and Raney concerning a fence he intended to build that would separate the property. The church wanted the fence to be shorter than Raney desired, and following a conversation, J. P. Wyatt reported that he "positively refused to change his plans."[100] Confronted with the reality that Raney was not going to cooperate with the church's plans, R. T. Vann suggested that the committee should scale back their plans to a structure that measured twelve-by-sixty on either side of the building. Vann's plan, though logical, was tabled until a later meeting, no doubt to see if the committee might be able to change Raney's mind.[101] Good news came two months

---

[96] Ibid., 12 January 1906 and 11 May 1906.

[97] Ibid., 6 June 1906.

[98] Ibid., 9 October 1903.

[99] Ibid., 8 July 1904. "Bro. Ray reported for the Com. On enlarging church and SS that it seemed next to impossible to accomplish the purpose owing to refusal of Mr. Raney to let us have the narrow strip of ground wanted on the south." The gentleman referenced was Richard Beverly Raney, the benefactor of the Olivia Raney Library.

[100] Ibid., 27 February 1903.

[101] Ibid., 8 July 1904.

later as the committee reported that the original plans could proceed and that a land exchange deal with Raney was imminent.[102]

By November the church authorized purchase of plans for a "two-story transcept building" from architect C. W. Barrett.[103] The following spring the committee reported that the architectural plans were completed and recommended "that the work of remodeling, refurnishing, and reseating be undertaken as soon as funds are secured." The estimated cost of the work was projected to be $18,000 [$447,000]—a figure that grew significantly as the work progressed.[104] The church selected an additional committee to raise the necessary funding and, by the end of the year, reported that $12,063 [$300,000] was secured in pledges.[105]

Work began on the building project early the following year. By a vote of twenty-seven to fourteen, the church approved the appointment of a building committee composed of J. E. Ray (chair), John S. Johnson, Thomas H. Briggs, C. J. Hunter, and J. D. Boushall. The work continued throughout the year. A note in the church records at the beginning of 1907 conveyed appreciation to the First Presbyterian Church "for their kindness in giving us the use of their church house for prayer meetings and other services for the last several months."[106] A final notation of thanks was conveyed to R. B. Raney, "expressing to him the appreciation of this church for his kindness in exchanging land and allowing debris on his lot while the church building was being enlarged."[107]

---

[102] Ibid., 9 September and 7 October 1904. No details of the land exchange are included in the church records.

[103] Ibid., 11 November 1904. The work that Barrett designed was nothing short of brilliant. Don Kline, a structural engineer and member of First Baptist Church of Raleigh, has studied the design of the building and its various renovations through the years. Concerning Barrett, Kline said, "[H]e deserves praise for conceiving the expansion and having carried it out. Designing a building from scratch is not easy, but working within the constraints of an existing building...gets higher marks in my book" (interview with Don Kline at First Baptist Church of Raleigh, 11 March 2011).

[104] Church Conference Records, 12 May 1905.

[105] Ibid., 20 December 1906.

[106] Ibid., 11 January 1907.

[107] Ibid., 11 October 1907.

Unfortunately, the church records do not reveal the exact nature of the work done in the enlargement process. An article in the *Biblical Recorder* reported that on Sunday, 22 September 1907, the congregation returned to their newly remodeled auditorium. The final cost for the work was approximately $32,000 [$754,000] and a debt of approximately $15,000 [$353,000] still remained to be paid. As for the work done, the article revealed that the seating capacity was "greatly increased" along with "one of the most conveniently arranged Sunday-school departments to be found in all the State."[108] An interesting glimpse into the church's value is given in the 1907 letter to the Central Baptist Association, where the total value of the church property was listed as $70,000 [$1.65 million] and the seating capacity was determined to be 1,200.[109]

The church's attention to local missions continued during Tyree's tenure as pastor. The Samaria Baptist Church, which in 1902 had requested to become a mission of First Baptist, had experienced enough growth as a mission to request that their status be changed, stating that they were "strong enough to sustain the ministry of the Gospel at this church by ourselves." The church granted letters of dismission for the Samaria membership, thereby ending their mission status.[110] Also, in 1905 the church began to investigate a new local mission opportunity located at the corner of North and Johnson Streets. Working with the city missions committee and the city missionary, First Baptist once again became a major supporter of the effort. A combination of contributions and a loan of $250 [$6,150] allowed the erection of a small chapel on the property, which was named for First Baptist deacon John S. Johnson, a primary force in the effort who died before its completion. Called the

---

[108] *Biblical Recorder* (Raleigh NC), 25 September 1907, 4. The writer alluded to the beauty of the work, saying, "It is generally confessed by all that it would hardly be foreseen by anyone, that the old First Church could be converted into such a thing of beauty and usefulness."

[109] Annual Letter to the Central Baptist Association (1907), contained in Church Conference Records, 7 September 1907.

[110] Church Conference Records, 6 October 1905.

John S. Johnson Memorial Chapel, it quickly began to grow and ultimately became the Johnson Memorial Baptist Church.[111]

Temperance Movement. The Temperance Movement, which began before the Civil War, eventually found its way to the city of Raleigh and to First Baptist Church. The church conference minutes from the meeting on 13 December 1907 refer to a motion to allow the Anti-Saloon League to use the auditorium during a prohibition campaign, an issue that was still hotly contested in Raleigh at that time.[112] In 1874 the city of Raleigh had held an election, which by a vote of 749–649 prohibited the sale of alcoholic beverages. The wet forces then challenged the election, resulting in a ruling that the election was invalid. Three years later the city voted overwhelmingly (480 to 1,248) against prohibition, but in 1886 the dry forces were able to pass a prohibition ordinance. N. B. Broughton, a member of First Baptist Church, was an important leader in the 1886 prohibition effort and the church was supportive as well. The city did not remain dry for long, however. Within two years liquor was being sold again in Raleigh. By 1902 at least twenty-five saloons possessed liquor licenses in the city.[113]

In 1902 a North Carolina branch of the Anti-Saloon League was formed. Among prominent First Baptist Church members involved in the Anti-Saloon League were N. B. Broughton (president of the North Carolina branch) and W. N. Jones. The nationally recognized Carrie Nation, outspoken crusader against alcoholic beverages of all types, made a visit to Raleigh in 1907. She drew large crowds and made several speeches. Nation did not limit her rhetoric to alcohol only. She also spoke out against tobacco use and Masonic lodges. As she prepared to leave the city, she turned her sharp rhetoric once more to tobacco use: "You are going to be rid of the dispensary but the great curse to North Carolina is this American Tobacco Company.... You need to drive the cigarette out."[114] Nation's visit in 1907 coincided with a statewide effort toward prohibition. N. B. Broughton was the Wake County organizer for the

---

[111] Ibid., 20 December 1905 and 7 September 1906. See also Morris, "The History of the First Baptist Church of Raleigh," 105.

[112] Church Conference Records, 13 December 1907.

[113] Johnson and Murray, *Wake: Capital County of North Carolina*, vol. 2, 28–29.

[114] *Raleigh News and Observer*, 31 July 1907, as cited by ibid., 30.

effort, which passed, and as of 1 January 1909 the state of North Carolina became dry—a decade before the 18th Amendment brought prohibition nationally.[115]

Death of Thomas Skinner. A final noteworthy event during Tyree's tenure was the death of First Baptist's beloved former pastor Thomas Skinner on 6 April 1905. Skinner's association with the church spanned fifty years and, with the exception of the two years' leave of absence during the Civil War (1863–1865) and the period from 1867 to 1879, Skinner spent most of his adult life in Raleigh. Following the resignation of his second tenure as the church's pastor, he lived out his retirement years as a member of the congregation, with his name appearing occasionally in the church records. Skinner's death came on a Sunday afternoon just a few hours after he attended the morning worship service.[116]

After serving eight years as the pastor of First Baptist Church, W. C. Tyree offered his resignation to the congregation on 9 September 1910 in order to become the pastor of First Baptist Church of High Point. His resignation letter, contained in the church records, was simple and direct: "Eight years ago I accepted your unanimous and hearty call to become your pastor, because I concluded that God would have me do so. I now resign this office because, after deliberate, careful and prayerful consideration, I am convinced that God would not have me remain longer."[117]

Five days later the church passed a resolution of appreciation for his ministry that contains a good summary of the church's progress during the previous eight years. The membership grew from 542 to 797. New additions included 228 baptisms and 260 by letter. The Johnson Memorial Mission had become a success, and the church renovations and addition of the Sunday-school building had been completed at a cost of approximately $32,000 [$745,000]. The church also drew attention to Tyree's leadership in the Baptist world beyond the local congregation, having served as a member of the State Mission Board, a trustee of both

---

[115] Johnson and Murray, *Wake: Capital County of North Carolina*, vol. 2, 30–31.
[116] Church Conference Records, 6 April 1905.
[117] Ibid., 9 September 1910.

Meredith and Wake Forest Colleges, and state vice-president of the Southern Baptist Convention Foreign Mission Board. Summarizing his ministry, the church declared, "To the present excellent condition of the church he has contributed in no small degree."[118]

* * *

First Baptist Church of Raleigh was in its ninety-ninth year when W. C. Tyree concluded his pastorate there. The end of his tenure provides a good place to pause and reflect over the century of accomplishment within the church. From a small gathering of committed Baptists, black and white, in the old State House in 1812, the church weathered several storms in the nineteenth century, including the Civil War and financial difficulties in the postbellum years, to emerge stronger by the beginning of the twentieth century. In addition to increased church membership, an active Sunday school boasted an average attendance of 823. During the previous twenty-five years, the church was instrumental in organizing or assisting at least six mission congregations, which grew into separate churches. Wake Forest and Meredith Colleges owed much to the church for its assistance as well. The founders' vision was by that time almost a century in the making. As the members looked back at the challenges of the nineteenth century, as well as the accomplishments, they were, doubtless, keenly aware that the next century would provide new challenges as well.

---

[118] Ibid., 14 September 1910.

6

Facing a New Century (1910–1938)

Americans had every reason to be optimistic as the twentieth century dawned. The horrors of the Civil War and Reconstruction were by then decades in the past. The Industrial Revolution and a seemingly unlimited supply of natural resources made the nation the richest on earth, as American wealth almost doubled in the decade between 1890 and 1900. The natural resources of the nation, as well as its technology, were being exported around the world by the beginning of the new century.[1] The average American in 1900, looking ahead to the new century, could not have imagined the changes that would come in the next three decades. The twelve-second flight piloted by Orville Wright at Kitty Hawk, North Carolina, in 1903 began an aviation revolution, and within three decades planes were crossing the Atlantic Ocean. Henry Ford's Model T and assembly line production of automobiles soon made the horse and buggy obsolete. Trolley cars made mass transit in cities much simpler. Electricity reached many rural areas by the 1930s. America was becoming "modernized."

The nation's optimistic spirit was evident in its newly elected president in 1900, William McKinley, who said, "I can no longer be called the President of a party. I am now the President of the whole people."[2] A year later, on 6 September 1901, McKinley's assassination brought the nation back to reality. There were still large problems that needed serious attention. Industrialism had produced a rich nation, but Americans were not equally wealthy. One percent of the population controlled 40 percent of the wealth. Blacks, women, and immigrants were still far from being treated as equal to white men. Unchecked capitalism created monopolies and corporations, which vanquished all competition. Crime and misery

---

[1] Winthrop D. Jordan and Leon F. Litwack, *The United States*, 7th ed. (Englewood Cliffs: Prentice Hall, 1991) 569.

[2] Jordan and Litwack, *United States*, 569.

festered in the large urban centers. The American worker, for all of his or her efforts, had still not achieved the "American Dream."[3]

And if the economic and social problems in America at the beginning of the twentieth century were not enough to spoil American optimism, World War I finally did the trick. Woodrow Wilson's efforts to steer a course of neutrality were successful for the first few years of the war, but America's isolationism changed in April 1917 after Germany resumed its unrestricted submarine warfare in the Atlantic Ocean. World War I was a devastation that brought twentieth-century technology to the battlefield to be used upon troops still trained in nineteenth-century tactics. When the war concluded in 1918, more than 50,000 American soldiers were dead—numbers that pale in comparison to Russia (1.7 million), Germany (1.8 million), France (1.4 million), Great Britain (0.9 million), and Austria-Hungary (1.2 million).[4] Given the tragic consequences of World War I, the hope was that the leading nations of the world would see that such devastation never happened again. The Treaty of Versailles did provide for a League of Nations to be formed (Woodrow Wilson's dream) so that local grievances could be settled by neutral nations to prevent war. Unfortunately, partisan politics in the United States Congress never allowed for American ratification of the peace treaty or the League of Nations. Without American participation, the league failed, and only a few decades later the world was at war once again.

Great social changes also occurred in the first three decades of the new century. The 16th and 17th Amendments to the Constitution were ratified by the states in 1913, creating the federal income tax and the direct election of senators, respectively. The 18th Amendment, ratified in 1919, finally brought the era of Prohibition, of which organizations such as the Anti-Saloon League and the Women's Christian Temperance Union had dreamed for decades. Most significantly, the 19th Amendment guaranteeing women's suffrage was ratified in 1920.

During the decade dubbed the "Roaring Twenties," Americans celebrated the new economic prosperity and security of the times in spite

---

[3] Ibid., 570.
[4] Ibid., 616–17.

of Prohibition. Yet the celebratory mood came to an abrupt halt on 29 October 1929 with the crash of the stock market. Following the crash the nation plunged into its worst economic depression ever. The nation elected Franklin Delano Roosevelt in 1932, and the following year Prohibition was repealed by the 20th Amendment to the Constitution. Roosevelt's New Deal helped to foster economic recovery as Americans gradually returned to work.

Christians in America, especially Protestants, experienced change in the first three decades of the twentieth century as well. In 1906 William J. Seymour, an evangelist and thirty-four-year-old son of former slaves, began a revival in a small mission on Azuza Street in Los Angeles, California, giving rise to the Pentecostal tradition—arguably the most important Christian movement of the twentieth century.[5] The Edinburgh Conference of 1910, originally intended as an effort to bring various Christian denominations together for interdenominational missionary support, led to the creation of the Ecumenical Movement. (The idea of finding common ground among all Christians still occupies the thoughts of many theologians and ministers today.) Fundamentalism developed as a conservative reaction to the rise of critical methodology in biblical studies, as well as to the optimism of nineteenth-century Liberalism. Fundamentalism made its way into the mainstream of American culture, and the nation found itself engrossed in a trial of a high-school teacher in Dayton, Tennessee, who broke Tennessee law by teaching the theory of evolution in his biology class. The "Scopes Monkey Trial," as it was dubbed, pitted the great agnostic ACLU attorney Clarence Darrow against guest prosecutor William Jennings Bryan. Darrow's surprise move of calling Bryan to the stand as a witness humiliated Bryan (who died of a stroke later that week in Dayton), but more importantly it shed light on the reactionary literalism of the Fundamentalists, forcing the movement to lose popularity for decades.[6]

---

[5] See Grant Wacker, *Heaven Below: Early Pentecostals and American Culture* (Boston: Harvard University Press, 2001) for the definitive history of that important movement.

[6] See Ray Ginger, *Six Days or Forever: Tennessee v. John Thomas Scopes* (New York: Oxford University Press, 1988) for a good presentation of the trial and the circus atmosphere that came to Dayton that year. See George M. Marsden,

Advances in technology made life easier for citizens of Raleigh in the first three decades of the twentieth century. By 1900 the telegraph had given way to the telephone. In 1907 there were seven small telephone companies serving Wake County, including three in Raleigh. During that year Southern Bell, Wake's largest phone company, merged with Interstate Telephone and Telegraph, creating a new company called Capital City Telephone Company. The name changed five years later to Southern Bell Telephone Company.[7] As a further sign of development, the railroad and streetcars were joined by a new form of transportation by 1900. Within the first three decades of the twentieth century the automobile became the preferred means of transportation in the city of Raleigh. The popularity of the car necessitated good roads. In 1903 Wake County implemented a road tax designed to provide funding for better roads. Four years later H. G. Holding, the county road superintendent, recommended that the county replace all wooden bridges with steel.[8] Raleigh resident Fred A. Olds caught the spirit of the transportation revolution on New Year's Eve 1912 when he said, "The first concrete road in the South has been built, as an object lesson, and there has become set in the minds of all thinking men a high purpose to take Raleigh's streets out of the mud and make them what they ought to be, and Raleigh men are joining with those outside to end forever the reproach of bad roads in Wake."[9]

When America became involved in World War I in 1917, the city of Raleigh did its part to support the war effort. Wake County provided a total of 1,647 men to the Army, 352 to the Navy, and nine to the Marine Corps. Twelve women from the county served in the nursing corps. A casualty list published in December 1918 indicated that 256 Wake County

---

Fundamentalism and American Culture: The Shaping of Twentieth-Century Evangelicalism 1870–1925 (New York: Oxford University Press, 1980) for a classic interpretation of Fundamentalism.

[7] K. Todd Johnson and Elizabeth Reid Murray, *Wake: Capital County of North Carolina*, vol. 2 (Raleigh NC: NC Wake County, 2008) 521–22.

[8] Ibid., 231–41.

[9] *Raleigh Times* (North Carolina), 1 January 1913; Olivia Raney Library Scrapbook, 176, as cited by Johnson and Murray, *Wake: Capital County of North Carolina*, vol. 2, 241.

soldiers were killed in action, eighty-four died from wounds, 140 died of disease, and seventy-four were wounded.[10] Furthermore, Raleigh was home to the military base Camp Polk during the war. The camp, located near the state fairgrounds, was one of the army's first tank training bases. Construction on the base began in fall 1918, and the war ended before its completion. In spite of the efforts of many citizens to keep the base in Raleigh permanently, the army decided to relocate. Nevertheless, during the short period it existed, Raleigh citizens were by and large supportive of the soldiers and the operations of the base.[11] Yet, despite those efforts of the city as a whole, not all of its residents supported America's involvement in the war. In one particular case, Floyd E. Simpkins, son of Primitive Baptist minister Elder W. A. Simpkins, was arrested on 9 August 1917 for threatening the life of President Woodrow Wilson. Allegedly, the younger Simpkins, while delivering bread to a store in Smithfield, said, "There ain't a damn bit of use of this war." He went on to say that if he were drafted, he hoped that Wilson would be the first person he "got a crack at." According to accounts, his father appeared at the hearing before John Nichols, the U.S. Commissioner, arguing that his son was only joking. The case was sent to a federal court but was dismissed.[12]

In addition to the war, a worldwide pandemic of Spanish influenza dominated much of the attention of Americans and Raleigh residents from 1917 to 1919. Estimates are that worldwide the pandemic attacked more than one-fifth of the world's population and killed more than fifty million.[13] North Carolina lost more than 3,000 people to the disease in 1917, with another 12,000 the following year. Finally, statewide deaths dropped to 6,000 in 1919. Wake County suffered from the disease more

---

[10] Johnson and Murray, *Wake: Capital County of North Carolina*, vol. 2, 416. See pp. 397–420 for a full discussion of Wake County and Raleigh during World War I.

[11] Ibid., 410–14.

[12] *News and Observer*, 10 August 1917, 1, and 16 August 1917, 5, as cited by ibid., 401.

[13] "The Deadly Virus: The Influenza Epidemic of 1918," National Archives and Records Administration, http://www.archives.gov/exhibits/influenza-epidemic/ (accessed 11 June 2010).

than any other county in North Carolina in October 1918, with 293 deaths reported in that month alone.[14]

The First Baptist Church of Raleigh 1911–1938

Thomas W. O'Kelley (1911–1927)

Following the eight-year successful pastorate of W. C. Tyree, the church once again needed to find a new pastor. On 7 October 1910 the church appointed a pastor search committee that worked for two months to secure a new pastor. On 14 December 1910 the committee recommended that the church call Dr. Thomas W. O'Kelley from St. Joseph, Missouri, at a salary of $3,000 [$69,900] per year along with use of the parsonage.[15] O'Kelly arrived in Raleigh shortly thereafter and presided over his first church conference as the new pastor on 1 February 1911.

Thomas Washington O'Kelley was born on 16 December 1861 in Hall County, Georgia. One of six children (all boys) born to Edward Washington and Elizabeth Barnes O'Kelley, Thomas and two of his siblings eventually became pastors. O'Kelley's opportunities for formal education were limited and meager. However, he was able to acquire enough education eventually to enroll at Mercer University, where he distinguished himself as an outstanding student, graduating with honors in 1889. Two years later he received the M.A. degree from Mercer. For one year he served as principal of Hiawassee High School in Hiawassee, Georgia, after which he joined the faculty at Mercer as professor of Latin.[16] In 1891 O'Kelley married his first wife, Mamie Alexander of

---

[14] Johnson and Murray, *Wake: Capital County of North Carolina*, vol. 2, 483. One Raleigh resident remembered: "[T]he coffins were stacked up like cordwood on the baggage trucks at the old train station. There was a lady in our neighborhood who came around to help. The hospitals were full to overflowing and there were loads of houses with everybody sick. She took soup to the sick, and helped lay out the corpses. When asked wasn't she scared, she said, 'No.'…but most people were scared. So many were sick we even had difficulty getting a preacher to bury a little two-year-old-baby girl" (quoted by Johnson and Murray, 483).

[15] Church Conference Records, 7 October and 14 December 1910.

[16] B. J. W. Graham, ed., *Baptist Biography*, vol. 2 (Atlanta: Index Printing Company, 1920) 244–45, http://books.google.com/books?id=QxwRAAA-

Maysville, Georgia, but she died two years after their marriage. He married his second wife, Rosa Bert Meriwether of Albany, Georgia, in 1900. Together they had three children: Thomas, Jr., Mary, and William.

The life of academia was not to be O'Kelley's calling. Converted to the Christian faith in 1879, he eventually felt a calling to preach. In 1888 he was ordained to the ministry by the First Baptist Church of Macon, Georgia, and began supplying the pulpit in various Georgia churches while teaching at Mercer. His first pastorate was in Hawkinsville, Georgia (1892–1893). Subsequent pastorates, prior to First Baptist, Raleigh, included the following: First Baptist Church, Griffin, Georgia (1893–1899); West End Baptist Church, Atlanta, Georgia (1899–1902); Second Baptist Church, Little Rock, Arkansas (1902–1904); and First Baptist Church, St. Joseph, Missouri (1904–1911). That O'Kelley preferred the pastorate to the academic world is evidenced by the fact that, though offered the presidency of Mercer University in 1913, he chose to remain as pastor of the First Baptist Church, Raleigh.[17]

It should come as no surprise, then, that O'Kelley was well known throughout Baptist life both before his tenure at First Baptist Church, Raleigh and while he served as the church's pastor. He served as a member of the board of trustees at the Foreign Mission Board of the Southern Baptist Convention and attended the annual sessions of the convention regularly. In 1913 O'Kelley delivered the convention sermon at the annual meeting—an honor generally reserved for the convention's best pulpiteers. He was supportive of Baptist higher education, especially Wake Forest and Meredith Colleges, because of their close proximity to the church. He was also a member of the board of directors of the *Biblical Recorder*.[18]

AIAAJ&pg=PA247&lpg=PA247&dq=Thomas+W.+O'Kelley+Raleigh+Baptist&source=bl&ots=D_Ai6Igpkx&sig=hpRteyI5GG7KwSyWb1V07iAUApY&hl=en&ei=PzMVTICGFYK0lQevjfXyCw&sa=X&oi=book_result&ct=result&resnum=1&ved=0CBwQ6AEwAA#v=onepage&q=Thomas%20W.%20O'Kelley%20Raleigh%20Baptist&f=false (accessed 13 June 2010). See also Church Conference Records, 12 July 1927, where a number of newspaper clippings concerning O'Kelley's life are attached.

[17] Newspaper clippings in Church Conference Records, 12 July 1927.

[18] Ibid.

The church was in good condition when O'Kelley assumed the pastorate. In the annual letter to the Central Baptist Association for 1911, it reported a total membership of 795. The membership of the Sunday school had grown to 902 with an average attendance of 363. The Woman's Missionary Society had a membership of 100, while the Young Ladies Missionary Society and the Sunbeams had memberships of forty-six and fifty, respectively. The church had seven ordained ministers as members: O'Kelley, R. T. Vann, Livingston Johnston, J. S. Farmer, C. F. Meserve, Hight C. Moore, and R. S. Stevenson. The total value of the property that year was estimated to be $70,000 [$1.63 million].[19] By all accounts, O'Kelley was deeply loved by the membership at First Baptist Church, Raleigh. Upon his death in 1927 one member of the church reportedly said, "He got closer to me than any pastor I ever knew." Another interpreter commented that "besides being eloquent in the pulpit, he had the common touch and the high and lowly felt equally at home in his presence and were equally the objects of his friendly interest."[20]

Centennial Celebration. The celebration of the church's centennial was one of the first big events in the life of the congregation after O'Kelley became the pastor. The grand event was celebrated over the weekend of 8–10 March 1912. The festivities opened on Friday evening at 7:30 with a worship service. Thomas H. Briggs and William A. Graham were featured speakers providing "Historical and Personal Reminiscences." Greetings from the pastors of five other Baptist churches in the city that had been organized as missions from the First Baptist Church were also included. Several former pastors, one of which was J. L. White, were also present to give greetings. The evening concluded with an address titled, "Incidents Connected with the Church, 1850–'55," by John Nichols.[21]

Three events occurred that Sunday of the centennial weekend. The worship service at 11:00 A.M. was devoted entirely to the church's anniversary. Three hymns, "Come Thou Fount of Every Blessing," "Glorious Things of Thee are Spoken," and "He Leadeth Me," suggested

---

[19] Annual Letter to the Central Baptist Association, contained in Church Conference Records, 8 September 1911.

[20] Newspaper clippings in Church Conference Records, 12 July 1927.

[21] Church Conference Records, 6 March 1912.

the theme of the service. The choir sang "Onward Christian Soldiers" as their anthem, and O'Kelley preached from I Samuel 7:12. He captured the enduring character of the congregation throughout its history with the following words: "We do not sneeze every time some theological professor takes snuff, nor do we go into convulsions when some upstart says that all old things must go. We just keep on in the even tenor of our way, knowing "nothing but Jesus and Him crucified."[22]

At 3:00 in the afternoon the sanctuary was again full for a special service presided over by Burton J. Ray, superintendent of the Sunday school, who recounted the history of the children's missionary societies. Reports were given from the Royal Ambassadors and the Young Ladies Missionary Society. The afternoon also featured a history of the Sunday school given by J. D. Boushall. He recalled the hesitation that some parents felt toward allowing their children to attend the Sunday school in the early years by telling the story of Sarah Williams, whose family members—who were not Baptist and perhaps lacked experience with or understanding of "Sunday School"—had forbidden her to attend Sunday school as a child "because they feared personal violence for her." The Sunday-school orchestra also performed and was "exceedingly entertaining" according to one account. The afternoon concluded with an address by W. A. Withers, a member of the First Presbyterian Church, who described the history of the Sunday-school movement in Raleigh.[23]

The highlight of the centennial celebration weekend came that evening. Thomas H. Briggs was the keynote speaker who provided a history of the church, giving particular attention to the pastors who had served the congregation. That was followed by Livingston Johnson, corresponding secretary of the Baptist State Convention and member of the church, who gave an address titled "The Relation of the Church to the Denomination." Finally, Mrs. Thomas H. Briggs provided a history of the church's Woman's Missionary Society, which by that time had become an

---

[22] "A Centennial's Close Sunday," *News and Observer* (Raleigh NC), 12 March 1912, 5. See also "Centennial Sketch of the First Baptist Church of Raleigh," *Biblical Recorder* (Raleigh NC), vol. 77, 13 March 1912, 1, 3. (This is an abstract of the history presented by T. H. Briggs.)

[23] *News and Observer*, 12 March 1912, 5.

important force for sustaining the church's vitality and upholding its commitment to missions.[24]

Within the first four years of O'Kelley's ministry, the church achieved a milestone. The annual letter to the Central Baptist Association from 1915 reported that the membership of the church had climbed to 1,003—the largest enrollment in its history up to that time.[25] The church treasurer's report for 1915 provides further insight into the life of the congregation at that time. According to the report there were 427 accounts, representing about 700 of the congregation, who contributed through the offering envelope system for the pastor's salary and other expenses. At the close of 1915 there was still $812 [$17,900] outstanding on members' pledges from that year. Individual contributions for the pastor's salary and expenses ranged from $1 [$22] to $156 [$3,440]. Still more than 300 members contributed nothing to the church expenses through the envelope system. The report ended by saying that "the finance committee would urge that every member of the church who can conveniently do so, to contribute through the envelope system in order that they may be given credit for the same on the church books."[26]

World War I. The first reference to World War I in the church records came one year before America's formal involvement. In April 1916 W. J. Peele made a motion that a special offering be collected at the evening worship service on 9 April, and that the money "be given to the fund for the relief of the Belgians, and that this departure against the rule of the church against special collections was made in recognition of the urgent need for aid to relieve these innocent victims of the great European War."[27] The members of First Baptist Church, like other patriotic citizens of the city, were supporters of the "war to end all wars." In September 1918 the church appointed a committee specifically to work with the soldiers of Camp Polk. The following month the deacons recommended that a portion of the Sunday-school building be devoted for use by soldiers at the camp for rest and relaxation, after a "Mr. Lang" from the

---

[24] Ibid.

[25] Annual Letter to the Central Baptist Association, contained in Church Conference Records, 6 August 1915.

[26] Church Conference Records, 7 January 1916.

[27] Ibid., 7 April 1916.

government "explained the desires and aims of the government in encouraging the rest rooms and club rooms for use of the soldiers."[28]

The women of the church were especially active in supporting the war effort. The Woman's Missionary Society agreed in September 1917 to participate with the national WMU to knit sweaters for the soldiers. The women also contributed a national flag for the sanctuary. Mr. and Mrs. W. A. Faucette provided a banner for the church honoring their two sons who were serving, which displayed a star for every member of the church serving in the war. The church held a special dedication service for the flags on 4 August 1918.[29] The women also joined the citywide effort to have all societies and book clubs join the American Red Cross and agreed to pay the $1 [$17] dues for any woman at First Baptist Church who could not afford to do so.[30]

A total of eighty-seven men from First Baptist Church volunteered or were drafted during the war.[31] Of those that served, four were killed in action: John E. Ray, Djalma Marshburn, Beverly Allen, and John C. S. Lumsden. (Lumsden was not formally a member of the church although his mother was.) John E. Ray died on 5 October 1918, five days after receiving wounds in combat. Ray, a captain, was an army medic and was wounded while giving aid to other wounded soldiers. In what was seemingly a cruel twist due to communication limitations, Ray's mother was initially informed by telegram that her son had sustained the loss of two fingers on his left hand. That telegram was followed by another that told her the wounds were not serious and he would be returning to duty. Unfortunately, Ray's injuries were more serious that what had initially been reported.[32] Ray had been a longtime member of the church and served as assistant junior superintendent of the Sunday school.[33] Djalma

---

[28] Ibid., 11 September and 7 October 1918.

[29] "Present Flag at Morning Service," *News and Observer* (Raleigh NC), 4 August 1918, 9.

[30] Minutes of the Woman's Missionary Society, 3 September 1917, 6 May 1918, and 3 June 1918.

[31] "Present Flag at Morning Service," *News and Observer*, 9. The names of the eighty-seven men are listed in the article.

[32] Ibid.; Johnson and Murray, *Wake: Capital County of North Carolina*, vol. 2, 408.

[33] "Honor Memory of Four Raleigh Boys," *News and Observer* (Raleigh NC), 30 June 1919, 12.

Marshburn, an early Navy aviator, died when his plane crashed after engine trouble off the coast of Ireland. Searchers found his body five days after the crash, on 20 May 1918. His cause of death was determined to be drowning.[34] Beverly Allen was killed in action on 29 September 1918, during fighting at the Siegfried Line. Originally a member of the National Guard, at the time of his death he was detached to a French mortar unit. Allen had been an active member of First Baptist Church and a member of the Young Men's Bible Class in the Sunday school.[35] John C. S. Lumsden served in the Army Aviation Corps. He was killed in aerial combat on 28 July 1918 over Chateau-Thierry, France. Eight enemy planes had attacked his squadron. One eyewitness described the episode:

> The enemy planes were diving on us from above, behind and from each side. Three times [I] saw Lumsden stop firing at enemies who were diving on our side and at us in order to swing his guns to the other side...[leaving] himself absolutely exposed and unprotected from the fire of the machine which was attacking us in order to keep the enemy from the machine which was performing the observation mission.... [W]hile he was thus fearlessly and purposely exposing himself to dangerous fire...the bullets from the enemy who was attacking struck him, one passing directly through his head from temple to temple.[36]

On 29 June 1919 the church held a memorial service during the 11:00 A.M worship service to commemorate the heroism of those four men. Speaking on behalf of the church, Thomas H. Briggs said that "reams and reams might be written of the valor of each for hardly did any North

---

[34] Ibid. See also "World War 1 at Sea: Casualties of the United States Navy—Naval Aviation," http://www.naval-history.net/WW1NavyUS-CasualtiesChronoxAviation.htm (accessed 21 June 2010).

[35] "Honor Memory of Four Raleigh Boys," *News and Observer*, 12.

[36] See Johnson and Murray, *Wake: Capital County of North Carolina*, vol. 2, 415–16. France awarded Lumsden with the Croix de Guerre, one of its highest military commendations. The citation received by his widow read: "First Lieutenant John C. Lumsden, 12th Aero Squadron, an excellent observer, having accomplished numerous missions with the infantry and the artillery, July, 1918, while protecting an infantry plane in combat with four enemy planes inside enemy lines, he brought down one of them and disabled another."

Carolinian die more bravely than did either of the four."[37] Briggs also read from a letter written by Ray before being wounded, in which he said that "death over there to make the world a better place to live in was to be chosen rather than success and indifference to duty here."[38] The church records made note of the event and described the service as "sweet and tender, and was an appropriate and fitting recognition and appreciation of the spirit of these fine young men who responded so cheerfully to duty's call and heroically gave their lives in the service of our beloved country."[39]

The 75 Million Campaign. In 1919 Southern Baptists developed an ambitious fundraising program—their largest ever to that point—called the 75 Million Campaign. Bolstered by the financial boom of the first two decades of the twentieth century, and by a new awareness of the needs around the world because of World War I, Southern Baptists, like other American denominational groups, sought expansion.[40] The program was designed to raise $75 million [$930 million] between 1919 and 1924. The convention went to great lengths to promote the program. George W. Truett, pastor of the First Baptist Church in Dallas, Texas, and Southern Baptists' most famous preacher at the time, was appointed the chair of a "Campaign Commission" of fifteen. L. R. Scarborough, president of the Southwestern Baptist Theological Seminary in Fort Worth, Texas, became the Southwide director and took a leave of absence from his post at the seminary in order to promote the program. State and associational leaders quickly came on board, and the editors of Baptist state newspapers joined the chorus of those promoting the program.[41]

---

[37] "Honor Memory of Four Raleigh Boys," *News and Observer*, 12.

[38] Ibid.

[39] Church Conference Records, 18 June 1919.

[40] H. Leon McBeth, *The Baptist Heritage: Four Centuries of Baptist Witness* (Nashville: Broadman Press, 1987) 618. Other denominational programs and amounts raised included "Men and Millions Movement" (Disciples of Christ, 1913, $6 million [$134 million]); the "Methodist Centenary Fund" (1916, $115 million [$2.32 billion]); the "New Era Movement" (Presbyterian, 1918, $13 million [$185 million]); "The Progress Campaign" (Reformed Church, 1918, $5 million [$71.2 million]); and the "New World Movement" (Northern Baptist Convention, 1919, $100 million [$1.24 billion]).

[41] Ibid., 618–19.

The last six months of 1919 were designated for a promotional blitz in the churches. July was to be "preparation," August "information," September "intercession," October "enlistment," November "stewardship," and from 30 November to 7 December, "victory week." Thousands of Southern Baptist pastors preached on the campaign and its necessity during those months. At the end of "victory week," pledges totaled $92,630,923 [$1.16 billion]—well beyond the initial goal of $75 million.[42] Southern Baptists were ecstatic. The future looked bright for Southern Baptists and their agencies immediately began to borrow money on the basis of the pledges in order to expand their work. Given that the program had designated five years for payment of pledges, no one thought there would be any problems collecting the money.

Unfortunately, the Southern Baptist euphoria did not last for long. The year 1919 saw an economic recession, brought on by a drop in agricultural prices, which had been inflated during the war. Crop prices dropped in half, and the total farm income was cut by more than half. Since most Southern Baptist churches were located in rural communities largely dependent upon agriculture, it soon became apparent that the convention was not going to be able to collect all the pledges that had been made. At the end of the five-year period, only $58,591,713.69 [$735 million] was raised, far short of the anticipated amount. While it was more than Southern Baptists had ever raised before, it was not near enough to cover the debts incurred by the agencies for their expansion. As a result the 1920s were a very difficult decade for Southern Baptists. And things only got worse in 1928 when it was revealed that Clinton S. Carnes, treasurer of the Home Mission Board, had embezzled $909,461 [$11.4 million] from the agency coffers. The crash of the stock market the next year almost led to bankruptcy for the convention. It would be several decades before the convention recovered its reputation and financial footing.[43]

In Raleigh the members of First Baptist Church embraced the 75 Million Campaign with great enthusiasm. The church records, when they first mention the campaign, reflect a feeling of excitement, as the church

---

[42] Ibid.
[43] Ibid., 619–20.

voted to allow its hymnals to be used for several rallies at Meredith College to promote the effort.[44] Shortly thereafter, the pastor, along with a committee consisting of W. N. Jones, J. J. Towler, and Thomas H. Briggs, selected V. O. Parker as the church's director for the campaign.[45] And by the end of the year the church had implemented an overhaul of its budget system to conform to the campaign. The following summarizes how the church budget was structured and changed by the 75 Million Campaign:

1st—Since the Seventy Five Million Dollar Fund is intended to cover all the objects of the Convention, not including pastors' salary, incidental expenses and local charity, and our membership having entered heartily into this move, we do not discontinue separate collections for the various Conventional objects, as heretofore taken, and enter into the general plan of the Seventy Five Million Campaign.

2nd—All the members of this church are expected to give of their substance to the support of the Seventy Five Million Dollar Fund, in which is included Foreign Missions, Home Missions, State Missions, Christian Education, Ministerial Relief, Orphanages and Hospitals. Any member desiring to designate his or her contribution to any one or more of these objects may do so.

3rd—The church treasurer, or financial secretary of this fund, shall keep accurate accounts of all moneys paid into his hands as such officer of the church, crediting each member with amounts paid, and shall render monthly statements to any and all members who are in arrears with their payments. In order to reach every member in making personal canvases, and for the collection of pledges, the finance committee shall be elected by the church and the membership shall be distributed among this committee.

4th—The church treasurer shall receive all moneys collected through the various organizations of the church, accurately accounting for same, and pay same to the treasurer of the Baptist State Convention. He shall also make regular monthly statements to the

---

[44] Church Conference Records, 8 August 1919.
[45] Ibid., 10 October 1919.

church showing receipts and disbursements of these funds. His accounts shall be audited by the church auditor annually.

5thUnder the general plan, all amounts paid by members under their notes previously given to the Million Dollar Move for Education, are to be credited to the member under his or her pledge given to the Seventy Five Million Dollar Campaign the same being included therein. All amounts paid by members for the objects of the Convention, named above, since May 1st, 1919 are to be credited to his or her pledge to the Seventy Five Million Dollar Campaign. The contributions of members are to be reckoned as due from the first day of November each year, and will be collected in accordance with the above plan.[46]

As expected, the members of Woman's Missionary Organization devoted themselves to the 75 Million Campaign and worked to sustain the church's level of energy and commitment to it. Sally Bailey Jones introduced the campaign to the women at their regular meeting in July 1919. In September the society encouraged the women to double what they usually gave in order to support the effort. In October the women eagerly anticipated the arrival of George W. Truett to the city, where he was scheduled to preach and promote the campaign. Finally, in November the topic for study at the women's monthly meeting was, "What a Woman Loses Who Does Not Take Part in the 75,000,000 Campaign."[47]

For the next five years the church actively promoted the 75 Million Campaign and the people gave generously. So how "successful" was the First Baptist Church in its efforts toward the campaign? The final report indicates that the church was very generous. Originally, the Southern Baptist Convention asked the church for an allotment of $115,000 [$1.43 million]. That number increased to $164,424.32 [$2.04 million] after the

---

[46] Ibid., 12 December 1919.

[47] Minutes of the Woman's Missionary Society, 7 July, 1 September, 6 October, and 3 November 1919. Truett returned to Raleigh in 1922 for a citywide revival, which lasted 1–12 March. Thousands came to hear the great preacher. Estimates were that more than 5,000 attended the final service of the revival on 12 March. See Church Conference Records, "The Truett Meeting," 1–12 March 1922.

members' pledges were tallied. The final amount given by the church was $145,258.86 [$1.82 million]. Although the church's goal was not achieved, the congregation gave $30,258.86 [$380,000], or 26.3 percent, above their allotment.[48]

Woman's Missionary Society. In 1920 the 19th Amendment to the Constitution was ratified, granting suffrage to women. But the women of First Baptist Church of Raleigh were already empowered in many ways. The Woman's Missionary Society had been an integral part of the church for decades. A careful examination of the records from the first three decades of the twentieth century provides evidence of just how important the organization was, not only to the church but to the city of Raleigh in general.

Commitment to missions was paramount to the women of the First Baptist Church. In 1911 the society expressed a willingness to raise $600 [$14,000] "for the salary of the missionary sent out from this church, Mrs. Calder Willingham."[49] Foy Elisabeth Johnson Farmer was born 6 October 1887 to Livingston and Frances Johnson. Her father was a minister and became the editor of the *Biblical Recorder* from 1917 to 1931. She attended the Baptist Female University (Meredith College), graduating with a B.A. degree in 1907. On 6 June 1911 she married Calder Truehart Willingham, son of Robert Josiah Willingham who served as Corresponding Secretary of the Foreign Mission Board from 1893 to 1914. The couple went to Kokura, Japan, as missionaries but Calder died in 1918. Foy returned to Japan as a widow but served only another two years when illness forced her to return to Raleigh in 1920.[50]

In 1922 Foy married James S. Farmer, who succeeded her father as editor of the *Biblical Recorder* in 1931. Almost immediately, she became active among the Baptists of North Carolina and Baptists throughout the South. She served three years as mission study chairwoman, three years as prayer chairwoman, and five years as vice-president of North Carolina

---

[48] That information is contained in a report pasted to the back of the Church Conference Records covering 1907–1929.

[49] Minutes of the Woman's Missionary Society, 4 December 1911.

[50] Mary Lynch Johnson, "Farmer, Foy Elizabeth Johnson," in *Encyclopedia of Southern Baptists,* ed. Lynn E. May, vol. 4 supplement (Nashville: Broadman Press, 1982) 2200.

Woman's Missionary Union. From 1942–1945 and 1946–1950, she was president of North Carolina WMU and also served as vice-president of the national WMU. From 1954 to 1960 she was a trustee of the Foreign Mission Board, and for twenty years (1943–1963), she was a director of the University of Shanghai. Additionally, she served as a trustee of Shaw University (1946–1953) and, from 1933 to 1963, as a trustee of her alma mater, Meredith College. Finally, she was the author of seven books. She died on 29 May 1971.[51]

The Woman's Missionary Society was proud of its involvement with Foy Johnson Willingham Farmer, not only because First Baptist was her home church but also because of her devotion to missions. During her seven years of service in Japan, she had maintained correspondence with the organization through letters. When she returned, the women welcomed her home with a reception and a bouquet of flowers. She spoke to the women that day of her work in Japan. The church where she and her husband had served began with nine members but had grown to twenty-one as a result of their efforts. She described her responsibilities, which included teaching a girls' class in the church, and she spoke of the eagerness of women in Japan to learn of Christ and how responsive they were to the gospel. She displayed six Japanese dolls given to her when she left and also modeled the way that Japanese women dressed. In an era before television, the Internet, and digital photography, meeting someone with items from a foreign country would have been almost as exciting as being there in person.[52]

Fannie E. S. Heck continued to have important influence among the Woman's Missionary Society of the church in the early years of the twentieth century. At the society's monthly meeting in September 1913, Fannie was invited to present a program on the topic, "The Needs of Our Society and How to Meet Them." She spoke about the history of both the Woman's Missionary Society and the children's societies, which were then active within the congregation, and how each organization had grown through the years. The most urgent needs, according to Heck, were for "greater spirituality," greater "enlistment" of new members,

---

[51] Ibid.

[52] Minutes of the Woman's Missionary Society, 2 September 1918.

and "a more enthusiastic missionary intelligence." She told the women that each meeting should be accompanied by a study of a missionary and encouraged mission study classes among the various groups. She ended with a plea "to the women to take their places in all the work, not only in our own church, but in associational and state work as well."[53]

Heck was president of the North Carolina Woman's Missionary Union from its beginning in 1886 until her death in 1915. In addition, she served as president of the national WMU from 1892 to 1894, 1895 to 1899, and 1906 to 1915. During her tenure as president of the North Carolina WMU, the organization grew from a humble beginning of seventeen societies giving less than $500 [$11,800] a year to the cause of Baptist missions, to more than 1,200 societies contributing almost $50,000 [$1.1 million]. She was instrumental in the organization of the Louisville Training School in Louisville, Kentucky, built for the purpose of educating young women.[54] Heck was also involved in social service work in the city of Raleigh as well as throughout the South. She was one of five women instrumental in the organization of the Raleigh Woman's Club and was its first president. She died on 25 August 1915, five years before the 19th Amendment to the Constitution was ratified. As great a leader as Fannie Heck was, she died having never voted in a national, state, or local election.[55]

The records from the Woman's Missionary Society provide the reader with a glimpse into the discussions among the women as well as the topics they studied. Over the years in the first several decades of the

---

[53] Ibid., (no date given) September 1913.

[54] "Miss Fannie Heck Enters Into Rest," *News and Observer* (Raleigh NC), 26 August 1915, 5. In 1953 the school became the Carver School of Missions, and ten years later its ownership was transferred to the Southern Baptist Theological Seminary, where it began to offer a master's degree in religious education with an emphasis in social work. In 1984 the name was changed once again to the Carver School of Social Work, where the master of social work degree was offered. In 1995, due to the domination of Fundamentalists on the seminary's board of trustees, the school was severed from the seminary and moved to Campbellsville University in Campbellsville, Kentucky. See Herb Hollinger, "Carver School of Social Work Given to Kentucky College," *Baptist Press*, 28 January 1998, http://www.bpnews.net/bpnews.asp?id=1934 (accessed 30 June 2010).

[55] "Miss Fannie Heck Enters Into Rest," *News and Observer*, 5.

twentieth century, they had numerous discussions about world affairs. In February 1919 Dr. Delia Dixon-Carroll, the first physician at Meredith College and the first female physician in Raleigh, conducted a program on "The Zion Movement and Its Effect on European Missions." The discussion included information about Theodor Herzl, the founder of modern Zionism, and his 1896 book *The Jewish State,* in which he argued for the creation of a separate Jewish nation in Palestine.[56] In February 1920 the society had another guest speaker, Mrs. T. P. Harrison, chairwoman for the Near East Relief Drive in Wake County, who spoke to the group about "the women and starving orphans of Armenia and Syria where the people are being so severely punished by the Turks."[57] In both June and November 1922 the topics discussed were the "Religious Status of Women in China" and "Women Living in Muslim Lands," both of which were accompanied by discussions of Taoism and Islam.[58] Roman Catholicism and the women of Latin America became the topic for discussion in December 1922.[59]

Because of their support for Baptist missionaries in foreign countries, the women of the society were keenly interested in learning about the world's religions. They studied Islam, Confucianism, Shinto, and Buddhism at various times along with Mormonism.[60] An interesting comment concerning Judaism is contained in the society's records on 6 March 1928: "the Jews, a people harder to convert to Christianity than the heathen, but work among them is a part of our duty."[61]

Another category of topics that interested the women of the society involved current social issues at that time in the United States. "Women in Educational Life" was the meeting topic in March 1916.[62] Immigration was a topic of concern as well, with subjects such as "The Duty of Christian America to the Children of Foreigners"—the topic in April

---

[56] Minutes of the Woman's Missionary Society, 3 February 1919.

[57] Ibid., 2 February 1920.

[58] Ibid., 5 June and 6 November 1922.

[59] Ibid., 4 December 1922.

[60] Ibid., 5 February, 4 March, 1 May, 7 May, and 4 June 1917; 5 June, 3 July, 7 August, 2 October, 6 November, and 4 December 1922.

[61] Ibid., 6 March 1928.

[62] Ibid., 6 March 1916.

1917.[63] The recently ended World War was in the background of the discussion on 3 March 1919 as the women considered "Our Women and War Work."[64] The Temperance Movement received attention on 5 May 1919 with the topic "The Relation of the Temperance Movement to Missions." A representative from the Women's Christian Temperance Union described how "the missionaries have found their greatest drawback to be beer and strong drink being introduced to the nations by American and British corporations."[65]

In September 1920 the women discussed the topic of the "Ministerial Relief Fund." Founded in 1918 as the Board of Ministerial Relief and Annuities, the organization originally concentrated on providing relief to retired ministers, their widows, and orphans.[66] Following the discussion the secretary recorded this comment: "If our pastors were more adequately paid for their services while they are laboring actively there would not be so much need of this fund. Half the number helped in this way are women widows of ministers who have

---

[63] Ibid., 2 April 1917. Immigration was the topic discussed on 6 June 1921, 2 May 1927, and 4 February 1929 as well.

[64] Ibid., 3 March 1919.

[65] Ibid., 5 May 1919. The interest in the Temperance Movement at that meeting in 1919 was not the only time that topic had been presented by the church. Two years earlier the church hosted a meeting of the Anti-Saloon League of North Carolina in which the featured speaker was the great William Jennings Bryan. One of the greatest orators in American history, Bryan whipped the capacity crowd into such a frenzy that on several occasions his speech had to be interrupted (once by Thomas W. O'Kelley) to calm the crowd from its boisterous applause and shouting, with reminders that the church had agreed to provide use of the sanctuary only on the condition that proper decorum be maintained, explicitly forbidding applause. (See "Bryan Champions Prohibition Cause in Strong Address," *News and Observer* (Raleigh NC), 16 January 1917, 1.)

[66] The agency began with an initial $100,000 [$1.42 million] gift from the Southern Baptist Sunday School Board and eventually secured a gift of $1 million [$14.2 million] from John D. Rockefeller and his son, John D. Rockefeller, Jr. For a brief history of the Board of Ministerial Relief and Annuities, which is now named "Guidestone Financial Resources," see "Facts about GuideStone," under "Press Kit," http://www.guidestone.org/newsroom/presskit/guidestonefacts.aspx (accessed 1 July 2010).

given the best years of their lives in service to the Master." The comment is then followed by, "Rescue the Perishing was the next hymn."[67]

The topics covered in the meetings of the Woman's Missionary Society present the modern interpreter with an opportunity to understand the thinking of the women of First Baptist Church in the early decades of the twentieth century. Those women desired to be engaged with the current events of their day. Many of them were community leaders in the city of Raleigh and were quite influential. That influence was apparent in the congregation as they became more empowered in the decision-making process of the church. No one spoke more eloquently about that than did Sallie Bailey Jones at a monthly meeting of the society in 1916. Her topic was "Women in the Christian Religion." The secretary provided the following summary of her presentation:

> Woman was created man's equal and a high standard for womanhood was given in the Old Testament. Miriam, the sister of Moses, who led her people was as divinely appointed as Moses, and Deborah, the prophetess was the first woman to rule a nation by divine appointment. With the coming of Christ there came a higher life for women and the gospel of a risen Christ was first heard by the disciples from Mary Magdalene. In later years the wives of the pioneer preachers made heroic sacrifices in the name of religion and the Christian home a great force for good.

Jones continued by describing Elizabeth Frye, a Quaker preacher "who did such splendid prison reform," and Mary Lyon, "whose efforts for the education of women were so untiring." She spoke of the first missionary society in America and the work of Ann Hasseltine Judson, "a splendid example of the heroic work of women."[68]

The men of the church soon recognized the strength and wisdom of the women, and that recognition led to a recommendation by the diaconate in 1925 to add twelve "deaconesses."[69] As described in chapter

---

[67] Minutes of the Woman's Missionary Society, 6 September 1920.

[68] Ibid., 2 October 1916.

[69] Church Conference Records, 10 April 1925.

4, the church named the first deaconesses as early as 1867. However, the women selected in 1925 were given a presence on the diaconate and, for the first time, became involved in the decision-making processes. According to the recommendation, the Woman's Missionary Society nominated the twelve women. The women selected were the following: Mrs. W. N. Jones, Emma Dowell, Mrs. C. E. Brewer, Mrs. C. W. Newcomb, Mrs. George Dowell, Mrs. Henry Bunch, Mrs. J. H. King, Mrs. John Briggs, Mrs. T. H. Briggs, Mrs. Thomas Burns, Mrs. R. T. Coburn, and Mrs. J. Rufus Hunter.[70] Unfortunately, the deaconesses did not participate in an ordination process like the male deacons. However, they were full, voting members of the diaconate. The records from the meeting of the diaconate on 9 June 1925 state the following: "It is with pleasure that we record the presence of the recently elected deaconesses at this, the first meeting since their election."[71] The first mention of an ordination service that included the women occurred at a deacons' meeting on 6 June 1936, when the pastor suggested setting aside a Wednesday evening for "ordaining newly elected deacons and deaconesses." Unfortunately, there is no record of the actual ordination service.[72]

The story of Susan Hatch serves as a further example of the dedication the women of First Baptist Church had to the Woman's Missionary Society. Susan Hatch, a longtime member of the society and supporter, died in spring 1920. At the meeting of the society on 12 April 1920, Mrs. T. H. Briggs delivered a memorial tribute to her life and dedication. In the tribute she recalled that Hatch had outlived all of her family. "What would Mrs. Susan's life have been without her church?" she asked. She continued by comparing Hatch to the "widow" in the gospels who gave the "widow's mite." Indicating that Hatch did not

---

[70] Ibid., 8 May 1925. Mrs. J. Rufus Hunter resigned the following month, but no reason is given.

[71] Minutes of the Diaconate, 9 June 1925. There is no formal statement in the church records indicating that the deaconesses were not ordained. However, it can be inferred from the entry in the Church Conference Records on 10 May 1925, describing the ordination service held for the newly elected deacons and three others who had been serving for some time but had not been ordained. Notably absent in this entry describing the ordination is any reference to the deaconesses.

[72] Minutes of the Diaconate, 6 June 1936.

have very much in the way of worldly goods, "her joy was that she had something more to give to her church" whenever she was able to make a little bit of money. "She came nearer giving the 'widow's mite' than anyone I know," said Briggs.[73] The following month the society's minutes reveal that Hatch left her entire estate to the organization—a total of $32.80 [$351]! The women were so moved by Hatch's dedication to their organization that they voted to purchase a tombstone for her grave in Oakwood Cemetery for a cost of $40 [$428.00].[74]

Addition of Church Staff. In 1919 the church indicated a desire to hire a pastoral assistant for Thomas W. O'Kelley. Although the church sought to hire someone sooner, it was not until four years later that the church hired D. R. Hamilton of New Orleans at a salary of $2,000 [$25,100] per year.[75] In a letter to Hamilton, O'Kelley described some of the expectations of the position: "One of my urgent needs is someone who can direct the young people's activities, a sort of educational secretary according to present day phraseology."[76] Hamilton began his duties in June 1923, but his tenure was short. He resigned in March 1924, and no reason is provided in the church records. The only statement about the resignation reveals that the church voted to pay him an extra $100 [$1,250] above his last paycheck, and "On motion of Bro. Carroll Weathers, the conference unanimously extended Bro. Hamilton a vote of appreciation for his work with us as assistant to the pastor."[77]

The following year a committee appointed to search for a new pastor's assistant reported that the church would hire Mary Smith of Charlotte for the position, making her the first female staff member to occupy a paid position full-time in the church's history. She began her duties in June 1925 and was well received by the congregation. She regularly reported her work to the church conference as well as to the Woman's Missionary Society. Her reports to the society actually provide

---

[73] Minutes of the Woman's Missionary Society, 12 April 1920.

[74] Ibid., 3 May and (no date given) August 1920.

[75] Church Conference Records, 7 February and 7 November 1919; 8 October 1920; 9 December 1921; 10 November 1922; and 9 March 1923.

[76] Thomas W. O'Kelley to D. R. Hamilton, TL, 23 February 1923, located in the "Sesquicentennial Scrapbook" of the Church Records.

[77] Ibid., 7 March 1924.

the most information about her work. For example, in December 1925 the records of the Woman's Missionary Society include Smith's end-of-the-year report, which describes how she had made numerous visits to the hospital and to visit other sick members as well as shut-ins and the needy of the community. Where needed, she provided "good cheer as well as material help." She gave clothing to children who were in need "so that they could attend school." The report indicated that "her deepest concern [was] for the young people of our church and she has made an earnest plea for their organizations, urging the support of our members," and concluded with the comment that her "work among us has meant much to us in many ways and hearty co-operation should be given her."[78]

It appears that Smith's responsibilities were mostly ministerial in nature. The church provided her an automobile for use beginning in 1927.[79] In summer 1928 she led the church in its very first vacation Bible school for the children.[80] She endeared herself to the congregation and served on the church's payroll until 1938.

Expansion of Facilities. By the 1920s it was apparent to the membership of First Baptist Church that the church needed to expand its education facilities. Numerous repairs to the church building and parsonage had recently been completed.[81] There were several impediments to constructing such a facility, however, not the least of which was accumulated debt. It was reported in April 1922 that the

---

[78] Minutes of the Woman's Missionary Society, 7 December 1925.

[79] Church Conference Records, 7 January 1927.

[80] Ibid., 6 June 1928.

[81] Ibid., 12 March 1920. Although the records from several years before are not completely clear as to the specific repairs and costs, it would appear that the church had carried a debt of several thousand dollars from repairs just after the turn of the century. From 1911 to 1920 various repairs were completed as needed, which included new carpet, repairs to the parsonage roof and new heating for the parsonage, a new sidewalk around the church, repairs to the church roof, repairs to the baptistery, the addition of pew racks for hymnals and envelopes, repair of the church windows, and new paint for the interior and exterior of the church. See Church Records, 6 January and 2 February 1911; 8 September 1912; 10 January, 12 September, and 19 December 1913; 10 September and 12 November 1915; 7 January and 11 February 1916; 8 June and 12 October 1917; and 11 July and 12 September 1919.

church debt was approximately $8,100 [$104,000].[82] Also, the church was in need of a new organ. The old one had been purchased in 1877. As early as 1915 a committee had been organized to contact Andrew Carnegie to see if he might be willing to provide a donation for a new organ; however, the committee's efforts were unsuccessful.[83] The church made an important decision in October 1921 when it approved a deacon's recommendation that a "campaign be undertaken" to raise funds for three projects: (1) payment of the church debt; (2) a new organ; and (3) a new education building.[84] The Committee on Ways and Means appointed to direct the campaign gave their first detailed report the following spring. Estimates were that a total of $68,000 [$870,000] would need to be raised to complete the three projects. The report continued by saying it was the committee's opinion that the membership of the church would not have the capacity to raise such a large amount of money. The committee recommended that the first priority, before purchasing a new organ or education building building, should be repayment of the debt the church had accumulated for fifteen years.[85]

Throughout the 1920s the church focused most of its attention on those three items as well as the 75 Million Campaign discussed above. The debt was paid, although the records do not provide the date upon which it was cancelled. In 1924 the church purchased a new organ from the Austin Organ Company for a total cost of $15,164 [$190,000].[86] It was dedicated at a special recital given by Dr. Dingley Brown, the church organist at the time who also served as the dean of music at Meredith College. By October 1925 the church was ready to take bids on the new building. Within a few months the church selected the Jewel Riddle Company of Sanford, North Carolina, as contractor and received an estimate of $44,950 [$550,000] as the projected cost of the project.[87] The

---

[82] Ibid., 7 April 1922.
[83] Ibid., 6 August 1915.
[84] Ibid., 7 October 1921.
[85] Ibid., 12 May 1922.
[86] Ibid., 9 May 1924.
[87] Ibid., 9 October 1925 and 12 February 1926.

four-story building, which greatly expanded the church's educational space, was completed in 1926.[88]

Death of Thomas W. O'Kelley. The decade of the 1920s was a decade filled with much growth and positive developments in the life of First Baptist Church. Unfortunately, it was also a decade that brought great sadness to the church with the untimely death of its pastor, Thomas W. O'Kelley. As late as 1925 things seemed to be positive for O'Kelley. On 24 January 1926, at the Sunday evening worship, the church honored him for his fifteenth anniversary as its pastor. Thomas H. Briggs delivered a historical sketch of O'Kelley's ministry titled "A Retrospect of Fifteen Years." W. N. Jones, J. H. Highsmith, and V. O. Parker gave anniversary greetings on behalf of the diaconate, Sunday school, and church, respectively. Outside guests included W. M. White, pastor of the First Presbyterian Church, on behalf of the Raleigh Ministerial Association; J. A. Ellis, pastor of the Pullen Memorial Baptist Church, on behalf of the Raleigh Baptist pastors; and C. E. Maddry, of the Baptist State Convention, on behalf of North Carolina Baptists. Finally, O'Kelley concluded the evening service with an address titled "The Forward Look."[89]

Whether he was aware of his illness at the anniversary celebration or not cannot be determined from the records. The first mention of his illness is found in the records of the diaconate, dated 15 August 1926, at a special called. meeting. T. H. Briggs reported that O'Kelley had been at "Connelly Springs" for more than a week and that his condition was "not as good as when he left home." The deacons voted unanimously to allow their pastor to "make arrangements to go at once to Clifton Springs, NY and remain as long as necessary, all expenses to be borne by the church and his vacation to be extended as long as necessary."[90] Unfortunately,

---

[88] Annual Uniformed Letter to the Central Baptist Association, in Church Conference Records, August 1927.

[89] "Fifteenth Anniversary of the Pastorate of Dr. Thomas W. O'Kelley," in Church Conference Records, 8 January 1926.

[90] Minutes of the Diaconate, First Baptist Church of Raleigh, 15 August 1926, located in the church archives. In the early twentieth century, Clifton Springs was known throughout the Eastern portion of the United States as a health spa, largely due to its sulfur springs and the religious enthusiasm that was pervasive in the

the treatment was not successful. In December 1926 O'Kelley tendered his resignation, but the congregation refused to accept it. However, just four months later it became apparent that his condition was not going to improve, and the church reluctantly accepted his resignation. In a move that shows the compassion of the members of the church and the love for their pastor, following acceptance of his resignation they bestowed upon him the title "Pastor Emeritus" and provided him a salary of $200 [$2,470] per month. The church also formed a search committee chaired by N. A. Dunn to select a new pastor. R. T. Vann, former president of Meredith College and a member of the congregation, was chosen to serve as interim pastor as long as necessary.[91] The beloved pastor died on 12 July 1927. According to the obituary in the *Raleigh News and Observer*, the cause of death was listed as "uraemic poisoning."[92] O'Kelley's tenure of sixteen years was the longest continuous tenure as pastor in the church's history at that point. Only Thomas E. Skinner, with a divided tenure of nineteen years, had a longer term.

John Powell Tucker (1927–1937)

At a special called meeting on 21 September 1927, following a search of only a few months, the pulpit committee recommended to the church the name of Dr. J. Powell Tucker from Selma, Alabama, to be the next pastor. Described to the congregation as "a man of pleasing personality and of marked ability," he was extended a unanimous invitation by the congregation to be its pastor.[93] Notification of Tucker's acceptance occurred at the regular church conference on 7 October 1927.[94]

Tucker was a native North Carolinian, born in Greenville on 8 February 1889, the son of James Henry and Mary Elizabeth Powell Tucker. His father was a well-known attorney who ultimately made his

---

area. (See "Historical Fact Sheet," under "Village of Clifton Springs," http://www.cliftonspringsny.org/history.htm (accessed 5 July 2010).)

[91] Church Conference Records, 11 March 1927.

[92] "Dr. T. W. O'Kelley Yields to Illness," *News and Observer* (Raleigh NC), 13 July 1927, 1.

[93] "Call Dr. Tucker as Pastor Here," *News and Observer* (Raleigh NC), 22 September 1927, 1.

[94] Church Conference Records, 7 October 1927.

career in Asheville. The Tuckers were prominent members of First Baptist Church, Asheville, where the elder Tucker served as a deacon and Sunday-school superintendent and authored the first history of the congregation. He also served as the president of the Western North Carolina Baptist Convention for three consecutive years from 1893 to 1896.[95]

The younger Tucker made a profession of faith and was baptized into the congregation at Asheville in 1900. He attended the prestigious Bingham Military School, located in Asheville at the time, and then received the B.A. from Wake Forest College in 1911. He completed his ministerial education at the Southern Baptist Theological Seminary. While he was a student at Southern, he was ordained by his home church in Asheville in 1913. The program for Tucker's ordination service reads like a "Who's Who" of Baptist life in the South at the beginning of the twentieth century. The sermon was delivered by C. B. Waller, pastor of First Baptist Church, Asheville at the time. B. W. Spilman, manager of the Southern Baptist Assembly at Ridgecrest, presented the charge to the candidate. Hight C. Moore, editor of the *Biblical Recorder*, presented Tucker with an ordination Bible. The ordination prayer was delivered by Charles W. Daniel, pastor of the First Baptist Church of Atlanta at the time. Following the "laying on of hands" by the ministers present, Prince E. Burroughs, educational secretary for the Southern Baptist Sunday School Board, presented the closing prayer.[96] Tucker had a long career serving as pastor to several prominent congregations in Southern Baptist life, including the following: First Baptist Churches of Springfield,

---

[95] "John Powell Tucker," under "Biographies," http://www.floridabaptist history.org/biographies/biographiest.html (accessed 6 July 2010). For information about the Tucker family and its contributions to the First Baptist Church of Asheville, see Charles W. Deweese, *The Power of Freedom: First Baptist Church Asheville, North Carolina, 1829–1997* (Franklin TN: Providence House Publishers, 1997) 16, 25, 58, 90–91, 98, 106–107, 110–11, 114–17, 120, 166, 174, and 337–38. The Western North Carolina Baptist Convention was an auxiliary of the Baptist State Convention of North Carolina from 1845 to 1857. It existed independently from 1857 to 1898 when it reunited with the mother organization.

[96] Deweese, *Power of Freedom*, 120–21.

Kentucky; Kershaw, South Carolina; Rock Hill, South Carolina; Selma, Alabama; and Orlando, Florida.[97]

The Great Depression. The records of the October 1927 meeting of the diaconate contain a statement that could have been considered an omen of things to come for Tucker and the church: "Bro. W. A. Yost made statement in regard to church finances, stating that collections on the church debt were coming in slowly and that the bank expected a reduction in our indebtedness."[98] Tucker's tenure at the church coincided with the Great Depression, the worst economic crisis in American history. That the church was beginning to have financial difficulty can be seen earlier in the year in the diaconate records, when the church rejected (for financial reasons) the requests of several smaller, local congregations for financial assistance. Prompted by the situation, George Marsh made a motion, which passed unanimously, "to restrict our charity work to members of the church, families connected in some way with the church or attending our church and to special cases."[99]

As the era of the Great Depression began, the church carried a significant amount of debt. The annual letter to the Central Baptist Association for 1928 indicates a debt of $19,800 [$248,000]. The following year brought a debt reduction of more than $6,000 [$75,100], but the total remained $13,500 [$169,000]. [100] The church debt and the financial crisis in the nation were of obvious concern to the membership of First Baptist Church. The deacons called a special meeting in June 1931 to consider the financial problems of the church. They divided the church roll among themselves and were instructed to canvass the congregation for pledges toward the budget for the year, which at that time was behind by $2,066 [$29,100]. The deacons were also encouraged to "secure pledges for the balance of the year from those who have not pledged."[101]

---

[97] "John Powell Tucker," under "Biographies," http://www.floridabaptist history.org/biographies/biographiest.html (accessed 6 July 2010).

[98] Minutes of the Diaconate, 4 October 1927.

[99] Ibid., 7 February 1928.

[100] Annual Letter to the Central Baptist Association, contained in Church Conference Records, August 1928 and 1929.

[101] Minutes of the Diaconate, 16 June 1931.

The impact of the depression on the church's financial well-being can be seen clearly in the amount of contributions made for missions. In 1929 the church reported to the Central Baptist Association that it contributed $48,233.53 [$604,000] toward missions, education, etc. That total had dropped considerably by 1932 to $12,726.98 [$200,000]. By 1933 the figure had declined even further to $8,616.22 [$143,000]. In 1934 the crisis seemed to have abated as the church's total mission expenditures rose significantly to $24,966.73 [$400,000].[102]

Internally, the church had to face difficult decisions about areas in the budget that needed to be cut. The deacons, in November 1930, considered cutting the new position of educational director, which had just been approved a few months before, although the position was ultimately retained for the time being. E. Powell Lee had just been hired by the church at a salary of $4,500 [$57,800] to serve as its first educational director a few months before.[103] The addition of Lee to the church staff, along with Tucker and Mary Smith, put greater pressure on the financial condition of the church. In that same November 1930 meeting of the deacons, they authorized the borrowing "for and in the name of First Baptist Church in such sum or sums as may be necessary in taking care of the existing church obligations."[104] The following month, in the presentation of the budget for the next year, the pastor's salary was cut from $6,500 [$83,500] to $5,900 [$75,800]. Mary Smith took a salary reduction as well.[105] Finally, the situation became so dire that Lee resigned from his position as educational director in March 1931.[106]

The Great Depression affected work among all Southern Baptists. The convention experienced its most serious financial crisis during the late 1920s and early 1930s. The Clinton S. Carnes situation (discussed

---

[102] Minutes of the Central Baptist Association, 1929, 35; 1932, 20; 1933, 17; and 1934, 17.

[103] Church Conference Records, 5 March 1930. Lee had considerable experience before coming to the position in Raleigh, having served in the same capacity at First Baptist Church, Macon, Georgia; Second Baptist Church, Atlanta, Georgia; and Southside Baptist Church in Birmingham, Alabama.

[104] Minutes of the Diaconate, 25 November 1930.

[105] Church Conference Records, 10 December 1930; Minutes of the Diaconate, 8 December 1931.

[106] Minutes of the Diaconate, 3 March 1931.

above) created a severe financial problem for the Home Mission Board, but other agencies had situations that were just as dire. In September 1930 L. R. Scarborough, president of Southwestern Baptist Theological Seminary in Fort Worth, presented a bleak report before the executive committee of the Southern Baptist Convention. With tears in his eyes he said, "Brethren, we are through at Southwestern…Here is my resignation and I turn over to you the seminary property. You'll have to sell it to pay our debts, and Southwestern will go out of existence."[107] He told of faculty salaries that had not been paid and of no money to pay the other seminary expenses. In a noble gesture, John R. Sampey, president of the Southern Baptist Theological Seminary in Louisville, Kentucky, responded to Scarborough: "I may lose my job for what I am about to say. Southern Seminary has some income from endowment on which we can live. I move that Southern Seminary's apportionment be cut and the difference given to Southwestern."[108] In addition to the Home Mission Board and Southwestern Seminary, the Foreign Mission Board also experienced deep financial troubles during the depression. By the time T. B. Ray became the executive secretary of the board in 1929, eighty-two missionaries had resigned from their appointments during the previous three years.[109] Overall, during the period from 1925 from 1929, while gifts to state conventions rose from $3.5 million [$42.8 million] to $5.5 million [$68.9 million], the Cooperative Program gifts going to national Southern Baptist causes dropped from $4.6 million [$56.3 million] to $2.2 million [$27.6 million]. The Southern Baptist Convention was in serious financial trouble.[110]

---

[107] Gaines S. Dobbins, *Great Teachers That Make a Difference* (Nashville: Broadman Press, 1965) 44, as cited by Jesse C. Fletcher, *The Southern Baptist Convention: A Sesquicentennial History* (Nashville: Broadman and Holman, 1994) 156.

[108] Fletcher, *Southern Baptist Convention*, 156. Fletcher reports that Dobbins recalled the episode taking place in 1933. But Robert Baker, who wrote the definitive history of the seminary, demonstrated that the date was 1930 (see Baker's *Tell the Generations Following: A History of Southwestern Baptist Theological Seminary, 1908–1983* (Nashville: Broadman Press, 1983) 255).

[109] Fletcher, *Southern Baptist Convention*, 156.

[110] Ibid., 155.

To confront the problem of debt among the Southern Baptist Convention agencies, the executive committee of the Southern Baptist Convention created the Baptist Hundred Thousand Club in April 1933. It was the brainchild of Frank Edward Tripp, who was a pastor from St. Joseph, Missouri. The goal was "the liquidation of the present debt of all the agencies of the Southern Baptist Convention."[111] The idea was simple: enlist 100,000 Southern Baptists who would agree to give $1 to the program above their regular offering to their respective church budgets. Tripp served as the general leader of the program and each state, association, and local church had a leader. In the first year of the program $37,588.28 [$602,000] was contributed. Within three years $191,296.88 [$2.86 million] had been raised, and by the end of the program in 1943 Southern Baptists contributed a total of $2,627,822.36 [$32.6 million]—a huge boost to aid Southern Baptists from their burden of debt.[112]

First Baptist Church, Raleigh, did their share for the Baptist Hundred Thousand Club. The first year that the church reported a total contributed to the campaign was 1936, when the contribution was $372.70 [$5,770]. By 1944 the total reported was $1,437.01 [$17,500].[113] The peak years for the church's contributions were 1942 and 1943, when the contributions totaled $2,053.34 [$27,000] and $2,204.55 [$27,300], respectively.[114]

Loss of Prominent Members. During Tucker's first year as pastor, the congregation experienced the loss of two of its most important members who had been leaders for decades. The first was Thomas H. Briggs, Jr., who died of heart failure on 7 May 1928. Born on 9 September 1847, Briggs became one of the most prominent members of the Raleigh community. He and his brother James A. Briggs (d. 1926) were the proprietors of Thomas H. Briggs and Sons Hardware Company, one of Raleigh's most successful businesses, founded by their father, Thomas H.

---

[111] Ibid., 158.

[112] Ibid., 158–59.

[113] The church continued to collect money for the program in 1944 even though the promotion of the program in the Southern Baptist Convention had formally ended in 1943.

[114] See the annual report of the church treasurer in the Church Conference Records for the years 1936, 1942, 1943, and 1944.

Briggs, Sr. His involvement at First Baptist Church had spanned decades. He was the grandson of one of the church's two charter deacons, John J. Briggs. He had been a member of the church for sixty-five years and an active Sunday-school member for even longer, serving as a teacher and eventually superintendent. He had also served on the diaconate for fifty years. Briggs had served not only his church but the greater Raleigh community as well. He was treasurer of Wake Forest College, his alma mater, for twenty years. He was also an early organizer of the Raleigh YMCA, as well as active in other civic and social circles.[115]

The second prominent member was Wesley N. Jones, who died on 20 October 1928. His death was also a blow to the congregation. He and his wife, Sallie Bailey Jones, had been important leaders not only at the First Baptist Church, but among all North Carolina Baptists. An attorney by profession, Jones had been chair of the diaconate at First Baptist Church for a number of years, chair of the Meredith College trustees, and the college's attorney from the school's inception. In addition, he had served as president of the Baptist State Convention (1905–1906) and for many years was a member of the Baptist State Convention Board of Missions. For more than thirty years he had also served as the attorney for Wake Forest College, his alma mater. Along with his contributions to his local church and denomination, Jones had been an important fixture in the Raleigh business and legal community, serving on various boards of businesses in the city.[116] The loss to the church of both Jones and Briggs left a leadership vacuum among the laity, which greatly affected the church during the decade of the 1930s.

Resignation of Tucker. J. Powell Tucker served as pastor of the First Baptist Church until 1937. He navigated the church through the turbulent decade of the Great Depression and provided stable leadership following the long pastorate of Thomas W. O'Kelley. Tucker's resignation came on 24 November 1937 at a special called meeting of the church. He told the congregation that evening that he had just accepted an offer to be the pastor of the First Baptist Church of Orlando, Florida. Tucker's

---

[115] "Thomas H. Briggs Dies At His Home," *News and Observer* (Raleigh NC), 8 May 1928, 1–2.

[116] "W. N. Jones Dies at His Home Here," *News & Observer* (Raleigh NC), 21 October 1928, 1–2.

resignation, while probably not forced, was possibly the result of some dissension in the church. The financial crisis of the 1930s had taken an emotional toll on the church. Evidence of disagreements within the congregation can be seen in a letter read to the deacons at their meeting on 7 September 1937. M. L. Shipman, a member of the congregation, had sent the letter to N. A. Dunn, the chair of the diaconate. Shipman began by indicating that after making a careful investigation, presumably within the congregation, he had concluded that "the First Baptist church is slumbering over a simmering volcano and only the wisest diplomacy can prevent an eruption that would be heard around the State." He mentioned the fact that a "large percentage of the membership" believed that "the reasons advanced for the displacement of Dr. Tucker are puerile and that the action of members of the Board of Deacons is most unfortunate." He counseled that a "cooling process" should occur in order to "create a more brotherly feeling in the hearts of the membership." If the deacons decided against a "watchful waiting" approach to the problem, then he advised bringing the issue before the entire congregation. Although he did not believe that "Doctor Tucker would approve this course," his supporters in the church would be supportive of such a course. Concluding, he warned that "there is no discounting the fact that serious consequences to the church are now impending…and unless a finer spirit of brotherhood shall be exercised it is going on the rocks."[117]

That letter to deacon chair N. A. Dunn raises more questions than it answers. One is left to wonder what Shipman means by the phrase, "slumbering over a simmering volcano." Furthermore, what does Shipman mean when he makes reference to Tucker's "supporters" and the "displacement of Dr. Tucker" by an "action of the Board of Deacons"? Unfortunately, there is no direct information available to answer the questions. It would appear that some kind of disagreement occurred between Tucker and the deacons, resulting in a tense relationship between pastor and diaconate. Yet neither do the church conference minutes nor the records of the diaconate contain any explicit mention of

---

[117] Minutes of the Diaconate, 7 September 1937. The original letter from Shipman is pasted inside the record book.

conflict between the deacons and Tucker or divisions within the congregation.

From the records of both the church conferences and the deacons' meetings, there was only one particular issue that may be construed as controversial and could have sown seeds of discontent between pastor and deacons. It was a proposal to restructure the diaconate and the method by which deacons were elected, which was really nothing other than an effort to establish a deacon rotation system—with deacons serving a four-year term then rotating off the diaconate. (The practice is quite common today among Baptist churches.) However, the effort failed and the following year, when brought up again, it failed a second time. Was Tucker perceived by some of the deacons as the architect of that effort in some way, thereby creating a power struggle between pastor and deacons that lasted for the next five years? Perhaps it is true, but again there is no direct evidence of it in the records.[118]

Whatever the issue, it is interesting that Tucker submitted his resignation within two months of Shipman's letter to the chair of the deacons. Also, the evening that Tucker read his letter of resignation to the congregation, Shipman moved that the congregation ask him to reconsider resigning. The motion was approved unanimously by the church. It would seem, therefore, that there may have been some tense relationships between the pastor and deacons (from what can be gathered by Shipman's letter), but certainly no open conflict existed that could be attributed to Tucker's resignation.[119]

Along with Tucker's resignation came the resignation of the church organist Mrs. Roger P. Marshall, who had served the congregation for more than eleven years. [120] One month later Hubert A. Tomlinson resigned from the diaconate after having served for two years. In his letter of resignation Tomlinson referenced the "many developments in the meantime, and particularly in consideration of the more recent trend of events," he believed it time for him to tender his resignation from the

---

[118] Ibid., 6 January 1931 and 6 September 1932.

[119] "Tucker Resigns Pastorate Here," *News & Observer* (Raleigh NC), 15 November 1937, 12.

[120] Church Conference Records, 8 December 1937.

diaconate.[121] The most serious staff loss to the congregation came a few months later when Mary Smith tendered her resignation as the pastor's assistant. She had served the church under two pastors for a total of thirteen years. Smith's reason for her resignation likely had to do with her health. The church records report that she died on 17 March 1939.[122]

* * *

The First Baptist Church of Raleigh weathered the First World War and the Great Depression and emerged financially stronger and determined to face the middle of the twentieth century and its challenges. It was a time for new leadership in the life of the congregation. Challenges were just around the corner. Fortunately, the church found capable leadership, and its indomitable spirit served it well as it entered the next several decades.

---

[121] Hubert A. Tomlinson to Brother Moderator, Ladies and Gentlemen, contained in Church Conference Records, 5 January 1938.

[122] Mrs. M. A. Smith to the Congregation, in Church Conference Records, 6 July 1938; Church Conference Records, 5 April 1939.

7

Preparing for a New Generation (1938–1960)

By the late 1930s the Great Depression had brought untold misery to millions of Americans. Franklin Roosevelt's landslide re-election in 1936 signaled American confidence in his ability to pull the nation out of the grips of economic disaster with the New Deal programs, but there was no quick solution to the problems. The Great Depression also brought a shift in the American psyche from the optimism of just a few decades earlier to one of pessimism and misery, as evidenced in the 1932 song "Brother, Can You Spare a Dime?":

> They used to tell me I was building a dream,
> And so I followed the mob;
> When there was earth to plow or guns to bear
> I was always there, right there on the job.
> They used to tell me I was building a dream
> With peace and glory ahead;
> Why should I be standing in line
> Just waiting for bread?[1]

By 1940 Americans had another worry on top of their economic woes. The devastation of World War I left the German people vulnerable to Adolf Hitler's promises to restore the German nation to greatness. In Italy Benito Mussolini represented another fascist threat to Europe. Stalin's blood purges in Communist Russia, a civil war in Spain, and Japan's aggressive actions in Asia gave Americans further concern. The world was about to be drawn into war for the second time in thirty years. This time Americans were even less eager to enter the fray than they had been in the previous war. Polls of public opinion in 1937 revealed that 70 percent of Americans thought it had been a mistake to enter World War I,

---

[1] "Brother, Can You Spare a Dime?," under "Songs of the Great Depression," http://www.library.csi.cuny.edu/dept/history/lavender/cherries.html (accessed 1 September 2010).

and 95 percent thought the nation should stay out of Europe's troubles if it came to war.[2] Yet public opinion took a turn with the Japanese attack on Pearl Harbor on 7 December 1941, and once again America was at war.

World War II changed the American people forever. Thousands of young men either volunteered for service or were drafted. More than 400,000 American soldiers died in the effort, and thousands more were wounded. The war effort back home brought gas and commodity rationing, which forced on the citizens a sense that they were participating in the sacrifice. Women by the thousands moved into factories to occupy jobs building tanks, jeeps, airplanes, and even ships, because so many men were serving in the armed forces. African Americans also served in the military, at first in segregated units but eventually alongside Caucasian soldiers.

The detonation of atomic bombs in Hiroshima and Nagasaki finally ended the war in the Pacific with Japan. With access to a weapon so destructive, America emerged as a leading superpower—a status few nations would dare to challenge. The American economy was strong once again because of the increased productivity during the war effort. Yet things were not so positive in other parts of the world. While the American economy had benefited, the war brought economic hardship to the Soviet Union, Great Britain, and France. Their colonial empires were also threatened by assorted nationalist actions in Africa, Asia, and the Middle East. Germany and Japan were devastated, and China was about to enter a bitter civil war.[3]

To compound the danger on the world scene, the Soviet Union exploded its own atomic bomb in 1949. That, coupled with the Soviet Union's refusal to cooperate with the other Allies in Europe following the war's end, led to the Cold War—a war characterized by espionage, subversion of foreign governments, and an arms race. The American fear that Communism would spread plunged the nation once again into war—this time in Korea. The Korean War lasted from 1950 to 1953 and

---

[2] Winthrop D. Jordan and Leon F. Litwack, *The United States*, 7th ed. (Englewood Cliffs: Prentice Hall, 1991) 695.

[3] Ibid., 729.

cost the United States another 53,000 soldiers. As might be expected, patriotism became an important value exhibited by Americans in the 1950s. Love of God was joined with love of country in the American state of mind during the administration of Dwight D. Eisenhower. The phrase "under God" was inserted into the Pledge of Allegiance in 1954. "In God We Trust," added to American coinage during the Civil War, became the nation's official motto in 1956.

The city of Raleigh continued to sustain growth and development during the middle decades of the twentieth century. In 1936 Raleigh had taken advantage of the Federal Theatre Project, one of the New Deal programs designed to promote live artistic performances throughout the country. The result was the birth of the Raleigh Little Theatre, and construction of its building, which has operated continuously for seventy-five years as a community theater. The theater's first performance was *The Drunkard*, a play promoting temperance that was originally written in 1844.[4]

The year 1943 brought the opening of RDU airport, a joint venture between the cities of Raleigh and Durham. The precursor to RDU was the Raleigh Municipal Airport, established in 1929. The airport established passenger and mail service in 1932 but business soon outgrew the small airfield. In 1938 the president of Eastern Airlines, Eddie Rickenbacker, convinced Raleigh and Durham they should begin work on a new airport. Work began on a parcel of land between the two cities in 1941 and the new airport opened in 1943, a transportation improvement that revolutionized the business environment in the Triangle.[5] Another milestone for Raleigh during the middle decades of the twentieth century came as developer Willie York overcame opposition from the Raleigh Garden Club and the residents of Cameron Park to create Cameron Village in 1949. Raleigh's first shopping center boasted more than 500,000 square feet of space and became highly successful. In the coming decades more shopping centers were built, and eventually enclosed malls were

---

[4] David Perkins, ed., *Raleigh: A Living History of North Carolina's Capital* (Winston-Salem NC: John F. Blair, 1994) 134–35.

[5] Ibid., 139–42.

added to a shopper's options. Cameron Village serves as a symbol of the economic boom following the postwar years in Raleigh.[6]

The First Baptist Church of Raleigh 1938–1960

Sydnor L. Stealey (1938–1942)

As 1938 began, the First Baptist Church of Raleigh embarked upon a search for a new pastor. Following the successful pastorates of Thomas W. O'Kelley and J. Powell Tucker would not be an easy task for the next pastor. The total membership of the church stood at more than 1,400, with a Sunday-school enrollment of more than 1,000.[7] The church budget for 1938 approved by the congregation was $30,000 [$457,000]. Clearly, First Baptist Church of Raleigh was a large, vibrant congregation in need of a gifted leader and capable preacher.

The church named a pulpit committee of fifteen members chaired by Will Wyatt soon after the start of the year.[8] Within four months the committee brought the name of Sydnor L. Stealey to the congregation with a recommendation that he be called as the next pastor. The church unanimously approved the choice of Stealey along with the salary recommendation of $4,200 [$63,900] per year, the use of the parsonage, and $200 [$3,050] moving expenses. The congregants promised their "love and support" along with "steadfast cooperation in the task of winning men and women to Christ, and in the advancement of His Kingdom in the earth."[9]

Sydnor Stealey was a rising star among Southern Baptists when he accepted the pastorate of First Baptist Church. He was born in Martinsburg, West Virginia, on 7 March 1897. His father, Clarence Perry Stealey, was also a Baptist minister and moved the family west to Oklahoma in 1909 where he founded and edited the *Baptist Messenger*,

---

[6] Ibid., 180–81.

[7] Annual Letter to the Central Baptist Association, contained in Church Conference Records, 22 September 1937.

[8] Church Conference Records, 9 February 1938.

[9] Ibid., 18 May 1938.

the state Baptist paper of Oklahoma.[10] Sydnor graduated from Oklahoma Baptist University (B.A., 1920) and the Southern Baptist Theological Seminary (Th.M., 1927; Ph.D., 1932). Following his graduation from college, he married Jessie Wheeler, also an Oklahoman, and became principal of a high school in Ringling, Oklahoma, from 1920 to 1922. Accepting a calling to ministry, he was ordained in 1922 and taught for two years at William Jewell College in Missouri. In 1925 he began his pastoral career in Missouri and within two years moved to Louisville, Kentucky, where he continued his education. He served several smaller churches in Kentucky while he was a seminary student, and upon graduation with his doctoral degree he became pastor of the First Baptist Church in Bloomington, Indiana (1932–1934). When called to Raleigh's First Baptist Church, he was serving as the pastor of the Bainbridge Street Baptist Church in Richmond, Virginia (1934–1938).[11]

Stealey's academic credentials were impressive, perhaps making him the most "scholarly" of the pastors to serve the church up to that point. As a graduate student at the Southern Baptist Theological Seminary he had worked as student assistant for the great E. Y. Mullins, who likely influenced his theology. Stealey's contacts at Southern and his love for the academic world would eventually take him away from First Baptist Church and back to the seminary where he joined the faculty full-time. Subsequently, by 1951 Stealey's reputation as a careful scholar and denominational leader led to an invitation to become the founding president of the Southeastern Baptist Theological Seminary in Wake Forest, North Carolina. He served as the seminary's president until 1963. Stealey died on 24 July 1969.[12]

---

[10] W. B. Shurden, "Stealey, Clarence Perry (1868–1937," in *Dictionary of Baptists in America*, ed. Bill J. Leonard (Downers Grove IL: Intervarsity Press, 1994) 259. Clarence Stealey was a well-known Fundamentalist leader among Southern Baptists in Oklahoma. He was an ally of the infamous J. Frank Norris, pastor of First Baptist Church in Fort Worth, in many of Norris's battles against Southern Baptists. It is interesting that Sydnor's life and theology, while remaining in the Southern Baptist tradition, took a different theological turn away from his father's rigid Fundamentalism.

[11] James H. Blackmore, "Stealey, Sydnor Lorenzo," in *Encyclopedia of Southern Baptists*, ed. Clifton J. Allen, vol. 3 supplement (Nashville: Broadman Press, 1988).

[12] Ibid.

The new pastor began his work in earnest in summer 1938. At one of his first meetings with the diaconate, he requested three things: (1) a new members' dinner held occasionally to foster greater awareness of the various ministries of the church, (2) the printing of some personal business cards and literature so that he might be able to promote the church's work, (3) and a request that he be given direct authority over the paid personnel of the church in order that the church staff may operate more efficiently. The deacons responded by approving only the first of the three requests and told the new pastor that he should use the "advisory committee" for other matters with which he may need assistance—an interesting rebuff of what might seem like simple requests.[13]

An important improvement to the church facility and a symbol of the modernization for the twentieth century during Stealey's tenure was the installation of an elevator. The idea first appeared in the church records in January 1939. Several months later the plan to raise the money necessary as a memorial to the late Thomas W. O'Kelley gave the project a boost. A report that $2,300 [$35,500] had been raised for the project was given in July 1939. By fall the elevator was installed and operational. The church held a dedication to the memory of O'Kelley in November of that year. A letter from O'Kelley's daughter was read at the dedication ceremony calling to the church's attention that one of his favorite hymns was "I'm Pressing on the Upward Way," which includes the lyrics, "Lord lift me up, and let me stand, by faith on Heaven's table land." She said, "I am sure that his blessed spirit…is happy today in the knowledge that many people who might not otherwise be able to enter the Lord's House…are being lifted into the sanctuary and so nearer the presence of God through the medium of a memorial which bears his name."[14]

Ecumenical Relations. For most of its history First Baptist Church has been ecumenical in its orientation toward other Christian denominations. That was clearly evident in the 1940s and 1950s. For instance, in March

---

[13] Minutes of the Diaconate, 6 September 1938.

[14] Church Conference Records, 4 January, 10 May, 5 July 1939; Mary O'Kelley Peacock to the Members of the First Baptist Church, Raleigh, North Carolina, LS, 22 November 1939. The original copy of the letter is contained in Church Conference Records, 8 November 1939.

1940 the church participated with Edenton Street Methodist Church in joint Holy Week services. The event was so successful that the two churches partnered with First Presbyterian Church for joint Sunday evening services during the summer months. The tradition of joint evening services in the summer continued for the next several decades, creating further good will between the churches. Eventually, the Episcopal Church of the Good Shepherd became a part of the event.

While the Baptists worshipped with the Methodists, Presbyterians, and Episcopalians on Sunday evenings in the summers, they also studied regularly about those traditions. Beginning in January 1945 Broadus Jones, Stealey's successor as pastor, implemented a series of seven Sunday-evening sermons titled "Contributions _____ Have Made to Religious History," with a different denomination highlighted each week. He began the series with the Episcopalians, then followed with Presbyterians, Methodists, Catholics, Lutherans, and finally Baptists. The final sermon of the series was delivered by Rabbi Harold Gelfman in honor of Brotherhood Week. The church bulletin for that Sunday contains the following description of the Rabbi's visit: "Its essential purpose is to unify the human family under the Fatherhood of God." The bulletin also noted that Broadus Jones had spoken the previous Friday evening at Temple Beth Or.[15]

Restructuring the Diaconate. Two years into Stealey's ministry the church gave approval to an organizational change that had been attempted almost a decade earlier. In 1931 a suggestion had been made to reorganize the diaconate, but the proposal had fallen short of the necessary votes needed for passage.[16] In December 1940 the deacons made a recommendation to the church that the diaconate be divided into two categories. Deacons older than the age of seventy were designated "members of the board for life." The remainder of the diaconate was to be composed of forty members: twenty-eight deacons and twelve deaconesses. One-fourth of that number would rotate off each year on 31 December. Seven new deacons and three new deaconesses were to be

---

[15] Church Bulletin, 18 February 1945. See also Church Bulletin, 7 January 1945 for a description of the series.

[16] Minutes of the Diaconate, 6 January and 3 February 1931.

elected each year at the regular church conference in December. No deacon or deaconess would be eligible for re-election until one year after the expiration of his or her term of office.[17] The same church conference that approved the new deacon rotation system also approved a report from the church's committee on committees that called for the chair of the diaconate to appoint deacons to serve as greeters at the front door during Sunday services, believing "that the Deacons of our church need to take a more active part in the activities and life of our church." The report also indicated that "the presence of such officers at the church door will add dignity and reduce confusion which sometimes occurs with visitors as well as our own members."[18]

The attention to the diaconate at First Baptist Church in that 1940 church conference reflects a tendency among many other Baptist churches in the early twentieth century. Historian Charles Deweese has shown that in the first half of the twentieth century, Baptist churches continued a trend begun in the previous century of defining the role of deacon as administrator. By the middle of the twentieth century, writers, and thus Baptist churches, began to encourage more involvement by deacons in the life of the congregation in a ministerial capacity, which included visitation of the sick, evangelism, and crisis care.[19] Howard B. Foshee's *The Ministry of the Deacon* became a classic guide to Southern Baptist churches regarding the role of the deacon in the postwar era of the twentieth century. Foshee expressed the conviction that the "actual authority of deacons is one of Christian influence rather than authority as a board of directors."[20]

Those actions on the part of the congregation reflect an attempt to bring more balance to the role of deacon at Raleigh's First Baptist Church.

---

[17] Church Conference Records, 4 December 1940. To begin the process, the chair and secretary of the diaconate selected by lot seven of the present deacons to serve one year, and the same number to serve two, three, and four years. They repeated the procedure with three deaconesses for each of the successive years.

[18] Ibid.

[19] Charles W. Deweese, *The Emerging Role of Deacons* (Nashville: Broadman Press, 1979) 49–60.

[20] Howard B. Foshee, *The Ministry of the Deacon* (Nashville: Convention Press, 1968) 24.

In the early years of the church's history, before the advent of the Woman's Missionary Society, the church minutes report deacon involvement in charity and other such matters in the congregation and community. While that did not stop completely when the women organized, the minutes of the church conferences, deacons' meetings, and Woman's Missionary Society meetings reflect a trend beginning in the late nineteenth century to relegate the charity work to the women, leaving the administrative tasks to the deacons. With the addition of deaconesses to the diaconate, it was only a short time before the church sought a more balanced role for its deacons.

Biblical Recorder. The subject of the *Biblical Recorder* became an item for discussion at the church conference on 9 July 1941. A presentation by its editor, John C. Slemp, concerned the paper's financial difficulties. A recommendation from the diaconate then followed, asking for the church to purchase 400 subscriptions for the remainder of the year and distribute those subscriptions among the membership. N. A. Dunn, chair of the diaconate and presiding officer over the church conference that day, vacated his seat as presiding officer and spoke a personal word of support about the *Biblical Recorder* to the church. The minutes of the meeting describe Dunn's words as "rather condemning [of] our membership for the lack of interest in our state denominational paper." Dunn called the congregation's attention to its long history of close relationship with the *Biblical Recorder* extending all the way back to the founding editor, Thomas Meredith, and the fact that all of Meredith's successors had been "affiliated with our church." Dunn also stressed the importance of reading the journal, "and thereby keeping informed concerning our church and denominational activities."[21]

The *Biblical Recorder* is one of the most successful and oldest of the Baptist state papers in the South. Founded by Thomas Meredith in 1833, the journal has published the news of Baptists in the South, and particularly in North Carolina, for more than 175 years. The *Recorder* was privately owned until 1938 when it was purchased by the Baptist State Convention of North Carolina. First Baptist Church, Raleigh and the *Biblical Recorder* have enjoyed a close relationship through much of their

---

[21] Church Conference Records, 9 July 1941.

shared history. Thomas Meredith's importance to the church was described in chapter 3. Upon his death in 1850 the church's pastor, T. W. Tobey, became the acting editor of the journal for almost two years. Since Meredith, the paper has employed fourteen editors: James D. Hufham (1861–1867); John H. Mills (1868–1873); Christopher T. Bailey (1875–1895); Josiah W. Bailey (1895–1907); Hight C. Moore (1908–1917); Livingston Johnson (1917–1931); James S. Farmer (1931–1938); George W. Paschal, (1938–1939), acting editor; John C. Slemp (1939–1941); Levy L. Carpenter (1942–1960); J. Marse Grant (1960–1982); R. Gene Puckett (1982–1998); Tony W. Cartledge (1998–2007); and Norman W. Jameson (2007–2010). The majority of the journal's editors throughout its history have been active members of First Baptist Church, Raleigh.

Resignation of Stealey. Compared to the long tenures of his predecessors, Stealey's tenure was relatively short. Word that he was in discussion with the Southern Baptist Theological Seminary about a possible faculty position leaked out earlier than he desired. The Sunday bulletin for 31 May 1942 contained the following statement by the pastor:

> The pastor regrets that news of the action of the Board of Trustees of the Southern Baptist Theological Seminary inviting him to the chair of Church History came to the congregation so unexpectedly in his absence. There are no controlling news agencies. President Sampey had spoken to me about the matter but the action of the Board was so uncertain that good judgment prevented my saying anything to you, for there was strong likelihood that nothing would come of it. Now, even yet, I cannot give my decision. A new president has been elected and I must await his action. I seek God's guidance to do what I ought to do. No man can be honest or happy otherwise. I know you will be patient and prayerful and helpful.[22]

By the next week, however, Stealey formally resigned as pastor of the church to become a professor of church history at Southern Seminary. In a handwritten letter addressed to "My Dear Fellow Workers," Stealey indicated that the contact from the seminary about the possibility came the previous December and that the decision to leave had been a "hard

---

[22] Church Bulletin, 31 May 1942.

decision" to make. He was convinced, nevertheless, that he should leave, "for I believe that my life can be more useful there than in any other place."[23] Stealey served on the faculty of the Southern Baptist Theological Seminary from 1942 to 1951. His success as a professor, according to one historian of the seminary, was attributed to the fact that he "endeared himself to many by his natural wit, homespun wisdom, and wise counsel."[24]

Broadus E. Jones (1943–1959)

The church was without a pastor for a year following Stealey's resignation. During the intervening period the church employed Charles Henry Durham, pastor emeritus from the First Baptist Church of Lumberton, North Carolina, to fill the pulpit as interim pastor.[25] In May 1943 the church called a meeting of the congregation where the pulpit committee presented the name of Broadus E. Jones, pastor of the First Baptist Church of Norfolk, Virginia, and recommended that he be called as the church's new pastor. They recommended that his starting salary be set at $5,000 [$62,000] per year with a $300 [$3,720] car allowance and use of the parsonage. The recommendation was accepted and Broadus began his tenure as pastor on 22 August 1943.[26]

At forty-seven years of age, Broadus Jones was a seasoned pastor with plenty of educational and ministry experience. He was born in Georgia in 1896. He graduated from Mercer University (A.B. degree) and the Southern Baptist Theological Seminary (Th.M.). He had served pastorates in Georgia and Kentucky while he was a student. Before coming to First Baptist Church of Raleigh, he had been the pastor of First

---

[23] S. L. Stealey to "My Dear Fellow Workers," LS, 7 June 1942, contained in the Church Conference Records, 7 June 1942.

[24] William A. Mueller, *A History of Southern Baptist Theological Seminary* (Nashville: Broadman Press, 1959) 222.

[25] C. H. Durham served as pastor of the Lumberton church on two different occasions: 1900 to 1914 and 1918 to 1941. His name was highly respected among Baptists in North Carolina. See http://www.fbclumbertonnc.com/history_beliefs (accessed 14 April 2011).

[26] Church Conference Records, 30 May 1943.

Baptist Church in Norfolk, Virginia, for eight years. [27] He died in 1972 after sixty years in ministry.

World War II. Jones's pastorate began during one of America's most serious and frightening periods. While America tried to maintain neutrality after the war began in Europe in 1939, the surprise attack on Pearl Harbor on 7 December 1941 brought Americans into the conflict. Thousands lined up to volunteer for the armed forces following the nation's formal declaration of war. Seemingly overnight, the country's economy changed and the high unemployment of the Great Depression was replaced by thousands of workers, including women, who went to work in factories to provide the goods and materials necessary for the war effort.

The first reference to World War II in the church's records came in a short entry from 10 July 1940, seventeen months before the United States formally declared war on the Axis powers. W. F. Marshall presented a request that the church express its support for the "British Baptist Mission fields which our brethren in England have been forced to give up on account of the war." [28] For the most part, however, the war was "over there" for the majority of the church members since no American soldiers were directly involved at that point.

The war effort did eventually become a part of the church's regular activities, actually a few months before the attack on Pearl Harbor. The church bulletin for 26 October 1941 reported that a "writing room for service men" had been established in the church "to assist soldiers and other service men who are visiting our city." The church provided space for two writing tables in two different Sunday-school classrooms, which were open on Saturday and Sunday afternoons for soldiers to use to correspond with loved ones. The chair of the committee established for that ministry, Mrs. T. M. Pittman, also made an appeal for families to host service men in their homes for a meal after the Sunday-morning worship services. [29] By late 1942 the church bulletin carried the following request: "Let prayer be made without ceasing for our soldier boys at

---

[27] Report of Pulpit Committee to First Baptist Church, Raleigh, North Carolina, contained in ibid.

[28] Church Conference Records, 10 July 1940.

[29] Church Bulletin, 26 October 1941.

home and abroad, and for our country in this our greatest of all wars. Our interest should not be half-hearted, but genuine and sincere."[30]

A large number of men and women from the church were involved in the armed services during World War II. In May 1943 the church bulletin printed a list of seventy-eight names under the heading "Our Men and Women in Service."[31] Several months later the deacons recommended that the church purchase American and Christian flags to be displayed in the sanctuary, along with another recommendation that the church contribute $25 [$310] to the USO Club in Raleigh.[32] By 1944 the number of church members serving in the armed forces had risen dramatically to 125. Since the number was too great to list altogether each week in the bulletin, in March 1944 the church began listing the names and addresses of ten of them each Sunday so that members of the congregation to could write letters to the soldiers from home.[33]

The Invasion of Normandy, the turning point of the war in Europe, provided much concern and discussion in the church records. On 21 May 1944 the church bulletin contained the following statement revealing the seriousness of the moment:

"D Day"
When the signal comes to the American people that our Armies have invaded Europe religious people all over America are requested to come immediately to their churches for a season of prayer. It will be the most fateful hour in the history of our world and never will prayers be so needed as then. No formal service will be held. Each individual in his own way in his own church will pray to his God on behalf of those whom he loves, and his country and the destiny of our world. The church will be open all day and until 9:30 at night. If the invasion signal comes after 9:30, the church will be open the following day on the same schedule."[34]

---

[30] Ibid., 15 November 1942.
[31] Ibid., 23 May 1943.
[32] Church Conference Records, 4 August 1943.
[33] Church Bulletin, 19 March 1944.
[34] Ibid., 21 May 1944.

Almost two weeks later the church bulletin reported that the following Wednesday evening service would be dedicated to the families of the men and women in the armed forces. The names of all of them were to be called publically. Excerpts from letters exchanged between families were also to be read in that special prayer service. The following week the Sunday bulletin indicated that approximately 250 were present for the service. By the end of June 1944 the church had a total of 146 men and women who were serving in the armed forces. The names of soldiers from the church killed in action were also reported. On 25 June Private Sage Upshaw was reported to have been killed in action, followed by an announcement of the death of Major James Jordan Bynum who was killed in August.[35]

After four long years of American involvement, the war finally ended in 1945 with VE-Day (8 May) and VJ-Day (2 September). Though it had taken a toll on the nation in soldier casualties, the war did finally bring the nation out of the Great Depression by sending Americans back to work. It also opened the eyes of the average American to the world at large. Thousands of soldiers and sailors, most of whom had never ventured very far from their birthplaces, saw the world firsthand. Many returned home, furthered their education through the G.I. Bill, and contributed to building the nation into a superpower.

Despite the difficulty of the war years, Southern Baptists had reason to celebrate more than just the conclusion of the war. By 1943, largely due to the efforts of the Hundred Thousand Club and active promotion of the Cooperative Program, the convention was finally able to declare itself free of debt, adding to the celebratory spirit as the war ended. Church contributions increased by almost $22 million [$262 million] in 1945 over the previous year—an omen of things to come in the postwar years.[36]

As 1945 dawned, Southern Baptists also prepared to celebrate their centennial. As early as 1939 the convention began to plan for a grand event to occur at the annual meeting scheduled for Atlanta in May 1945. The focus of the centennial celebration was to be an evangelistic

---

[35] Ibid., 4 June, 11 June, 25 June, and 3 September 1944.

[36] Jesse C. Fletcher, *The Southern Baptist Convention: A Sesquicentennial History* (Nashville: Broadman and Holman, 1994) 173–75.

emphasis with a goal of winning one million converts. While the goal was not achieved completely, more than 500,000 converts were reported at the conclusion of the campaign, making it the largest and most successful evangelistic effort of its kind in Southern Baptist history. Unfortunately, the celebratory event for which they had planned did not occur. A government ban on large group meetings in 1945 forced the convention to cancel its annual session where the centennial was to be celebrated. The convention's centennial was also overshadowed by the nation's merriment over the war's end. The commemoration finally happened the following year at the annual meeting in Miami, but the eagerness of the moment had passed.[37]

The Southern Baptist Convention centennial spirit was not lost on the membership of Raleigh's First Baptist Church. In anticipation of the 100th year, the church bulletin on 19 November 1944 carried the following statement:

> The year 1945 marks the one hundredth year of service for the Southern Baptist Convention. The Centennial Crusade now being planned by the Executive Committee "aims to complete, celebrate, climax, and crown a century of organized service for Christ." The objectives center in evangelism, enlistment, education, stewardship, and rehabilitation. What could be more worthy goals for our Church in the anticipation of a new unspent year?[38]

Postwar Missions and Finances. A commitment to missions was at the heart of the membership of First Baptist Church during the Broadus Jones years, as had been the case throughout its history. In the late 1940s the church began to assume the annual salary of one Foreign Mission Board missionary. The church records note that in 1946 the salary of "Dr. McMillan, the Church Missionary" [was] to be increased to $1,000 [$9,600] for 1947.[39] Unfortunately, no further information exists as to when the church first committed to it, but the minutes of the church conferences and the Woman's Missionary Society reveal that the program

---

[37] Ibid., 175.
[38] Church Bulletin, 19 November 1944.
[39] Church Conference Records, 4 September 1946.

continued long after McMillan's retirement in 1955. In addition to the annual salary, the church also sent to the McMillans a monetary gift each Christmas.

Hudson and Lelia Memory McMillan served the Foreign Mission Board as missionaries to China and then to the Bahamas from 1913 to 1955. Both were native North Carolinians. Henry was born in Wagram, while Lelia's birthplace was Whiteville. Henry graduated from Wake Forest College in 1908 with an A.B. degree, and then received the Th.M. and Th.D. degrees from the Southern Baptist Theological Seminary. The couple married in 1913 just before departing for China. Lelia was educated at Meredith College, graduating in 1908 with a major in music. She taught music for several years at Buies Creek Academy (now Campbell University) before she and Henry were married.[40]

Following the McMillans' retirement from the Foreign Mission Board in 1955, the church continued the missionary support program by committing to provide the annual salary for Winfield and LaVerne Applewhite. The Applewhites, originally from Statesville where Winfield practiced medicine, were appointed as medical missionaries to Indonesia by the Foreign Mission Board in December 1955. Winfield was originally from Atlanta. He graduated from Baylor University with a major in chemistry and then attended medical school at Vanderbilt University. He completed his internship at the U.S. Marine Hospital in New Orleans and served in the Pacific in the U.S. Army Medical Corps during World War II. LaVerne Viverette was a native of Mississippi. She graduated from Blue Mountain College and then completed a degree in religious education from New Orleans Baptist Theological Seminary. First Baptist Church of Raleigh paid the salary for Winfield Applewhite, whose mother was a member of the church, while Statesville's First Baptist Church assumed the salary of LaVerne.[41] The Applewhites served in Indonesia until their retirement in 1985.

One of the Southern Baptists' most ambitious expansion programs in the postwar years was launched at the annual gathering of the

---

[40] Biographical sketch of the McMillans printed in the Church Bulletin, 28 December 1947.

[41] "Applewhites Appointed Missionaries," *Biblical Recorder* (Raleigh NC), 7 January 1956, 17.

Southern Baptist Convention in 1953. The program focused on increasing the Sunday-school rolls in Southern Baptist churches and was given the catchphrase, "A Million More in '54." Robert E. Naylor, president of Southwestern Baptist Theological Seminary from 1958 to 1978, defended the success of the program against the "snide remarks" made by some who in subsequent years mocked the catchy slogan. Naylor said, "I took it seriously and so did a multitude of other Southern Baptists." He called it "one of the greatest years in winning people to Christ in the history of the Convention."[42] By most standards the program was successful, adding more than 600,000 new members to Southern Baptist Convention Sunday schools.[43]

First Baptist Church took "A Million More in '54" seriously as well. In September 1953 the church bulletin announced the endeavor, calling it "the most gigantic effort to reach people ever attempted by our denomination." The church sought a 30 percent increase in Sunday-school enrollment, emphasizing a "program of visitation" of church members who were not also members of the Sunday school.[44] Unfortunately, "A Million More in '54" did not prove to be as successful at First Baptist Church, increasing the Sunday-school enrollment by only 6 percent.[45]

In 1946 the church adopted a "Modified Unified Budget Plan," which represented a substantial administrative change in the budgeting process. It gave the church a unified budget covering all the ministries in the congregation rather than several unrelated budgets. It also allowed for a smoother budget process and eliminated potential duplication of resources and competition between the various entities of the church's

---

[42] Robert E. Naylor, *A Messenger's Memoirs: Sixty-One Southern Baptist Convention Meetings* (Franklin TN: Providence House Publishers, 1995) 93.

[43] David S. Dockery, *Southern Baptist Identity: An Evangelical Denomination Faces the Future* (Wheaton IL: Crossway Books, 2009) 272, http://books.google.com/books?id=peVqpjimF5UC&printsec=frontcover&source=gbs_ge_summary_r&cad=0#v=onepage&q&f=false (accessed 25 September 2010).

[44] Church Bulletin, 20 September 1953.

[45] See the Annual Letter to the Raleigh Baptist Association in Church Conference Records, 9 September 1953 and 3 November 1954. Sunday-school enrollment for 1953 was 1,150. That increased to 1,222 in 1954.

ministries. Fifty percent of the money collected was designated for internal expenses, while the other 50 percent was to be used for causes outside the church, such as the Cooperative Program. Money collected above the amount needed for the budget was earmarked for building expenses and expansion. One treasurer could then preside over the unified budget instead of several treasurers administrating multiple budgets. The church selected W. A. Yost to be the first treasurer responsible for the unified budget.[46]

For contributions, the members to the church continued to use the envelope system adopted decades earlier. Members were allowed to designate all or part of their contributions, but undesignated funds were to be divided upon the 50/50 basis between the local church and the Cooperative Program. Contributions given as a memorial were not considered part of the unified budget. The four offerings promoted by the WMU during the year (home missions in March, Heck memorial in June, state missions in September, and foreign missions in December) continued. No special collections, however, were allowed without the church's consent, except those collected under the auspices of the WMU.[47]

The new fiscal arrangement allowed the budget-planning process to be more streamlined and efficient. A special committee appointed by the finance committee was commissioned to prepare a draft of the budget each year. Various organizations and ministries in the church were asked to present their budget requests for the next year in writing to that committee. When a draft of the budget was completed, it was presented to the full finance committee for approval, then to the Diaconate, and finally to the church conference for final approval.[48]

Worship. Indications are that Broadus Jones gave careful attention to worship planning during his tenure at the church. That is apparent through examination of the church bulletins from the period of his pastorate, and also in the prominence given to the music ministry. Since

---

[46] Church Bulletin, 18 August 1946; Church Conference Records, 7 August 1946. There is a notation that the financial system in the church at that time utilized between twenty and thirty treasurers to handle the money collected.

[47] Ibid.

[48] Ibid.

the purchase of a new organ in 1877, the church devoted (and continues to do so to this day) numerous resources and efforts to providing quality music for the worship services. In 1948 organist and choirmaster Frederick Stanley Smith resigned after ten years of service to the church's music ministry. Shortly thereafter he was replaced by Dr. Harry E. Cooper. The following month the church employed a bass soloist named Joseph Bouchard, an alumnus of the Boston Conservatory who had served on its faculty for three years before moving to Raleigh. During his time in Boston, Bouchard served as the bass soloist at the Old South Church. In addition to the service he gave to First Baptist Church, Raleigh, Bouchard also taught private lessons in Raleigh and served on the music faculty at Campbell College.[49]

In 1949 Jones suggested implementation of a special time for dedication of babies, which would be separate from the regular Sunday-morning worship service. While infant dedication is fairly routine within Baptist churches today, especially on Mother's Day, half a century ago the church feared it would be confused with infant baptism. Jones, however, believed it would provide an opportunity for First Baptist Church to minister to families and bring families into a closer relationship with the church. The deacons first discussed the issue and finally approved the pastor's request "with dissenting votes."[50] The following evening the church conference approved the measure, indicating that the dedication service would be held once per year in the Sunday-school auditorium. The chair of the diaconate, W. H. Weatherspoon, assured the congregation "that there would be nothing in this service that would resemble infant baptism," but that the "main purpose of the service is to bind parents more closely to the church which in reality would be a rededication of parents." Interestingly, C. J. Curry, a member of the diaconate, expressed his thoughts to the church conference, stating that while he had initially opposed the idea when it was first discussed among the deacons, upon further reflection he

---

[49] Church Bulletin, 31 October 1948.

[50] Minutes of the Diaconate, 6 September 1949. It is interesting that the record reads: "On the motion of Carroll Weathers, the recommendation was adopted with dissenting votes, including that of Mrs. J. S. Farmer." Farmer was the widow of former *Biblical Recorder* editor J. S. Farmer.

believed "that such a service would be a benefit."[51] Church bulletins for the remainder of Jones's tenure as pastor routinely promoted the infant dedication services, which always took place following the Sunday-morning worship service.

Race Relations. The women from First Baptist Church during the postwar years deserve special recognition, not because they were necessarily more active than other organizations in the church, but because of the nature of their work. Their attention given to the issue of race—years before the beginning of the Civil Rights Movement—is noteworthy. As early as February 1943 a program topic was titled, "Witnessing for Christ Across the Barriers of Race." The speaker that day emphasized that "there was no race distinction in the heart of God when he created and sent his Son for man's salvation, so there must be none in our dealings with other races."[52]

Foy Valentine, in his study of Southern Baptists and race relations in the first half of the twentieth century, found that during the 1940s "Southern Baptists showed a remarkably broad and progressive interest in the improvement of race relations."[53] Beginning in 1941 the national WMU set aside $10,000 [$146,000] for the purpose of encouraging closer cooperation with African-American Baptist women in promotion of missions. In summer 1940 the national WMU promoted several interracial institutes throughout the South (Jackson, Mississippi; Macon, Georgia; and Montgomery, Alabama) for the purpose of fostering mutual support and cooperation between white and black Baptist women.[54] The idea caught on in North Carolina the following summer as the first "Negro Institute" was held at Shaw University in Raleigh. Originally

---

[51] Church Conference Records, 7 September 1949.

[52] Minutes of the Woman's Missionary Society, 15 February 1943.

[53] Foy Valentine, *A Historical Study of Southern Baptists and Race Relations, 1917–1947* (New York: Arno Press, 1980), 188, http://books.google.com/books?id= ac_hd2oO2agC&pg=PA29&lpg=PA29&dq=Southern+Baptist+Convention+1947+ race&source=bl&ots=2afn10n4MS&sig=jZoEC5tfPqsax8Nbdqav-gvx1DY&hl=en&ei=mCelTPSyFIX7lweJ1Zi0DA&sa=X&oi=book_result&ct=result &resnum=2&ved=0CBoQ6AEwAQ#v=onepage&q=Southern%20Baptist%20Conv ention%201947%20race&f=true (accessed 30 September 2010).

[54] "W.M.U. Interracial Institutes," *Biblical Recorder* (Raleigh NC), 23 August 1944, 3.

conceived to be a yearly event, the women were unable meet in 1942, but the institutes resumed in 1943 and continued yearly into the 1950s.[55] The records of the Woman's Missionary Society of the First Baptist Church indicate strong support for the "Interracial Institutes." That was due in large part to the leadership of Foy Farmer, who served as the president of the North Carolina Woman's Missionary Union from 1942 to 1945 and 1946 to 1951. From May 1945 until March 1946 she served as the interim and corresponding executive secretary.

In summer 1947 both the Social Service Commission and the Committee on Race Relations presented reports at the annual meeting of the Southern Baptist Convention that were unanimously approved by the messengers. Those two reports set forth eight principles of conduct that encouraged all Southern Baptists to work toward racial reconciliation.[56] The women from First Baptist Church at the November 1947 meeting of the Woman's Missionary Society pledged support of those eight principles. At their meeting that month, Mrs. Albert Haskins, Jr. presented a program titled "Racial Discrimination." She encouraged the women to "undertake to live up to the eight points on the program outlined by the S.B.C." She then presented the following principles to the women and urged them to "pray for guidance in racial problems":

1. To consider the Negro as a real person
2. To strive to conquer prejudice
3. To teach our children to conquer prejudice
4. To protest against injustice to Negroes
5. To stimulate a deep desire for all Negroes to enjoy privileges as granted in the Constitution
6. To be just in dealings with individuals of other races
7. To strive to promote community good will

---

[55] See "1943 Negro Institutes," *Biblical Recorder* (Raleigh NC), 23 June 1943, 17; "Approaching Negro Institutes," *Biblical Recorder* (Raleigh NC), 7 July 1943, 17; "Negro Institutes Highly Successful," *Biblical Recorder* (Raleigh NC), 4 August 1943, 17; and "Two Interracial Institutes in July," *Biblical Recorder* (Raleigh NC), 2 May 1953, 15.

[56] "Report of Committee on Social Service and Civic Righteousness" *Biblical Recorder* (Raleigh NC), 1 October 1947, 3.

8.To help build up Negro churches, Sunday Schools and missions[57]

Matters related to race continued to be a topic at the Woman's Missionary Society meetings of First Baptist Church throughout the decade of the 1940s. In March 1949 Miss Lottie Tucker spoke on the topic "Misplaced Tensions" at a meeting of the Eliza Yates Circle. She told the women assembled that day that "race is no problem with God, to whom all colors are the same." Another woman, identified in the record only as "Miss Currin," followed by discussing the tendency many whites had to "stereotype all members of other races or nationalities; to judge all by the one or two we knew, or knew of." She urged the women to rise above their prejudices "by knowing the members of other races or nationalities."[58] The following year a guestspeaker, Dr. N. C. Newbold, the North Carolina Director of Negro Education at the time, presented a program on "Negro education" at the general meeting of the church's Woman's Missionary Society. He emphasized the fact that Christians have a "duty to assure the Negro...an equal chance in education."[59]

The women of First Baptist Church were remarkably progressive in their promotion of racial reconciliation during the postwar years. Interestingly though, as the Civil Rights Movement began in the 1950s the records of the church's Woman's Missionary Society do not reflect a strong continuation of those attitudes. That does not necessarily reflect a change in attitude as much as it may suggest that the women believed, as the issue of race became more controversial in society, their best approach was to promote reconciliation in a quieter manner. Furthermore, it is also worth noting that although First Baptist Church (Wilmington Street) was located diagonally across the state capitol grounds from the church, there is very little indication of interaction between the two churches during this era. That changes, however, as noted in the next chapter.

Renovation of Facilities. First Baptist Church launched a major building renovation project during the Broadus Jones tenure. Reflecting the postwar economic boom, financial contributions during Jones's

---

[57] Minutes of the Woman's Missionary Society, 17 November 1947.
[58] Ibid., 8 March 1949.
[59] Ibid., 21 August 1950.

pastorate grew from $45,000 to $140,000 [$558,000 to $1.03 million], making that period most conducive to a capital campaign. [60] As early as 1942 the possibility of air conditioning the church building was presented though no action was taken on the matter.[61] Throughout the 1940s the church records report various miscellaneous repairs performed, such as painting the sanctuary and Sunday-school building in 1945.[62] During spring 1948 the deacons began to discuss the major repairs needed for the entire church structure.[63] In May, after several months of discussion, the church hired an architect to make a survey of the repair needs and to submit drawings and cost estimates.[64] By the middle of 1950 the church had spent a total of $70,618.60 [$629,000] on numerous repairs and improvements on the building. That figure can be broken down and itemized as follows: $60,583.04 [$540,000] for alterations and improvements to the building; $4,340.81 [$38,700] for architectural fees; $4,696.96 [$41,800] for new chairs in the adult Sunday-school department; and $997.79 [$8,890] for various other miscellaneous repairs.[65]

---

[60] *The Struggles and Fruits of Faith: Sesquicentennial Celebration* (Raleigh NC: First Baptist Church, 1962) 50. This small history of the church was prepared by the church in celebration of the church's sesquicentennial.

[61] Church Conference Records, 6 August 1942.

[62] Ibid., 8 August and 3 October 1945.

[63] Minutes of the Diaconate, January, February, March, and April 1948.

[64] Church Conference Records, 5 May 1948.

[65] Jesse M. Page to W. H. Weatherspoon, attached to Minutes of the Diaconate, 7 October 1950. A further breakdown of the repair work is included in the letter: "$33,638.77 [$300,000] To Davidson & Jones, General Contractors for materials, labor, and fee. The work included improvements to the adult department, kitchen, labies [*sic*] toilet, young peoples department, and other repairs to the church plant; $2,874.14 [$25,600] to Vickers & Ruth, plumbing and heating contractors for plumbing and heating work; $8,873.00 [$79,100] to Beaman's Inc., Greensboro, N.C. for modern fold doors used in the adult and young peoples department; $544.32 [$4,850] to Westinghouse for water coolers; $1,008.94 [$8,990] to Bernhard's for electric fixtures; $760.00 [$6,770] to Sumter Art and Leaded Glass Company for repairing and cleaning art glass windows; $15.00 [$134] to William A. Brickhouse for removing a tree; $1,248.86 [$11,100] to Baker & Brown, roofing contractors for repairs to roof; $375.00 [$3,340] to Stone's of Raleigh for stage draperies and equipment; $7,646.00 [$68,100] to A. C. Horne Company for waterproofing exterior stucco of building; $57.85 [$515] to Fleming Hester for a change in electric wiring to put electric service to the building on one meter,

In late 1951 the church approved further renovations, this time specifically in the sanctuary. The work included air conditioning, new lighting, new paint, new carpet, and repairing and refinishing the pews. By early 1952 the deacons recommended the organization of two committees: the "Auditorium Improvement Committee" and a "Building Fund Committee." The building fund campaign began in March 1952.[66] By the following year, the scope of the project had grown significantly. A report to the church conference in April 1953 indicated that the costs would total $103,200 [$828,000]. The church approved the report and also approved borrowing the additional funds necessary.[67] By early 1954 the cost of the project had grown even further. The church authorized an additional $15,000 [$120,000] to be borrowed, raising the total debt for the project to $80,000 [$639,000]. The total cost of the entire renovation project had reached $140,000 [$1.12 million].[68] As a memorial to her husband, Mrs. J. Rufus Hunter donated the money necessary for the sanctuary lighting. J. Rufus Hunter, a faithful member and loyal deacon, had died in 1951 at the age of eighty-six. He had been a member of First

---

resulting in a saving of current charges; $1,175.00 [$10,500] to C. R. Miller for repairs to the steeple roof; $106.34 [$947] to Martin Millwork Co. for materials in connection with repairs to steeple roof; $2,259.82 [$20,100] to Montgomery-Green for kitchen equipment."

[66] Minutes of the Diaconate, 9 October 1951; Church Conference Records, 12 December 1951, and 9 January and 6 February 1952. See also Church Bulletin, 9 March 1952, for the formal announcement of the "Auditorium Improvement Campaign." The total amount needed for the project reported to the congregation was $75,000 [$606,000].

[67] Church Conference Records, 22 April 1953. The following month on 20 May in a special called meeting, the church unanimously approved a motion to borrow $65,000 [$521,000]. The specific work that took place in the sanctuary included: heating and air conditioning, $54,000 [$433,000]; new electrical wiring, $16,500 [$132,000]; miscellaneous repairs and construction, $7,000 [$56,100]; painting and decorating, $3,200 [$25,700]; new pews, $14,500 [$116,000] (a few months later the total grew by $6,090 [$48,800] to allow for new pew cushions); and new carpet, $7,500 [$60,200].

[68] Ibid., 10 February 1954.

Baptist Church for more than fifty years and the gift of the new lighting was a fitting memorial to his life and service to the church.[69]

Several other final projects capped off the renovations that had taken most of the decade of the 1950s to complete. In 1956 a waterproofing contractor was hired to work on the exterior of the building. Also, the church spent $900 [$7,100] to ground the steeple—a precaution taken as a result of the devastating fire that destroyed the Edenton Street Methodist Church on 28 July 1956.[70] In 1957 it became apparent that the organ, originally purchased in 1924, was in need of a major overhaul. The work was completed at a cost of $32,000 [$244,000], which increased the value of the organ to $85,000 [$648,000]. The final major expenditure by the church was the purchase of a lot adjacent to the church property for a value of $170,000 [$1.25 million] in 1959, just after Jones's resignation.[71] The final tally of the renovation work completed during the last decade of Broadus Jones's pastorate was approximately $200,000 [$1.47 million]. So successful was the church's ability to raise the money that when he resigned as pastor in 1959, the indebtedness was only $25,000 [$184,000].[72]

Broadus Jones resigned as pastor of First Baptist Church in July 1959 because of illness. Just one month shy of sixteen years, Jones's tenure was the second longest continuous pastorate in the church's history, bested only by Thomas W. O'Kelley. During those years the church staff became the largest in the church's history with a pastor, pastor's assistant, educational director, church host, organist, choir director, two secretaries, two paid soloists, a custodian, and a maid. As mentioned earlier, the budget increased from $45,000 to $140,000, reflecting the economic boom of the postwar years.[73] As also mentioned, major renovations totaling

---

[69] A plaque on the wall at the back of the sanctuary commemorates the life of J. Rufus Hunter and the gift of the lighting given by his wife in his memory.

[70] Church Conference Records, 12 August 1956. According to the *News and Observer*, the cause of the Edenton Street Methodist Church fire was a lightening strike on the church's steeple (see Charles Craven, "Edenton Street Church Destroyed by Flames," *News and Observer* [Raleigh NC], 29 July 1956, 1).

[71] *Struggles and Fruits of Faith*, 50.

[72] Ibid.

[73] See document titled, "Growth and Development Under the Leadership of Broadus E. Jones," located in Church Conference Records, 9 December 1959.

approximately $200,000 were completed and almost paid for by the time Jones resigned. Sunday-school enrollment increased from 801 in 1943 to 1,124 in 1959, while the total number of church members increased from 1,637 to 1,798.[74]

* * *

As the decade of the 1950s closed and the 1960s loomed on the horizon, the church reflected upon the ministry of Broadus E. Jones and concluded: "While attention is called to the growth in a material way...the greatest contribution of Broadus Jones was his spiritual leadership and guidance for the members of our congregation."[75] The next decade would test the founders' vision in ways it had never experienced before, and such events called for a successor to Broadus Jones who would equal his intellect and pastoral skills. Raleigh's First Baptist Church would not have to look very far to find such a man.

---

[74] Annual Letter to the Raleigh Baptist Association, Church Conference Records, 9 December 1959.

[75] "Growth and Development Under the Leadership of Broadus E. Jones."

8

Embracing a Changing World (1960-1987)

In his inaugural address on 20 January 1961, John F. Kennedy said that "the world is very different now." While other words in his speech that day became immortalized, no other phrase captured any better the transformation the nation was about to experience over the next decade. The "torch has been passed to a new generation," and for those who lived through it, some may have wondered at the end of the decade if the light of the torch had been extinguished.

As Kennedy occupied the Oval Office, he assumed his predecessor's headaches with Cuba. A botched CIA attempt in 1961 to overthrow the Castro regime (known as the Bay of Pigs) humiliated the young president, even though the operation had been planned by the Eisenhower administration. The following year the Soviet Union, possibly emboldened by the Bay of Pigs fiasco, deployed nuclear missiles on the island of Cuba, which threatened to bring the world to the brink of nuclear holocaust. Most Americans did not know of the crisis until Kennedy's television broadcast to the nation on 22 October 1962, when he declared that any launch of such missiles toward any nation in the Western Hemisphere would be regarded as an attack on the United States and would elicit a full retaliatory strike. The crisis was averted following a naval blockade of Cuba and backdoor diplomacy. Kennedy's firm stand against the Soviets established his foreign policy *bona fides*, but his shocking assassination in Dallas, Texas, on 22 November 1963, plunged the nation into mourning and fear for the future.

Lyndon B. Johnson became the thirty-sixth president following Kennedy's assassination and led the nation through the middle years of the 1960s. Elected president in 1964 after defeating Senator Barry Goldwater, Johnson brought important social change to the nation by ushering through Congress legislation dubbed "the Great Society." The "Great Society" legislation included expansive social reforms such as the creation of Medicare and Medicaid, environmental laws, support for public broadcasting and for education, and an initiative to alleviate poverty, which he called the "War on Poverty." Johnson also signed the long-anticipated Civil Rights Act in 1964—arguably the most important social legislation of the 1960s. The public support for Johnson's presidency began to wane after the midterm elections of 1966 because of the continuing escalation of the war in Vietnam. By 1968 Johnson, challenged in the Democratic primaries by Eugene McCarthy and later Robert F. Kennedy, knew that he would not be able to secure the nomination of the party. In a speech before the nation on 31 March 1968, Johnson withdrew from the presidential election, leaving Kennedy, McCarthy, Hubert Humphrey, and George Wallace as the top choices for the party.

Many Americans might have assumed the nation was coming apart in spring 1968. On 4 April in Memphis, Tennessee, Martin Luther King, Jr. was assassinated as he was leaving his motel room to speak at an evening event. When news of King's assassination was reported, riots broke out in scores of cities including Chicago, Washington, and Los Angeles. Robert Kennedy heard the news on his way to a campaign event in Indianapolis and gave an impromptu speech, recalling King's commitment to nonviolence and pleading for calm in the midst of the tragedy. But only two months later, after winning the California Democratic Primary, Robert Kennedy was assassinated following a victory speech before supporters gathered in the ballroom of the Ambassador Hotel in Los Angeles.

Richard Nixon, the Republican candidate, won the election of 1968 against Hubert Humphrey who represented a badly fractured Democratic Party, but Vietnam dominated the headlines of the day as the decade closed. By 1970 the Pentagon had long since known that the war was unwinnable. Yet even after Nixon's attempts to draw down troop numbers, the United States still had more than 300,000 troops in Vietnam. Nixon still achieved reelection in 1972 by landslide, but by the next year his administration was embroiled in the Watergate scandal, which ultimately ended with his resignation in disgrace as Congress prepared impeachment proceedings.

The election of Jimmy Carter to the presidency in 1976 brought a wave of optimism to the beleaguered nation following the turmoil of the 1960s, the horrors of Vietnam, and the scandal of Watergate. Carter was the first Southern Baptist ever elected to the presidency. Formerly the governor of Georgia, Carter made a name in Georgia politics by his honesty, integrity, and success as a peanut farmer. His genuine commitment to faith, exemplified by his active membership in the Plains Baptist Church in Plains, Georgia, captured the attention of Americans hopeful for change in Washington. Carter achieved significant milestones during his presidency. One such milestone highlighted the Camp David Accords, which created lasting peace between Israel and Egypt. Other milestones highlighted successful negotiations such as the SALT II treaty with the Soviet Union (lowering tension even further between the two super powers) and the return of the Panama Canal to Panama. Domestically, he created the Departments of Education and Energy. He also created an energy policy, which encouraged conservation and development of new energy technologies. Perhaps the greatest of his successes related to his promotion of human rights, both at home and abroad, which continues to the present through the work of the Carter Center in Atlanta. But in spite of his successes, Carter's presidency was ultimately doomed by the inability to negotiate the release of American hostages in Iran who were taken when the Iranian revolution began in 1979. A failed military rescue effort created a narrative about his administration—that it had weakened America's military—and ultimately led to the landslide election of Ronald Reagan in 1980.

The Reagan administration brought a seismic shift to American politics and culture with its emphasis on free enterprise as opposed to government intervention. Reagan's election also coincided with the rise of the "Religious Right" in American politics—a force that would influence political elections for years to come. Reagan emphasized a strong national defense, and many interpreters consider that to be one of the factors that brought an end to the Cold War and the downfall of the Soviet Union. Still, the Reagan administration was not without controversy. The Iran-Contra scandal was the most serious scandal from his presidency and led to indictments of several of his top aides.

The city of Raleigh underwent transformation while sustaining growth during that era as well. In 1962 the legislature moved out of the state capitol to new facilities located a few blocks away. The new structure provided 200,000 square feet of space and was not without controversy. The structure ended up costing the taxpayers $6.2 million [$44 million], and some critics dubbed it "Baghdad-on-the Neuse," while others lampooned it as the "Taj Mahodges," after Governor Luther Hodges, whose administration conceived the idea.[1] The business and commerce sector of the capital city received a major boost in 1965 when IBM announced it would move into the Research Triangle Park. Other businesses arrived in Raleigh in the 1960s including Exide, Aerotron, Corning Glass, Action Corporation, Athey Products, Duraw Manufacturing, Mallinckrodt, Litho Industries, Crown Zellerback, and Inco Electro Energy.[2]

The state capitol received much-needed repairs in the early 1970s as the general assembly provided more than $500,000 [$1.99 million] for the project, which gave the old building a complete makeover both inside and out. The goal of the project was to restore the building as nearly as possible to its original appearance. The State Department of Archives and History, as well as architect William A. Dodge, III, oversaw the work, which occurred between 1972 and 1975. By 2 June 1975 the work was completed, and the building was declared a national historic landmark.[3]

Another important state landmark to receive a makeover was the governor's mansion. For decades the mansion had been in need of work. For example, in 1925, upon his election, Governor Angus McLean refused to move into the structure because he believed it to be unsanitary. The health department concurred, and money was appropriated for heating, insulation, and plumbing work. By 1971 the legislature began to discuss the possibility of a new structure. Those favoring a complete renovation of the original structure prevailed, and in 1975 the $575,000 [$2.29 million] project was complete.[4]

---

[1] James Vickers, *Raleigh, City of Oaks: An Illustrated History* (Woodland Hills CA: Windsor Publications, 1982) 129.

[2] Ibid.

[3] Ibid., 132–33.

[4] Ibid., 133. For a complete history of the governor's mansion, see William Bushong, *North Carolina's Executive Mansion: The First Hundred Years* (Raleigh NC: Executive Mansion Fine Arts Committee and the Executive Mansion Fund, Inc., 1991).

For most of the twentieth century Raleigh has been able to weather the economic storms that created problems in other cities. Because of the large number of state employees, the city came through the Great Depression better than other cities. During the recession that hit the nation in 1975, unemployment figures in North Carolina reached 10.8 percent but reached no higher than 5 percent in Raleigh. The same held true with the larger recession that hit the nation in the early 1980s.[5]

The First Baptist Church of Raleigh 1960–1987

Following the resignation of Broadus A. Jones, the pulpit committee worked for less than a year before bringing a recommendation on 10 January 1960 that the church hire thirty-eight-year-old John M. Lewis to be the next pastor.[6] The committee did not have to look very far for Lewis. For the previous two years he had served as an associate professor of religion and director of student religious activities at Meredith College. He had occupied the pulpit of First Baptist Church on several previous occasions, such that the congregation already knew and respected him. It is no surprise, then, that his name arose to the top of the list early in the search process. Church members were encouraged to submit names of any possible candidates for the position. Lewis's name was suggested by "many members," prompting the committee to declare: "It should be reported to you that the committee would have brought its recommendation much earlier had it not felt morally obligated to pursue the many other good suggestions which you submitted."[7]

John Lewis was a native Floridian born in Miami on 15 December 1921. He attended Stetson University where he received a B.S. degree in history in 1943. As a student at Stetson, he was active in the varsity

---

[5] Vickers, *Raleigh, City of Oaks*, 135–36.

[6] Church Conference Records, 10 January 1960. I am following the chronological outline for the Lewis pastorate presented in *The Dream Lives On: Celebrating 175 Years of Witness and Ministry in North Carolina's Capital City* (Raleigh NC: First Baptist Church, 1987) 15–36.

[7] Church Conference Records, 10 January 1960. The members of the search committee were Everette Miller (chair), Earle Hostetler, W. H. Weatherspoon, Mrs. E. L. Layfield, Jesse Helms, Bill Simpson, Mrs. H. A. Wood, Coite Jones, Edgar Wyatt, Albert Haskins, Roy Purser, and Mrs. L. R. Harrill.

debate team, the Little Theater, and numerous clubs, including the History and International Relations Clubs. He was president of both the Stetson and Florida State Baptist Student Unions and was the student body president during his senior year.[8] Lewis also served as pastor of a small Baptist congregation in Longwood, Florida, from 1941 to 1943. Most importantly, Lewis met his future wife, Jean Morris, during his student days at Stetson. Lewis continued his studies at the Southern Baptist Theological Seminary in Louisville, Kentucky, where he completed the Th.M. (1947) and the Th.D. (1952) degrees. His doctoral work concentrated in the area of theology where he served as a teaching fellow to Dr. Dale Moody. During his seminary years he served as pastor of the David's Fork Baptist Church in Lexington, Kentucky (1943–1950), and First Baptist Church of Taylorsville, Kentucky (1950–1952). In 1952 Lewis was called to be the pastor of the Montrose Baptist Church in Richmond, Virginia, where he ministered until 1956. During those years he became active in denominational life, serving as a member of the executive committee of the Richmond Baptist Association and a trustee of the Foreign Mission Board of the Southern Baptist Convention. Lewis also taught Bible in the evenings for students attending the University of Richmond Night School.[9]

In 1956 Lewis had the opportunity to return to Southern Seminary as a faculty member. For two years he was an associate professor of Christian theology. Then in 1958 he left Louisville for Raleigh where he joined the faculty of Meredith College.[10] The church allowed Lewis to complete spring semester 1960 at Meredith College before assuming the pastoral duties full-time in June, but the young pastor wasted no time in his effort to lead the congregation into its next era. The first meeting of the diaconate he attended was on 5 April 1960, during which he requested a report from each deacon and deaconess by the next meeting describing: (1) the three strongest characteristics of the church, (2) the

---

[8] Biographical information obtained from Southern Baptist Historical Library and Archives, Nashville, Tennessee.

[9] Ibid.

[10] Ibid.

three weakest characteristics of the church, and (3) three or more items whereby the church could grow and advance.[11]

By May the church became aware that Lewis was intent on engaging issues in modern American culture. The church bulletin on 15 May 1960 indicated that he would be teaching the Sunday-evening seminar that night on the topic "Religion, Politics, and the White House"—an indication that he was thinking of the religious issues swirling around the Kennedy/Nixon election that year.[12] By September, as the election neared, Lewis conducted two Sunday-evening seminars titled "Responsible Citizenship: The Catholic Way," and "Responsible Citizenship: The Protestant Way." The congregation's interest in the sessions is indicated by a report that "several hundred" were present at the first of the two seminars.[13]

Sesquicentennial Celebration. In 1961 the church began to make plans for its sesquicentennial celebration that was to occur the next year. Herbert Weatherspoon was appointed chair of the steering committee to plan for the event. The church generously provided $5,000 [$35,900] to cover the expenses—an indication that the anniversary would be celebrated in style.[14] By February 1962 the plans were almost finalized. Lewis reported to the congregation that speakers had been secured for what would be a week-long event with special services each evening. The church invited choirs from Campbell and Meredith Colleges and Southeastern Baptist Theological Seminary to participate. Special invitations were extended to the church's former pastors, and they were asked to assist in a special communion service during the event. Invitations were extended to the other churches in Raleigh, and perhaps most importantly, an invitation was extended to the First Baptist Church, Wilmington Street for a joint worship service.[15]

The week of festivities began on Sunday morning, 4 March 1962, with the church's monthly observance of communion followed by a communion meditation delivered by John Lewis. Other guest preachers

---

[11] Minutes of the Diaconate, 5 April 1960.
[12] Church Bulletin, 15 May 1960.
[13] Ibid., 25 September and 2 October 1960.
[14] Church Conference Records, 10 May 1961.
[15] Ibid., 8 February 1962.

for the week included Carlyle Marney, pastor of Charlotte's Myers Park Baptist Church; Glenn L. Archer, executive director of Protestants and Other Americans United for Separation of Church and State; Roy O. McClain, pastor of Atlanta's First Baptist Church; and Baker James Cauthen, executive secretary of the Foreign Mission Board of the Southern Baptist Convention. The Honorable Brooks Hays was originally scheduled to deliver the sermon on Thursday evening of the week's festivities. Hays was special assistant to President Kennedy for intergovernmental services and a former congressman from the Fifth District of Arkansas. A dedicated Southern Baptist layman, Hays had served a term as president of the Southern Baptist Convention from 1957 to 1958. Unfortunately, due to a death in his immediate family, Hays was unable to be present for the service. In his place, James T. Cleland, dean of the Chapel at Duke University, delivered the evening message.[16]

The Campbell College Choir, the Meredith College Chorus, and the Southeastern Baptist Theological Seminary Choir provided special music for the week's worship services. Former pastors Sydnor Stealey and Broadus Jones participated in two of the worship services respectively. Douglas Branch, executive secretary of the Baptist State Convention of North Carolina, was present, as was Robert L. Costner, secretary of Missions from the Raleigh Baptist Association. William S. Hicks and Harry Wood, former members of First Baptist Church whom the congregation had ordained years before, were present. Hicks was the executive director of the Council of Churches of Greater Bridgeport, Connecticut, and Wood was pastor of the First Baptist Church of Leaksville, North Carolina. Albert Edwards and Howard P. Powell, pastors of First Presbyterian Church and Edenton Street Methodist Church, respectively, were included in the week's worship services, and members of their churches were deemed special guests of the congregation during the week. Finally, Charles Ward, pastor of the First Baptist Church, Wilmington Street, along with the deacons from the church, was present and participated in one of the services. Lewis and Ward developed a strong friendship throughout Lewis's tenure as pastor,

---

[16] "Sesquicentennial Program," included in Church Conference Records, 14 March 1962.

and there would be numerous annual gatherings between the two churches for fellowship and celebration of mutual heritage.[17]

The sesquicentennial celebration included a few other items to complement the worship services during the week. The Sunday-evening seminar on 4 March focused on the history of the church, with several longtime members comprising a panel to reminisce and tell stories of interest. Also, a historical room with memorabilia from the church's history was on display. Edgar M. Wyatt and Mrs. W. Hal Trentman were co-chairs of the project. A "Historical Album," prepared by Mrs. C. D. Baucom, was one of the feature exhibits on display in the room. WRAL-TV broadcast a special show highlighting the church's history and heritage in the city, which aired on Sunday afternoon, 4 March, at 5:30 P.M. The worship services during the week were broadcast live over WPTF radio. Finally, a small history of the church was prepared and published for distribution among the membership.[18]

L. R. Harrill, the church clerk at the time, reflected on the anniversary celebration in a summary report presented to the monthly church conference following the sesquicentennial. He quoted one of the speakers from the week who said, "Tradition makes good ballast but very poor cargo." Harrill then encouraged the church to "reflect on the past history and achievements" and "move into the future with hope and enthusiasm using…past achievements as stepping stones for greater achievements in Christian service."[19] The church had no way of knowing it at the time, but the current events of that era were about to force the greatest internal crisis since the congregational split in the early nineteenth century.

Civil Rights and Conflict. By 1963 civil rights had become the dominant social issue in American society. On 16 April Martin Luther King, Jr. was arrested in Birmingham, Alabama, and wrote the famed "Letter from Birmingham Jail," criticizing the moderate voices sympathetic with the movement. The following month Americans were horrified as they saw the television images of Birmingham protesters (includ-

---

[17] Ibid.

[18] Ibid.

[19] Quoted from a report titled, "Sesquicentennial Celebration March 4–11, 1962," included in ibid. Harrill did not indicate the identity of the quote's source.

ing women and children) being viciously attacked by firehoses and police dogs. Mississippi's NAACP field secretary, Medgar Evers, was murdered in his driveway by Ku Klux Klansman Byron De La Beckwith on 12 June. On 28 August hundreds of thousands of people gathered in Washington, D.C. at the Lincoln Memorial to hear Martin Luther King's "I Have a Dream" speech. Finally, on 15 September, again in Birmingham, four little girls were killed when a bomb exploded at the Sixteenth Street Baptist Church minutes before church services were to begin.

The Civil Rights Movement was in full swing in Raleigh that year also. Bishop Vincent C. Waters of the Raleigh Catholic Diocese had previously taken an important early step toward civil rights by ordering all Catholic schools in the Diocese to be fully integrated following the *Brown v. Board of Education* ruling by the United States Supreme Court in 1954. Accordingly, Cardinal Latin High School received eight African-American students in 1955. Segregation of the public schools, as well as other facets of society, took much longer. To speed the desegregation process along, African Americans in the city formed the Raleigh Citizens Association to encourage voter registration, and local chapters of the National Association for the Advancement of Colored People (NAACP) and the Congress of Racial Equality (CORE) were created. In May 1963 African-American students from Shaw University and St. Augustine's College, along with supportive white students from NCSU and other area schools, conducted sit-in demonstrations at several local businesses, including the S&W Cafeteria, the Sir Walter Hotel, the Ambassador Theatre, Gino's Restaurant, and the Statehouse dining room. The demonstrations resulted in mass arrests of more than 150 protestors during the second week of May. On 10 May more than 500 protesters marched to the governor's mansion and interrupted a concert being given by the North Carolina Symphony. Governor Terry Sanford refused to discuss the issue on the spot, but made a commitment to meet with protest leaders in his office at a later date. On 26 July Mayor William G. Enloe, the owner of the Ambassador Theatre, created a community relations committee to facilitate the gradual integration of the city's facilities.[20]

---

[20] Vickers, *Raleigh, City of Oaks*, 131.

The membership of First Baptist Church of Raleigh was keenly aware of its bi-racial history as those events unfolded. The church had just been reminded of that during the 150th anniversary, which included the attendance of Reverenc Charles Ward and the deacons from the First Baptist Church, Wilmington Street. Yet while the issues of race and desegregation were swirling around in its community and society at large, the First Baptist Church was still caught by surprise on 7 April 1963 when Charles A. Earle, a black student at Shaw University, presented himself before the congregation and requested membership. John Lewis was away from the church that morning preaching in Wilmington. Dr. Bill Smith, state secretary of the Baptist Student Department and a member of the church, was leading the worship service. It was Palm Sunday and there was no sermon, the service consisting mainly of music. Earle came forward during the singing of the final hymn, traditionally called the "invitation hymn" in a Baptist church. Ironically and perhaps appropriately, the title of the invitation hymn that morning was "Beneath the Cross of Jesus."[21]

The church's constitution and bylaws contained a statement under Article II—Membership, which said, "In any instance where serious objection is voiced from the floor, the case shall be referred, without discussion, to the minister and the deacons for investigation and report."[22] Accordingly, the church did not give Earle the customary vote that morning when he came forward, as was the typical practice in the church. Instead, the congregation referred the matter to the deacons, plunging the church into what John Lewis would later describe as "the greatest struggle of my career."[23]

The church's attention turned immediately to Earle's request for membership. Within two days the deacons formed an eleven-member committee to examine Charles Earle's application for membership.

---

[21] Ibid.

[22] "Constitution and By-Laws of the First Baptist Church," contained in Church Records, 8 August 1962.

[23] *Dream Lives On*, 17. For a good analysis of the entire episode, see Charlie Nichols, "The Road to Integration at First Baptist Church of Raleigh," unpublished manuscript, in the archives of First Baptist Church, Raleigh, North Carolina. Nichols's work and organization were helpful for my discussion below.

Robert N. Simms, chair of the diaconate, called the situation "a serious matter for Baptists and other Christians here and in the world." He recommended the formation of a special committee composed of all former chairs of the diaconate, the present chair, and the pastor to investigate the matter quickly and bring a recommendation to the church.[24]

The following Sunday was Easter, prompting Lewis to wait until 21 April to respond from the pulpit to the situation. That response came in the form of a sermon titled, "Come, Let Us Reason Together," reportedly one of his best sermons ever. Taking as his text Isaiah 1:11-20, Lewis began by updating the congregation on the events that had transpired over the previous two weeks. He visited with Earle, "as I would do in any similar situation," to discuss his desire for church membership. He indicated that the committee had met several times during the previous two weeks and had interviewed Earle. Because Lewis's schedule required him to be out of town during the next two weeks, a called church conference for the purpose of hearing the report was delayed until he returned. He also told the congregation he was aware that there were different opinions over the issue and pleaded with them for mutual respect among one another, because "one of the great values we are responsible for preserving in this hour is the freedom of conscience and private judgment." Concluding his introduction, Lewis said, "I see my task this morning not as one who seeks to present any one single possible solution of our problem, but rather to review…what I consider to be the pertinent questions and ramifications which you may wish to consider in regard to your own judgment."[25]

Following his introduction, Lewis presented three points. First, he reminded the church of its history as a biracial congregation, with nine white members and fourteen black slaves as the charter members. He

---

[24] Minutes of the Diaconate, 9 April 1963. The members of the committee were: Robert N. Simms (chair), John Lewis, J. J. Combs, T. W. Brewer, W. L. Wyatt, Sr., R. B. Carpenter, W. H. Weatherspoon, Roy Purser, Coite Jones, Everette Miller, and E. H. Hostetler.

[25] John M. Lewis, "Come, Let Us Reason Together" (sermon, First Baptist Church, Raleigh NC, 21 April 1963), located in the archives of the First Baptist Church, Raleigh, North Carolina.

noted the incident in 1849 when the church excommunicated J. G. Buffaloe for his involvement in the slave trade. Finally, he described the 1868 founding of the First Baptist Church, Wilmington Street, composed of the former African-American members of First Baptist Church, and reminded the congregation that segregation developed in the South following the Civil War and Reconstruction. Lewis concluded the section by asking three questions: "(1) Shall race be a barrier to one's membership in our church? (2) What are the personal and particular circumstances to be considered in the present case? (3) What effect will our decision have on our church and the cause of Christ in general?"[26]

Lewis then reminded his congregation about the nature of the church. The church is responsible to the lordship of Christ. As such, it has the task of proclaiming salvation to the world. The gospel is "for all…universal in scope and centers in a personal relationship between the believer and Jesus Christ," which is the only requirement for membership in a congregation. He spoke of the early days of the Christian movement and how both Jews and Gentiles came together under Christ's lordship, and that Paul had reminded the Galatians that in Christ "there is neither Jew nor Greek, there is neither bondman nor freeman, there is neither male nor female." The pastor also mentioned the church's task in missions and carrying the gospel to the world. The careful listener in the congregation that day would have been able to discern Lewis's true feelings on the matter by hearing his words in this section of the sermon:

> We are being repeatedly told by our foreign missionaries that the failure to solve the race problem in America is daily weakening our witness in Foreign Missions. We are compelled with compassion to take into account, therefore, the impact made on citizens of other countries amongst whom we labor and preach the Gospel. We are concerned also for students from nations all over the world studying in our country and watching the church in America. When any church seems to sanction racial discrimination in contradiction to what is preached and practiced on the Foreign Mission field, many feel that the entire cause of Christ is thereby weakened.[27]

---

[26] Ibid. For a discussion of the Buffaloe incident, see ch. 3 above.
[27] Ibid.

Charles Earle was a student at Shaw University from Jamaica. In the statement above, Lewis was clearly calling the church to its mission and task under the lordship of Christ. And yet, strategically he knew it would not have been wise to bluntly tell the congregation what they ought to do in an explicit way. Effective leader that he was, he knew the church needed to discover the truth for itself.

The final portion of Lewis's sermon evaluated the two possibilities that lay before the church on the matter. He encouraged the members, however their consciences were to lead them, to ask several questions of themselves: "How the decision will strengthen the work of the church? How the decision will strengthen and help the work of missions? How it is a witness to the Gospel and to the nature of the church? How it will mean the strengthening of God's work here in our own congregation?" Lewis trusted that the faithful members who heard his words that day could only come to one conclusion, especially in light of those questions: To deny membership to someone on the basis of skin color could not possibly be a positive thing for the church, missions, or the church's witness.[28]

After working for several weeks, the special committee was finally able to present its report to the deacons at their monthly meeting on 14 May. The report was presented in two parts: (1) a statement of the facts of the investigation and (2) a recommendation that the application for membership of Charles Earle be rejected. The committee determined after an interview with Earle that he was twenty-three years old and a citizen of Jamaica. He was a student at Shaw University where he was a senior and president of the student body. Earle also told the committee that as a boy he was baptized and became a member of the East Queen Street Baptist Church in Kingston, Jamaica. Earle had been at Shaw for three years. For one year, after he left Jamaica, he attended college in Tyler, Texas, where he said he joined an African-American Baptist church. He was active in the Shaw chapter of the NAACP and had taken part in the recent protest activities in the city.[29] Just four nights prior to the deacons'

---

[28] Ibid.

[29] Statement of Committee as to Facts, Minutes of the Diaconate, 14 May 1963.

meeting, Earle was an active participant in the protest at the governor's mansion and had been quoted as a student leader in a news account of the story.[30]

Earle also told the special committee that he had heard John Lewis preach on occasion at Shaw University, he had enjoyed his preaching, and he liked First Baptist Church. He indicated that he had visited other white Baptist churches in the city, including Pullen Memorial and Forest Hills, and that he had visited the First Baptist Church on Wilmington Street, but said that he had never tried to join any of those churches. Most importantly, he told the committee that his desire to join the church "has no connection with the picketing activities in which he has been engaged; that it was not a part of any student plan." Furthermore, he indicated that he "wants to advance the cause of Christ and that if his joining [the] church would not do that, or would cause any trouble or difficulty…he would withdraw his application for membership."[31]

Supplementary to the interview with Earle, the committee's report adds several other facts. They discovered that Earle had received a student loan from the Home Mission Board of the Southern Baptist Convention in the amount of $375 [$2,660], and the funds were to be repaid unless he "gives his life to definite Christian service." His letter of agreement with the Home Mission Board dated 2 November 1962 indicated that he was a member of "Kettering Baptist." The report gives no indication as to the location of "Kettering Baptist Church." Finally, the committee included in its report the fact that, while since 1868 the First Baptist Church of Raleigh had received no African Americans into its fellowship as members, there had been numerous occasions when African Americans had been welcomed in various worship services.[32] Following a lengthy discussion of the report, T. A. Upchurch made a motion, seconded by James A. Graham, that the report be approved and recommended to the church conference. In a split vote, the board voted

---

[30] Bob Lynch and Roy Parker, Jr., "Negroes Boo Governor at Mansion," *News and Observer*, 11 May 1963, 1.

[31] Statement of Committee as to Facts.

[32] Ibid.

forty-two to nineteen to accept the committee's report and recommend to the church that the membership request of Charles Earle be rejected.[33]

The long-awaited church conference to vote on Earle's request for membership occurred the following evening, 15 May. More than 500 members of the church assembled for the meeting—the largest number ever to gather for a church conference at First Baptist Church. One participant, Zua Moore, recalled, "There were people that I did not know belonged to the church who were there, and I had been there since 1942."[34] Other observers confirmed the presence of some people who seldom were seen at the church worship services. Bill Simpson reflected, "There was one fellow who came, he and his wife...he came that night, and that is the only time I saw him after high school...and we finished high school in 1943."[35]

Originally conceived, the plan for the meeting was to be simple. Paper ballots were distributed that included only two options: "For accepting the applicant" and "Against accepting the applicant."[36] Robert N. Simms, the chair of the diaconate, moderated the meeting, which began with a reading of the report of the special study committee and its recommendation to the deacons to deny Earle's membership. Simms added some additional information he received earlier in the day by an anonymous phone call, which asserted that Earle was a member at the Fayetteville Street Baptist Church in the city, a largely African-American Baptist church. The new information seemed to contradict the information Earle gave to the committee concerning his church membership and led to further suspicions of his motive. When Simms became aware of that information, he informed neither the full diaconate nor the pastor. He also neglected to contact Charles Earle to verify the

---

[33] Minutes of the Diaconate, 14 May 1963.

[34] Zua and Jack Moore, interview by Charlie Nichols, 26 November 2006, quoted in Nichols, "Road to Integration at First Baptist Church of Raleigh," 5–6.

[35] Bill Simpson, interview by Charlie Nichols, 24 November 2006, quoted in Nichols, "Road to Integration at First Baptist Church of Raleigh," 6.

[36] Report to Board of Deacons, Minutes of the Diaconate, 14 May 1963.

accuracy of the information, all procedural issues that John Lewis believed should have been handled differently.[37]

When Simms opened the floor for debate, the scene turned ugly. Zua Moore reflected, "It was a fight. People were ugly, booing anybody who wanted to bring him in.... A lot of them wouldn't stand up and speak.... It was really bad."[38] As it turned out, only two people that evening had the opportunity to express their opinion—both in favor of accepting Earle as a member of the church. Just as Al Haskins stood, intending to speak in favor of accepting Earle, Jesse Helms, a member and deacon in the church, suddenly stood up behind Haskins. He began to shout over Haskins, not speaking out against Earle, but to "call for the question," which, if approved by the body, would end debate and move the church immediately to voting. Haskins, who ironically was the brother-in-law of Robert N. Simms, protested. But Simms chose to recognize Helms instead. Upon the rejection of a substitute motion to extend the debate by thirty minutes, the original motion to end debate passed on a voice vote, and the conference then moved to voting.[39] Shouts of protest could be heard from the assembled members. The ballots were cast and, by a vote of 367 to 147, Charles Earle's application for membership was rejected.[40]

While the abrupt end to the discussion was surprising to most, John Lewis was probably the most frustrated. Robert Simms promised the pastor the opportunity to speak to the congregation before the voting took place. Lewis was not given that opportunity even though he had prepared remarks explaining that he did not agree with the report of the special committee. Instead, Lewis believed the right course for the church was to receive Charles Earle into the membership. It was to be a strong statement of support for Charles Earle. Because Lewis was unable to state his opinion and reasoning to the congregation, he thought it important

---

[37] Nichols, "Road to Integration at First Baptist Church of Raleigh," 6. See Church Conference Records, 5 June 1963, for Lewis's thoughts on the matter.

[38] Zua and Jack Moore, interview by Charlie Nichols, 26 November 2006, cited in Nichols, "Road to Integration at First Baptist Church of Raleigh," 7.

[39] Nichols, "Road to Integration at First Baptist Church of Raleigh," 7.

[40] Ibid. See also James Hall, "Church Rejects Negro Applicant," *News and Observer* (Raleigh NC), 16 May 1963, 36.

that his views on the matter be retained in the church records. Accordingly, at the June 1963 church conference Lewis requested that his prepared remarks become a part of the permanent records of the church.[41] After a few other separate issues of business, the church prepared to adjourn the meeting. John Lewis rose and encouraged the congregation to continue to support the church with the same level of enthusiasm shown that evening. He concluded by saying, "Let this be water under the bridge. Let us continue together to strengthen the program of this church in the community."[42]

It would appear that the major stumbling block for the congregation regarding Earle's request for membership concerned his activities in the local Civil Rights Movement, perhaps more so than the color of his skin. His name was well known to members of the church who read the local newspaper regularly. Was his request for membership a legitimate desire on the part of a Baptist Christian to join a local Baptist church? Or was Earle's motivation to be an "agitator" and gain press attention? [43] In his interview with the special investigative committee, he maintained that his desire was pure. John Lewis accepted Earle's explanation. When church members complained to Lewis that Earle was "just testing us," Lewis said, "Right—let's pass the test."[44] In the end the issue came down to the fact that the special committee and the majority of the congregation did not believe the testimony of Charles Earle. Contrary to Earle's assertions to both Lewis and the committee, the majority of the members believed that his activism could not be separated from his desire to join the church. Bill Simpson, an eyewitness to the episode, said, "So many members felt like when Charles Earle came in there was the publicity aspect of it."[45]

---

[41] Church Conference Records, 5 June 1963.

[42] Ibid., 15 May 1963.

[43] "Agitator" is used here only to pose the question as it was conceived by members of the church at that time.

[44] Ernest B. Furgurson, *Hard Right: The Rise of Jesse Helms* (New York: W. W. Norton and Co., 1986) 227, as cited by Nichols, "The Road to Integration at First Baptist Church of Raleigh," 3.

[45] Bill Simpson, interview by Charlie Nichols, 24 November 2006, cited in Nichols, "The Road to Integration at First Baptist Church of Raleigh," 10.

Did the church "pass the test"? The answer to that question is not easily discernable, even after almost half a century. It is very easy to look back from the perspective of fifty years with a judgmental eye upon that episode. The fact of the matter is that very few white Baptist churches in the South in 1963 would have admitted Earle. The First Baptist Church of Raleigh could probably best be characterized as cautiously progressive through the era of Civil Rights. The congregation was not ready for the "test" in 1963. Given time, however, the church did change. In 1970 Kenneth Osei, a student at St. Augustine's College from Ghana, was admitted to the membership of the church without any protest.[46] And progress in racial equality within the congregation has continued to the present. In 2006 Ebele Achonu, a black, female member, was elected to serve on the diaconate. Much of the change must be credited to John Lewis and his pastoral leadership. He obviously believed that the Earle incident created a teachable moment for the church. And it is also to his credit that there was no mass exodus of members following that painful episode.

A final note of interest concerns the role that Jesse Helms played in the affair. Helms had been a member of the church for years serving in many leadership roles, most notably as a deacon. His roots in the church were long. He and his wife, Dot, were married there in 1942. It is no secret that during the years that Jesse Helms was a commentator for WRAL television in Raleigh, and later while he served the state of North Carolina as a United States senator, he frequently opposed efforts toward desegregation and civil rights. It is also no secret that Helms opposed the desegregation of white churches during the Civil Rights Movement. One biographer, William A. Link, indicated that while serving as a deacon at First Baptist Church, he "refused to seat black people and warned other ushers" that this might be a "potential problem."[47] There is evidence that he even threatened to leave the church if it ever integrated. And yet,

---

[46] "Black Admitted to Congregation," (no source given), 20 December 1970, clipping included in file "Race Relations," located in the archives of First Baptist Church, Raleigh.

[47] Jesse Helms to R. B. Carpenter, 11 January 1956, as cited in William A. Link, *Righteous Warrior: Jesse Helms and the Rise of Modern Conservatism* (New York: St. Martin's Press, 2008) 51.

according to Link, Helms's thoughts on the matter were much more complicated than his detractors have expressed. Helms believed that if African Americans truly desired to worship in a white church, he would fellowship with them. But "he believed that nearly all black visitors to white churches were primarily interested in causing 'strife and dissension.'"[48] That seems to have been Helms's approach to the Charles Earle matter, although the role he played behind the scenes is not clear from the extant records. Helms remained at the church until 1966 when he and his family joined the Hayes Barton Baptist Church. Helms's reason for leaving involved his son, who had cerebral palsy and wanted to join the Boy Scout Troop at Hayes Barton, and also the fact that Hayes Barton was located just a few blocks from the Helms family home.[49]

The Elliott Controversy. As the Charles Earle situation played out at First Baptist Church, the Southern Baptist Convention was embroiled in a controversy that had lasting implications for decades into the future. The so-called "Elliott Controversy" centered on the publication of a book titled *The Message of Genesis*, by Ralph H. Elliott in 1961. In the book, published by Broadman Press, Elliott argued for a symbolic interpretation of Genesis 1–11 rather than a strictly literalist view, angering many Fundamentalists in the Southern Baptist Convention who held to a literalist interpretation of the Bible. Elliott was a young professor at the recently formed Midwestern Baptist Theological Seminary in Kansas City—the newest of the Southern Baptist seminaries—which added fodder to the fire. "Why was a professor employed at a Southern Baptist seminary advocating such liberal ideas about the Bible?" the Fundamentalists asked. Elliott was eventually dismissed from his post at the seminary, and in 1963 the Southern Baptist Convention issued a revision of its 1925 Baptist Faith and Message in an

---

[48] Link, *Righteous Warrior*, 51. Link said that Helms likened himself to Jesus driving away the money changers from the temple in the gospels. He believed that African Americans seeking to join white churches during the Civil Rights Movement were "using church as a 'potential bartering place.'"

[49] Ibid., 127.

attempt to appease Fundamentalists who sought stronger doctrinal parameters around the convention.[50]

It should be noted here that although John Lewis was a few years ahead, he and Ralph Elliott were both students at the Southern Baptist Theological Seminary in the 1950s and no doubt knew one another. It is also important to recognize that when Lewis became pastor of the church, he continued a tradition that stretched back at least as far as the era when Sydnor Stealey was the pastor—that of seeking to educate the congregation on theological issues and encouraging the laity to think theologically about world crises, events in the denomination, and of course, personal life struggles. The church bulletin from 14 May 1961, for example, contained an announcement that Lewis and the associate pastor, Donald Niswonger, would be teaching two theological discussion groups on Sunday evenings during the months of June and July. Furthermore, the groups would meet before the union worship services with the Methodist and Presbyterian churches. Niswonger was to teach a class on *An Interpretation of New Testament Ethics,* by Reinhold Niebuhr, while Lewis was to teach on *Present Trends in Christian Thought,* by L. Harold De Wolf.[51] Throughout his ministry at the church, Lewis continually attempted to provide theological education to his congregation, not just in his sermons but through similar seminars at various times. That resulted in a congregation who was more sophisticated theologically than the typical Southern Baptist Church and laid the groundwork for later important decisions the church would

---

[50] For the history of the Elliott Controversy from Elliott himself, see Ralph H. Elliott, *The "Genesis Controversy" and Continuity in Southern Baptist Chaos: A Eulogy for a Great Tradition* (Macon GA: Mercer University Press, 1992). For a complete objective analysis of the controversy, see Jerry L. Faught, "The Genesis Controversies: Denominational Compromise and the Resurgence and Expansion of Fundamentalism in the Southern Baptist Convention" (Ph.D. diss., Baylor University, 1995). For a concise analysis of the controversy, see Walter B. Shurden, *Not a Silent People: Controversies That Have Shaped Southern Baptists* (Macon GA: Mercer University Press, 1995) 69–81.

[51] Church Bulletin, 14 May 1961.

make about its connections with the Southern Baptist Convention in the 1990s.[52]

With that information in mind, we can return to the Elliott Controversy, which reached a crescendo at the annual gathering of the Southern Baptist Convention in San Francisco in 1962. Lewis attended the convention that year and, when he returned, decided to use a Sunday-morning sermon to address the controversy. On 15 July he preached a sermon about the nature of the Bible titled "Beyond the Sacred Page." The bulletin that morning gave the explanation that "today's message is the Pastor's report and evaluation of two motions passed by the Convention in San Francisco."[53] It would not be the last time that Lewis would address conflict in the Southern Baptist Convention to the church. The Elliott Controversy was just the beginning of a bitter war between Fundamentalists and Moderates that would eventually result in a complete takeover of the convention's agencies and seminaries in an

---

[52] On 7 October 1962 the church bulletin reported that Niswonger would be starting a weekday class called "A History of Christianity." The class lasted for a number of weeks. In November 1962 the Sunday-evening seminars dealt with the world's religions, again showing a remarkable effort to educate the congregation. Lewis was not beyond using a sermon for didactic purposes also. On 24 February his evening sermon was titled "Kierkegaard: Truth as Encounter."

[53] Church Bulletin, 15 July 1962. At the San Francisco convention, messengers passed several motions that pertained to the Elliott matter. The first called for the executive committee of the convention to create a special committee to present a confessional statement modeled after the 1925 "Baptist Faith and Message." The second and third motions, presented by Fundamentalist pastor K. Owen White of Houston, Texas, were copied in the church bulletin and commented upon in Lewis's sermon on 15 July. The first said, "That the messengers to this Convention, by standing vote, reaffirm their faith in the *entire* Bible as the authoritative, authentic, infallible Word of God." The other, quoted in the bulletin, said, "That we express our abiding and unchanging objection to the dissemination of theological views in any of our seminaries which would undermine such faith in the historical accuracy and doctrinal integrity of the Bible, and we courteously request the Trustees and administrative officers of our institutions and other agencies to take such steps as shall be necessary to remedy at once those situations where such views now threaten our historic position." (For a fuller discussion of the issue, see *Southern Baptist Convention Annual*, 1962, 65, 68, as cited by Shurden, *Not a Silent People*, 73–74.)

effort to rid the denominational leadership of so-called "liberals." Lewis's term of service as pastor corresponded with most of that conflict.

Expansion of Facilities. In late 1964 the church began to plan for its future needs, including facilities and property. At the church conference in October the membership approved the creation of a Long-Range Planning Committee and asked the committee to look at three specific matters: (1) investigate whether the church could obtain adjoining property; (2) if more property on the present site was not available, explore and investigate other locations in the city where the church might consider moving; and (3) develop a plan for utilization of the current location if additional property is available.[54] The next summer John Lewis attended a conference at Ridgecrest that specifically targeted the unique challenges encountered by downtown Baptist churches. When he returned, he gave the deacons a report and agreed to provide a brief written report to the members of the church.[55] By 1965 the sentiment in the congregation appears to have leaned toward remaining at the present location. Willis Harvey made a motion that the pastor and chair of the diaconate communicate with the Long-Range Planning Committee, and other committees as well, "to consider First Baptist Church's role as a downtown church and to give special consideration for our downtown responsibilities in 1966."[56] Also, in 1965 the church began to discuss the possibility of erecting a new education building.[57] Six years earlier the church had the fortune of acquiring adjoining property from Charles Johnson for $170,000 [$1.25 million].[58] Although unable to purchase

---

[54] Church Conference Records, 21 October 1964.

[55] Minutes of the Diaconate, 10 June 1965.

[56] Church Conference Records, 31 October 1965. It was a special called church conference for the purpose of approving the 1966 budget.

[57] See ibid., 21 July 1965, where an excerpt from a letter from W. L. Wyatt is read establishing a memorial to his late wife. He wanted to fund a ladies' parlor in a new education building. If a contract on a new building did not happen within ten years of his own death, the money would be given to Meredith College. Also see Deacons' Meeting Minutes, 8 December 1965 report, noting that a memorial to her husband had been established by Mrs. E. L. Layfield to furnish the Jones-Brewer-Berean Classroom in a new education building.

[58] See Church Conference Records, 30 August 1959.

additional land from the state in 1965, the church still had room to expand in its present location.[59]

After working for almost three years, in May 1967 the Long-Range Planning Committee presented its final report to the congregation. The report, given in great detail, provided recommendations in the areas of programs (preaching, teaching, missions, fellowship, music, giving, and cooperation with other Christians), staff, facilities, and financial support. As expected, the most noteworthy recommendation from the committee related to facilities, calling for major renovation to the sanctuary and the construction of a new education building. The report ended with a strong statement about the commitment needed to be a successful congregation in a downtown area: "While all churches strive to keep their programs attractive and inviting, the downtown church is especially confronted with the necessity of maintaining a program worthy of a trip downtown by its members and worthy of a visit by the passing public.... A mediocre church cannot survive in a downtown area."[60]

The church wasted no time implementing the Long-Range Planning Committee recommendations. Within four months a building committee was selected, and in January 1968 the church retained the architectural firm of Haskins and Rice to produce plans for the renovation and building projects.[61] Another important step was to secure the services of Ketchum and Company, a professional fundraising firm employed to

---

[59] In June 1965 the church approved a committee to investigate the possibility of purchasing the "Raney property" from the state, located between the church structure and Hillsborough Street. The state refused to sell the lot to the church. The following year the church acquired property designated as the "Bradshaw property" across Edenton Street from the church lot. The cost was $320,000 [$2.18 million]. There were conversations in 1966 about the possibility of an exchange of properties with the state but those plans never materialized.

[60] Report and Recommendations of the Long-Range Planning Committee, 13, contained in Church Conference Records, 17 May 1967. Members of the Long-Range Planning Committee were J. Everette Miller (chair), C. C. Cameron, J. J. Combs, William H. Simpson, and W. H. Weatherspoon.

[61] Church Conference Records, 20 September 1967 and 24 January 1968. The members of the building committee were J. J. Combs (chair), Charles D. Barham, William B. Dewar, Mrs. Carl Goerch, Rufus A. Hunter, Mrs. C. Gordon Maddrey, J. Everette Miller, James Lloyd Norris, Anna Riddick, Melton E. Valentine, Edgar W. Wyatt, and John M. Lewis (*ex-officio*).

help raise an initial goal of $1 million [$6.16 million] for the project.[62] The church appointed L. R. Harrill to head the building fund campaign.[63] In January 1969 the church sponsored three "Interpretive" dinners for families to come and hear about the proposed project, and then make pledges and contributions. Families whose last names began with the letters A–F came to the Tuesday evening dinner, G–Q gathered on Wednesday evening, and R–Z came on Thursday.[64] The twelve-week campaign was deemed a success. When completed, more than $1 million in cash and pledges were raised. L. R. Harrill said he "had never experienced anything quite so rewarding as the campaign and he wanted to convey a warm 'thank you.'"[65]

So successful was the initial fundraising effort that in March 1969, the church instructed the building committee to request that the architects proceed with drawing plans for a new education building, with an unfinished basement, a partially finished top floor, and minimum necessary renovations to the sanctuary. The total cost of the project was not to exceed $1,539,000 [$9 million].[66] Albert Haskins, one of the architects and a member of the church, presented the plans to the church in August. The church clerk said that Haskins's presentation was given "in a most sincere and moving atmosphere," where he "thanked the church, on behalf of Mr. Richard Rice and himself, for the job assigned to them."[67] At the end of the year John Lewis told the congregation he appreciated its commitment to the project. He said that 1969 was a "year of commitment and dedication," 1970 would be the "year of building expectation, sacrifice, and reorganization," and 1971 would be a "year of building completion, rejoicing, and expansion."[68]

---

[62] Ibid., 16 October 1968.

[63] The members of the building fund committee were L. R. Harrill (chair), Dorothy Austell, Albert M. Calloway, R. B. Carpenter, Ivie L. Clayton, Coite H. Jones, Claude F. Gaddy, Roy M. Purser, J. Gordon Riddick, Charles Lee Smith (*ex-officio*), Ruth Wilson, Edgar M. Wyatt (*ex-officio*), and William L. Wyatt, Jr.

[64] Church Bulletin, 12 January 1969.

[65] Church Conference Records, 19 February 1969.

[66] Ibid., 19 March 1969.

[67] Ibid., 13 August 1969.

[68] Ibid., 21 December 1969.

The plans were completed by January 1970, and the church was ready to accept bids on the project. The architects recommended that the building committee invite six or more contractors to bid on the plans. A revised estimate placed the anticipated cost at $1,671,400 [$9.23 million]. Commenting on the moment, John Lewis said that the church had made "an historical decision" that evening—a reference no doubt to the fact that the church had not undertaken a building project of that magnitude since the original structure was built in 1859. The excitement was dampened a few months later when it became apparent that the lowest bid exceeded the architects' estimate by $459,104 [$2.54 million], requiring the architects to make revisions to the original plans. Eventually, after a second round of bidding, the church negotiated a contract with Davidson and Jones Contractors on a cost-plus-10-percent basis. The total of the contract was $1,181,000 [$6.52 million], with additional subcontractor and architectural fees totaling $649,542 [$3.59 million]. The grand total of the building project was $1,830,542 [$10.1 million].[69]

The decision reached by the church was not easy. Two church conferences were needed to allow the congregation to express its concerns. In an expression of his commitment, John Lewis publically gave $500 [$2,760] toward the project and made this appeal: "We have waited for 158 years for this decision. The future of our church is in the balance, and we cannot afford to fail now. God has given the members of this congregation the money to do the work. It is now a question of being realistic."[70]

The building process continued in August 1970 when the church agreed in special conference to borrow $1,200,000 [$6.63 million]. Groundbreaking ceremonies occurred on 6 September 1970 and the construction proceeded during the next fourteen months. However, just before the completion of the project, a delay of approximately one month was necessary because of the discovery of termite damage to the southeast corner of the main sanctuary roof structure. The damage in

---

[69] Ibid., 21 January, 15 April, 15 July, and 22 July 1970. See also *The Dream Lives On*, 23–24.

[70] Church Conference Records, 22 July 1970.

three short blocks of wood (critical supports for the three arches joining at that point) was so severe that structural engineers were amazed the roof had not collapsed. If the southeast corner of the roof had collapsed, it is very likely that the entire sanctuary would have collapsed. The damage was repaired by shoring up the roof and installing steel plates, bolts, and concrete. The final plastering and painting were done so well that the work is almost unrecognizable.[71] The church was able to occupy the new education building on 14 November 1971. Finally, on 15 April 1973 a grand celebration was held as the new building and the renovated sanctuary were dedicated.[72] Two months later J. J. Combs, chair of the building committee, gave a final report of the committee's work. The first meeting of the committee occurred on 10 October 1967, with the final meeting on 19 June 1973—a total of fifty-three meetings. The final amount of money spent was $1,872,819.33 [$9.04 million].[73] Although left unfinished at the time, the third floor of the education building was finally completed in 1977.

Further Baptist Controversy. The skies darkened further in the Baptist world as the decade of the 1960s closed and a new decade began. The Elliott Controversy was never really settled sufficiently, even after the Baptist Faith and Message Statement was passed by the Southern Baptist Convention in 1963. Another conflict over one Baptist scholar's interpretation of Genesis erupted in December 1969, following the release of volume 1 of the Broadman Bible Commentary series. Originally the brainchild of Clifton J. Allen, editorial secretary of the Baptist Sunday School Board, and William J. Fallis, head of the book editorial department, the commentary series was to be composed of twelve volumes comprising an exposition and commentary on the entire Bible.

---

[71] Don Kline, interview with the author, 4 April 2011.

[72] Church Conference Records, 25 April 1973. The ceremony occurred on Palm Sunday. The dedication of the fellowship hall (where worship services had been held while the sanctuary was being renovated) took place at 10:00 A.M., and the members then processed into the newly renovated sanctuary carrying palm branches and singing "Forward Through the Ages." See *Dream Lives On*, 25.

[73] Church Conference Records, 20 June 1973.

Volume 1, which covered Genesis and Exodus, was co-authored by G. Henton Davies and Roy Honeycutt, respectively.[74]

Davies was a well-known Baptist Old Testament scholar from England who served as principal of Regents Park College at Oxford. His academic and Baptist credentials were impeccable. Yet very shortly after the release of the commentary, Fundamentalists in the convention took exception to Davies's interpretation of Genesis 22:1–19, wherein God commanded Abraham to sacrifice his son Isaac. While acknowledging that many interpreted the text literally, Davies preferred a more symbolic reading of the text, arguing, "Indeed, what Christian or humane conscience could regard such a command as coming from God?"[75] Over the next two years the controversy played out on the editorial pages of Baptist state papers as well as the annual convention gatherings. Ultimately, a new author, Clyde Francisco, was enlisted to rewrite the Genesis section of the commentary, resulting in a revision of volume 1. The Broadman Bible Controversy, as the Elliott Controversy had before, served to highlight the theological differences that existed in the Southern Baptist Convention between Fundamentalists and Moderates. The congeniality of the two camps—largely due to a shared commitment to missions—was in the process of unraveling.[76]

On the heels of the Broadman Bible Controversy at the national level came the "Baptism Controversy" within the Baptist State Convention of North Carolina. In 1971 M. O. Owens, a pastor and Fundamentalist leader in North Carolina, became concerned that there were Baptist churches in the state receiving new members into their congregations without requiring believer's baptism by immersion. His

---

[74] Jerry L. Faught, "Round Two, Volume One: The Broadman Commentary Controversy," *Baptist History and Heritage* 38/1 (Winter 2003): 94–114.

[75] G. Henton Davies, *Genesis*, The Broadman Bible Commentary, vol. 1 (Nashville: Broadman Press, 1969), 198, as cited by ibid., 98. It is noteworthy that Lewis invited Davies on several occasions to preach and teach at First Baptist Church. For several years in the late 1970s, Davies served as visiting professor of religion at Meredith College. (See Minutes of the Diaconate, 18 January 1978.)

[76] That is the thesis of Bill Leonard, *God's Last and Only Hope: The Fragmentation of the Southern Baptist Convention* (Grand Rapids MI: Wm. B. Eerdmans, 1990). This book remains one of the best interpretations of the conflict between Fundamentalists and Moderates in the Southern Baptist Convention.

proposed solution was to add an amendment to the constitution of the Baptist State Convention that would exclude churches from membership in the convention if they did not require immersion of their members. The ensuing controversy created an acrimonious environment in the convention for the next three years. When the amendment came to a vote in the 1971 convention, 54 percent of the messengers voted in favor of it. However, a two-thirds majority was required to amend the constitution. Owens pressed the matter once more in 1972, when again it failed to garner the needed majority.[77]

Although the First Baptist Church of Raleigh did require immersion for full membership at the time, John Lewis was nevertheless opposed to the Owens effort in the Baptist State Convention. Just before the gathering of the convention in 1971, Lewis discussed his reasons for being opposed to the proposed action, although the church records do not record his words. Then in 1972, when the issue resurfaced, Lewis used the "Pastor's Paragraphs" section of the church bulletin to explain his thoughts again. There were two amendments scheduled to be debated at the annual meeting in 1972. The first, a repeat from the previous year, called for the exclusion of churches from the Baptist State Convention that did not require immersion for membership. The second sought to make it mandatory that voting messengers to the convention be immersed members of Baptist churches. Lewis, who was in his first term as president of the general board of the Baptist State Convention, argued that "the issue is not immersion." Instead, "conventions must stay clear from exercising any doctrinal, creedal or ecclesiastical control over participating churches."[78]

---

[77] David T. Morgan, *The New Crusades, The New Holy Land: Conflict in the Southern Baptist Convention, 1969–1991* (Tuscaloosa: The University of Alabama Press, 1996) 23–24. Morgan's book, overlooked by many Baptist scholars, provides the best analysis of the background leading up to the crisis in the Southern Baptist Convention, generally thought to have begun in 1979 with the election of Adrian Rogers to the presidency. Morgan argues that the issues that led to Rogers's election in 1979 actually began with the Elliott controversy and gained momentum during the 1960s and 1970s.

[78] "Pastor's Paragraphs," Church Bulletin, 12 November 1972. During much of Lewis's pastorate the church newsletter was attached to the Sunday bulletin,

ACTS Committee. In summer 1969 the youth began to initiate conversations within the congregation about how the church might be more actively involved in meeting human social needs in downtown Raleigh. The result was the formation of the ACTS Committee.[79] One of the most significant projects promoted by the ACTS Committee was to establish a cerebral palsy day care center to operate in the new education building. The United Cerebral Palsy Association of North Carolina provided all personnel, equipment, funding, etc., while the church provided the facilities. The church gave final approval for the project in December 1971.[80]

As the decade of the 1970s progressed, the ACTS Committee moved to other projects as well. In May 1973 the committee asked the congregation for approval to establish a "crisis closet" to serve the needy who came to the church requesting food or clothing. The old fellowship hall underneath the sanctuary served as the location. The junior and senior high youth helped to prepare the space for the ministry.

The ACTS Committee also helped motivate the church to approve the Infant-Toddler Center. The church unanimously approved the concept at its November 1974 church conference, but not without considerable discussion. Donna Toms, the chair of the ACTS Committee at the time, indicated that her committee would study the administrative issues related to such an endeavor following the church's approval. She told the church that Edenton Street Methodist Church had a similar program with a long waiting list. In particular, there was need for a center to be established for those from the age of infancy to three years old. By September 1975 the Infant-Toddler Center was fully operational.[81]

---

maximizing the opportunity to communicate announcements, etc. with the largest number of members while saving postage expense.

[79] See *Dream Lives On*, 23, and Church Conference Records, 18 June 1969. "ACTS" was the acronym for "All Christians to Serve." The original members of the committee were O. H. Dillard (chairman), William Lassiter, Ed Vick, Mrs. Raymond Brown, Mrs. Joe Elkins, Mrs. Carl Goerch, Austin Lewis, and Donna Crocker.

[80] Church Conference Records, 15 December 1971.

[81] Ibid., 20 November 1974 and 7 May 1975.

Two years prior in September 1973, the church had the opportunity to purchase another lot adjoining the church property called the "Rogers property." Claude Gaddy was instrumental in negotiations with the Rogers family for the property. Originally, the property was offered for lease to the Baptist Sunday School Board as a location for a new Baptist bookstore, but because of the expense of leasing the land, the board decided to build in another location. The property was then sold to the church for $352,800 [$1.7 million]. Although it increased the church's indebtedness to $1,141,000 [$5.51 million], the purchase proved to be beneficial, giving the church ownership of more property to be used for parking.[82] The following year the church sold the Bradshaw property to the state for $433,225 [$1.88 million], which was applied to the church debt.[83]

Bold Missions Thrust. The Southern Baptist Convention closed out the decade of the 1970s with a special missions emphasis called "Bold Missions Thrust," a challenge that "every person in the world shall have the opportunity to hear the gospel of Christ in the next 25 years."[84] The plan, approved in 1977, was to last for three years and utilize the resources of the convention as well as local churches and laity. The first mention of Bold Mission Thrust at First Baptist Church occurred in the church conference minutes from January 1978, with a notation that the pastor would appoint a Bold Mission Task Force. Two months later Don Kline was selected to chair the committee, signaling the commitment of the church to the program.[85]

One of the most visible expressions of Bold Mission Thrust at First Baptist Church was a partnership created with the West Monmouth Baptist Church in Freehold, New Jersey, which was approved in October 1978. The West Monmouth Baptist Church was organized with help from the Home Mission Board of the Southern Baptist Convention. It had just recently become self-supporting and had a membership of 141 at the

---

[82] Ibid., 20 June 1973.

[83] Ibid., 26 June 1974.

[84] Albert McClellan, "Bold Mission Thrust," in *Encyclopedia of Southern Baptists*, ed. Lynn Edward May, vol. 4 supplement (Nashville: Broadman Press, 1982) 2125–26.

[85] Church Conference Records, 25 January and 22 March 1978.

time. The church's pastor was David Leary, a North Carolinian originally from Ahoskie. First Baptist Church committed to help the new congregation with financial contributions, as well as through mission trips by the youth and adult laity. Speaking to his congregation at First Baptist, John Lewis indicated that the young church "needed encouragement and help from older established churches like our own."[86]

Fundamentalist Takeover of the Southern Baptist Convention. By the end of the decade the conflict between Fundamentalists and Moderates in the Southern Baptist Convention erupted into a full-scale war. That war would eventually force Moderates to form their own organization for missions and theological education—called the Cooperative Baptist Fellowship.[87] As mentioned above, the Elliott Controversy and the conflict over the first volume of the Broadman Bible Commentary highlighted the theological differences between Fundamentalists and Moderates in the Southern Baptist Convention. Fundamentalists insisted that the nature of the Bible should be understood with the word "inerrant." They believed that each word of the Bible had been dictated by God to the original writers, and that in its original manuscripts the Bible was completely free from any errors–whether theological, historical, or scientific. Free from all error, so they claimed, the Bible should be interpreted literally, and when it conflicted with, for example, the theory of evolution, the Bible should be believed instead of modern science. Moderates, on the other hand, were fine with understanding the nature of the Bible as having been "inspired" by God, but chose not to

---

[86] "Pastor's Paragraphs," in Church Bulletin, 12 November 1978. Shortly after this column was written, John Lewis traveled to New Jersey where he met with the church's pastor to determine further needs. While there, he presented from First Baptist a check to the congregation for $1,200 [$3,950] to be used to purchase a 16-mm projector and screen for the church.

[87] For a good, concise discussion of the conflict in the Southern Baptist Convention between Fundamentalists and Moderates post-1979, see Shurden, *Not a Silent People*, 83–112. For a concise history of the Cooperative Baptist Fellowship, see Walter B. Shurden, "The Cooperative Baptist Fellowship," in *The Baptist River: Essays on Many Tributaries of a Diverse Tradition*, ed. W. Glenn Jonas, Jr. (Macon GA: Mercer University Press, 2006) 243–68.

use the word "inerrant." That position was attacked by Fundamentalists who claimed that Moderates did not "believe the Bible."

Those and other differences were not resolved in any meaningful way. The result was that in June 1979, at the annual meeting of the Southern Baptist Convention in Houston, Texas, Adrian Rogers was elected as convention president. Rogers, a Fundamentalist pastor of Bellevue Baptist Church in Memphis, Tennessee, was the first of a string of Fundamentalists elected to the position over the next eleven years. The power of the presidency was not lost on the Fundamentalists. Paul Pressler, an appellate judge from Houston, and Paige Patterson, the president of the Criswell Center for Biblical Studies at the time, were the architects of "The Takeover," as it later came to be called. They understood that the president had the power to appoint the committee on committees, which in turn appointed a committee that selected trustees for all the agencies in the convention. The plan was simple. Control of the presidency for a decade would in turn guarantee that Fundamentalists could have a majority on the trustee boards of the agencies. By 1990 the Moderates, tired of the political wrangling year after year only to lose, chose to break away and form the Cooperative Baptist Fellowship.

John Lewis was keenly aware of the issues that confronted the Southern Baptist Convention. He had been involved in Baptist life beyond the local church level for his entire career, having served in numerous leadership positions on both the state and national levels. At the time of the Houston convention in 1979, Lewis was in the middle of a four-year term as a member of the powerful executive committee of the Southern Baptist Convention. When he returned from Houston, it did not take him very long to respond to what he witnessed. Writing to the congregation in the church newsletter, Lewis issued a scathing rebuttal of the concept of biblical inerrancy. He argued that such a view "takes us back into the dark ages of Medieval scholasticism, and the out-moded Aristotelian science, which the church erroneously championed as part of the divine revelation. It calls for a crucifixion of one's intellect, and to falsely choose between the truths of modern science and a distorted interpretation of the Bible."[88]

If anyone doubted where Lewis stood on convention issues, that article clearly placed him on the side of Moderates. Lewis continued to speak out about convention issues and the growing power of Fundamentalism until his retirement in 1987.[89]

Last Years of Lewis's Pastorate. The year 1980 began with the church observance of the 20th anniversary of the pastorate of John Lewis. For several weeks in January and February, the church celebrated Lewis's ministry. As a special gift, the church granted Lewis a sabbatical leave, which began on 24 February. Lewis and his wife traveled to Egypt and Greece and then settled in England for three months. Here Lewis was able to attend lectures at Oxford University and exchanged pulpits for one month with Reverend Gethin Abraham Williams, a British pastor from Sutton Baptist Church near London.[90]

During the last five years of John Lewis's pastorate, the church returned once again to its earlier ministry of establishing a mission congregation. In February 1983 the deacons passed a motion to recommend that the church "consider favorably" sponsoring a new church in the Northwest Raleigh area in cooperation with the Raleigh Baptist Association.[91] The church unanimously approved the idea and selected a steering committee for the project. The Raleigh Baptist Association requested that the church commit $5,000–$10,000 [$10,800–$21,500] per year for two years, as well as ten families from the church who would help get the church started. The first worship service for the church was held at Ravenscroft School in September 1983. Thomas Bland, a professor at Southeastern Baptist Theological Seminary at the time, served as the mission's first pastor. By spring 1984 the mission was ready

---

[88] "Pastor's Paragraphs," in Church Bulletin, 15 July 1979. Lewis also authored a book on the subject of biblical authority. See John M. Lewis, *Layman's Library of Christian Doctrine: Revelation, Inspiration, Scripture* (Nashville: Broadman Press, 1985).

[89] See, for example, "Pastor's Paragraphs," in Church Bulletin, 17 and 24 May 1981; 13 June 1982; and 19 May, 2 June, and 9 June 1985.

[90] *Dream Lives On*, 29–30.

[91] Minutes of the Diaconate, 16 February 1983.

to purchase property and begin a building project. Alan Sasser was selected by the congregation as the first full-time pastor. In June 1984 the mission requested that it be constituted into a self-sustaining church. Today, Greystone Baptist Church is a thriving congregation in the North Raleigh area.[92]

Another important mission initiative, which has grown into one of First Baptist's most important contributions to downtown ministry in Raleigh, began during the last five years of Lewis's tenure. At a deacons' meeting on 16 April 1983, Sonia Moore, mission action drector of the WMU, proposed that the basement area under the sanctuary be used as a clothes closet for the city's homeless and less fortunate. The following month the deacons approved the plan and the church's clothing ministry was born.[93]

In 1986 John Lewis announced his intention to retire at the end of March 1987, which coincided with the church's 175th anniversary. In his weekly column in the church newsletter, Lewis indicated that it had become "time to live off the interest earned by a thousand memories, so many which you have provided in our pilgrimage of faith, love and hope shared in the work of God's great kingdom."[94] Lewis's retirement announcement came almost eighteen months after the death of his wife, Jean.[95]

When his retirement finally became a reality in 1987, Lewis had served the congregation for twenty-seven years—the longest tenure of any pastor in the church's history. His ministry had been fruitful. When he assumed the pastorate of the church, there were 1,748 members. The church had a budget of $190,000 [$1.38 million] and a total indebtedness

---

[92] *Dream Lives On*, 32–34.

[93] Minutes of the Diaconate, 16 April and 18 May 1983.

[94] "Pastor's Paragraphs," in Church Bulletin, 14 September 1986.

[95] Jean Lewis deserves to be recognized for her importance as a co-laborer with her husband, John, during his twenty-seven years as pastor of the church. Her energy and personality were integral components to the couple's ministry together. The education building constructed during his pastoral tenure was eventually named the "John M. Lewis Education Building." He was also awarded the title *Pastor Emeritus* upon his retirement. In 2010, recognizing Jean's contribution during those years, the church appropriately renamed the building the "John and Jean Lewis Education Building."

of $195,250 [$1.41 million]. During his tenure the church raised the money to build a new education building and renovate the sanctuary at a cost of more than $1.8 million. In 1987, when Lewis retired, the total membership of the church was approximately 1,300[96] with a budget of approximately $750,000 [$1.42 million].[97]

Lewis died on 15 December 2007, more than twenty years after he retired. His obituary revealed the special qualities about his life that made him so beloved as the church's pastor:

> His career touched the lives of countless friends, families, students and professional associates. He is cherished for his intellect, his compassion, his courage of conviction, and his steadfast integrity. He, along with like-minded others, guided the members of the Raleigh church to open its doors to the faithful of any race or creed during the early days of the civil rights movement, thereby helping the wider community along the same path. His unwavering belief in, and tireless activism for, the bedrock Baptist principles of local church autonomy, priesthood of the true believer, and cooperative fellowship remain beacons for all Baptists today. He was a poet, artist, and amateur astronomer whose interests included chess, philosophy, classical music, travel, golf, and communing with the mysteries of the sea, all of which greatly informed his life and ministry.[98]

At a memorial service where the church mourned his loss, Dan Day, then pastor of the church, said, "John Lewis's rich baritone voice and courtly gentleman's demeanor were accurate but dim indicators of the depth of the man himself; for within John there was the soul of a poet, the curiosity of a scientist, the playfulness of a child, and the mind of a meticulous scholar, all wrapped round the heart of a kind and principled Christian."

* * *

---

[96] Report of the Future Focus Committee, contained in Church Conference Records, 24 June 1987.

[97] Church Conference Records, 22 October 1986.

[98] *News and Observer* (Raleigh NC), 18 December 2007, 8b.

The conclusion of Lewis's tenure as pastor coincided with the church's 175th anniversary. The next twenty-five years brought a further challenge to the founders' vision. The church was about to be met with significant obstacles related to the well-being of its building and its commitment to historical Baptist principles. With its long track record of faithfulness in the midst of challenge, the church was poised to call a new pastor and embrace the next era.

9

Being Baptist in a New Way (1987–2012)

In a speech at the Brandenburg Gate in West Berlin on 12 June 1987, President Ronald Reagan uttered the now famous words, "Mr. Gorbachev, tear down this wall!" Although the wall separating East and West Berlin stood for another two years, and its destruction came at the hands of the East German people rather than the Soviet Union, these words still captured the mood of the United States in the late 1980s as the Cold War came to an end. Since the end of World War II, the United States and the Soviet Union had been opponents in a global effort to promote competing ideologies of capitalism and communism, respectively. The competition had been dangerous, and at least once (the Cuban Missile Crisis in 1962) the two nations could have engaged in full-scale nuclear war. The fall of the Soviet Union in 1991 ushered in a new era in American history, one free from concerns about a competing superpower.

Despite the Iran-Contra Scandal that engulfed the Reagan White House during his second term, Ronald Reagan remained one of the most popular presidents in American history. His popularity helped his vice-president, George H. W. Bush, to be elected to the presidency in 1988. Bush is widely regarded today as a "moderate" Republican, having signed into law a number of important pieces of legislation, including the Americans with Disabilities Act (1990), a re-authorization of the Clean Air Act (1990), and the Immigration Act of 1990—a measure which increased legal immigration into the United States. Bush also led a multination coalition supported by the United Nations to attack Iraqi military forces in 1991 that had invaded the smaller neighboring country of Kuwait, an important American ally in the region. The Gulf War ended shortly through a cease-fire negotiated with Iraq's leader, Saddam Hussein.

More controversially, at home Bush appointed Clarence Thomas to succeed Thurgood Marshall on the United States Supreme Court in 1991. While Thomas was widely regarded as conservative in his judicial philosophy, it was his confirmation hearing before the Senate Judiciary Committee that captured the nation's attention for several days. Anita Hill, a former legal associate with Thomas, claimed he had sexually harassed her in the workplace. The salacious nature of her testimony and the charges she brought against him made his confirmation hearing one of the most controversial in history. The Senate nevertheless confirmed Thomas by a vote of fifty-two to forty-eight in 1991.

By 1992 the political winds in the nation were blowing from a different direction. The Republicans had held the White House for twelve years. Bill Clinton, Democratic governor of Arkansas, was elected President that year largely by capturing the attention of younger voters. He became the first president from the "Baby Boomer" generation. His campaign theme song, "Don't Stop Thinking about Tomorrow" by Fleetwood Mac, conveyed the optimism of his campaign. Clinton presided over a long period of economic growth, one of the longest of the twentieth century. His administration, however, was tainted by scandal—most notably, the Monica Lewinsky scandal. In his grand jury testimony at the height of the scandal, Clinton committed perjury when asked about his adulterous relationship with Lewinsky. The House of Representatives passed two articles of impeachment against him in 1998: (1) lying under oath and (2) obstruction of justice. The Senate, however, refused to find him guilty and he remained in office for his full term.

Fresh on the heels of the Clinton-Lewinsky scandal, the presidential election of 2000 became one of the most acrimonious in American history. Clinton's vice-president, Al Gore, was the Democratic candidate while George W. Bush, son of Clinton's predecessor, was the Republican nominee. Early on election night, the major news networks projected that Gore would be the winner when Florida was called in his favor. But the race was so close in Florida that, within an hour, it was taken out of the Gore column and returned to "toss-up" status. It took several weeks of vote-counting, political wrangling, and eventually a ruling from the United States Supreme Court in the case *Bush v. Gore* to declare George W. Bush the ultimate victor in the bitter race.

On 11 September 2001, barely nine months after George Bush assumed the presidency, the nation suffered the worst terrorist attack in American history. Terrorists hijacked four passenger jets that morning that had departed for the West Coast from Boston, Newark, and Washington, D.C. Two of the planes were deliberately flown into the twin towers of the World Trade Center, causing their collapse. One plane was crashed into the Pentagon. The passengers of the fourth plane attacked the hijackers, leading to the crash of the plane in a rural Pennsylvania field. More than 3,000 Americans died on that day.

America went to war against Al Qaeda in Afghanistan in 2002 in retaliation for the 9/11 attacks. Intelligence reports determined that the mastermind was Osama Bin Laden, a Saudi national. Bin Laden had been bitterly opposed to American presence in the Middle East—particularly America's support for Israel. Bin Laden built the Al Qaeda terrorist network and resided with his terrorist training camps at the time in Afghanistan. The following year American forces also launched an attack on Iraq, based largely on claims that Saddam Hussein had weapons of mass destruction and might potentially use them against American troops still stationed in the region since the first Gulf War. That two-front war drained American financial resources, caused thousands of American casualties and untold numbers of Afghan and Iraqi civilian deaths, and sparked a bitter debate in American society that remains to the present. Hussein was captured by American forces in 2003, tried by the new Iraqi government, and executed in 2006. Osama Bin Laden, was killed in a raid on his compound by Navy Seals in May 2011. The majority of American troops have left Iraq, while the war in Afghanistan continues.

Just four years after the 9/11 attacks, one of the worst natural disasters in American history occurred on 29 August 2005. Hurricane Katrina, a powerful category-3 storm, came ashore near the area of New Orleans, Louisiana, bringing with it a huge storm surge that devastated much of the Gulf Coast from Florida to Louisiana. The storm killed more than 1,800 people and caused more than $100 billion in property loss, with the majority of the damage suffered by the city of New Orleans.

The presidential election of 2008 was historic. George W. Bush had completed his two terms as president, and his vice-president, Dick Cheney, was not running, making that election the first open election since 1952. Barack Obama won the Democratic primary and became his party's nominee, overcoming a hotly contested primary challenge from

Hillary Clinton, wife of former president Bill Clinton. The Republican nominee was longtime Arizona senator John McCain. Obama's election made him the first African American ever elected to the presidency. He assumed the presidency during the worst economic slowdown since the Great Depression, making his first term challenging when coupled with the two-front wars still being waged in Iraq and Afghanistan.

The decade of the 1990s marked a significant milestone for the city of Raleigh. In 1992 the city celebrated its bicentennial. To commemorate the celebration, the city commissioned artist David Benson, who produced a giant acorn sculpture located at Moore Square in keeping with the city's nickname the "City of Oaks." The copper and steel acorn is ten feet tall and weighs 1,250 pounds. It is dedicated to the late John Watkins, who dreamed up the idea and spearheaded the effort to enlist local businesses to pay for the expense of its creation. The giant acorn has become a part of Raleigh tradition since the bicentennial—it has been dropped from a crane at midnight for Raleigh's "First Night" celebrations on New Year's Eve since.[1]

Natural disaster struck Raleigh as well as other parts of Eastern North Carolina when, in the early morning hours of 6 September 1996, Hurricane Fran blew ashore from along the Atlantic coast as a category-3 storm. After coming ashore the storm blew inland along the I-40 corridor, leaving a wake of destruction. The storm was responsible for thirty-seven deaths and more than $2.2 billion in property damage.[2] Three years later, on 16 September 1999, Hurricane Floyd swept through the state, again causing tremendous devastation. In North Carolina alone, Floyd was responsible for thirty-five deaths, 7,000 destroyed homes, and more than $3 billion in damages.[3]

An important advancement for the city of Raleigh occurred in 1997 when the Hartford Whalers of the National Hockey League moved the

---

[1] See "Raleigh Drops Giant Acorn with Lift from Southern Crane," 8 February 2011, http://www.constructionequipmentguide.com/Raleigh-Drops-Giant-Acorn-With-Lift-From-Southern-Crane/15690/# (accessed 15 March 2011).

[2] See "Hurricane Fran, September 1996," http://www4.ncsu.edu/~nwsfo/storage/cases/19960906/ (accessed 21 March 2011).

[3] See "Hurricane Floyd, September 1999," http://www4.ncsu.edu/~nwsfo/storage/cases/19990915/ (accessed 4 April 2011).

team to Raleigh and became the Carolina Hurricanes. The move prompted the city to construct the Raleigh Entertainment and Sports Arena (later renamed the RBC Center), which serves as the home arena for the Hurricanes as well as the home basketball arena for the North Carolina State Wolfpack. The venue also hosts numerous concerts and other entertainment events each year. Skeptics wondered whether professional hockey would be popular enough in Raleigh for the city to support the team. They were proved wrong in 2006 when the Carolina Hurricanes won the coveted Stanley Cup. The National Hockey League recognized Raleigh's love of the sport by awarding the 2011 NHL All-Star Game to the city, which brought an estimated $11.4 million in revenue from outside visitors. The city also received national acclaim for its preparation and hospitality.[4]

During the first decade of the new millennium, the city of Raleigh made efforts to revitalize its downtown district. Plans included a new convention center and hotel, the opening of Fayetteville Street to traffic once again (it had been closed since 1977), and a commuter rail system. By the end of the decade some progress had been made, but some of the work had to be cancelled or delayed due to the economic recession beginning in 2008.[5]

The First Baptist Church of Raleigh 1987–Present

W. Randall Lolley (1988–1990)

With a tenure lasting twenty-seven years, John Lewis served as pastor of the First Baptist Church of Raleigh longer than any of the other

---

[4] See Josh Saffer, "NHL All-Star Weekend Was a Boon," *News and Observer* (Raleigh NC), 8 March 2011, http://www.newsobserver.com/2011/03/08/1037226/nhl-all-star-weekend-was-a-boon.html# (accessed 15 March 2011); and Michael Farber, "Venue Will Go Down as Biggest Star of NHL's All-Star Weekend," *Sports Illustrated*, 30 January 2011, http://sportsillustrated.cnn.com/2011/writers/michael_farber/01/30/all.star.game/index.html (accessed 15 March 2011).

[5] Tim Nelson, "Economy Stalls Downtown Revitalization," 13 February 2009, http://abclocal.go.com/wtvg/story?section=news/local&id=6657254 (accessed 15 March 2011).

pastors in the church's history. Shortly after his retirement became effective, the church bestowed upon him the honorary title "pastor emeritus."[6] The committee selected to search for the next pastor had a responsibility like no other committee before it in the church's history. While a great number of Southern Baptist pastors might have been interested in the position, the reality was that only a few had the experience, wisdom, pulpit skills, and leadership qualities that following John Lewis demanded.

Lewis gave the church plenty of time to prepare for his departure, and he helped guide the process of nominating a search committee for the church to approve because, after twenty-seven years, most of the active members of the church would have had very little experience concerning how to approach a search for a pastor. On 19 November 1986 the church selected nine members to serve on the committee: Charles Barham (chair), Mary Lily Gaddy (vice-chair), Ralph Cavin, Austin Connors, Stan Crocker, Barbara Huggins, Jim Millen, Jane Purser, and Edgar W. Wyatt. The congregation also employed Malcolm Tolbert, professor of New Testament at Southeastern Baptist Theological Seminary, to be the interim pastor, thereby providing capable pastoral and preaching leadership during the interim.[7]

As expected, the committee was thorough in its work. For example, as the church was considering the proposed 1988 budget, a question arose concerning the proposed salary package for a prospective new pastor. Although no candidate had been selected by that point, Charles Barham reported to the congregation that the proposed figure was comparable to the pastoral salary packages of nineteen "top" North Carolina Baptist churches. After a sixteen-month search, the committee recommended the name of Dr. W. Randall Lolley to the church on 6 April 1988.[8]

Although much of his career was spent in North Carolina, Lolley was born in Troy, Alabama, in 1931. He attended Samford University in Birmingham where he graduated magna cum laude with his bachelor's

---

[6] Church Conference Records, 25 March 1987.

[7] Ibid., 19 November 1986.

[8] Ibid., 28 October 1987 and 6 April 1988.

degree in 1952. That same year Clara Lou Jacobs, also a native Alabaman, became his wife. Together the newlyweds left for Wake Forest, North Carolina, where he enrolled at Southeastern Baptist Theological Seminary, established by the Southern Baptist Convention only two years earlier. He received his B.D. degree (equivalent to a master of divinity today) from the seminary in 1957 and a year later completed the Th.M., graduating summa cum laude. Following graduation, Lolley enrolled at Southwestern Baptist Theological Seminary in Fort Worth, Texas, where he completed the Th.D. in 1964.[9]

Prior to assuming the pastorate of First Baptist Church of Raleigh, Lolley had been the president of Southeastern Baptist Theological Seminary (only thirty miles away) since 1974, but had resigned his position in October 1987 following a series of conflicts with Fundamentalists who had gained control of the board of trustees. Lolley, along with the seminary's dean, Morris Ashcraft, and six administrators, resigned from their positions to protest a new trustee policy that mandated hiring only faculty who affirmed biblical inerrancy.[10]

In many ways Lolley was a "perfect fit" for First Baptist Church of Raleigh. He was one of the most admired Baptists of his day, noted especially for his preaching skill. He also had a wealth of pastoral experience. Beginning during his college days in Alabama, Lolley served three churches in the state before graduation: Reece Baptist Church, Piney Grove Baptist Church, and Good Hope Baptist Church. After moving to North Carolina for seminary, he became pastor of the Pine Ridge Baptist Church in Poplar Springs, North Carolina, serving from 1954 to 1958. He left Poplar Springs to join the staff of First Baptist Church of Greensboro as assistant pastor, a position that gave him his

---

[9] "Report of the Senior Minister Search Committee," Church Conference Records, 27 July 1988. Lolley's doctoral work at Southwestern Baptist Theological Seminary concentrated in the areas of philosophy of religion and ethics. Both John Newport and T. B. Maston served as his advisors. See Randall Lolley, e-mail message to author, 19 March 2011.

[10] For a short account of Lolley's clash with Fundamentalists at Southeastern, see David T. Morgan, *The New Crusades, the New Holy Land: Conflict in the Southern Baptist Convention, 1969–1991* (Tuscaloosa: The University of Alabama Press, 1996) 137–38. See also http://www.religiousherald.org/index.php?option=com_content&task=view&id=4786&Itemid=53 (accessed 11 April 2011).

first taste of pastoral ministry in a large urban congregation. Just a couple of years before completion of his Th.D., Lolley became pastor of the First Baptist Church of Winston-Salem, where he served from 1962 to 1974. Lolley's pastoral experience, administrative skills, personality, and pulpit prowess generated enthusiasm at the First Baptist Church of Raleigh. When the committee presented his name to the church, the vote to call him as pastor was unanimous.[11]

Master Planning Committee. In June 1987, one year prior to Lolley's selection as John Lewis's successor, the church heard and approved a major report from the Future Focus Committee. Active since its appointment in 1986, the committee provided the first in-depth study of the congregational needs, and it was timed appropriately to be presented at the conclusion of John Lewis's tenure as pastor. Part one of the committee's final report provided a profile of the community and the church, containing results of a congregational survey that revealed five areas of congregational concern: (1) the selection of a new pastor to lead the church in a positive way, (2) the development of a more effective outreach program targeting both members and non-members, (3) a continued commitment to be a "downtown church" ministering uniquely in that setting, (4) the development of a more informed membership specifically in the area of mission and stewardship, and (5) an evaluation of the facility needs for the church and a plan to make necessary improvements. The second part of the report—presented several months later—provided a list of the needs and goals of the church as it looked toward the future. Each of these needs, along with corresponding goals, was grouped within the framework of the church's six commissions at the time (administration, education, fellowship, mission and witness, social ministries, and worship). The Future Focus Committee's findings represent an impressive report that provides an important glimpse into how the church viewed itself as it neared the end of the twentieth century, and what it believed were its most important needs. It was the first major study of its kind completed since the 1960s.[12]

---

[11] Church Conference Records, 6 April 1988.

[12] "Future Focus Committee Report," January 1987, Church Conference Records, 24 June 1987. The membership of the committee represented some of the major leaders of the church at the time: Marie Andrews, Austin Connors, JoAnn

By June 1988 another committee grew out of the Future Focus Committee called the Master Planning Committee. Chaired by Ed Vick, that committee was tasked with the responsibility of looking at the needs of the church for the future—primarily the preservation and maintenance of the building. By 20 November 1988 Vick reported that the committee had concluded that the help of a professional consultant was needed because "it is beyond the capabilities and expertise of this committee...to proceed with plans in certain areas."[13] Following approval by both the deacons and the finance committee, the congregation approved the employment of the architectural firm of Haskins, Rice, Savage, and Pearce to assist the Master Planning Committee in their assessment of the church's structural needs.[14]

Ten months later, the Master Planning Committee presented a detailed report to the diaconate. The primary concern, according to the committee, was the preservation of the sanctuary. The report indicated that there was rotting on the roof trusses that needed to be repaired. It suggested that the church replace the carpet in the sanctuary, at least on the first floor. The steeple needed to be inspected and repaired. The sanctuary needed to have a sprinkler system installed. The "clothes closet," which housed the church's clothing ministry, underneath the sanctuary needed some renovations. The Lewis Building needed a new roof to replace the current flat roof. The kitchen area needed renovations, and the committee suggested that more space was necessary for the children's ministry. The choir loft needed further study with a view toward enlargement. Finally, the organ needed to be renovated, and the console needed replacement. A second phase or "wish list" of items included the possibility of a family life center, but it was acknowledged

---

Cooper, Mary Lily Gaddy, Jerry Helms, John Hiott, Kay Huggins, Don Kline, Mabel Claire Maddrey, Clint Neal, Jackie Pittman, Gene Puckett, Jane Purser, Betty Singletary, Donna Toms, Ed Vick, and Ed Wyatt.

[13] Minutes of the Diaconate, 20 November 1988. The committee members' names (in addition to Chairman Ed Vick) were Sam Carothers, Edythe Crocker, Carolyn Dickens, Clint Galphin, Karl Lewis, Sonia Moore, Robert Ponton, Lee Smith, and Thomas Toms, with *ex-officio* members Ivie Clayton and Hayden James.

[14] Church Conference Records, 30 November 1988.

that that part of the report was "hypothesis because wishes and needs may change…before this phase is implemented."[15]

The report estimated that the first phase of necessary repairs and renovations would cost approximately $1.5 million. Phase two, or the "wish list," was projected at the same amount. The deacons approved the report and recommended to the congregation that (1) the report become the "Master Plan for First Baptist Church"; (2) a Capital Campaign Committee be appointed to conduct a feasibility study, secure a professional fundraising firm, and conduct a capital campaign to raise the money necessary; (3) the church employ Haskins, Rice, Savage, and Pearce as the architectural firm to draw the plans for the improvements; and (4) upon completion of the capital campaign, the church select a building committee to carry forth the work.[16] The church conference approved the Master Plan and requested that sometime during 1990 the moderator bring to the conference consideration of a capital campaign.[17] The master plan set the stage for a series of major renovations to be completed in various stages in the church throughout the next several years.

Southern Baptist Convention Issues. The shift toward Fundamentalism in the Southern Baptist Convention continued to be an issue of major concern as Randall Lolley became the church's pastor. Only two months after he assumed the pastoral charge of the church, the annual meeting of the Southern Baptist Convention occurred in San Antonio. The meeting that year stands out in the history of the "takeover" era (1979–1990) for two reasons. First, Moderates, with their presidential candidate, Richard Jackson, got closer to winning the presidency of the convention that year than any other year. Jackson, well known and respected in both Moderate and Fundamentalist circles, was pastor of the North Phoenix Baptist Church in Phoenix, Arizona. The Fundamentalist candidate was Jerry Vines, pastor of the First Baptist Church of Jacksonville, Florida.

---

[15] Minutes of the Diaconate, 18 September 1989.

[16] Ibid.

[17] Church Conference Records, 29 November 1989. The Capital Campaign Committee was appointed in May 1990. See Church Conference Records, 23 May 1990.

When the votes were tallied, Moderates were just 692 votes shy of winning.[18]

The other event that made San Antonio memorable was orchestrated by Randall Lolley. During the discussion devoted to resolutions, the messengers, by more than a thousand-vote majority (54.75 percent), approved the infamous "Resolution No. 5," which carried the formal title, "Resolution on the Priesthood of the Believer." Rather than an affirmation of the Priesthood of the Believer, the resolution was more a statement for pastoral authority, concluding with a quote from Hebrews 13:17: "Obey your leaders, and submit to them; for they keep watch over your souls, as those who will give an account." Moderates were outraged. Baptist historian Walter B. Shurden referred to it as "the resolution that virtually de-baptistified the SBC."[19] Gene Puckett, editor of the *Biblical Recorder* and member of First Baptist Church of Raleigh, called it "nothing short of heresy to a genuine Baptist."[20] Nothing captured Moderate outrage about the resolution any better than Randall Lolley's march to the Alamo at the conclusion of the session, followed by several hundred Moderate protestors who ceremoniously tore up their voting ballots.[21] Lolley was already a martyr in the eyes of Moderates, and this remonstrance, staged so effectively, now afforded him hero status.

Within several months of the San Antonio convention, the diaconate decided it was time for the church to begin to engage the situation in the Southern Baptist Convention more actively. At the church conference on 1 March 1989, the deacons presented a motion that the moderator select an "ad hoc Committee on Responsible Denominationalism" with a term of three years, "the purpose of which will be to monitor developments on all levels of the denomination (local, state, national, and international) with a view toward informing the congregation and making

---

[18] Morgan, *The New Crusades*, 93.

[19] Walter B. Shurden, *Not a Silent People: Controversies That Have Shaped Southern Baptists* (Macon: Smyth and Helwys, 1995) 100.

[20] Quoted in Morgan, *The New Crusades*, 94.

[21] Ibid.; Shurden, *Not a Silent People*, updated ed., 101.

recommendations for responsible participation."[22] The committee presented a preliminary report to the deacons on 25 June 1989 and then a finalized report to the church conference eleven months later. The committee recommended five items to the church: (1) the church should remain a part of the Southern Baptist Convention and continue to contribute to the Cooperative Program but on a reduced level, "giving directly to specific causes that are congruent with our values and beliefs"; (2) the church should reaffirm its support for missions and special offerings, which the committee also suggested increasing; (3) the church should increase its financial support for the Baptist State Convention of North Carolina; (4) the church and its membership "should work diligently to restore the mutual trust, respect and confidence between our Southern Baptist churches and the SBC"; and (5) the church should keep all its options open concerning its missions and cooperative giving since circumstances change and the need for modification may arise.[23]

The significance of the congregation's acceptance of that report should not be diminished. The suggested changes that went into effect for the 1990 budget represent an important modification of the church's relationship with the Southern Baptist Convention. Almost since the birth of the Southern Baptist Convention in 1845, First Baptist Church of Raleigh could be counted as a loyal supporter. Yet the acceptance of that report from the Committee on Responsible Denominationalism was the first step in a long road over the next several years that would lead to a formal parting between the church and the Southern Baptist Convention.

Resignation of Randall Lolley. During the Sunday-morning worship service on 11 February 1990, Randall Lolley announced his resignation as pastor of First Baptist Church of Raleigh to become the pastor of First

---

[22] Church Conference Records, 1 March 1989. The first members of the committee were Bill Kibler (chairman), Tom McCrary, Phillip Cave, Starr Gardner, Murphy Osborne, Donna Toms, Bill Simpson, Jane Purser, and Mary Lily Gaddy. The senior minister and chair of the diaconate were *ex-officio* members.

[23] "Report of the Ad Hoc Committee on Responsible Denominationalism," in Church Conference Records, 23 May 1990. The report presented to the church conference was much briefer than the five-page report presented to the diaconate. See Minutes of the Diaconate, 25 June 1989.

Baptist Church of Greensboro. He had served in the position for only twenty-two months. Quite naturally, most of the congregation was surprised. Lolley had two major reasons for leaving First Baptist Church, Raleigh. He said that the chair of the minister search committee at First Baptist Church, Greensboro had contacted him toward the end of 1989 and had asked him for a meeting. The Greensboro committee was disappointed by the fact that one of the main prospects it had considered had turned it down. Lolley said, "The evening I met with them I honestly thought I was to discuss how they could focus their search after that disappointment. Fact is they wanted to talk with me about becoming their pastor."[24] Since Lolley had been on the staff at the Greensboro church for two years just after graduation from seminary, he had an emotional attachment with the church, which led to a second reason for the resignation. He said, "The more I talked with that committee, the more I felt that since I was a 'wounded healer' from the events at Southeastern prompting my resignation, and they were 'wounded healers' attempting to recover from their pain, it might just work together for good to go and help them."[25] Lolley's move from Raleigh to Greensboro, therefore, involved his close connection with First Baptist Church, Greensboro, as well as his recent painful exit from the presidency at Southeastern Seminary, and the close geographical proximity between the seminary and Raleigh.

The deacons were saddened that Lolley was leaving; nevertheless, they were very complimentary.[26] One deacon sensitive to Lolley's feelings "spoke about Dr. Lolley and his pain over being so close to Southeastern Seminary and how much he appreciates there being understanding and sympathy on the deacons' part."[27] An

---

[24] Randall Lolley, e-mail message to author, 19 March 2011.

[25] Ibid.

[26] Minutes of the Diaconate, 11 February 1990. This was a called meeting of the diaconate whereby Lolley explained his reasons for the resignation. Along with the reasons given in the correspondence mentioned above, Lolley added that he was concerned the Future Focus program (the "master plan" discussed above) would need sustained, long-term leadership—longer than he projected he could stay at his age.

[27] Ibid.

acknowledgment of Lolley's love for First Baptist Church of Raleigh is evidenced by the fact that upon his retirement from full-time ministry, he and his wife reunited with the membership of the church in 1997. Lolley said, "Lou and I never considered joining any other church in Raleigh upon our return here.... One of the reasons was silently to say to those wonderful people, "It was not you; it was us who needed a bit of space away from our pain."[28]

R. Wayne Stacy (1990–1995)

Following Lolley's resignation, the church once again called upon Dr. Malcolm Tolbert to be the interim pastor. Tolbert committed to serve the church from May through December 1990. The church also selected a pastor search committee composed of Bill Simpson (chairman), Austin Connors, Edythe Crocker, Starr Gardner, Hayden James, Bill Kibler, Clint Neal, and Betty Singletary. *Ex-officio* members were Doris Baldwin (chair of the personnel committee), Howard Shell (chair of the finance committee), and Mary Lily Gaddy (chair of the diaconate).[29] It took the committee less than a year before recommending to the church the name R. Wayne Stacy as the next pastor. Stacy accepted the congregation's unanimous call on 31 October 1990.[30]

Wayne Stacy was a native Floridian. He was born on 19 October 1950 in West Palm Beach and educated at Palm Beach Atlantic College where he received his B.A. degree. He continued his education at the Southern Baptist Theological Seminary, completing both the M.Div. and the Ph.D. degrees. Stacy's doctoral work concentrated in the area of New Testament, with Frank Stagg serving as his primary advisor. Stacy had a significant amount of both pastoral and academic experience before accepting the call to the Raleigh pastorate. He came to Raleigh from the faculty of Midwestern Baptist Theological Seminary where he had served as associate professor of New Testament since 1986. He was a professor of biblical studies and philosophy at Palm Beach Atlantic College in West Palm Beach, Florida, from 1985 to 1986. He served as senior pastor of the

---

[28] Randall Lolley, email message to author, 19 March 2011.

[29] Church Conference Records, 28 February 1990.

[30] Ibid., 31 October 1990.

North Stuart Baptist Church in Stuart, Florida, from 1980 to 1985. From 1978 to 1979 he was an instructor in New Testament and a Garrett Teaching Fellow at the Southern Baptist Theological Seminary. He also served as pastor of the First Baptist Church in Austin, Indiana, from 1973 to 1979. He had begun his ministry experience as associate pastor of Crossroads Baptist Church in West Palm Beach, Florida, where he served from 1971 to 1973.[31]

Early Support for the Cooperative Baptist Fellowship. The conflict between Fundamentalists and Moderates in the Southern Baptist Convention came to a head in summer 1990. That year the Moderates made one last push to win the presidency at the annual meeting in New Orleans. Moderates pitted Dan Vestal, pastor of the Dunwoody Baptist Church in Atlanta, Georgia, against Fundamentalist candidate Morris Chapman, pastor of First Baptist Church of Wichita Falls, Texas. Moderates worked for almost a year from state to state, encouraging churches to send their full complement of messengers to the meeting. They placed Carolyn Crumpler Weatherford, who until 1989 had served as executive director of the national WMU, in nomination for the office of first vice-president. They believed that her popularity among women throughout the South might enlarge the Moderate vote. Their hopes were dashed, however, when the votes were tallied revealing the largest margin of loss for the Moderates since the controversy began in 1979.

Following defeat in New Orleans, Dan Vestal called for Moderates to come to Atlanta in August 1990 in order to dialogue about the future. More than 3,000 people attended that first meeting, which began on 23 August 1990 and lasted for three days.[32] First Baptist Church, Raleigh had

---

[31] Information gathered from the *curriculum vitae* of R. Wayne Stacy, located in a file titled "Dr. R. Wayne Stacy," located in "Pastors and Wives" box in the Archives of First Baptist Church, Raleigh, North Carolina.

[32] Walter B. Shurden, "The Cooperative Baptist Fellowship," in *The Baptist River: Essays on Many Tributaries of a Diverse Tradition*, ed. W. Glenn Jonas, Jr. (Macon: Mercer University Press, 2006) 247. That was not the first organization to grow out of Moderate distaste for the Fundamentalist takeover. Earlier, in 1987, some Moderates created the Southern Baptist Alliance (later named "The Alliance of Baptists"). The alliance remains an active and viable Baptist organization reflecting the progressive wing of Baptist life. It is generally regarded as more progressive on some social issues than the Cooperative Baptist Fellowship. For

an early interest in the new Moderate Baptist organization, soon called the Cooperative Baptist Fellowship. By November 1990 the committee on Responsible Denominationalism recommended a change to the fourth-quarter Cooperative Program giving. At the Atlanta meeting in August, the disaffected Moderates had created a financial plan by which churches could bypass the Southern Baptist Convention and support the new organization. Instead of sending Cooperative Program money to the Southern Baptist Convention in Nashville, where it would then be distributed to the various Southern Baptist Convention agencies, Moderate churches could send the money to Atlanta where the new organization could distribute the money to the agencies. That allowed Moderate churches to sidestep Southern Baptist Convention agencies, such as the Executive Committee, that they disagreed with, but still support agencies like the Home and Foreign Mission Boards.[33]

In March 1991 the Committee on Responsible Denominationalism presented a report concerning a "Statement on Baptist Mission Funding," which the committee hoped the church would affirm. The committee chair Bill Kibler said that twenty-six churches in North Carolina had currently affirmed the statement. The goal was to gather fifty churches in support and then hold a press conference to publicize the coalition. The document was a statement of protest against the continued tactics of the Fundamentalists in the Southern Baptist Convention; it was also a proclamation that the supporting churches could "no longer, in good conscience, fund the new agenda for Southern Baptists." That document promoted the new funding mechanism described above and concluded by saying, "we claim this action as a free church in a free state under the conviction that freedom in Christ is our most cherished gift from God

---

example, in 2004 the Alliance of Baptists issued a public statement of support for gay marriage. See "Statement on Same Sex Marriage," The Alliance of Baptists, 17 April 2004, http://www.sitemason.com/files/e10jfO/statementsamesexmarriage 2004.pdf (accessed 19 March 2011). While there may be some local churches supportive of the Cooperative Baptist Fellowship that have similar stances on gay marriage, the fellowship as an organization has expressed no support.

[33] See Church Conference Records, 28 November 1990, and "Moderates Create New Funding Mechanism for SBC Fellowship; Set Spring Convocation," *SBC Today* (September 1990): 1, as cited by Shurden, "The Cooperative Baptist Fellowship," 248.

and our most distinguished Baptist hallmark." Following the presentation by the committee, the church conference voted to affirm the statement. [34]

Building Renovations. By May 1992 the church was ready to launch a "Capital Campaign Drive for Sanctuary Preservation" plan. The initial goal was to raise $300,000 for various needs in the sanctuary, which included installation of a sprinkler system ($110,000), window rehabilitation ($33,000), structural repairs ($25,000), new carpet in the sanctuary ($22,000), new chairs in the choir loft ($11,500), air circulation changes in the choir loft ($10,000), roof repairs ($10,000), new lighting in the choir loft ($5,000), and contingencies ($43,000).[35] Two months later Ivie Clayton, chair of the Capital Campaign Committee, reported that with 250 pledges the church had surpassed the goal—for a total of $314,000. He reported that work would begin soon on the designated projects.[36]

On 27 January 1993 the congregation received a detailed report from the Sanctuary Preservation Committee appointed to oversee the work. Max Baldwin, chair of that committee, reported that significant progress had been made. He reported that restoration of the stained-glass windows was almost completed. A contract had been awarded to Austin Organs, Inc. for a new organ console, expected to be delivered in the later half of 1993. Another contract had been awarded to the engineering firm of Bass, Nixon, and Kennedy to draw up plans and oversee the installation of a sprinkler system in the sanctuary; improve the lighting, heating, and air-conditioning in the choir loft; and make other structural repairs that may be needed. Two companies were identified to bid on replacing the carpet in the sanctuary.

Baldwin told the church that the committee was sensitive to the "special and historical significance of our sanctuary." He also made it clear that the committee also did not want to disrupt the use of the sanctuary any more than would be necessary, but that the sanctuary may need to be closed for two or three weeks. Finally, Baldwin informed the

---

[34] "Statement on Baptist Mission Funding," in Church Conference Records, 27 March 1991.

[35] Church Conference Records, 17 May 1992.

[36] Ibid., 22 July 1992.

congregation that with the "repair of old structures," there could be surprises—repairs might take longer or be more expensive than initially thought.[37] As it turned out, Baldwin was correct. In February 1994 the Sanctuary Preservation Implementation Committee reported that the cost of the renovations would be approximately $450,000 rather than the originally anticipated $300,000.[38]

Work continued throughout 1994. In August the committee provided a progress report. It indicated that a contract was about to be signed with a company to begin work on the steeple repairs, and it anticipated that the work would be complete by December. Also, due to condensation in some areas of the ceiling of the sanctuary, the committee reported that some of the ductwork needed to be replaced and that a contract had been awarded for that job. In addition, there continued to be problems with leaking along the walls of the sanctuary, particularly in the southeast corner, which still needed work. Finally, chairs were purchased for the choir loft and were expected to arrive within twelve weeks. Sanctuary renovations were eventually completed during 1995.[39]

Resignation of Wayne Stacy. After four and a half years as pastor, Wayne Stacy submitted his resignation on 28 June 1995, to be effective at the end of July. Stacy left the church to return to full-time teaching as a New Testament professor at Gardner-Webb University.[40] In his letter of resignation to the church, he indicated that teaching had always been his "first best gift," and while "[p]astoral ministry was something I knew how to do, it is not the place in which I find my greatest vocational joy." He was affirming to the congregation, thanking the members for their support and especially their "faithfulness as listeners each week" to his sermons. "If good preaching is…dialogical rather than monological,

---

[37] "Report from the Sanctuary Preservation Implementation Committee to Church Conference," located in ibid., 27 January 1993.

[38] Church Conference Records, 23 February 1994.

[39] "Report from the Sanctuary Preservation Implementation Committee," in ibid., 24 August 1994. There is no direct information given in the church records for 1995. Since there were no reports given during the year, the assumption can be made that the work was completed.

[40] Church Conference Records, 28 June 1995.

you've been a wonderful 'dialog partner,'" he said in closing.[41] Stacy eventually became the dean of the M. Christopher White Divinity School at Gardner-Webb in 1997 and served in that role until 2003, when he returned to the pastorate at Southside Baptist Church in Jacksonville, Florida.[42]

J. Daniel Day (1996–2007)

Within one month of Wayne Stacy's resignation, the church selected a new pastor search committee. The members were Matt Bullard (chair), Ed Vick, Max Baldwin, Charles Apperson, Jeff Hobart, Elizabeth Chamblee, Maria Neal, Carolyn Dickens, Gwen Cavin, and Pearl Poole.[43] The committee worked for the next year, and on 25 August 1996 it recommended the name of J. Daniel Day to the congregation to be the next pastor of the church. Day was overwhelmingly accepted by the church by a vote of 480 to three. In a humorous note, the secretary for the diaconate made this notation about the events surrounding Day's arrival at the church:

> Mr. Smith reported that right before our new pastor was presented to the church lightning struck the church steeple knocking out the public address system of the church, alarm system, etc. Several electrical panels were also damaged. The total cost is $2,500 for the P.A. system and $4,000 to $5,000 for other damage. Our insurance has a $1,000 deductible. Also the basement was flooded. Bolton Company had repaired the drain and said it operated but that a larger machine was required to complete the job. Mr. Smith said there was a lot of water damage to the church.[44]

---

[41] "Dr. Stacy Resigns," *Biblical Recorder,* 1 July 1995, 12. The resignation letter is found on the church's specialized page attached to the *Biblical Recorder.* A copy is located in the Archives of First Baptist Church, Raleigh, North Carolina.

[42] Greg Warner, "Stacy Expected to Leave Gardner-Webb Divinity School for Jacksonville Pulpit," 18 December 2003, http://www.dev.abpnews.com/index. php?option=com_content&view=article&id=2608:stacy-expected-to-leave-gardner-webb-divinity-school-for-jacksonville-pulpit&catid=45 (accessed 22 March 2011).

[43] Church Conference Records, 26 July 1995.

[44] Minutes of the Diaconate, 15 September 1996.

Thankfully, Day's tenure as pastor was not as "stormy" as this notation might suggest! The "Mr. Smith" referred to in the quote was Reverend Paul Smith, longtime minister of music and administration. Smith's value to the church should be recognized. He served on the staff from 1978–1999. His service to the church spanned the pastorates of John Lewis, Randall Lolley, Wayne Stacy, and Dan Day, making him a valuable member of the staff and congregation.

J. Daniel Day was a native Oklahoman, born in 1942 in Okmulgee, Oklahoma. He graduated from Oklahoma Baptist University in 1963 with his B.A. degree. Following, his call to ministry led him to Southwestern Baptist Theological Seminary where he completed the B.D. (later changed to M.Div.) in 1966. Just before completion of his B.D., Day married Mary Carol Rogers in July 1965. They had twin sons (John and Douglas) on 29 December 1968. Day remained at the seminary and completed the Th.D. (later changed to Ph.D.) in 1973 in the area of biblical theology. Before his call to the Raleigh church, Day held pastorates at First Baptist Church, Ruston, Louisiana (1972–1980); First Baptist Church, McAlester, Oklahoma (1980–1985); and First Baptist Church, Columbia, Missouri (1985–1996).[45]

Further Building Repairs. The congregation thought that all the necessary repairs to the building had been completed during Wayne Stacy's tenure.[46] Unfortunately, for the next decade a variety of regular upgrades on the structures along with widespread renovations would be necessary.

In November 1996 Mrs. Donnie Helms, chair of the Properties Committee, brought to the church conference a detailed report that specified "critical needs to the church's heating and cooling systems as well as to the church roof for waterproofing."[47] The deacons took up the

---

[45] Dan Day, e-mail message to author, 21 March 2011.

[46] In addition to the Church Records, correspondence with Dan Day, Don Kline, and Fannie Memory Mitchell provided helpful insight into the details and sequence of the repairs discussed in this section. The correspondence took the form of e-mails dated 10 April 2011 (Fannie Memory Mitchell), 12 April 2011 (Dan Day), and 17 April 2011 (Don Kline).

[47] Church Conference Records, 20 November 1996.

matter at a meeting on 16 February 1997, where discussions focused not only on the heating and cooling system issues and roof sealing, but also on electrical problems that needed urgent attention. The projected cost of the repairs given to the deacons that evening was $750,000.[48] Ten days later the church conference appointed an ad hoc committee that began to focus on the matter.[49] Within two months the congregation learned that the bids for work on the roof indicated that the work "is to be much more involved and consequently more expensive than originally anticipated."[50] In July the situation became even worse. During the church conference the congregation was informed that a recent storm had caused water damage to the sanctuary balcony and foyer when lightning struck the steeple, causing a sprinkler pipe to burst, flooding everything below it. Although no pews were damaged, the antiphonal organ pipes in the balcony sustained damage and needed to be dismantled and dried out. The repair process to the organ, the report says, could take up to a year.[51] By fall, scaffolding was assembled in the sanctuary in order to complete the necessary repairs.[52]

The scope of the repairs proved to be more serious than originally thought, and when coupled with other building needs, the congregation decided that an organized plan for repairs and financial support was needed. Consequently, the Cary architectural firm of Sears, Hackney, Keener, and Williams, Inc., which specialized in building renovation work, was retained in spring 1997. Several committees in the church worked with the architectural firm to develop a plan to address all of the problems that were identified. In February 1998 the church conference heard and approved a "Summary Report Regarding Major Maintenance and Equipment Deficiencies." The report identified three categories of problems: (1) safety problems, including basement flooding and electrical hazards; (2) mechanical weaknesses related to heating and cooling; and (3) water leakage in roof areas and structure walls. The report also stated that renovations were required in the kitchen and preschool areas,

---

[48] Minutes of the Diaconate, 16 February 1997.
[49] Church Conference Records, 26 February 1997.
[50] Ibid., 23 April 1997.
[51] Ibid., 23 July 1997.
[52] Minutes of the Diaconate, 21 September 1997.

coupled with attention to security concerns related to the Garth area.[53] The estimated cost of the work was $2.5 million.[54] Upon hearing the report, the church approved hiring Cargill and Associates as consultants with the church to begin a capital campaign to raise the money, a campaign that ultimately proved to be very successful.[55]

Daniels and Daniels Construction Company of Goldsboro, North Carolina, became the general contractor for the first major phase of the overall plan, which was to include: safety and drainage matters, heating and air conditioning, selected roofing repairs, and renovation of the kitchen and preschool areas. Unfortunately, soon after the repair and renovation work began, a large portion of the Lewis Building's fireproofing (which was asbestos-based) had to be removed or abated. The discovery of asbestos in unanticipated places forced the removal of all electrical wiring, ductwork, ceilings, and lighting. This added extensive costs to the project and forced the church to vacate its facilities until the painstaking work could be completed.[56]

For most of 2000 the church's activities were spread throughout several locations in the city. The church rented office space in North Raleigh for church staff and other administrative needs. The Sunday-morning worship services and Sunday-school classes were held at Meredith College. Edenton Street United Methodist Church graciously allowed the congregation use of its building for Wednesday-evening activities. St. John's Baptist Church housed the Infant-Toddler Center, and for a short period of time Our Savior Lutheran Church hosted the weekday children's program. Vacating the building also forced the church's other activities, such as recreational and social programs, to be relocated. Finally, the church's clothing ministry was temporarily suspended.[57]

---

[53] The "Garth" refers to an enclosed area between the sanctuary and Lewis Education Building, comprised of both pavement and grass covering an old section of the basement.

[54] "Summary Report Regarding Major Maintenance and Equipment Deficiencies," Church Conference Records, 25 February 1998.

[55] Church Conference Records, 27 January 1999.

[56] Don Kline, e-mail correspondence with the author, 17 April 2011.

[57] Ibid.

In August 2000, after approximately nine months away from their beloved church building, the congregation was in the process of preparing to return to the newly renovated facility when a most unfortunate event occurred that easily could have been disastrous. Two homeless men broke into the church on the night of 12 August.[58] They went into the office of the Infant-Toddler Center and discovered a checkbook whereby they proceeded to write themselves checks. Attempting to destroy evidence of their presence, they started a fire in the office, which did not spread due to the recent installation of new fireproof partitions. Before they left, they also went into the basement under the sanctuary where the church clothing ministry was housed and started a second fire on the old stage. Fortunately, the fire did not spread rapidly enough to catch the old wood flooring of the sanctuary above. The sprinkler system installed in the sanctuary a few years before, along with the rapid response from the Raleigh Fire Department, prevented the sanctuary from total destruction.[59] The costs for the first portion of the long building project totaled $5,268,000.[60]

When finally able to return to its building, the church showed its gratitude to those whose aid had been helpful during the period dubbed "The Adventure" by many in the congregation. For Meredith College, "as a continuing recognition for the interrelationship of our heritage," the church established the "First Baptist Church, 99 N. Salisbury Street, Raleigh, North Carolina Scholarship," with an initial gift of $10,000.[61] For Edenton Street United Methodist Church, First Baptist provided a gift of three liturgical banners with brass hangers and inscriptions, which completed a set of banners already begun by the Edenton Street Church. The cost of that gift was $6,081.[62] First Baptist committed $1,800 to St. John's Baptist Church for safety renovations, which allowed its children's

---

[58] See "United States of America v. Curtis Lee Terry; United States of America v. Ronnie Williams," http://ftp.resource.org/courts.gov/c/F3/257/257.F3d.366. 00-4902.00-4856.html (accessed 2 April 2011).

[59] Don Kline, e-mail correspondence with the author, 17 April 2011.

[60] Ibid.

[61] "Recommendation of the Transition Adventure Task Force," Church Conference Records, 23 August 2000.

[62] Ibid.

areas to complete safety regulations for infant day care facilities.[63] A contribution of $500 was also sent to Our Savior Lutheran Church as a way of thanks for the short period of time that it hosted the weekday children's program. Finally, letters of appreciation were sent to several other organizations and churches that were helpful during that period.[64]

In the midst of that project the church made an interesting discovery that part of its drainage system had been built on a small portion of land belonging to the state of North Carolina adjacent to the Lewis Education Building. Approximately fifty-five feet of the building also rested on state property. Through friendly and reasonable negotiations the church was able to purchase 1,035 square feet of land to rectify the problem.[65]

A second phase of the long building project involved a complete replacement of the electrical system in the sanctuary. This included the chandeliers and lighting controls. In addition, the old ceiling of the clothing ministry was replaced with fireproof materials so that the timber floor of the sanctuary above might be protected. This forced the evacuation of the sanctuary for two months in 2005. Unlike the closing of the sanctuary in 2000, on this occasion the church worshipped in the fellowship hall with two Sunday-morning services until the work was completed.[66] The general contractor for this multifarious project, which lasted from April 2005 to January 2006, was Sparrow Construction Company of Raleigh. The cost was $808,000. The work "proceeded well for a renovation of such an old facility."[67]

The third portion of the project involved the water infiltration problems of the building. Because the building was close to 150 years old, several months of investigative work were required to establish exactly how to proceed and what materials were necessary. All former waterproofing materials were removed from the outer walls, which were then repaired and coated with newer, stronger materials. This was done with great care in order to maintain the original appearance of the walls. The roof also received significant waterproofing work as many sections

---

[63] Ibid.

[64] Ibid.

[65] Church Conference Records, 24 January 2001.

[66] Ibid., 27 April and 24 August 2005.

[67] Don Kline, e-mail correspondence with the author, 17 April 2011.

were either replaced or reworked. Seager Waterproofing, Inc. of Greensboro and Hamline Roofing Company of Raleigh did the work for this project. The total cost was just under $1,500,000 and the work was completed between March and November 2006.[68]

Finally, three much smaller projects were completed: restoring and protecting the sanctuary windows, replacing most of the roof of the Lewis Education Building, and renovating the two elevators, both of which were forty years old. The total cost of these projects was $538,000 and they were completed by March 2011.[69]

Japanese Ministry. The Japanese Ministry began in 1982 with the appointment of an ad hoc committee comprised of Luther Copeland (chair), Louise Copeland, Mabel Claire Maddrey, Sonia Moore, and Marc Mullinax. Jo Ellen Ammons was an *ex-officio* member of the committee due to her role as chair of the Commission on Mission and Witness. Because of their status as retired missionaries to Japan, Luther and Louise Copeland were important to the success of the ministry.[70]

Following a survey of the Japanese community in the Raleigh area, the committee determined that there were significant areas of ministry the church could provide. Consequently, in fall 1982 the Japanese American Cultural Exchange program began for both Japanese and American women.[71] The goal of this ministry was "to promote friendship and understanding between Japanese and American women."[72] The ministry provided weekly gatherings where both Japanese and American women could share fellowship, aided by a Japanese interpreter. They shared customs with one another, hosted parties, and shared meals in homes together.[73]

In fall 1983 the church initiated a Bible class in the Japanese language. Luther Copeland served as the first teacher for the class, which

---

[68] Ibid.

[69] Ibid.

[70] "The Japanese Ministry in First Baptist Church, Raleigh, N.C.," Church Conference Records, 28 October 1998.

[71] Ibid.

[72] "The Japanese Cultural Exchange, First Baptist Church, Raleigh, North Carolina," Church Conference Records, 28 October 1998.

[73] Ibid.

eventually grew into a larger ministry to the local Japanese community. In 1990 Yasushi and Kaoru Tomono became members of First Baptist Church. Trained in law and theology in Japan, Yasushi Tomono came to the United States to further his ministry training at an American seminary. He enrolled at Southeastern Baptist Theological Seminary and received a scholarship provided through a cooperative effort between First Baptist Church and the Baptist State Convention of North Carolina. At the end of 1991 First Baptist Church entered into an agreement with the Baptist State Convention of North Carolina and several local Baptist associations to form a nonprofit corporation to fund a ministry to the Japanese community in North Carolina. Tomono was employed part-time to lead this ministry. The church's commitment for the year 1992 was $10,000—$8,800 came from designated gifts, with the remaining amount provided by the Japanese mission that had formed within First Baptist Church.[74] The ministry enjoyed success throughout the 1990s. At the church conference in October 1998, the church received impressive statistics related to its growth: attendance of approximately thirty in the Japanese worship services; eighteen Japanese people baptized into the membership of First Baptist Church; and 220 individuals who had attended the mission and later returned to Japan. In addition, more than 150 adult Japanese, along with many children, had been present at the last annual Christmas service in 1997.[75]

A transition for the Japanese Ministry occurred in 2002. In March the church heard a report that the nonprofit corporation was going to dissolve. Later that year First Baptist Church adopted a plan for its Japanese mission to become a self-sustaining church by 2007.[76] To date,

---

[74] "The Japanese Ministry in First Baptist Church, Raleigh, N.C." The associations participating in the cooperative venture with First Baptist Church and the Baptist State Convention were Atlantic, New River, New South River, Wilmington, and Raleigh. See Church Conference Records, 20 November 1991. By 1998 support from the nonprofit corporation grew beyond these associations to include the Pilot Mountain and Yates Baptist associations. See "The Japanese Ministry in First Baptist Church, Raleigh, N.C."

[75] "The Japanese Ministry in First Baptist Church, Raleigh, N.C."

[76] Church Conference Records, 27 March and 28 August 2002.

the Japanese mission is not a self-sustaining church, although that does remain a future goal.

Severing Ties with the Southern Baptist Convention. At a meeting of the diaconate on 14 June 1998, pastor Dan Day expressed to the deacons gathered that evening his grave concerns about the recent meeting of the Southern Baptist Convention. The convention meeting that year marked the beginning of efforts to revise the convention's confessional statement titled the "Baptist Faith and Message." Southern Baptists first produced the confession in 1925 during the Evolution Controversy. In 1963, during the Elliott Controversy, the convention modified the confession. By 1998, with the convention firmly in Fundamentalist control, the messengers voted to amend the confession by adding an article on "The Family." The new article evoked a firestorm of opposition from Moderate ranks because it contained a statement that said, "A wife is to submit herself graciously to the servant leadership of her husband even as the church willingly submits to the headship of Christ. She, being in the image of God as is her husband and thus equal to him, has the God-given responsibility to respect her husband and to serve as his helper in managing the household and nurturing the next generation."[77] The newly added article also contained the statement, "children from the moment of conception, are a blessing and heritage from the Lord"—an obvious allusion to the abortion debate.[78]

Following Day's expression of concern, Ed Vick made a motion that the matter be referred to the Denominational Relations Committee, in order that they may consider the possibility of "further distancing ourselves from the Southern Baptist Convention."[79] Ray Goodman moved that all "First Baptist literature and the sign outside the front of the church bear the words 'Affiliated with the Cooperative Baptist Fellowship.'"[80] Both motions were approved by the church conference ten days later.[81]

---

[77] "The Baptist Faith and Message," http://www.utm.edu/staff/caldwell/bfm/1963–1998/18.html (accessed 28 March 2011).

[78] Ibid.

[79] Minutes of the Diaconate, 14 June 1998.

[80] Ibid. The Southern Baptist Convention produced a revision of the Baptist Faith and Message in 2000, which further angered Moderates. For a good

The Denominational Relations Committee worked for the next four months to study the question of whether or not the church should sever its ties to the Southern Baptist Convention. Over the summer they held four listening sessions. A total of 335 people either participated in one of the listening sessions or corresponded with the committee in writing. By 2 September 1998 the committee indicated that it would present a resolution to the next church conference recommending a course of action.[82]

The historic meeting occurred in the church sanctuary on 23 September 1998. Carolyn Dickens served as moderator. Mary Jon Roach, chair of the Denominational Relations Committee, began by introducing the committee members and reviewing the process since the deacons' meeting the previous 14 June. Robert Newton, chair of a subcommittee tasked with preparing the congregation for the proposed action, recalled the efforts made to that end. Roach then read letters from the church's three previous pastors, John Lewis, Randall Lolley, and Wayne Stacy, affirming the proposed action. The committee's proposed resolution recommended that First Baptist Church sever its ties with the Southern Baptist Convention. Because of the historic nature of that action by the church, the full text of the "Resolution on Identity" deserves to be included below:

> Whereas, the identity of the First Baptist Church of Raleigh, North Carolina, from its founding one hundred and eighty-six years ago in 1812 has always embraced and cherished the authentic and mainstream Baptist heritage; and

---

discussion of the changes to the document in 2000, see "1963 and 2000 Baptist Faith and Message Statements: Comparison and Commentary," http://texas-baptists.org/files/2010/08/bfmcomp1.pdf (accessed 28 March 2011). Baptist historian Doug Weaver called the 2000 revision of the Baptist Faith and Message the "crowning achievement of the victory against Moderates." See C. Douglas Weaver, "Southern Baptists," in *The Baptist River: Essays on Many Tributaries of a Diverse Tradition*, ed. W. Glenn Jonas, Jr. (Macon: Mercer University Press, 2006) 65.

[81] Church Conference Records, 24 June 1998.

[82] Ibid., 2 September 1998.

Whereas, First Baptist Church, Raleigh, founded with 23 charter members, bequeathed to us our Baptist identity through witnessing, ministering, and magnifying the presence and spirit of Christ in their generation; and

Whereas, First Baptist Church, Raleigh, has historically rooted its life in the Bible as the inspired and authoritative Word of God for faith and practice, to be interpreted by each individual as led by the Holy Spirit within this fellowship of believers, and with Jesus Christ as the only criterion by which the Bible is to be interpreted; and

Whereas, we have characteristically interpreted the Scriptures without the encumbrance of biblical literalism and consistently exercised our freedom of self-governance, thereby enabling us to honor the ministry of gifts of women as well as men and to ordain women as deacons of this church since 1874 and, since 1982, as ministers of the gospel; and

Whereas, our ancestors founded First Baptist Church, Raleigh, two years before the founding of the Triennial Convention, the first national Baptist organization in the United States, eighteen years before the formation of the Baptist State Convention, and thirty-three years before the organization of the Southern Baptist Convention; and

Whereas, First Baptist Church, Raleigh, has led in the establishment of numerous local congregations and has always exercised its cherished local church independence within the bounds of a broader Baptist interdependence, enthusiastically cooperating and liberally contributing to joint missionary, educational, and benevolence efforts through the Raleigh Baptist Association, the Baptist State Convention of North Carolina, and the Southern Baptist Convention; and

Whereas, we do affirm our faithfulness to Christ and to the extension of His kingdom as we have done throughout the years by continuing to participate in missions, education, and benevolences both in our city, our state, and to the ends of the earth, and by praying for and financially supporting those who serve in Christ's name where we cannot be present in body; and

Whereas, current authoritarian trends in the Southern Baptist Convention disregard our Baptist heritage and compromise essential freedoms of biblical interpretation, the autonomy of every local church, the priesthood of all believers, and the right of all people to worship God in their own way, without interference from government; and

Whereas, we reaffirm our commitment to our Baptist heritage and freedoms, under Christ our Lord, and honor the right of every Baptist church to choose its own guiding principles;

Be it therefore RESOLVED that we, the members of the First Baptist Church of Raleigh, North Carolina, meeting in conference September 23, 1998, after years of faithful cooperation, do reaffirm our commitment to the Raleigh Baptist Association and the Baptist State Convention of North Carolina; and we also reaffirm the traditions and fellowship we share with Baptist churches throughout the South, the nation, and the world, and will continue to support with our prayers, our presence, and our financial means the ministries within that community which reflects our convictions;

Be it further RESOLVED that, regretfully, we no longer identify our church with the Southern Baptist Convention.[83]

With the presentation of the "Resolution on Identity" to the assembled members, the time for discussion came. A lengthy discussion on the resolution ensued. After an amendment to the resolution, the congregation voted by secret ballot and overwhelmingly approved it by a vote of 264 in favor and twenty-three against. The First Baptist Church, Raleigh, no longer identified itself with the Southern Baptist Convention.[84]

The historic nature of that action by the church should not be missed. The First Baptist Church of Raleigh was never on the sidelines in Southern Baptist life. Since the formation of the Southern Baptist Convention, the church had always been among the leading churches in North Carolina in supporting the convention, whatever the cause. Members of the congregation, both clergy and laity, had for decades served at all levels of leadership in Southern Baptist life. For most of the convention's history, the church sent messengers to the annual meetings. But as Fundamentalism began to gain a foothold in convention ranks, beginning in the early 1960s and continuing until the total onslaught that began in 1979, the church wisely followed the events with interest. Pastors John Lewis, Randall Lolley, Wayne Stacy, and Dan Day all desired that the church be informed about convention matters. In fact, for

---

[83] "Resolution on Identity," Church Conference Records, 23 September 1998.
[84] Church Conference Records, 23 September 1998.

most of the twentieth century, the church's pastors encouraged the laity continually to be informed about theological issues and denominational concerns. Therefore, the action taken that September evening in 1998 was not an impulsive decision on the part of the congregation. It was the result of a local Baptist congregation that came to believe the convention had left it, not that it was leaving the convention. In other words, the church that night expressed its firm belief it was remaining true to its Baptist distinctiveness, and that it was actually the Southern Baptist Convention that had abrogated that identity.[85]

Change of Membership Requirements. In 2001 the church began to examine the possibility of changing its membership requirements. During that year the Constitution and Bylaws Committee received a formal request for a revision of the church's policy concerning the rebaptism of professed Christians—specifically those who sought membership in the church from other denominations that observed different baptismal policies. In consultation with the pastor, the committee believed that if any change in the current policy were to be presented, congregational education would first be necessary. Accordingly, the Constitution and Bylaws Committee requested that the Discipleship Training Committee address the issue by including a Wednesday evening seminar class on baptism. The result was a four-part series titled "Baptists and Baptism" led by Bob Mullinax, a member of the congregation and former executive director of the Council on Christian Higher Education at the Baptist State Convention of North Carolina.[86]

Other more urgent matters, such as a revision of the church's deacon election procedures, forced the Constitution and Bylaws Committee to put the possibility of revising the membership requirements on

---

[85] The historic nature of the break between First Baptist Church and the Southern Baptist Convention was highlighted in an article in the *New York Times.* See Rick Bragg, "Old Baptist Church, Women and All, Is Set to Leave Fold," *New York Times,* 25 July 1998, http://query.nytimes.com/gst/fullpage.html?res=9A05E5DD1139F936A15754C0A96E958260&pagewanted=all (accessed 17 April 2011). The article focused on the opinion of a longtime congregation member, ninety-one-year-old Mabel Claire Maddrey, and was published a few weeks before the church made the decision to leave.

[86] "Background Information Regarding the Proposed Baptismal Policy Change," Church Conference Records, 19 November 2003.

the "back burner." But in 2003 the issue resurfaced. Because two years had passed since the original discussion, the committee believed that further congregational education was necessary. Subsequently, three Wednesday-evening sessions on the topic of baptism occurred in summer 2003. These sessions were promoted and well attended. Bill Leonard, dean of the Wake Forest Divinity School, spoke on the topic, "Baptist Understandings and Traditions Regarding Baptism," at the first session. The second Wednesday evening in the series featured a panel of spokespersons from Edenton Street United Methodist Church, Sacred Heart Cathedral, First Presbyterian Church, and Christ Church. The spokespersons all shared insights from their traditions. The final Wednesday session was a town hall meeting whereby members were invited to share ideas, concerns, and suggestions. As that last session concluded, an informal show of hands suggested that the Constitution and Bylaws Committee should prepare a recommendation for the church to consider allowing non-immersed Christians to become members of the church without rebaptism.[87]

The result was an additional sentence to the article on "Membership" in the church Bylaws, which allowed membership to professing Christians from other denominations who have been baptized by means of different baptismal practices. The additional sentence permitted membership by "Statement of experience and faith, if the person has been baptized in another Christian tradition; immersion is always to be offered but not required of these candidates."[88] The church approved the addition to the Bylaws in church conference on 19 November 2003.[89]

Resignation of Dan Day. Dan Day turned sixty-five in 2007, and after eleven years as pastor of the First Baptist Church of Raleigh, he announced his retirement. Just two months before the retirement announcement, Day delivered a message during the church's observance of its 195th anniversary. In that sermon, he said:

---

[87] Ibid.

[88] Ibid.

[89] Church Conference Records, 19 November 2003.

I have a dream for this church. It does not have to do with budgets or buildings or programs or any of the things people are most impressed by. My dream is that this church 195 years from now—in the year 2157—will still be a church committed to freedom. My dream is of a church that encourages people to search scripture for themselves and to ask the awkward questions and to follow their conscience-driven answers. My dream is of a church that refuses to muffle its pastor, telling her or him what to preach. My dream is of a church that knows God is not served by "poking religion down anyone's throat," be it by court order or manipulative gimmicks. And my dream is of a church where the members are not the least bit embarrassed to say right out loud anywhere: "Jesus is the one who sets us free—and if you'll let him set you free, you will be free indeed!"[90]

As Day transitioned out of the role as pastor, the church was in the process of discussing whether or not to continue its financial support for the Baptist State Convention of North Carolina. In recent years Fundamentalists have captured control of the convention on the state level in much the same way that they gained ascendency in the Southern Baptist Convention. In both cases the Moderate voice was completely silenced. As of this writing, no formal action had been taken in a church conference to discontinue financial support for the BSC, but very little money makes its way into BSC coffers anymore.

In some sense, then, the church has almost come full circle in its two centuries. There was no Baptist State Convention or Southern Baptist Convention in 1812. But as these entities were established with the help of the church, it has made its own decisions about whether to support them and how much to contribute. Throughout its history First Baptist Church, Raleigh has sought to be informed of all the issues in Baptist life and then make its own decisions, beholden to no one except the lordship of Christ.

* * *

---

[90] J. Daniel Day, "Baptists' Best Treasure," *Baptist Heritage Update* 23 (Spring 2007): 11.

Day's words provide a good conclusion to the first 200 years of the church's history and a springboard into the next century. The founders' vision was nurtured by the faithful members of the First Baptist Church, Raleigh for two centuries. As the church faces a new century, great challenges lay ahead—challenges not only for the local church or the Baptist denomination, but for the Christian religion itself. Where will the next century lead and how will the vision be nurtured?

10

Celebrating Two Centuries

Throughout this book I have referenced the "founders' vision." What was that vision? There are no extant records that reveal to us any efforts on their part to predict what their congregation would look like two centuries later. If we somehow were able to get into a time machine and travel back to that March weekend in 1812, we might ask someone like John, Moses, Dolly, or Siddy to imagine what their new church would be like in 200 years. It is interesting to speculate about what John might have imagined. Would his vision for the church be different from Siddy's? I suspect it might. They might be able to tell us some things they hoped for. But as far as we know from the records that survive, there were no such prognostications on their part. They just established a Baptist community of faith out of their desire to serve Christ in the relatively new city of Raleigh, where they lived and spent their lives building their church for the next generation. The "founders' vision" then became what each successive generation of First Baptist Church members did with what they inherited. Now, as we look backward from the perspective of 200 years, we can see that the founders' vision was carefully nurtured by each successive generation.

The great Presbyterian pastor Peter Marshall had a well-known sermon titled "Keepers of the Springs." He began the sermon with a story about a how a small town grew and developed at the base of a mountain. On the mountain above the town lived a man who took it upon himself to be the "Keeper of the Springs." Whenever he found a spring as he walked through the woods on the mountain, he would clean out the fallen leaves, silt, mud, branches, or anything else that polluted the water as it flowed down toward the town. Because of the vigilance of this man, the water in the town was always clear, clean, and refreshing.

Millwheels were whirled by its rush.
Gardens were refreshed by its waters.
Fountains threw it like diamonds into the air.

Swans sailed on its limpid surface and
Children laughed as they played on its banks in the sunshine.[1]

One day the city council examined the budget for the town and saw the salary for a "Keeper of the Springs." The council members questioned the expense and suggested that a reservoir might be built above the town, which would be more economical than paying the salary of the man. So the "Keeper of the Springs" was deemed unnecessary and the town built its reservoir. The new reservoir filled with water, but after a short time, things were no longer the same. The water was not as clean as before. With no one to clean the water at its source, a scum began to develop in the reservoir and the unpurified water that came into the town began to cause problems. Eventually, the town's water became a cause for health concerns, forcing the city council to admit its error and rehire the "Keeper of the Springs." Within a short time, the water in the town was once again clean and pure.[2]

Borrowing Marshall's metaphor, the founders' vision is akin to the "spring" in the mountain town. The "keepers" have been the pastors and laity of the church, thousands of Baptist, Christian women and men who through the years affiliated with the church, then gave of their time, money, and talents to "keep" the founders' vision. The vitality of the congregation that continues to occupy the structure at 99 Salisbury Street stands as a testimony to the success of the "keepers."

On 19 April 2009 the church elected Dr. Chris Chapman as the pastor to lead the congregation into the next century. A native North Carolinian, Chapman spent much of his early years in Louisville, Kentucky. He attended the University of Kentucky where he earned the B.A. degree in social work and psychology in 1982. He then continued his education at the Southern Baptist Theological Seminary, earning the M.Div. in 1987. While a seminary student, Chapman worked on the ministerial staff of Broadway Baptist Church in Louisville. Following his marriage to Dana White, the couple moved to Danville, Virginia, where he served as associate pastor of the Moffett Memorial Baptist Church for

---

[1] Peter Marshall, "Keepers of the Springs," in *The Best of Peter Marshall*, ed. Catherine Marshall (New York: Chosen Books, 1983) 66.

[2] Ibid., 66–67.

two and a half years. Chapman then moved to Warrenton, North Carolina, to serve for two years as pastor of the Warrenton Baptist Church. During this time, he enrolled at Union Theological Seminary in Richmond, Virginia, to begin work on a Doctor of Ministry degree. In 1992 he became the pastor of Ginter Park Baptist Church in Richmond, serving for six years, during which time (1996) he completed his D.Min. degree. In 1998 he moved to North Carolina again where he became the pastor of the Knollwood Baptist Church in Winston-Salem. It was from this pastorate that he left to become the pastor at First Baptist Church, Raleigh.[3]

Chapman's first sermon as the new pastor at First Baptist Church was titled "Opening Our Hearts to Each Other," preached on 21 June 2009. Drawing his text from 2 Corinthians 6:1–13, Chapman included these words,

I have the sense that this is a church full of people who genuinely love and care for each other.... I also have the sense that your heritage has been to relate to your ministers in the very same way. So, on this first Sunday I have the privilege of serving as your pastor, I want to make clear my yearning for this same kind of relationship, and, taking a cue from the Apostle Paul...I want to invite us to consider making a commitment to how we will relate to each other over time. I want to invite us to do more than the minimum of thinking and working together, gathering for worship and conducting the business of the church, even studying scripture and doing missions. I want to invite us to open our hearts to each other, that we may experience the kind of intimacy God seeks with us and intends for us, and in turn, model this way of relating for a world of lonely and isolated people.[4]

It did not take Chapman long to discover one of the key reasons for the longevity of First Baptist Church, indeed the secret to how the church has been able to keep the founders' vision: harmonious fellowship. While

---

[3] Chris Chapman, personal e-mail correspondence with author, 5 April 2011.

[4] Christopher C. F. Chapman, "Opening Our Hearts to Each Other," sermon preached at First Baptist Church, Raleigh, 21 June 2009, obtained by personal e-mail correspondence with author, 31 March 2011.

this congregation through the years has had disagreements on occasion, there has been only one crippling controversy. Back in the 1830s, the controversy discussed in chapter 2 almost destroyed the church. Since then, even during times of disagreement the church has been able to preserve a sense of unity and fellowship, a rarity for many Baptist congregations. This quality has in turn produced considerable energy and financial resources for ministry in the city, state, and world.

It is also noteworthy that in the church's history there is no record of a pastor ever having to be terminated by the church. Baptist churches are autonomous; they determine their own policies and make their own decisions about clergy. It is not uncommon for a congregation as old as First Baptist Church, Raleigh to have at least several pastoral terminations in its history. The fact that there are none in this church's history is a credit to the harmony that has existed through the years between pastor and laity. There have been conflicts at times. A careful "reading between the lines" in the records will bear this out. But even in those instances a sense of the greater good prevailed. The harmonious relationship between pastor and laity throughout the history of First Baptist Church stands as a legacy worth celebrating.

The members of First Baptist Church, Raleigh have never forgotten their commitment to the Baptist tradition. This is evidenced by the number of members who have served the denomination (locally, regionally, and nationally) in various capacities. For example, at least six members have served as presidents of the Baptist State Convention of North Carolina: Patrick W. Dowd (the first president), Colonel J. M. Heck, Major A. B. Graham, Jr., C. T. Bailey, Dr. J. Clyde Turner, and Wesley N. Jones. Throughout its two centuries, this congregation has had a clear understanding of what it means to be Christian in a Baptist way. No clearer evidence of its Baptist commitment can be seen than in the congregational decision, painful as it was, to discontinue its support for the Southern Baptist Convention. The action of the church that night shows evidence of a congregation with a clear understanding of Baptist polity and practice.

The location of First Baptist Church so close to the North Carolina state governmental offices makes it a unique church as well. Throughout its history one governor was a member in the nineteenth century, while in the mid-twentieth century a future governor attended the church while a college student at North Carolina State University (W. W. Holden and Jim Hunt, respectively). The church has also had members who eventually became United States senators (Jesse Helms and Josiah Bailey). The church's second pastor, Josiah Crudup, served one term as a United States congressman. Jim Graham, longtime commissioner of agriculture in the state, was a member and deacon in the church for years. Numerous other politicians have worshipped in the church for Sunday morning services, funerals, weddings, or other special civic events. William Jennings Bryan, the most famous orator of his day, once preached from his pulpit at a temperance crusade. Although the church has been in the vicinity of power, it has never sought to exploit its access to power nor has it ever attempted to manipulate the structures of power for its own selfish benefit. On the contrary, First Baptist Church, Raleigh has been a good neighbor to state governmental complex and has consistently remained as a living witness to the way of Christ.

What lies ahead for the First Baptist Church of Raleigh? Of course, the answer to that question is only speculation. It is clear that the founders' vision is still alive and well 200 years later. This church is a healthy congregation still standing tall in the city of Raleigh. There is every reason to believe that its members will continue to be the "keepers of the spring." The twenty-three founders can rest eternally in peace knowing that their efforts to build a Baptist Christian congregation 200 years ago in the nascent city of Raleigh were not in vain. The founders' vision is still being nurtured.

Index